# OXFORD LEGAL HISTORY SERIES

*General Editors*

PAUL BRAND
JOSHUA GETZLER
DANIEL HULSEBOSCH
AND
AMALIA KESSLER

Priests of the Law

# OXFORD LEGAL HISTORY SERIES

*General Editors*

*Paul Brand, Joshua Getzler, Daniel Hulsebosch, and Amalia Kessler*

This series presents original work in legal history from all periods. Contributions to the series analyse diverse legal traditions, including common law; *ius commune*, civilian, and canon law; colonial, imperial, and international law; and customary, religious, and non-Western cultures of law. The series embraces methods ranging from doctrinal and juristic analysis through to every variety of historical, social-scientific, and philosophical enquiry. A leading purpose of the series is to investigate how legal ideas and practices operated in larger historical contexts. Our authors trace changes in legal thought and practice and the interactions of law with political and constitutional institutions and wider movements in social, economic, cultural, and intellectual life.

# Priests of the Law

*Roman Law and the Making of the Common Law's First Professionals*

THOMAS J. MCSWEENEY

OXFORD
UNIVERSITY PRESS

OXFORD
UNIVERSITY PRESS

Great Clarendon Street, Oxford, OX2 6DP,
United Kingdom

Oxford University Press is a department of the University of Oxford.
It furthers the University's objective of excellence in research, scholarship,
and education by publishing worldwide. Oxford is a registered trade mark of
Oxford University Press in the UK and in certain other countries

Published in the United States of America by Oxford University Press
198 Madison Avenue, New York, NY 10016, United States of America

British Library Cataloguing in Publication Data

Data available

Library of Congress Control Number: 2019946449

ISBN 978–0–19–884545–4

Printed and bound by
CPI Group (UK) Ltd, Croydon, CR0 4YY

Links to third party websites are provided by Oxford in good faith and
for information only. Oxford disclaims any responsibility for the materials
contained in any third party website referenced in this work.

*To Abby, Sean, and Charlotte*

# Preface

I first became interested in the history of lawyers as a law student. Our profession is a strange one. My *Doktorvater* is fond of saying that law school is designed to replace your brain with an entirely new one. The degree to which law school fundamentally transforms people is debatable, but I think law school is, at the very least, designed to make people *think* that they have been changed; a friend once observed that the only organization that does a better job than a law school of convincing you that you have been transformed into something different is the Marine Corps. We separate the world, by way of a curious analogy to the clergy, into lawyers and laymen. In law school I began to wonder how we got this way. When I got to graduate school, I became interested in the processes by which people who work with law have constructed the image of the lawyer as someone separate and different from people who perform other types of work.

These kinds of questions kept coming back to me when I read the thirteenth-century treatise *On the Laws and Customs of England*, more commonly known as *Bracton*. I am the kind of person who is interested in the kinds of things that interested the authors of *Bracton*. I like to tell my property students that my class will teach them to see the world as it truly is. When they walk down Duke of Gloucester Street in Colonial Williamsburg, they will no longer see boxwood hedges and blooming crape myrtles. Rather, they will see a combination of beautiful, abstract property interests: possessory estates, future interests, easements, and covenants. And yet, when I read *Bracton*, I found that I was less interested in what its authors wrote about the law than in why they wrote it at all. What compelled this group of justices in England's central courts to spend what must have been a large amount of their spare time, working long into the night watches, writing a massive treatise? I hope to show that *Bracton* is at least as much about the justices who wrote it, and how they wanted to perceive themselves and their work, as it is about teaching anyone how servitudes worked in thirteenth-century England.

This book would not have been possible without the support of the many people who devoted their time and energy to helping me develop as a scholar. Many different institutions have been generous in their support for this project. I have had a number of academic homes while I have worked on this project, starting with the history department at Cornell University, where *Priests of the Law* began life as my doctoral dissertation. That was followed by two years as a visiting assistant professor on the faculty at Cornell Law School. From there I moved to William & Mary Law School, where I feel particularly fortunate to have a dean and faculty who have supported me as a historian of medieval law. A number of individuals and organizations have provided financial support for this project, as well. I would especially like to thank fellow William & Mary alumnus Joseph J. Plumeri for his support for the Plumieri Award for Faculty Excellence, which helped me complete this book manuscript. The Huntington Library in San Marino, California, provided me with a grant to spend a month working with their legal manuscripts. The Graduate School at Cornell University, the Mario Einaudi Center for International Studies, and the Bibliographical Society of America sent me to England for a fruitful summer in the archives. The staff at Cambridge University Library, the British Library, the National Archives in Kew, the Wren Library at Trinity College, Cambridge, the library at Trinity Hall, Cambridge, and Lincoln's Inn Library in London all gave me valuable access to their collections, and for that I am extremely grateful. The Anglo-American Legal Tradition project at the University of Houston has also been a wonderful resource and I would like to thank all who have worked on that project for the work they have done to make the treasures of the British National Archives more accessible.

There are a number of people who influenced my thinking about this project as I was developing it. I have presented portions of this book project at various conferences, colloquia, and workshops, including the 2015 Hurst Summer Institute in Legal History, the annual meetings of the American Society for Legal History in 2010 and 2016, the 2013 British Legal History Conference in Glasgow, the 2015 Law and Governance in Pre-Modern Britain Conference at the University of Western Ontario, the London Legal History Seminar, the 2018 Medieval Studies conference at the University of Wisconsin, the International Medieval Congress at Leeds, the International Congress on Medieval Studies at Western Michigan University, the annual meeting of the Charles Homer Haskins Society, the William & Mary Legal History Seminar, the William & Mary Medieval and Renaissance Studies Colloquium, the European History Colloquium and the Medieval Studies Student Colloquium at Cornell University, and the faculty speaker series at Cornell, Emory, and St. Louis University law schools. I appreciate the feedback I have received from the participants in all of these events. I would additionally like to thank the student editors at the Temple Law Review and the Buffalo Law Review. My first two law review articles, both on *Bracton*, appeared in those publications. I have adapted parts of each of those pieces and incorporated them into this book.

I have been a part of two wonderful writing groups, one of which was generously funded by the Society for the Humanities at Cornell, and my friends in both of those groups—Eliza Buhrer, Abigail Fisher, Sarah Harlan-Haughey, Ada-Maria Kuskowski, Guillaume Ratel, and Melissa Winders—have given me wonderful feedback. I have learned much about writing good scholarship while reading their work on late medieval theories of cognition, the criminal networks of English coiners, nature in English outlaw literature, the world of the French coutumiers, the construction of truth in early modern French courts, and aristocratic courtesy in the Welsh marches. I also need to thank the "half-bakers" group of junior faculty at William & Mary Law School, including Jeff Bellin, Jay Butler, Chris Griffin, Tara Grove, Alli Larsen, Sarah Rajec, and James Stern. This wonderful group of people gave me some good advice on the introduction to this book when I was stuck.

I have had some outstanding students, both at William & Mary and Cornell, and several have made direct contributions to this book. In particular, I would like to thank my research assistants, Kristi Breyfogle, Gwen Brown, Ryan Schuster, and Evan Steiner. Sarah Spencer, who was the founding president of the William & Mary Legal History Society and a tireless promoter of legal history at William & Mary Law School during her three years here, also deserves thanks for bringing certain things to my attention that helped my argument in Chapter 7.

Several scholars have generously volunteered their time to give me comments and advice on the manuscript at various stages. The members of my dissertation committee gave me important guidance as I worked on this project. I hope each them will recognize something of their own scholarship in this work. Bernadette Meyler's guidance in thinking about legal texts as literary productions has been a major influence on my scholarship. Duane Corpis pushed me to think about the social side of intellectual history. David Powers first got me thinking about the relationship between judges and jurists, and the interactions between the different kinds of texts they produce. I would also like to mention Charlie Donahue, David Seipp, Tom Green, Dick Helmholz, and Karl Shoemaker, who gave me excellent comments in the later stages.

There are two people in particular who deserve special thanks: the two Pauls who have helped me to shape this project. Without their patient mentoring and meticulous work in reading and commenting on the text, it would not be where it is today. Paul Brand, my editor at the Oxford Legal History series, has been a wonderful mentor and has used his encyclopedic knowledge of law in the thirteenth century to prevent me from falling into a number of errors. I owe an unrequitable debt to Paul Hyams, my *Doktorvater*, for taking me on as a graduate student, for shaping me as a scholar, for challenging me, for encouraging me, and for writing more letters of recommendation than I can count. I hope I prove to be worthy of the faith they have both placed in me.

On a more personal note, my mom and dad were very supportive, as well. It was nice to be close to them, as well as my grandparents and my sister's family, while I was working my way through graduate school.

I have saved the most important person for last: my wife, Abby, who has patiently stood by me and given me her love and support through law school, graduate school, my VAP, the job market, and the quest for tenure. It has worked out well for us. We are now back in Williamsburg with two future William & Mary alumni of our own, Sean and Charlotte, who were both born while I was working on this book. They turned me into a coffee drinker, but they have also kept me grounded while I have worked, long into the night watches, towards tenure and to finish this project.

My study of history has given me a certain degree of humility about my own role in the grand sweep of history. In order to really be remembered by later generations, one has to be both exceptional and lucky. Even being the Roman emperor or president of the United States does not, by itself, guarantee one a place in our society's historical imagination. For a historian of the middle ages, the kind of mark one can make is quite a bit more modest. Historical knowledge proceeds incrementally. We each build upon what others have written. My hope is that this book will contain something in it that is useful to a historian of another generation, and that she will unlock more of the mysteries of *Bracton*.

# Table of Contents

# List of Abbreviations

| | |
|---|---|
| AALT | *The Anglo-American Legal Tradition* <http://aalt.law.uh.edu/> |
| Azo, *Summae* | Azo, *Summa Codicis . . .(Institutionum et Digestorum) & Brocardica* (Vico Verlag 2008), reprint of *Summa Azonis Sive Locuples Iuris Civilis Thesaurus* (Venice 1581) |
| *Bracton* | Woodbine, GE (ed) and Thorne, SE (tr), *Bracton on the Laws and Customs of England*, 4 vols (Belknap Press 1968–77) |
| BNB | Maitland, FW (ed), *Bracton's Note Book*, 3 vols (CJ Clay & sons 1887) |
| CM | Matthew Paris, *Chronica Majora*, 7 vols (Henry Richard Luard ed, Rolls Series, Longmans & Co, 1872-83) |
| *Corpus Iuris Canonici* | Friedberg, E (ed), *Corpus Iuris Canonici*, 2 vols (Bernhard Tauchnitz, 1879–81) |
| CPR | *Calendar of the Patent Rolls of the Reign of Henry III Preserved in the Public Record Office, 1232–1272*, 4 vols (His Majesty's Stationery Office 1906–13) |
| CR | *Close Rolls of the Reign of Henry III Preserved in the Public Record Office*, 13 Vols (His Majesty's Stationery Office 1902–38) |
| CRR | *Curia Regis Rolls Preserved in the Public Record Office*, 20 vols (Her Majesty's Stationery Office 1922–2006) |
| CUP | Cambridge University Press |
| *Digest of Justinian* | Watson, A (tr), *The Digest of Justinian*, 4 vols (Revised edn, University of Pennsylvania Press 1998) |
| EHR | English Historical Review |
| *Glanvill* | Hall, GDG (ed and tr), *The Treatise on the Laws and Customs of the Realm of England Commonly Called Glanvill* (Reprint edn, Clarendon Press 2002) |
| *Justinian's Institutes* | Birks, P, and Mcleod, G (trs), *Justinian's Institutes* (Cornell University Press 1987) |
| LQR | Law Quarterly Review |
| MCL | Brand, P, *The Making of the Common Law* (Hambledon Press 1992) |
| ODNB | *Oxford Dictionary of National Biography* (Online edn, OUP 2008) |
| OUP | Oxford University Press |
| RLC | Hardy, TD (ed), *Rotuli Litterarum Clausarum in Turri Londinensi Asservati*, 2 vols (Record Commission 1833–44) |
| RLP | Hardy, TD (ed), *Rotuli Litterarum Patentium in Turri Londinensi Asservati*, 2 vols (Record Commission 1835) |

SR      Luders, A, Tomlins, TE, France, J, Tauton, WE, and Raithby, J (eds), *The Statutes of the Realm: From Original Records, etc.* (1101–1713), 11 vols (London, 1810–28)
SS      Selden Society
TNA     The National Archives (United Kingdom)

# A Note on the Sources

Where an English translation of a text exists I have generally followed that translation, but I have modified other scholars' translations in places, particularly where I want to highlight the use of a particular word in the Latin. Where I quote passages from the Bible, I use the Douay-Rheims version, the English version which is closest to the Latin Vulgate. Most of the people referenced in this book bear toponyms based on their place of origin. These place names are spelled in various ways in the medieval texts. For the sake of consistency, I have used modern spellings of the place names, i.e., "Pattishall" rather than "Pateshull."

# Introduction

Sometime in the middle decades of the thirteenth century, a justice working in the courts of the English king wrote, "law is called the art of what is fair and just, of which we are deservedly called the priests, for we worship justice and administer sacred rights."[1] The words appear in a treatise that bears the title *De Legibus et Consuetudinibus Angliae* (*On the Laws and Customs of England*) or *De Legibus et Consuetudinibus Anglicanis* (*On English Laws and Customs*). *De Legibus*—which is known today as *Bracton*, after the man who was presumed for seven centuries to have been its author—has achieved a reputation for being one of the foundational texts of the common law. Lawyers, judges, and academics occasionally dust off this ancient tome when they want to make the case that a particular rule or principle has been a part of our common-law tradition from its beginning, or close to it.[2] This book will be less concerned with what *Bracton* can tell us about the law of the thirteenth century, however, than in what it can tell us about the people who wrote it, those people who the author of the sentence above describes as the law's priests. The author of this sentence supposes himself to be part of some community and, through the use of the word "we," hints that he imagines that his reader is a member of that same community. He never explicitly defines the "we," however. Who were these priests of the law?

*Bracton* was written over several decades, between the 1220s and the 1260s, and its authors were justices working in the courts of the king. Martin of

---

[1] "Ius ergo derivatur a iustitia, et habet varias significationes. Ponitur enim quandoque pro ipsa arte, vel pro eo quod scriptum habemus de iure, quod ius dicitur ars boni et aequi, cuius merito quis nos sacerdotes appellat. Iustitiam namque colimus et sacra iura ministramus." *Bracton*, vol 2, 24. I have provided a bit more of the Latin for context. As we shall see, the author did not so much write this sentence as adapt it from an earlier source.

[2] It was cited in a supreme court opinion as recently as 2018, when Justice Gorsuch, in his dissent in *Sveen v. Melin*, cited *Bracton* for the principle that "Because legislation often disrupts existing social arrangements, it usually applies only prospectively." *Sveen v. Melin*, 138 S Ct 1815, 1826 (2018). It is interesting for the purposes of this book to note that Justice Gorsuch was actually citing to a provision of Roman law that had been worked, without attribution, into the text of *Bracton*. The statement that "every new constitution ought to impose a rule on future things and not on things past" is probably a paraphrase of a provision from Justinian's *Codex. Bracton*, vol 3, 181. It was probably worked into an already-complete passage at some later point in the editing process; it appears to have been inserted mid-sentence and is not directly relevant to the material around it.

*Priests of the Law.* Thomas J. McSweeney, Oxford University Press (2019). © Thomas J. McSweeney.
DOI: 10.1093/oso/9780198845454.003.0001

Pattishall (d. 1229), who was an important justice in the 1210s and 1220s, may
have started the project. His clerk, William of Raleigh (d. 1250), who would
become the chief justice of the court *coram rege*, the court that would later be
known as the King's Bench, was probably the primary author. Raleigh's clerk,
Henry of Bratton (d. 1268), who became a justice of the court *coram rege* himself, appears to have edited the treatise and added his own material to it. The
central argument of this book will be that the justices who wrote *Bracton* were
the first people in the history of the common law to think of themselves as
legal professionals. It will build upon the work of several scholars who have
examined the beginnings of the legal profession in England. Ralph Turner's
magisterial work, *The English Judiciary in the Age of Glanvill and Bracton,
c. 1176-1239*, gives us a very detailed account of the early judiciary, and the
stages by which full-time justices came to dominate the work of the king's
courts.[3] C.A.F. Meekings and David Crook pick up where Turner left off in
their detailed narrative history of the court *coram rege* from 1234 up to 1272.[4]
Paul Brand has written on the judiciary in the reign of Edward I (1272–1307)
and, in particular, the "emergence during the course of the reign of a much
more recognizably 'professional' judiciary."[5] Although his focus is on the last
decades of the thirteenth century, Brand examines changes that took place in
the courts and the judiciary, some of which reach back into the first half of the
century. Brand's *Origins of the English Legal Profession* deals primarily with the
origins of two other groups of legal professionals, the serjeants and attorneys,
people who worked for clients in the royal courts. These groups were coales-
cing around the same time the *Bracton* authors were writing, in the middle
decades of the thirteenth century.[6] I am indebted to all of these scholars for
the detailed work they have done in reconstructing judicial careers in the thirteenth century. This book will build upon their work to illuminate the process
by which justices of the early thirteenth century came to think of themselves
as legal professionals. When these scholars discuss the professionalization of
the judicial bench, they tend to focus either on the development of expertise

---

[3] Ralph V. Turner, *The English Judiciary in the Age of Glanvill and Bracton, c. 1176-1239* (CUP 1985)
(hereafter Turner, *English Judiciary*).

[4] CAF Meekings and David Crook, *King's Bench and Common Bench in the Reign of Henry III* (Selden
Society 2010) (hereafter, Meekings and Crook, *King's Bench and Common Bench*).

[5] Paul Brand, "Edward I and the Transformation of the English Judiciary" in MCL, 135 (hereafter
Brand, "Transformation").

[6] Paul Brand, *The Origins of the English Legal Profession* (Blackwell 1992) 54–55 (hereafter Brand,
*Legal Profession*). Brand notes that a reference in Matthew Paris' *Chronica Majora* under the year 1239
to the king obtaining the services of all of the serjeants of the Common Bench seems to indicate that the
serjeants were an identifiable group of professionals by that time. Ibid, 55. There is evidence that some
people were practicing in the courts regularly enough to be considered professionals as early as the
1220s. Ibid.

or on structural changes within the courts that placed them on a more regular footing.[7] Turner and Brand show us, for instance, that by the early decades of the thirteenth century more of the central royal courts' work was being done by justices who served continuously for long periods of time and that many justices began their careers as judicial clerks, gaining experience in the courts before they ascended to the bench.[8] Expertise is not the only mark of a professional, however. This book will focus on another aspect of professionalization, the justices' self-perception. The justices who wrote *Bracton* are interesting figures not just because they had developed expertise in the law, but because they actually thought of themselves, first and foremost, as people who worked with law.

This book will examine *Bracton* and the other writings produced by the *Bracton* authors for evidence of the ways the justices thought about themselves. *Bracton* is a massive tome; it fills more than 1,200 pages in its modern edition and generally fills a very large single volume in its medieval manuscripts.[9] It draws on many sources. Those sources included numerous forms of writs— the small pieces of parchment that kept the royal administration running in the thirteenth century—as well as legislative acts, such as Magna Carta and the Provisions of Merton, and cases decided in the royal courts. The authors borrowed from earlier English sources, such as the *Glanvill* treatise, written in the late 1180s, just a few decades after the reforms of Henry II's reign. Its authors also probably had access to even earlier works, such as the *Leges Edwardi Confessoris*, an early twelfth-century composition that claims to recount the laws of a late Anglo-Saxon king. They may have known Latin translations of genuine Anglo-Saxon law codes.[10]

---

[7] Brand notes, for instance, that there was a growing tendency throughout the thirteenth century towards fewer justices who served longer periods of time on the bench and who did so to the exclusion of other types of work. These tendencies became much more pronounced in Edward I's reign, but the trend towards specialization appears to have begun as early as John's reign, if not before. Brand, "Transformation" (n 5) 141–44. This tends to show that justices were specializing and developing expertise in the work of the royal courts. Brand also notes that there is some evidence that there were attempts to place justices on regular salaries as early as 1218. Salaries became more common in the ensuing decades until, in the 1250s, most justices were receiving them. Ibid, 144–47.

[8] Brand, *Legal Profession* (n 6) 27–29. Brand argues that the development of a professional judiciary helped create the conditions necessary for a professional bar to develop. Ibid, 32.

[9] The treatise known as *Glanvill* is much smaller. *Glanvill* fits easily in a single volume of 177 pages in its modern edition, with fewer words per page. It is slightly more than one-tenth the size of *Bracton*.

[10] HG Richardson, "Studies in Bracton" (1948) 6 Traditio 61, 75–78 (hereafter Richardson, "Studies in Bracton"); TFT Plucknett, *Early English Legal Literature* (CUP 1958) 53 (hereafter Plucknett, *Legal Literature*); Wiebke Fesefeldt, *Englische Staatstheorie Des 13. Jahrhunderts: Henry De Bracton Und Sein Werk* (Musterschmidt Verlag 1962) 82; Paul Brand, "The Date and Authorship of Bracton: A Response" (2010) 31 Journal of Legal History 217, 220–22, 225 (hereafter Brand, "Date and Authorship").

The *Bracton* authors did not rely exclusively on English sources for their treatment of the "laws and customs of England," however. They also relied on another textual tradition: the tradition of Roman and canon law. In the twelfth and thirteenth centuries, the study of Roman law experienced a revival in those parts of Europe that, centuries before, had comprised the Western Roman Empire. The revival had begun in Italy. Bologna became the premier center for the study of Roman law and its close cousin, canon law. People from every corner of Latin Christendom—those parts of Europe and the Mediterranean world that recognized the pope as the head of the Church—traveled to learn at the feet of the doctors of Bologna. From Northern Italy, the study of Roman and canon law quickly spread. The first teacher of Roman law in England, Master Vacarius, arrived in the 1140s.[11] Vacarius' students, along with English scholars returning from continental schools, established their own schools in England. Oxford arose as one such center of learning in the last decades of the twelfth century.

Roman and canon law were taught together in the universities—indeed, they are often referred to as the "two laws," a loose translation of the medieval Latin phrase "*utrumque ius*"—and helped to knit together a shared educated culture throughout Europe. To the people who traveled, often at great danger and expense, to learn them, they were the universal laws of Christendom. Canon law was the law of the one, holy, catholic, and apostolic Church. It was binding law wherever the pope had authority and, by the turn of the twelfth century, popes were taking a very broad view of their authority. Roman law could also be understood as a universal law. Roman law was the law of the Christian empire. Just as canon law was regarded as the universal law of the *sacerdotium*, the priestly power exercised by the pope, Roman law was regarded by many as the universal law of the *regnum*, the secular power exercised by kings and emperors.[12] The ordinary gloss to Gratian's *Decretum* tells us that, although the main text of the *Decretum* says that the law of the Quirites—an archaic term for "Romans"—binds only the Romans, it actually binds all people, because "all subject to the Roman Empire are called Romans" and "The emperor is prince of the entire world."[13] This gloss implies that Roman law applies to the entire world as a positive law, but students of Roman law were more likely to think

---

[11] Jason Taliadoros, *Law and Theology in Twelfth-Century England: The Works of Master Vacarius (c. 1115/20-c. 1200)* (Brepols 2006) 3–4 (hereafter Taliadoros, *Law and Theology*).

[12] For a discussion of *sacerdotium* and *regnum* or *imperium*, see Jacques Le Goff, *Medieval Civilization, 400-1500* (Julia Barrow tr, Barnes & Noble Books 2000) 264–68.

[13] Ordinary Gloss to D.1 c.12, *nulli*; Gratian, *The Treatise on Laws with the Ordinary Gloss*, (Augustine Thompson and Katherine Christensen trs, Catholic University of America Press, 1993) 12. Not all jurists of the twelfth and thirteenth centuries would have agreed. The thirteenth-century canonists Laurentius Hispanus and Hostiensis both argued that the law of the Romans did not apply in the kingdoms of their own time. Laurent Mayali, "Ius Civile et Ius Commune dans la Tradition Juridique Médiévale" in

of it as a universal law in a somewhat different sense. Roman law was a sort of Platonic form of law. Medieval scholars referred to it, at times, as *ratio scripta* (written reason).[14] As the most rational form of law humans had produced, it approached the natural law. To many of its students, it had normative value. The laws of their own realms should, ideally, reflect its universal glory.

The authors of *Bracton* had, at their disposal, a broad range of texts of Roman and canon law. *Bracton* borrows much of its organization from the *Summa Institutionum* (*Summa on the Institutes*), of Azo, one of the leading doctors of Bologna. In addition to the work of Azo, the authors of *Bracton* used, quoted from, and cited to the primary sources of Roman law, those sixth-century compilations made at the command of the Emperor Justinian: the *Institutes*, *Digest*, and *Codex*.[15] They used the works of canonists, as well. They surely knew Gratian's *Decretum*, the textbook that essentially established canon law as an academic discipline at Bologna in the middle decades of the twelfth century. They knew more recent texts, such as an *ordo judiciarius*, a procedural manual, written by the Bolognese jurist Tancred, completed around 1216.[16] They knew and used Raymond of Peñafort's *Summa de Casibus* (*Summa of Cases*) and his *Summa de Matrimonio* (*Summa on Marriage*), both written in the 1220s or 1230s.[17] They likely knew the *Decretals of Gregory IX*, a major collection of papal decretals completed by Raymond in 1234.[18] They were also familiar with the work of English canonists. The *Summa Aurea* (*Golden Summa*) of William of Drogheda, a contemporary of the *Bracton* authors who taught Roman and canon law at Oxford until his untimely death at the hand of one of his servants in 1245, figures prominently in the treatise.[19] Despite the prevalence of texts

---

Jacques Krynen (ed), *Droit Romain, Jus Civile, Et Droit Français* (Presses de l'Université des Sciences Sociales de Toulouse 1999) 205.

[14] Laurent Mayali, "Romanitas and Medieval Jurisprudence" in Michael Hoeflich (ed), *Lex Et Romanitas: Essays for Alan Watson* (Robbins Collection 2000) 134.

[15] Close to 500 individual texts from the *Digest* and *Codex* are quoted in the treatise. They are only occasionally marked as quotations, however. *Bracton*, vol 1, xxxvi. Usually they are worked into the text without attribution to the source. I have counted thirty-four citations to texts of Roman- or Canon-law sources in the treatise, although the exact number depends on what one counts as a citation. See *Bracton*, vol 2, 45, 46, 53, 98, 101, 185, 295, 303, 305, 320, 323, 324, 362, 363, 367, 429; vol 3, 68; vol 4, 276. Most of those citations are in the format a civilian would have used to cite the text. See *Bracton*, vol 2, 53, 98, 303, 323–24. Some, however, simply cite "a *lex*" or "the *Institutes*." See, e.g., *Bracton*, vol 2, 46, 367.

[16] Nicholas Vincent, "Henry of Bratton (*alias* Bracton)" in Mark Hill and RH Helmholz (eds), *Great Christian Jurists in English History* (CUP 2017) 32 (hereafter Vincent, "Henry of Bratton").

[17] HG Richardson, "Tancred, Raymond, and Bracton" (1944) 59 EHR 376–84; Naomi D Hurnard, *The King's Pardon for Homicide before A.D. 1307* (Clarendon Press 1969) 70.

[18] Fritz Schulz, "Bracton on Kingship" (1945) 60 EHR 136, 167.

[19] HG Richardson, "Azo, Drogheda, and Bracton" (1944) 59 EHR 22 (hereafter Richardson, "Azo, Drogheda, and Bracton"). For a good summary of the literature on the sources of *Bracton*, see Vincent, "Henry of Bratton" (n 16) 32–33.

of the Bolognese masters in the treatise, its authors probably never travelled to Bologna. They interacted with the luminaries of Bologna through their texts and their students, some of whom had returned to England to teach. Through the circulation of texts and students, the greatest of the doctors of Bologna developed rock-star-like reputations that spanned Latin Christendom. In the writings of the English scholar Thomas of Marlborough, who studied at Bologna in the first decade of the thirteenth century, we find Azo described as "lord of the lords of the laws of Bologna."[20]

It was in these texts that the authors of *Bracton* found a template for the legal professional. *Bracton* was written primarily for the justices and clerks of the royal courts, and it is designed, in part, to convince those justices and clerks that they are part of the broader legal culture of Latin Christendom, the culture defined by the two universal laws. The phrase with which this chapter began, "law is called the art of what is fair and just, of which we are deservedly called the priests, for we worship justice and administer sacred rights," is presented in the treatise as if these are the words of the author. The author of *Bracton* is speaking these words to his reader and he draws himself and his reader into a single community defined by that "we." We know that the authors of the treatise were justices of the central royal courts and, just a few paragraphs before the quotation appears in *Bracton*, the text defines its audience as apprentices who are preparing to sit as royal justices in England.[21] *Bracton*'s audience, the "we" who are "deservedly called priests" of the law, are the justices and clerks of the English king's central royal courts.

These words draw the author and the reader together into a community and define that community as a group of people who are both masters and servants of the law. I think it does something else, however. The phrase "law is called the art of what is fair and just, of which we are deservedly called the priests, for we worship justice and administer sacred rights," is actually derived from Roman law, and the author of this passage likely expected that his reader would know that. It originated with the Roman jurist Ulpian (d. 223 C.E.). For Ulpian, the "we" in the sentence was comprised of people like himself, the jurists who were teaching and consulting on the law of Rome during its classical period. Ulpian's words were transmitted to scholars in medieval Europe through Justinian's *Digest*, a sixth-century compilation of the works of the most important jurists of the classical era.[22] They were later included, in a slightly modified version,

---

[20] "Legum dominorum dominus Bononiae." Richardson, "Azo, Drogheda, and Bracton" (n 19) 22.
[21] *Bracton*, vol 2, 20.
[22] D.1.1.1.

in Azo's *Summa on the Institutes*, the *Bracton* authors' probable source for the quotation.[23]

As we shall see in later chapters, the authors of *Bracton* imagined their reader as someone who was well-versed in Roman law. Anyone who had studied Roman law in the thirteenth century would likely have encountered Ulpian's words, either in Azo or in the *Digest*.[24] In the context of *Bracton*, the "we" referred to the justices and clerks of the royal courts, but it also would have evoked, in the mind of the reader, the jurists of civil law working in the universities of Western Christendom. The "we" thus draws the justices and clerks of the royal courts together into a single community, but also draws them into community with the jurists of the civil law who were expounding this sacred and universal law throughout Christendom.

This book will argue that the authors of *Bracton* were the first people in the history of the common law, at least that we know of, to grapple with the idea of what it means to be a legal professional, and that they found their model for the legal professional in the civilians' and canonists' ideal of the jurist, the *iuris peritus* or *iuris prudens*. Roman law gave the authors of *Bracton* a way of imagining themselves, in a particular time and place, as part of a universal endeavor. In *Bracton*, they found a way of attaching universal significance to the mundane work of the English royal courts. Through their writing, they transformed themselves into jurists of the universal law. In making this argument, this book will explore three themes. First, it will explore the relationship between the two laws and the early common law. The degree to which the common law was, in its first century, influenced by Roman and canon law is one of the central questions with which historians have wrestled over the last century. The debates in this field have largely stalled, however, in disagreements over whether particular rules, doctrines, and procedures of the early common law were inspired by the two laws. I hope to offer a new way forward in these debates by arguing for a different kind of civilian and canonist influence on the early common law, which I hope will open new avenues of inquiry for this central question of common-law scholarship.

That new way forward implicates the second and third themes of the book. The second deals with the ways in which the common law was developing in the early thirteenth century. At the time these justices started writing *Bracton*, the common law had already developed its own technical terminology, quite different from the terminology used in Roman and canon law, and had already

---

[23] Azo, *Summae*, 1043, 47–48 (commentary on Inst.1.1.pr.).
[24] D.1.1.1.

diverged quite a bit in substance and procedure from the two laws. It had not developed much when it came to higher-level questions, however. The 1220s to 1260s were a period of experimentation and contestation when it came to thinking about just what the common law was, where it resided, and who should control it. This meant that there was more space for civilian and canonist influence on the common law in the realm of higher-level thinking about law than in the realm of rules, doctrines, and procedures. I hope to demonstrate that the kind of civilian and canonist influence we find in *Bracton* and related texts is influence of this higher-order sort.

That brings us to the third theme, which is methodological. The historians who have debated the level of connection between the early common law and Roman and canon law have tended to focus on demonstrating that rules, doctrines, and procedures that became central features of the common law were originally borrowed from Roman or canon law. In this book, I will offer a different way of thinking about influence from one legal system to another. When we look at the common law as an amalgam of practices rather than a set of rules, doctrines, and norms, influence from the two laws becomes more apparent. When I say that the common law is an amalgam of practices, however, I do not refer to the practices of litigants in using the law or of justices in applying it. The practices I examine in this book are the practices of using, reading, and producing texts in the royal courts of the thirteenth century. The authors of *Bracton* had extensive knowledge of Roman and canon law, probably acquired in the schools. Instead of transplanting rules and doctrines to the royal courts, however, they brought particular ways of *doing* law with them from their study of Roman law. In the schools they had learned to think of law as a textual practice; they then adapted the textual practices of the schools to their work in the courts. They re-imagined the records of the legal proceedings that took place in their courts, the plea rolls, as the *consilia* of jurists, for instance. These very tangible textual practices gave them space to imagine the work of the English royal courts as one constituent part of the universal culture of the two laws and to imagine themselves as members of an order of jurists that spanned the Christian West.

## Roman Law, Canon Law, and Common Law

The degree to which the early English common law interacted with and was influenced by Roman and canon law has occupied historians for more than a century. Traditional narratives of English exceptionalism—and its subset, common-law exceptionalism—have set the terms of the debate and made the issue of Roman- and canon-law influence one of the central questions of the literature on the early common law. Some scholars have argued that England was precocious in its legal development and, as a result, largely avoided the kind of Roman- and canon-law influence that continental legal systems experienced. According to these scholars, by the time Roman and canon law were developed enough to influence English law, they found in England an established system of royal courts that were impervious to penetration by foreign ideas.[25] Alternatively, some scholars argue that the two laws were central to the early development of the common law. Frederic William Maitland's theory that Roman and canon law partly inspired Henry II's new writs in the 1160s is still being debated.[26] Recently scholars have argued for Roman- and canon-law influence on some of the pillars of the common law, such as Magna Carta and trial by jury.[27]

[25] Raoul van Caenegem is a proponent of this view. RC Van Caenegem, *The Birth of the English Common Law* (2nd edn, CUP 1988) 106. Over a century ago, Heinrich Brunner offered an influential version of this thesis. Brunner thought that England was precocious in its development, and had incorporated a bit of Roman law in the early stages. According to Brunner, this small reception of Roman law had "operated as a sort of prophylactic inoculation, and had rendered the national law immune against destructive infection." Heinrich Brunner, "The Sources of English Law" in *Select Essays in Anglo-American Legal History*, vol 2 (Little, Brown, and Company 1908) 42. Brunner's metaphor still has some currency among legal historians. See John Hamilton Baker, *An Introduction to English Legal History* (4th edn, Butterworths 2002) 28.

[26] Richard Helmholz has stated that "It is now generally agreed that [the assize of novel disseisin] was suggested by Roman law notions mediated through the canon law." RH Helmholz, "The Early History of the Grand Jury and Canon Law" (1983) 50 University of Chicago Law Review 613, 626 (hereafter Helmholz, "Grand Jury"). Charles Donahue, on the other hand, states that "Recent work with the origins of [the writ of right, the assize of novel disseisin, and the assize of mort d'ancestor] would suggest that they have little to do, in their origins, with the [Roman] concepts of ownership and possession." Charles Donahue, "*Ius Commune*, Canon Law, and Common Law in England" (1991-92) 66 Tulane Law Review 1745, 1759. I tend to think that it is still an open question. Donahue largely follows S.F.C. Milsom, who argued that the early writs were primarily about relations between lord and vassal, and therefore came out of a very different tradition of thought than the Roman concepts of ownership and possession. This tradition of thought was, indeed, incompatible in many ways with the Roman categories of ownership and possession. SFC Milsom, *The Legal Framework of English Feudalism* (CUP 1976). There is a bit of room between these two positions. It is possible, for instance, that Henry II's writs were not influenced by the two laws' distinction between ownership and possession, but that the counsellors who were developing them and the justices who were applying them did turn to Roman law to fill in some of the specifics, such as whether the winning plaintiff could also recover his chattels by the assize of novel disseisin. Donald Sutherland, *The Assize of Novel Disseisin* (Clarendon Press 1973) 23–24 (hereafter Sutherland, *Novel Disseisin*). John Hudson has recently referred to the assize as an exercise of "judicial bricolage," which incorporated some ideas from Roman and canon law. John Hudson, *The Oxford History of the Laws of England, Volume II: 871-1216* (OUP 2012) 612.
    For two recent summaries of the literature on the possibility of civil- and canon-law influence on the early assizes, see Anne J Duggan, "Roman, Canon and Common Law in Twelfth-Century England: The Council of Northampton (1164) Re-Examined" (2010) 83 Historical Research 379, 397–99; Joshua C Tate, "Ownership and Possession in the Early Common Law" (2006) 48 American Journal of Legal History 281.

[27] Helmholz, "Grand Jury"; RH Helmholz, "Magna Carta and the *Ius Commune*" (1999) 66 University of Chicago Law Review 297 (hereafter Helmholz, "Magna Carta and the *Ius Commune*"); Mike Macnair, "Vicinage and the Antecedents of the Jury" (1999) 17 Law and History Review 537 (hereafter Macnair, "Vicinage"); Kenneth Pennington, "The 'Ius Commune', Suretyship and Magna Carta" (2000) 11 Rivista

The debate between the two sides has largely reached a stalemate.[28] Kenneth Pennington, coming at the issue from the direction of canon-law studies, has argued that this is primarily because scholars of the early common law "Balkanize" medieval legal systems in anachronistic ways. Pennington argues that medieval people did not create the kinds of impermeable boundaries between fields of knowledge that we do today. Different bodies of knowledge, such as law and theology, were not as firmly divided as our modern academic disciplines, and, in the absence of the nation-state, medieval people did not draw the kinds of national boundaries around legal systems that we see in the modern world.[29] Law was law, and universal principles that happened to come out of the discourses of Roman and canon law would not have been rejected by people who served in the English royal courts simply because they came from Roman and canon law.

This kind of anachronistic Balkanization certainly has influenced the way scholars have thought about the early history of the common law. Common lawyers have been particularly insular at various points in their history, and that insularity has led to some strange thinking about the relationship between the early common law and the two laws. Historians' focus on the possible civilian and canonist influence on the early common law is part of a broader process of trying to understand England in a larger geographical and cultural context, to move away from a literature in which England is as insular in its law, politics, and culture as it is in its geography. Even if England's legal system developed along somewhat different lines from the legal systems of the continent, it must still be significant that England, as well as continental realms, experienced a "legal revolution," as Harold Berman put it, in the twelfth and thirteenth centuries.[30] Legal treatises proliferated everywhere in Europe in the thirteenth century, from texts like *Bracton* to the German *Sachsenspiegel*

---

internazionale di diritto comune 255 (hereafter Pennington, "Suretyship"); Ken Pennington, "Reform in 1215: *Magna Carta* and the Fourth Lateran Council" (2015) 32 Bulletin of Medieval Canon Law, new series 97 (hereafter Pennington, "Reform in 1215").

[28] For some responses to the above literature, see John Hudson, "Magna Carta, the *Ius Commune*, and English Common Law" in Janet S Loengard (ed), *Magna Carta and the England of King John* (Boydell Press 2010) (hereafter Hudson, "Magna Carta"); Thomas J McSweeney, "Magna Carta, Civil Law, and Canon Law" in Daniel Barstow Magraw, Andrea Martinez, and Roy E Brownell (eds), *Magna Carta and the Rule of Law* (American Bar Association 2014); Charles Donahue, "Biology and the Origins of the Jury" (1999) 17 Law and History Review 591 (hereafter Donahue, "Biology").

[29] Pennington, "Suretyship" (n 27) 255–57.

[30] Berman argues that many kingdoms simultaneously developed distinct legal institutions, professional bodies of lawyers, and a general sense that law is a discrete field of thought. Harold J Berman, *Law and Revolution: The Formation of the Western Legal Tradition* (Harvard University Press 1983) 7–11 (hereafter Berman, *Law and Revolution*).

and the French *coutumiers*. Some scholars have argued that this revolution resulted, at least partly, from common responses to common problems throughout Europe. Thomas Bisson, for instance, has argued that the institutions of public power—including the institutions of the law—came about in response to a twelfth-century crisis in lordship, in which too many petty lords were attempting to exercise coercive power, leading to violence.[31] Common problems partially explain the revolutions in law and government we see in the thirteenth century, but the striking similarities in response to these common problems hint that there must be something else going on, as well. The Church, as one of the few institutions that had a presence throughout Western Europe in the Middle Ages, looms large in the story of this revolution. Berman argues that the kingdoms of Europe were, in essence, forced to respond to a more assertive papacy, which was increasingly operating through the medium of law. Kings staked out their own jurisdiction by responding in kind, with legal arguments for royal power, and created secular systems of justice modeled on canon law.[32]

Scholars of Roman and canon law have suggested that the influence of the two laws can help us explain these Europe-wide developments. Manlio Bellomo has argued that by the end of the twelfth century Roman and canon law together constituted a common law of Europe, often referred to by historians as the *ius commune*.[33] According to scholars such as Bellomo and Pennington, people trained in the methods of the *ius commune* carried those methods over into their work in the secular courts. The *ius proprium*, the law of a particular place, thus reflected the *ius commune*, helping to create a common legal culture, even in the local or regional courts of Europe.[34] These scholars have made important contributions to our understanding of the legal revolution of the twelfth and thirteenth centuries, and why such similar processes occurred throughout Europe.

---

[31] Thomas N Bisson, *The Crisis of the Twelfth Century: Power, Lordship, and the Origins of European Government* (Princeton University Press 2009) 182–278.

[32] Berman, *Law and Revolution* (n 30) 86–87.

[33] Manlio Bellomo, *The Common Legal Past of Europe, 1000-1800*, (Lydia G Cochrane tr, Catholic University of America Press 1995) (hereafter Bellomo, *Common Legal Past*). For reasons discussed in Chapter 2, I generally will avoid using the term "*ius commune*" to refer to Roman and canon law collectively.

[34] At times, arguments over the influence of the *ius commune* in the Middle Ages can take on a political valence. Bellomo is quite open about the fact that he has a political agenda in arguing for a robust, Europe-wide legal culture in the Middle Ages. Bellomo wants to replace the many national legal cultures of present-day Europe with a common European legal culture of the kind that existed in the Middle Ages. Bellomo, *Common Legal Past* (n 33) 29–33. This issue is particularly pressing in England, given the debates about whether England is properly a part of Europe. Many of the proponents of Britain's withdrawal from the European Union argued that England has a political and legal culture that is distinct from the traditions of the continent.

The problem is that there is little direct evidence that the architects of the early common law borrowed rules and doctrines from Roman and canon law. Scholars have been able to find very little Roman- and canon-law terminology in the texts surrounding the English king's courts of the twelfth and thirteenth centuries. The argument that many of Henry II's writs—the assize of novel disseisin, for instance—are based on Roman or canon law is based on similarities in the way they operated. No one has been able to point to a single word in the assize of novel disseisin drawn from Roman or canon law.[35] Raoul van Caenegem likewise pointed out that "it is no doubt significant that Magna Carta . . . contains no Roman terminology."[36] That is a bit of an overstatement, but just a bit.[37] Richard Helmholz admits that there "is no 'smoking gun'" to prove Roman- and canon-law influence on Magna Carta.[38]

People in thirteenth-century England actually held a range of views on the issue of whether rules and doctrines from Roman and canon law should, could, or should not be adopted into the common law of the realm. There were people in England who, as Helmholz says "desired actively to advance the fortunes of the *ius commune* in England."[39] This kind of normative commitment to Roman and canon law certainly could have led some people in England to try to reform the rules of the Common Law to align more closely with those of Roman and canon law.[40] There were likely people in England who, as Pennington suggests, were trained in the methods of Roman and canon law and saw no barrier to importing its rules and methods into the common law.[41] As Charles Donahue notes, however, "That leaves . . . a rather large number of people who counted and who neither knew nor cared about Roman-canonical

---

[35] Donald Sutherland, who thought that the drafters of the assize borrowed heavily from the Roman interdict *unde vi*, conceded that "the terminology of novel disseisin owes nothing to those passages of Justinian's *Corpus* that deal with the interdict." He thought that, "The designers of the assize used Roman law as a source of suggestions but not as a model to be copied." Sutherland, *Novel Disseisin* (n 25) 24.

[36] RC Van Caenegem, *An Historical Introduction to Private Law* (DEL Johnston tr, CUP 1992) 181. Van Caenegem noted that other texts of the period did include Roman terminology. By this he meant the *Glanvill* and *Bracton* treatises, on which there will be more discussion below.

[37] Magna Carta contains no terminology that we can unambiguously attribute to Roman law. Helmholz, in a brilliant and thorough article, demonstrated that there is some terminology in Magna Carta that might be derived from Roman law. Helmholz, "Magna Carta and the *Ius Commune*" (n 27) 368. John Hudson has demonstrated that all of the terms have other possible sources, sources that he thinks more likely than Roman law. Hudson, "Magna Carta" (n 28) 108. Magna Carta also contains six chapters (chapters 1, 22, 52, 53, 57, and 63) that unambiguously draw upon canon law. All of them deal with ecclesiastical issues, where this would be appropriate.

[38] Helmholz, "Magna Carta and the *Ius Commune*" (n 27) 359.

[39] Ibid, 367.

[40] Some of those involved in the debate over subsequent legitimation and the council of Merton could be described in this way. See below, pp 13–4.

[41] Pennington, "Reform in 1215" (n 27) 124.

procedure."[42] Indeed, some of those people who mattered were hostile to the idea that common law should incorporate elements of Roman and canon law. There were people who, in essence, thought that the norms of Roman law *could* be followed in England's secular courts. There were also those who thought that Roman law was, in some sense, universal, and that it *should* be followed in England's secular courts. But these discourses about Roman law coexisted with discourses that held that the norms of Roman and canon law were irrelevant, or even inimical, to the practice of England's secular courts.

The debate over the legitimacy of a child whose parents married after his birth is a case in point. From at least the late twelfth century, when the royal courts needed to know whether someone was legitimate or a bastard, they would write to his bishop.[43] To determine a person's legitimacy, it was necessary to know whether his parents were married, and the formation of marriage was within the exclusive jurisdiction of the ecclesiastical courts. We know that the king instructed his justices in 1234 that, from then on, in that subset of legitimacy cases in which a party was alleged to be a bastard because he was born before his parents' marriage, the justices were to send a letter to the bishop asking a slightly more specific question than whether the person in question was legitimate: "born before marriage or after."[44] They were to ask this narrow question because, according to canon law, a child born before marriage became legitimate at the moment his parents married, while under English law, he remained a bastard.[45] Thus, if the justices simply asked the bishop if the child was legitimate, he would answer yes even in circumstances where, under English law, the child would be considered illegitimate. A long and distraught letter from Robert Grosseteste, the Oxford scholar and newly elected bishop of Lincoln, to William of Raleigh—the primary author of *Bracton* and, at the time, the chief justice of the court *coram rege*—attests to the cold response some of the bishops gave to this method of inquiry.[46] Grosseteste argued that the rule applied in the royal courts was contrary to natural law, divine law, canon law, and civil law. His argument was based on the grounds that canon

---

[42] Donahue, "Biology" (n 28) 596. Donahue is responding specifically to Mike Macnair's claim that Henry II's adoption of trial by jury may have been inspired by forms of proof at canon law. See Macnair, "Vicinage" (n 27).

[43] *Glanvill*, 87–88 (VII, c. 14–15); Paul Brand, "Law and Custom in the English Thirteenth Century Common Law" in Per Anderson & Mia Münster-Swendsen (eds), *Custom: The Development and Use of a Legal Concept in the Middle Ages* (DJØF Publishing 2009) 27 (hereafter Brand, "Law and Custom").

[44] BNB, vol 1, 106–107; Brand, "Law and Custom" (n 43) 28. This formulation appears in *Bracton*, as well: "mittatur loquela ad ordinarium loci et fiat inquisitio per hæc verba utrum videlicet talis natus fuerit ante sponsalia sive matrimonium vel post." *Bracton*, vol 4, 297.

[45] *Bracton*, vol 4, 297.

[46] BNB, vol 1, 108.

law is a positive law superior to secular law—he quotes Gratian's *Decretum* for the notion that a secular law that is prejudicial to the law of the Church has no force—and that the canon-law rule in this case was in accord with reason, while the rule applied in the royal courts was not.[47] Thus, for Grosseteste, the canon-law rule of subsequent legitimation represented both a superior positive law and *ratio scripta*.[48] The other bishops agreed. According to *Bracton*, a group of bishops protested that "those born before espousals or marriage were as legitimate as those born after marriage in the eyes of God and the Church" and that they could not answer the question posed in the king's writ, condemning some people who were not bastards in their eyes to lose their land in the royal court, without "prejudice to Holy Church."[49]

Matters came to a head at the great council of the realm held at Merton Priory in 1236. It would appear that the lay lords were unmoved by Grosseteste's arguments that canon law was a superior positive law and that it represented good reason. Various accounts tell us that "all the earls and barons answered with one voice that they did not wish to change the laws of England, which have been used and approved."[50] It is possible that the magnates feared the retroactive application of this rule would cast some uncertainty upon their own land tenure; some families would have an elder bastard somewhere in the family tree who had been disinherited.[51] Even if they had a good reason to object, the language that the roll uses here does not imply that they objected on the ground that the barons preferred the English rule to the canonical rule, but rather that they preferred English law, the laws "which have been used and approved," to

[47] Robert Grosseteste, *The Letters of Robert Grosseteste, Bishop of Lincoln* (FAC Mantello and Joseph Goering trs, University of Toronto Press 2010) 118; Robert Grosseteste, *Roberti Grosseteste Episcopis Quondam Lincolniensis Epistolae* (Henry Richards Luard ed, Longman, Green, Longman, and Roberts 1861) 88–90.

[48] Brand points out that Grosseteste may have been worried that this line of argument would not have much resonance with Raleigh. Grosseteste also claimed that the English had previously followed a version of the rule of subsequent legitimation, appealing to the customs of the realm rather than the dictates of canon law. Raleigh replied that such a rule had not been applied even as far back as the reign of Henry II. Brand, "Law and Custom" (n 43) 28.

[49] "Ad quod omnes episcopi dixerunt quod omnes illi qui nati fuerunt ante sponsalia vel matrimonium ita erunt legitimi sicut illi qui nati fuerunt post matrimonium, quoad deum et quoad ecclesiam, nec voluerunt nec potuerunt sine præiudicio ecclesiasticæ dignitatis respondere ad breve super huiusmodi inquisitione facienda de bastardia sic obiecta . . ." *Bracton*, vol 4, 296.

[50] "Et omnes Comites et Barones una voce responderunt quod nolunt leges Angliae mutare que usitate sunt et approbate." SR 1, statutes section, 4; BNB, vol 1, 110–11; *Bracton*, vol 4, 296.

[51] Sara McDougall has recently suggested that the rules the barons sought to protect at Merton were of relatively recent origin, part of a trend in the late twelfth and early thirteenth centuries towards the dispossession of bastards. If societal and legal norms concerning a bastard's ability to inherit were in flux in this period, it is entirely possible that some of the barons feared relatively strong claims from relatives who had been born out of wedlock. Sara McDougall, *Royal Bastards: The Birth of Illegitimacy, 800-1230* (OUP 2017) 185.

canon law. The text does not necessarily indicate that the barons were hostile to canon law, but it does indicate that they felt no need to bring the common law into conformity with it, either on the ground that it was superior to secular law or on the ground that it was closer to natural reason.

Roger of Thirkleby, chief justice of the Common Bench, made an even stronger statement of distaste for canon law in 1251. The monastic chronicler Matthew Paris records his objection to the *non obstante* (notwithstanding) clauses that were sometimes used in royal letters and writs. Occasionally Henry III would issue a writ that ordered his officials to do something notwithstanding some prior grant or preexisting privilege to the contrary. In 1228, Henry ordered his eyre justices in Hampshire to hear an assize of novel disseisin against some men of Southampton "notwithstanding that the Lord King conceded on this occasion [i.e., this particular eyre] to the men of Southampton that pleas pertaining to the aforesaid vill of Southampton should be pleaded within that same vill."[52] As the eyre justices were then sitting at Winchester, the order to hear the case directly contravened a privilege Henry had granted to the burgesses of Southampton.[53] Matthew suggests that by 1251, the king had been using these clauses often enough to draw criticism.[54] He tells us that Thirkleby, at that time the senior justice of the Common Bench, gave a speech in which he said, in grandiose and pseudo-Biblical style, "Alas, alas, that we should have seen these days. Behold, even now the civil court is polluted by the example of the ecclesiastical [court], and a brook is poisoned by a sulphurous fount."[55] If Matthew reports the speech accurately, Thirkleby clearly associated the *non obstante* clause with the ecclesiastical courts—the king may have been following the example of papal letters—and he did not like what he saw.[56] Although he is talking about the practices of the courts, not the field of knowledge known as canon law, one gets the sense that Thirkleby would have been hostile to the notion that English law should reflect canon law. Matthew Paris also shows contempt for Roman law in a forged papal bull he includes in his chronicle for the year 1254. The bull laments that the study of Roman

---

[52] "[N]on obstante eo quod dominus rex hac vice concessit hominibus de Suhamt' quod placita ad predictam villam Suhamt' pertinentia infra eandem villam placitentur." CR 1227–31, 33; FM Powicke, *King Henry III and the Lord Edward: The Community of the Realm in the Thirteenth Century* (OUP 1966) 324 (hereafter Powicke, *Henry III*).

[53] The order was given on April 4th. The eyre sat at Winchester from April 3rd to May 5th, when it moved to Southampton. David Crook, *Records of the General Eyre* (Her Majesty's Stationery Office 1982) 85 (hereafter Crook, *General Eyre*).

[54] Powicke, *Henry III* (n 52) 324–25.

[55] "Heu, heu, hos utquid dies expectavimus. Ecce jam civilis curia exemplo ecclesiasticae coinquinatur, et a sulphuero fonte rivulus intoxicatur." CM, vol 5, 211.

[56] Powicke, *Henry III* (n 52) 325.

law has overtaken the study of philosophy and theology, so that "these lawyers, or rather devils" have taken the offices of the Church for themselves and
"show themselves not the servants of Him who was crucified, but the heirs of
Lucifer."[57] This is pretty standard thirteenth-century anti-lawyer invective.[58]
What is more interesting is that the bull continues on to say that in the kingdoms of France, England, Scotland, Wales, Spain, and Hungary, where "the
causes of the laity are decided not by imperial laws, but by the customs of
laymen," civil law should no longer be taught at all.[59] The author of this forgery
does, of course, recognize that the canons of the Church apply in these countries, as they do throughout Christendom, but the idea that Roman law was a
law that the laws of these kingdoms should emulate would have been anathema
to him.

One of my goals for this book will be to shift the conversation about early
interaction between the common law and the two laws away from rules and
doctrines. *Bracton* and the other texts created by the same group of justices
give us some purchase for examining the nature of the relationship between
the early common law and the two laws. Written by a known group of justices
with a particular agenda, *Bracton* and related texts open up the possibility of
examining both the mechanisms of Roman-law influence on the common law
and the reasons why justices, in the second quarter of the thirteenth century,
turned to Roman law. *Bracton* and the other texts produced by this group provide a rich archive for thinking about the ways people working in the king's
courts of the thirteenth century interacted with the two laws. Through these
texts, we can catch a glimpse of a group of people working in the royal courts
of the early thirteenth century who thought that the two laws were central to
their work. These justices did not look on the two laws primarily as a treasury
of good doctrine to be applied in the royal courts or as a justification for changing certain rules they wanted changed. Although they did not adopt the
rules and doctrines of the two laws as their own, neither was their use of the
two laws merely ornamental. They looked to Roman and canon law for ways
of understanding the work they were doing in the royal courts. It gave them

---

[57] Matthew Paris, *Matthew Paris's English History*, 3 vols (JA Giles tr, Henry G Bohn 1852-54) vol
3, 440–41 (hereafter Matthew Paris, *English History*); CM, vol 6, 294; Hector L MacQueen, *Common
Law and Feudal Society in Medieval Scotland*, (Edinburgh Classics Edition, Edinburgh University Press
2016) 1.
[58] For further examples, see below p 72.
[59] Matthew Paris, *English History* (n 57) vol 3, 440–44. "Praetera, cum in Franciae, Angliae, Scotiae,
Walliae, Hispaniae, et Hungariae regnis causae laicorum non imperatoriis legibus sed laicorum
consuetudinibus decidantur." CM, vol 6, 295.

a framework for thinking about the common law, as well as a framework for thinking about who they were.

## Before the Common Law Was the Common Law

The authors of *Bracton* used the two laws less as a gap-filler in fields of law where common law had not yet developed any doctrine than as a template for understanding their work in the royal courts. They used Roman and canon law to think through higher-order questions about the nature of the common law and where it, and its justices, fit into the broader constitution of Christendom. There was space for Roman and canon law to enter into discussions about the common law at these higher levels of abstraction because, although the king's courts developed their own language and procedures fairly early, when it came to higher-order questions the common law was much slower to develop. Scholars usually treat Henry II's reforms of the 1160s and 1170s as the "birth of the common law," yet even fifty years later, there was still no consensus on how to think about what the royal courts were doing. People in England had not settled on a collective term for the law the royal courts administered; "common law" would not become the dominant term until late in the thirteenth century.[60] The variety of terms in use before then hint at contested understandings of that law.

Our story begins in the years immediately following Magna Carta. As David Carpenter has demonstrated, the period between 1216 and 1227 was an important period for the development of English ideas of good government.[61] King John had died, leaving his minor son, Henry III, on the throne. Magna Carta had been an occasion to think about the division of power within the realm. Henry III's minority offered a continuing opportunity. The king's courts were at the center of many of the debates about the nature of authority in England. Some people viewed the royal courts through the lens of kingship, and saw them as very closely connected to the person of the king. Kings, their officials, and their justices regularly issued pardons that were said to be for the salvation of the king's soul, suggesting a close link between the

---

[60] There are a few scattered uses in the late twelfth century or the early thirteenth, but the phrase did not settle into the familiar *comune ley* or *lex communis* until the 1270s. Brand, "Law and Custom" (n 43) 21; John Hudson, *Oxford History of the Laws of England, Volume II, 871–1216* (OUP 2012) 853; John Hudson, *The Formation of the English Common Law* (2nd edn, Routledge, 2018) 14 (hereafter Hudson, *Formation*).

[61] DA Carpenter, *The Minority of Henry III* (University of California Press 1990) 2–4 (hereafter Carpenter, *Minority*).

king and his courts.[62] King John, whose reign would have been on everyone's mind in the 1220s, had maintained a greater degree of personal control over the administration of royal justice than his predecessors. From the reign of John's grandfather, Henry II, a royal court began to sit permanently at Westminster, detached from the royal household.[63] During the reign of John's elder brother, Richard, this court, later known as the Common Bench or Court of Common Pleas, became an independent institution, no longer associated directly with the exchequer.[64] But starting in 1207, John began to remove cases from the bench at Westminster, reserving them to himself. In 1209, he closed the Westminster bench completely and brought the justices to his side.[65] The central court would follow the king and often sit in the king's presence. In Ireland, where the local English lords were much more powerful vis-à-vis the king than they were in England, John made claims of a special relationship between the king and the law a central feature of his attempts to assert royal authority. In 1209, he issued a decree for Ireland in which he asserted a special type of royal authority, qualitatively different from the lesser authority exercised by the Anglo-Irish lords. He commanded that no one in Ireland buy or sell with any coins but the king's. The minting of coins was an important prerogative of kingship and a demonstration of the exceptional quality of royal power; only the king could mint coins. In the same text, John commanded that no case involving a free tenement was to be heard unless the plaintiff had acquired a writ from the king or his justiciar, placing jurisdiction on a level with the minting of coins as a mark of sovereignty.[66] In 1210, John visited Ireland at the head of a mighty army in an attempt to awe his Irish magnates into submission. The sight of the royal host, arriving on 700 ships with 800 knights and 1,000 sergeants and crossbowmen, must have been truly impressive.[67] But John's entourage did not just contain knights and crossbowmen. It contained some of the most prominent justices of the royal courts. Simon of Pattishall, who may have been accompanied by Martin of

---

[62] Thomas J McSweeney, "The King's Courts and the King's Soul: Pardoning as Almsgiving in Medieval England" (2014) 50 Reading Medieval Studies 159–75.

[63] Paul Brand, "'Multis Vigiliis Excogitatam et Inventam': Henry II and the Creation of the English Common Law" in MCL, 86–89.

[64] Turner, English Judiciary (n 3) 68–73.

[65] Ibid, 135.

[66] Colin Veach, Lordship in Four Realms: The Lacy Family, 1166-1241 (Manchester University Press 2014) 135; RLP 1, part 1, 76. During Henry III's minority, the sheriff of Cornwall appointed judges to hear petty assizes, rather than reserving those cases for the king's justices. This was viewed by the king's guardians as an attack on the king's authority. Carpenter, Minority (n 61) 212.

[67] SD Church, "The 1210 Campaign in Ireland: Evidence for a Military Revolution?" in Christopher Harper-Bill (ed), Anglo-Norman Studies XX: Proceedings of the Battle Conference, 1997 (Boydell Press 1998) 48, 54.

Pattishall, then his clerk, was among the "men discerning and learned in the law" who witnessed John's proclamation that "English laws should be held in Ireland."[68] John seems to have thought that the provision of the king's justice, not just a display of military might, was important in the establishment of his rule in Ireland.

This kind of thought, that the justice administered by the king's courts was personal to the king, and a mark of his sovereignty, may be behind the phrase *lex regni* ("the law of the realm"), contained in chapters 42 and 45 of Magna Carta. *Lex regni* attaches the law to notions of kingship; *regnum* in Latin, usually translated as "realm," can also be translated as "royal authority."[69] Carpenter has argued that a different phrase, *lex terrae* ("the law of the land"), which made its way into other chapters of Magna Carta, may have been preferred by the barons.[70] The phrase *lex terrae* detaches law from notions of kingship, giving the reader the impression that the law is something that arises out of the ground.[71] There was a growing sense in the early thirteenth century that the king's courts were, and should be, somewhat separate from the king. As early as the 1170s, the exchequer official Richard FitzNigel could distinguish between the "common law of the realm" (*communi regni iure*) and the "arbitrary will of the king."[72] A blanket pardon issued in 1189 by Eleanor of Aquitaine for the soul of her recently deceased husband, Henry II, similarly makes distinctions between prisoners who have been imprisoned for violations of the forest

---

[68] It is even possible that William of Raleigh accompanied Simon of Pattishall. He may have been working in the royal courts at this point. Paul Brand, "Ireland and the Literature of the Early Common Law" in MCL, 445–47.

[69] David Carpenter, *Magna Carta* (Penguin 2015) 245–47 (hereafter Carpenter, *Magna Carta*). The *Glanvill* treatise, written by someone working in the royal courts in the late 1180s, similarly uses the term *ius regni*. *Glanvill*, 72 (VII, c. 1); Hudson, *Oxford History* (n 60) 651.

[70] Carpenter, *Magna Carta* (n 69) 246–47.

[71] John Hudson argues that the decision to use *lex terrae* as opposed to *lex regni* or vice-versa may not have been as significant as Carpenter supposes, at least in some chapters. Hudson points out that the Articles of the Barons uses the word *regnum* in a way that does not attach it to royal power. In particular, it speaks about the "peace and liberties [that the articles create] between the king and the realm (*regnum*)," implying that the *regnum* is a corporate entity separate from the king. John apparently did not like this usage. Magna Carta changes many of the references to "the realm" to "our realm," adding the possessive pronoun to indicate that the realm is not a body separate from the king, but something that belongs to the king. John Hudson, "From the Articles of the Barons to Magna Carta," in Elisabeth van Houts (ed), *Anglo-Norman Studies XXXVIII: Proceedings of the Battle Conference, 2015* (Boydell Press 2016) 12. This may have been more important to John than the difference between *lex regni* and *lex terrae*, which may have been regarded as interchangeable statements, neither of which necessarily implied that the law was connected to royal power without the possessive "our". It would not be going too far, however, to say that the phrase *lex regni* had the potential to be interpreted as connecting the law to kingship, while *lex terrae* clearly distanced it from the exercise of royal power.

[72] "Legibus quidem propriis subsistit, quas non communi regni iure set voluntaria principum institutione subnixas dicunt . . ." Emilie Amt and SD Church (eds), *Dialogus De Scaccario, and Constitutio Domus Regis: The Dialogue of the Exchequer, and the Establishment of the Royal Household* (Clarendon Press 2007), 91 (I, c xi); Hudson, *Formation* (n 60) 14.

law or "through the royal will," on the one hand, and those who have been imprisoned "by the common right (*commune rectum*) of the county or the hundred, or by appeal."[73] The former were to be "freed quit," but the latter would be
freed only if they found pledges who could guarantee that they would appear
in court to be tried at some point in the future.[74] It appears that Eleanor did not
think it was fully within the king's power to forgive those accused by the juries
of presentment in the county or the hundred or by private parties via the appeal
of felony. This is perhaps why it was so jarring to the barons that John kept such
tight control of the courts. Charges that John had decided cases by will rather
than by judgment were central to the barons' complaints in Magna Carta in
1215.[75]

The barons did not like many of the things that King John did with his courts,
but the courts themselves were actually quite popular institutions. This is why,
although Magna Carta generally attempted to limit royal power, when it came
to royal justice, the drafters of the charter seem to have wanted more of it, not
less. They called for the king's justices to visit the counties four times a year to
hear the three main petty assizes, far more often than they had been visiting.[76]
The courts continued to be popular after John's death. Civil war broke out just
a few months after King John assented to Magna Carta. When John died in
October of 1216, his side was losing the war, and it looked like the Angevin line
might very well end with him, to be replaced by a Capetian dynasty. As unlikely
as it seemed, the Angevin loyalists would ultimately win some major victories
and end the war in 1217. Military victory did not put an end to England's political troubles, however. John left a government led by William Marshal and the
papal legate to run the country on behalf of the nine-year-old King Henry III.
During Henry III's minority, many of the magnates questioned the right of the
king's guardians to rule. Some sheriffs refused to surrender their shrievalities
on the theory that they could only be removed by a king, and the king, as a
minor, was not yet competent to make that decision. They held their own

---

[73] Roger of Howden, *Chronica Magistri Rogeri De Hovedene*, vol 3 (William Stubbs ed, Rolls series,
Longman & Co 1870) 4 (hereafter Roger of Howden, *Chronica*); Hudson, *Oxford History* (n 60) 473.
Paul Brand has suggested an alternate reading to me. It is possible that *commune rectum* (common
right) is actually a corruption of *commune rettum* (common accusation). This reading may indeed be
the correct one, as the passage would then be contrasting two types of accusation, the common accusation of the county or hundred, likely a reference to the jury of presentment, and accusation by an
individual in the appeal. The general point, that the king lacks absolute power to pardon those who
have been imprisoned through the ordinary process of the royal courts, while he may pardon those
imprisoned through his arbitrary will or through the process of his justices of the forest, still stands,
however. I would like to thank Professor Brand for this suggested reading of the passage.

[74] Roger of Howden, *Chronica* (n 73) vol 3, 4; Hudson, *Oxford History* (n 60) 473.

[75] Carpenter, *Magna Carta* (n 69) 223–25.

[76] Ibid, 44–45 (Magna Carta, c 18).

courts and administered royal justice without permission from the central government.[77] The young king's guardians were anxious to reassert royal authority in a way that did not alienate the magnates. They turned to the courts to do it.

In 1218, the government sent out the first eyres to visit the counties since the civil war. The king's guardians intended the eyre to act as a display of royal power; the justices were to take an oath from all knights and free tenants to obey the king and the laws and customs of the realm.[78] At the same time, the eyres were a display of unity and reconciliation. They carried out popular policies. The annalist of Waverly Abbey commented that the eyre justices observed and enforced the terms of Magna Carta, righting the wrongs of John's reign.[79] The eyres returned land to former rebels who had lost it during the war.[80] Judicial commissions were even used to move against some of John's henchmen, such as the wildly unpopular mercenary and adventurer Falkes de Breauté.[81]

The choice of justices to lead these eyre circuits was significant. Each of the eyre circuits contained, in addition to magnates who had fought for John and his son Henry in the civil war, at least one prominent person who had opposed John: a magnate who had fought with the rebels or a bishop who had suffered in exile on account of the king's excommunication.[82] The king's guardians also used the central court at Westminster to bring rebels back into the king's fold. In October of 1218, William d'Aubigny, earl of Arundel, who had fought on both sides at various points in the war, was appointed to the Westminster bench for a term, and was listed as the senior justice in the final concords of the court.[83] William d'Aubigny had no special qualification to be a justice. He had never served on an eyre or as a justice of the bench. From Easter term 1220 to Easter term 1221, Robert de Vere, earl of Oxford, one of the most important rebel leaders, sat as senior justice of the Common Bench.[84] Again, de Vere's primary qualification for the position was the fact that he had been a rebel and could bring a degree of reconciliation to the realm by taking control of the royal courts, an institution John had held so tightly to himself. Neither served on the bench for very long, and their seniority was probably simply an honor accorded to them on account of their status. But in both cases, I suspect the appointment was a symbolic measure. The courts brought together the great men

---

[77] Carpenter, *Minority* (n 61) 212, 337.

[78] Ibid, 98.

[79] Ibid, 402.

[80] Ibid, 56.

[81] Ibid, 357; Carpenter, *Magna Carta* (n 69) 230.

[82] Carpenter, *Minority* (n 61) 101; Nicholas Vincent, *Peter des Roches: An Alien in English Politics, 1205-1238* (CUP 1996) 168.

[83] Carpenter, *Minority* (n 61) 80, 101.

[84] Ibid, 180.

of the realm, who had been on opposite sides of the war, to exercise the king's justice as part of the same bench.

In the eyre circuits of 1218, the crown and the magnates came to a sort of compromise in the struggles over who owned the courts. They were not the only people contending for control of the courts, however. Another group was represented on these eyre circuits: the professional justices of the royal courts. The professional justice was a relatively new phenomenon in 1218. Starting in the last decade of the twelfth century, a group of justices came into the royal courts who, unlike justices of previous generations, served in the courts full-time. Where justices of the previous decades had been magnates, prelates, or royal servants who served only occasionally in the courts, these new justices devoted their careers to judicial work and not much else.[85] By the second decade of the thirteenth century, there were even some justices who spent their entire careers in the royal courts, starting as clerks before being elevated to the bench. The circuit that visited Yorkshire and Northumberland, for instance, included several justices of this type. It had the bishop of Durham, Richard Marsh, at its head. Next in the order of precedence came Robert Vipont, an important northern baron and royal servant. Third came Martin of Pattishall, a professional who had been serving in the royal courts for at least seventeen years in 1218, most of that as a clerk to the justice Simon of Pattishall. Last comes Roger Huscarl, who was one of John's regular justices from at least 1210.[86]

The professional justices usually come second, third, or fourth in the order of precedence, but there is reason to think that they were running the show, even if bishops, abbots, and magnates were formally put at the head of these commissions. The articles of the eyre, the set of instructions that the king sent out with his eyre justices, were almost always entrusted to one of the professionals.[87] *Bracton* itself may give us some indication that the professional justices were regarded as the real leaders of the circuits, at least by their fellow professional justices. *Bracton* contains more than 500 citations to cases decided in the royal courts. When the authors of *Bracton* do cite to these eyres of the early part of Henry III's reign, they always pair the non-professionals with one of the professionals. The abbot of Reading, the bishop of Durham, and two earls all appear paired up in the case references with either Martin of Pattishall or William of

---

[85] Ralph Turner identified a group of eight justices in particular who, by the middle years of Richard I's reign, were doing judicial work along with occasional work for the exchequer, but were not doing other types of work for the king. Turner, *English Judiciary* (n 3) 77, 81, 85–86.

[86] Crook, *General Eyre* (n 53) 75.

[87] See ibid, 71–75. In the case of the bishop of Durham's circuit, the close roll claims that the articles were entrusted to the bishop, but the patent roll claims they were given to Pattishall. Ibid, 75. It would have been more in keeping with the other eyre circuits to give them to Pattishall.

Raleigh. But while the professional justices are sometimes cited on their own, the non-professionals never appear on their own. Pattishall, Raleigh, Seagrave, and other professional justices are treated as authorities in the treatise. It records what they "used to say."[88] *Bracton* records their professional opinions on points of law and, sometimes, the debates between them. It never records the opinions of the magnate justices. *Bracton* tells us of a case "of the eyre of the bishop of Durham and Martin of Pattishall in the county of York in the third year of king Henry," the same 1218 eyre mentioned above.[89] This was an eyre in which Pattishall did not come second in the order of precedence, but third. It seems that the mention of the bishop of Durham is simply meant to indicate which eyre of Martin of Pattishall is being cited—much like the reference to the "last eyre of Martin of Pattishall in Lincoln" found just a few pages later—not to ascribe any kind of authority to the bishop of Durham.[90] There may have been some eye-rolling on the part of the professional justices, as men who had been at the king's side administering his justice for years were now subordinated to men who had little experience in what was already becoming quite technical work. It may very well have been the eyres of 1218 to 1222—along with the appointment of magnates to head up the Common Bench—that prompted the statement at the beginning of *Bracton* that "these laws and customs are often dragged into misuse by men of little wisdom and small learning who ascend the judgment seat before they have learned the laws, and stand amid doubts and the confusion of opinions, and are frequently subverted by the greater men who decide cases according to their own will rather than by the authority of the laws . . ."[91] In this context, where the magnates and the crown were trying to work out between them who should control the common law, a group of royal justices appears to have tried to make the case that they were the law's masters. Within a few years of these eyres, they had begun to write the *Bracton* treatise, in which they claimed a special relationship to the law. The law may be the law of the realm or the law of the land, but either way, they were its priests.

---

[88] *Bracton*, vol 2, 327, 368; vol 3, 128; vol 4, 360.

[89] *Bracton*, vol 3, 376.

[90] Ibid, 389.

[91] "[H]uiusmodi leges et consuetudines per insipientes et minus doctos, qui cathedram iudicandi ascendunt antequam leges didicerint, sæpius trahantur ad abusum, et qui stant in dubiis et in opinionibus et multotiens pervertuntur a maioribus, qui potius proprio arbitrio quam legum auctoritate causas decidunt . . ." *Bracton*, vol 2, 21. I have made some minor amendments to Thorne's translation. I am grateful to Paul Hyams for suggesting the translation of "insipientes et minus doctos" as "men of little wisdom and small learning," which I think captures the author's tone more effectively than Thorne's translation as "unwise and unlearned." There are other possibilities for the impetus behind this statement, including Raleigh's correction of the justices of the Common Bench during his term as chief justice of the court *coram rege* discussed below at p 40.

## The Mechanisms of Influence

To summarize the argument thus far, scholarship on the influence of Roman and canon law over the early common law has reached something of a stalemate. I think this is because its focus has been limited, for the most part, to the discussions of particular common-law rules and doctrines that might have been borrowed from the two laws. I hope that this book will open us up to new ways of thinking about influence and how it might have worked, particularly when it comes to higher-order questions about law, an area where the common law was not very well developed in the early thirteenth century and where it was probably more susceptible to influence from other legal discourses. But if Roman and canon law influenced the way people thought about the common law, how did this influence occur? What were the mechanisms of influence?

This book seeks to put the people back into the story of the legal revolution. The legal revolution appears to have played out in many different places in Latin Christendom at roughly the same time. Roman and canon law played some role in the development of secular law in many different kingdoms. But while this revolution in law was a phenomenon that transcended political and cultural boundaries, it manifested itself in different ways in different places, often for reasons that were specific to the locality. If Roman and canon law exerted influence over the common law, it was because there were people in England who wanted Roman and canon law to exert an influence over it. I will argue that the authors of *Bracton* were people who, for reasons specific to the way English judicial careers were developing in the early and middle decades of the thirteenth century, saw canon law and, more particularly, Roman law as attractive models for the work they were doing in the royal courts. They used Roman law to make the case that the common law was a body of knowledge that should only be applied by justices who had mastered it through a long period of study and practice.

Sir Henry Maine, in his famous *Ancient Law*, claimed that *Bracton* "put off on his countrymen as a compendium of pure English law a treatise of which the entire form and a third of the contents were directly borrowed from the Corpus Iuris."[92] Other scholars have argued that the authors of *Bracton* were eager to reform English law to bring it into line with Roman law or that they used Roman law to fill in gaps in the developing common law.[93] There are instances

---

[92] Henry Sumner Maine, *Ancient Law* (16th edn, John Murray 1897) 82.

[93] Paul Hyams, *King, Lords, and Peasants in Medieval England: The Common Law of Villeinage in the Twelfth and Thirteenth Centuries* (Clarendon Press 1980) 84; Frederic William Maitland (ed), *Select Passages from the Works of Bracton and Azo* (SS vol 8, Bernard Quaritch, 1895) xx (hereafter Maitland, *Bracton and Azo*); *Bracton*, vol 1, xxxii.

in which *Bracton* fills gaps in English law with civilian doctrines. For the most part, however, *Bracton* uses Roman and canon law in a slightly different way. The authors of the treatise were not interested so much in bringing English law into line with Roman law as they were in demonstrating that English law *already was* in line with Roman law. They worked hard to show that the rules applied in the English courts were perfectly in accord with those of the two laws, even when this was manifestly not the case.

Since the authors of *Bracton* were not, for the most part, adopting the rules and doctrines of Roman and canon law, I hope to move the debate over learned-laws influence on the early common law away from the realm of rules and doctrines and to open a window to another type of influence that has been little studied. In fact, I will shift the focus of the debate away from the history of legal ideas altogether. The authors of *Bracton* did think about law, but they did something even more interesting than that: they began to act like jurists. They had been trained in Roman and canon law in England's schools, where they would have been imbued with the notion that law was, at least in part, a textual practice; the community of scholars of Roman and canon law was a community built upon a shared set of texts and a shared set of textual practices. The justices who wrote *Bracton* learned in their study of Roman and canon law that the way to be a jurist was to write like a jurist, so they began to emulate the textual practices of the schools in their own work in the courts.

Their motivations for emulating the textual practices of the jurists were likely personal. In his *Renaissance Self-Fashioning*, Stephen Greenblatt describes the ways in which people living in the sixteenth century consciously constructed the self through their writing.[94] Something like that appears to be going on in the writing of *Bracton* and the plea roll collections. There are certainly differences. Scholars have noted that medieval people tended to understand themselves not so much as unique individuals, but as exemplifying certain "types." Aaron Gurevich noted that even those medieval authors who emulated the style of St. Augustine's *Confessions*, such as Peter Abelard and Guibert of Nogent, rejected the most individualistic and introspective elements of that style. In place of deep introspection they employed a device not found in the *Confessions*: they compared themselves to model characters from the Christian or classical past who they found in various "authoritative" texts, such as the Bible.[95] They understood themselves through the medium of these exemplars.

---

[94] Stephen Greenblatt, *Renaissance Self-Fashioning: From More to Shakespeare* (New edn, University of Chicago Press 2005) (hereafter Greenblatt, *Self-Fashioning*).

[95] Aaron Gurevich, *The Origins of European Individualism* (Katharine Judelson tr, Blackwell 1995) 93.

The exemplars themselves would often be typified as bishop, king, or knight. As Jacques Le Goff points out, individual people are regularly described in medieval literature as having generic physical characteristics that fit their type.[96]

It would be easy to make too much of this evidence. None of this actually proves that medieval people did not or could not understand themselves as individuals. It does, however, show that the group or the type was important in describing or understanding the individual. Indeed, identification with a type was regarded by some as having implications for one's salvation. Sermons of the thirteenth century might divide society into several dozen "estates," each with its own duties and path to salvation.[97] The problem for the professional justices of the early thirteenth century was to determine which "type" or "estate" they belonged to. The early medieval typology that divided society into those who pray (oratores), those who fight (bellatores), and those who work (laboratores) did not contain a clear space for them.[98] In the justices' lack of an obvious type, a clear place in society, we can see some similarities to the sixteenth-century figures Greenblatt examines. Greenblatt argues that people such as Thomas More were driven to active self-fashioning partly because they were "displaced in significant ways from a stable, inherited social world."[99] As Greenblatt notes, "None of the figures inherits a title, an ancient family tradition or hierarchical status that might have rooted personal identity in the identity of a clan or caste."[100] Pattishall, Raleigh, and Bratton were similar. They did not inhabit a clearly defined space within English society. They were clerics, but as we shall see in Chapter 2, their clerical status was probably not as important to their sense of identity as we might think, as movement between the categories of cleric and layman was fairly easy in the early thirteenth century.[101] In addition to not having a defined type, they came from relatively obscure families. These men—as Ralph Turner describes them, "men raised from the dust"—rose to important posts within the royal administration, where they would have interacted with, and indeed had the power of judgment over, earls,

---

[96] Le Goff, Medieval Civilization (n 12) 279–80.

[97] Ibid, 262.

[98] For the history of this tripartite division of society, see ibid, 255–60. It is interesting to note that Azo of Bologna actually did try to fit people who work with law into the tripartite scheme, under two different headings. As noted above, he employed Ulpian's quotation that transformed jurists into priests. He also developed his own argument, based on the opening words of Justinian's Institutes ("Imperial Majesty should not only be graced with arms but also armed with laws . . ."), that lawyers (advocati) should be regarded as knights (milites), since "the emperor is said to be armed with laws" and "we believe that not only those who fight with sword and breastplate serve our imperial authority, but also lawyers." Justinian's Institutes, 33; Azo, Summae, 1044.

[99] Greenblatt, Self-Fashioning (n 94) 7–8.

[100] Ibid, 9.

[101] See below, p 98.

barons, bishops, and abbots.[102] They had the ear of the king, but they were entirely dependent upon him, as they served only during his pleasure.[103] They could not rely on the prestige of their heritage for their authority. An earl or abbot who was sitting in the king's court would not have identified himself primarily as a royal justice, but would have taken his identity from his role as an earl or abbot. These new justices had little else to draw upon apart from their identity as the king's justices. Their identity came from the fact that they were, first and foremost, people who worked with law. That was a new notion in the early thirteenth century. The question of where they fit into the realm must have weighed heavily on their minds.

There were some possibilities for the royal justice of the thirteenth century. As we will see in Chapter 2, there were parallels between the work of the justice, who spent a good deal of his time looking after the king's interests, and the work of the steward. The steward was a well-known type in thirteenth-century England, both from the Bible and from the management of lordly and royal estates. But the justices who wrote *Bracton* did not identify with this type. The judge was a more obvious type, and one that had resonance for the authors of *Bracton*. *Bracton*, in a passage that can only be described as a fire-and-brimstone sermon on the perils of judging, draws on Biblical images of God as the just judge who will punish unjust judges on the day of judgment.[104] The authors of *Bracton* did not identify solely with the judge, however. They wove together the judge and another type, the jurist, to create their own version of the royal justice. They found, in the image of the jurist, a way of thinking about a person who works primarily with law, and one that carried quite a bit of authority and prestige. Jurists were not important people because they worked for kings, popes, and emperors, although many did hold office in the church or the secular administration and could draw additional prestige and power from those offices. They were important because they "professed knowledge of the civil law," as the *Digest* put it.[105] Indeed, kings, popes, and emperors sought to tap into their prestige by employing and consulting them.

The justices who wrote *Bracton* attempted to transform themselves into jurists through their writing. Sixteenth-century scholars often turned to autobiography to deal with their lack of a clear place in their society. Autobiography

[102] Ralph V Turner, *Men Raised from the Dust: Administrative Service and Upward Mobility in Angevin England* (University of Pennsylvania Press 1988).

[103] Ryan Rowberry, "The Origins and Development of Judicial Tenure 'During Good Behaviour' to 1485" in Travis R Baker (ed), *Law and Society in Later Medieval England and Ireland: Essays in Honour of Paul Brand* (Routledge 2018) 181.

[104] *Bracton*, vol 2, 21–22; Maitland, *Bracton and Azo* (n 93) 17. See also *Bracton*, vol 2, 305–09.

[105] D.1.2.35; *Digest of Justinian*, vol 1, 7.

was not a common genre in the thirteenth century, however, and the justices did not turn primarily to explicitly introspective writing to identify themselves as jurists. Rather, they acted out this new type. Writing happened to be the way to act out this identity in the thirteenth century. Jurists of the thirteenth century were defined by the types of texts they produced. The authors of *Bracton* thus had a dialectical relationship of sorts with the texts they produced. They produced the texts, but the texts, at the same time, defined them as jurists.

In his biography of Gerald of Wales, Robert Bartlett states that, although Gerald discusses the exercise of royal power extensively in his works, it would be misleading to think of him as laying out a "political programme" that he "hoped to see realized."[106] He was far from the centers of political power and must have known that his works were not going to directly influence policy. I think the same is true of the *Bracton* authors. The were not laying out a program for thinking about the common law and they probably had not planned their literary corpus from beginning to end in a bid to influence the way people in power thought and talked about the common law. As I argue in the next chapter, they were writing primarily for themselves and for people like them, who worked in the royal courts. These civilian-inspired textual practices were probably not intended to raise up the professional justice so much as to help these justices define themselves and their work.

## Organization

The book begins with an introductory chapter, in which I introduce our cast of characters and set out a chronology of their careers. Chapters 2 and 3 are concerned with the ways in which the *Bracton* authors thought about law. The authors of *Bracton* were familiar with Roman and canon law. They may have learned their law from texts, but they likely had some formal education in the two laws. Chapter 2, "Law as Text," will discuss the new kinds of discourses about law the *Bracton* authors would have encountered in their study of the two laws. The focus will be on how these justices began to think of law as a textual practice and to imagine communities of legal professionals that were constituted around texts. This was not necessarily an obvious way to think about law in the thirteenth century. In England's county and manor courts, much of the law was contained in the collective memory of the suitors of the court, not in authoritative texts. Thus, the fact that *Bracton*'s authors studied Roman and

---

[106] Robert Bartlett, *Gerald of Wales: A Voice of the Middle Ages* (New edn, Tempus 2006) 62.

canon law would have led them to think about law in a different manner from many of their colleagues in the central royal courts, who had come to the judiciary through the county administration.

Chapter 3, "Thinking About Law," will take a closer look at *Bracton* and how its authors perceived the place of Roman law in their work in the royal courts. The authors of *Bracton* thought of the two laws and the early common law as part of the same body of knowledge. Indeed, they wanted to demonstrate that the common law was a part of the broader legal culture of Christendom; it was not an insular affair. The law they administered was not just the law of the realm, limited to those places and people ruled by the king of England. Rather, it was one local instantiation of the universal law of Latin Christendom, a local instantiation which diverged in its specifics from what they had learned in the texts of Roman and canon law, but that could still fit within the universal law's four corners. But *Bracton* isn't primarily about reforming English law along the lines of Roman and canon law; it is about demonstrating that English law is already one local manifestation of these universal laws. Rather than using Roman and canon law to fill gaps in their own law or to justify changes to their law, the authors of *Bracton* took English law as a given and instead worked hard to demonstrate that the law they applied in the king's courts was in perfect accord with the rules of the two laws.

Chapters 4, 5, and 6 are about the ways the authors of *Bracton* thought about the texts they produced. In these three chapters, I argue that the *Bracton* authors assimilated their own practices of textual production to the practices of the civilians and canonists in the schools. Thus, where in Chapter 3 we see the authors of *Bracton* attempting to assimilate the substantive law they were applying in the king's courts to the substantive law of the two laws, in the chapters following it we see them assimilating genres of texts they were producing in the king's courts to genres of texts that were current in the two laws. Chapter 4, "From Classroom to Courtroom," will examine the practice of collecting cases from the plea rolls, the records of cases heard by the royal courts. Raleigh and Bratton produced several collections of cases drawn from the plea rolls, one of which, known today as *Bracton's Note Book*, survives. It provides a fascinating window into the ways in which these justices were transforming, through the production of certain types of texts, the mundane administrative work of the royal courts into a type of learned discourse. Raleigh and Bratton took plea roll entries out of their original context and remade them in the image of the texts they had encountered in the schools.

In *Bracton's Note Book* we see the same group of people who wrote *Bracton* editing plea roll entries into texts that look something like the texts they would have encountered in their study of Roman and canon law. Unfortunately, the *Note Book* does not tell us why they were doing this. Since the *Note Book* and *Bracton* were written by the same group of justices and clerks, however, we can read *Bracton* and the *Note Book* together to help us to understand how the authors of these texts thought about plea roll entries. *Bracton* contains over 500 citations to cases decided in the royal courts, often citing to a specific place where the case can be found on a plea roll. Chapter 5, "Cases and the Dialectic," will examine the ways in which the authors of *Bracton* construct the plea roll entry as an authoritative text. The authors of *Bracton* use and treat citations to plea roll entries and citations to the authoritative texts of Roman law— Justinian's *Digest, Codex,* and *Institutes*—in very similar ways. The authors of the treatise adopt similar citation methods for both, and speak about them in similar terms. In the schools, certain texts were regarded as authoritative. If those texts appeared to conflict with each other, the jurist's goal was, as the introduction to Justinian's *Digest* put it, to "reflect[] upon the modes of diversity with a subtle mind" to find a solution that resolves the contradiction.[107] This chapter demonstrates that the authors of *Bracton* applied to their case records the same methods of harmonization and reconciliation that they had learned to apply to the authoritative texts of Roman and canon law. By applying the schools' dialectical methods of reconciliation to these case records, the *Bracton* authors indicated that they were applying the notions of an authoritative text current in Roman and canon law to the texts that they produced through their work in the king's courts.

In Chapter 6, "The Genres of Authority," we see that the way the authors of *Bracton* thought about texts was related to the way they thought about what it meant to be a royal justice. In the process of reconstituting the plea roll entry, the justices transformed themselves into jurists. In *Bracton*, the plea roll entry is assimilated to genres of civilian and canonist texts that were specifically associated with jurists. One of the authors of the treatise compares the cases drawn from the plea rolls to *consilia* and *responsa*, texts in which an important civilian or canonist jurist gave his opinion on a legal matter. The plea roll entry and the jurist's *consilium* are texts with very different aesthetics. But there were some similarities in the textual conventions of these two types of texts, such as the use of the word "judgment" to describe what the author of the text is doing. The justices who created *Bracton* and the *Note Book* emphasized these similarities between the genres to make the rather far-fetched case that the plea roll entry *is* the opinion of a jurist on a point of law. They took these texts, which the royal

---

[107] D.Const. Tanta.15; *Digest of Justinian* (pages unnumbered in this part of the text).

courts had already been producing for decades when Martin of Pattishall and William of Raleigh entered the courts, and read them through the lens of the texts they had encountered in the schools, connecting their work in the courts with the culture of the two laws. This was not an obvious way to read plea roll entries. Indeed, it required quite a bit of reading against the grain to transform these judicial records into jurists' opinions, and to transform the justice of the royal courts into a jurist.

By the 1250s, Pattishall, Raleigh, and Bratton had been working to create a literature for the royal courts for about thirty years. In Chapter 7, "A New Plea Roll for a New Audience," we will see the results of this process. This chapter will examine some surviving rolls of cases heard by Henry of Bratton. Bratton appears to have internalized the notions that plea rolls were authoritative texts and that the justices who wrote them were jurists. As a result, Bratton began to approach his own rolls differently, crafting them for a potential audience who would be interested in the legal principles his cases represented, much as modern justices of the United States Supreme Court think about law students as an audience when drafting important opinions. In his rolls and the treatise, we see Bratton trying to position himself as the obvious heir to the great justices Martin of Pattishall and William of Raleigh.

The culture of textual production that these jurists tried to create did not survive the thirteenth century. In the second half of the century, English legal literature became more insular in its outlook. By the fourteenth century, few of the justices had much training in Roman and canon law. In place of learned jurists trained in the tradition of the two laws, the king increasingly turned to serjeants who had spent their careers pleading cases in the king's courts to fill vacancies on the bench. But *Bracton* and the plea roll collections represent an important moment in the history of the common law, when people were reflecting on what law is and how it should be practiced. Through *Bracton* we can catch a glimpse of people who were thinking about what it meant to administer the law of the king's courts, in a time before the common law was the common law. In these texts, we see the justices of the royal courts turning to the two laws for inspiration. They did not, for the most part, turn to the two laws to find rules and doctrines, however. They turned to them to understand the essence of the law they administered and, ultimately, to understand themselves. Their vision of the legal professional was an exclusive one; *Bracton* and the other texts produced by this circle present the justice or clerk as a learned person. As we will see in the next chapter, *Bracton* assumes both easy access to court records and a high level of knowledge of Roman and canon law. The treatise does not seem to embrace the pleaders and attorneys who were working in the courts within the circle of priests of the law. But if the authors of *Bracton* defined their community narrowly in some ways, in others they defined it very broadly. The authors of *Bracton* took a cosmopolitan view of their work. The repurposed phrase, "law is called the art of what is fair and just, of which we are deservedly called the priests, for we worship justice and administer sacred rights," would have acted for the reader as a link between the justices and clerks who worked in the courts in Westminster and the jurists of the civil law, the original subjects of the passage, most of whom lived in distant lands the reader would never visit, and who would be known to him only through their texts.[108] *Bracton* presented this small group of people, working in the courts of the king of an island realm, with a way of imagining themselves as part of a broader legal culture. Through their writing, the authors of *Bracton* transformed themselves from servants of the king to priests of the law.

---

[108]  *Bracton*, vol 2, 24; D.1.2.35; *Digest of Justinian*, vol 1, 7.

# 1

# Setting the Stage

Although part of my purpose in writing this book is to take the *Bracton* treatise out of the center of the story and to demonstrate that it was just one part of a larger program of textual production, the composition, editing, and re-writing of *Bracton* will be an important part of the narrative thread of this story, and so it is important to set the stage by first introducing the justices who wrote *Bracton* and giving an account of the writing process. There is a great deal of scholarly debate about who wrote *Bracton* and when it was written. It is now generally accepted that *Bracton* was written in stages and that Henry of Bratton, whose name was attached to the treatise at some point, was not the primary author of the first recension of the treatise. In this chapter, I will give a brief account of the careers of the three justices who were most likely to have been involved in the writing of *Bracton*—Martin of Pattishall, William of Raleigh, and Henry of Bratton—and then attempt to synthesize the most recent scholarship on the dating of *Bracton* into a coherent narrative of its history between the 1220s and the 1280s. The short version of this account is that there were likely at least three recensions. The first, which I will call *Raleigh*, was probably "complete" by 1236, although it may have been rather disorderly, with much material written into the margins and even on odd scraps of parchment slipped between the pages. The second recension, which I will call *Bratton*, was probably written by Henry of Bratton in the early 1250s. It likely existed in a single, but much more orderly, manuscript. The third, the text we know today as *Bracton*, is likely a creation of the 1270s or 1280s, which combined material from both *Raleigh* and *Bratton*. The account is contestable, as most of the evidence we have for this process is indirect, but it will help to establish a timeline to which the rest of the chapters can refer.

## Our Cast of Characters

*Bracton* is named after the royal justice Henry of Bratton, to whom it was attributed as early as 1278.[1] Bratton almost certainly worked on the treatise but,

---

[1] Paul Brand, "The Age of Bracton" in John Hudson (ed), *The History of English Law: Centenary Essays on "Pollock and Maitland"* (British Academy 1996) 74 (hereafter Brand, "Age of Bracton"). For the discrepancy between "Bratton" and "Bracton" see below, p 43.

*Priests of the Law*. Thomas J. McSweeney, Oxford University Press (2019). © Thomas J. McSweeney.
DOI: 10.1093/oso/9780198845454.003.0002

as Samuel Thorne has demonstrated, could not have written the majority of the text, much of which had been written in the 1220s and 1230s, before Bratton had begun his career as a clerk in the king's courts. The primary author of the treatise was probably William of Raleigh. Bratton had served as Raleigh's clerk and maintained close connections with his mentor until Raleigh's death in 1250. It is possible, however, that Martin of Pattishall, whom Raleigh had served as a clerk in the 1210s and the 1220s, was the original driving force behind the treatise. Others may have worked on the treatise whose identities are now unknown. But while we cannot identify the entire universe of people who had some role in the writing of *Bracton*, we can be fairly certain that at least Raleigh and Bratton worked on the text and there is a decent chance that Pattishall played some role in the early stages of the writing process. These three men were important figures in the royal courts of the thirteenth century.

Martin of Pattishall hailed from the village of Pattishall in Northamptonshire. Pattishall was the home of another prominent royal justice, Simon of Pattishall. The two do not appear to have been related, but the hometown connection probably helped Martin to secure Simon's patronage. Martin served as Simon's clerk for at least fifteen years. Simon of Pattishall has been called the first professional justice in the royal courts. He served continuously in the courts for about twenty-five years.[2] Beginning his service as a justice under Richard I in 1190, probably thanks to the patronage of Geoffrey Fitz Peter, Simon served as a justice of the bench at Westminster, as the chief justice of John's court *coram rege*, and in every eyre visitation of Richard's and John's reigns.[3] His contemporaries appear to have thought of him as an important person. According to the chronicler Matthew Paris, Simon "at one time sensibly guided the reins of justice of the whole realm."[4] He was trusted by King John, although in the confusion of the civil war between the king and his barons Simon was dismissed, arrested, and reconciled to the king within a very short period of time. Despite John's inconstancy, it seems that Simon was loyal to his lord to the last and, after his reconciliation, was even appointed to sit as a justice for a special assize in 1216. Later that year he finally retired and probably died shortly thereafter.[5]

---

[2] Paul Brand, *The Origins of the English Legal Profession* (Blackwell 1992) 27 (hereafter Brand, *Legal Profession*).

[3] Ralph V. Turner, *The English Judiciary in the Age of Glanvill and Bracton, C. 1176-1239* (CUP 1985) 105 (hereafter Turner, *English Judiciary*); Ralph V Turner, "Pattishall, Simon of (d. c.1217)," ODNB, <www.oxforddnb.com/view/article/21544> accessed June 19, 2017.

[4] "Simonis de Pateshulle, qui quandoque habenas sane moderabatur totius regni justiciarii . . ." CM 3:296.

[5] Ralph V Turner, "Pattishall, Simon of (d. c.1217)" (ODNB, September 23, 2004) <www.oxforddnb.com/view/article/21544> accessed June 19, 2017.

Thus, when Henry III's regents restored the courts after the war, it was not Simon, but his former clerk, Martin of Pattishall, who was guiding the reins.

We know little of Martin of Pattishall's early life, before he joined the court. That may imply that he was of rather humble origins and that he owed his entry into royal service to patronage rather than to family influence.[6] Martin was in Simon of Pattishall's service by 1201, when a note on an eyre roll tells us that "This roll is to be handed to Martin the clerk of the lord Simon of Pattishall."[7] A man identified as "Martin the Clerk" also acted as an attorney for several litigants between 1203 and 1206.[8] In 1208, he was an attesting witness to a ratification of an agreement made by King John. He is listed last on the list of witnesses, which probably indicates that he drafted the document.[9] Martin appears to have had special responsibilities in the king's courts. A record of 1206 tells us that the names of people who have been attached are written "in Martin's book," hinting that Martin was responsible for keeping a special record of all those who had been attached.[10]

Martin became one of the dominant figures in the royal courts from the late 1210s through the end of the 1220s. He helped to reconstitute the royal courts after the barons' war ended in 1217. When the first eyres were sent into the counties in 1218, Martin was appointed to the panel of justices who were sent on a circuit through the North-Eastern counties. The feet of fines list the justices sitting at any given term in order of precedence.[11] Martin was always listed first among the professional justices at the Bench at Westminster in feet of fines.[12] Martin, a cleric, was elevated to the prestigious post of dean of St. Paul's Cathedral in London at the time he retired from the Bench, about a year before his death.[13]

---

[6] Turner, *English Judiciary* (n 3) 210–11.

[7] Doris Mary Stenton, *Rolls of the Justices in Eyre for Lincolnshire 1218-9 and Worcestershire 1221* (SS vol 53, Bernard Quaritch 1934) xvii (hereafter Stenton, *Rolls for Lincolnshire and Worcestershire*).

[8] Turner, *English Judiciary* (n 3) 211.

[9] He is also the only clerk to witness the document; the rest of the witnesses are all royal justices. Stenton, *Rolls for Lincolnshire and Worcestershire* (n 7) xvii.

[10] CRR, vol 4, vii, 177; Stenton, *Rolls for Lincolnshire and Worcestershire* (n 7) xvii.

[11] Feet of fines were records of final concords, essentially settlements, that were kept by the court. Final concords made in the court were drawn up in the form of a tripartite chirograph. Each party kept one copy of the record of the settlement. The court kept the copy at the bottom of the sheet of parchment, the foot. For more on chirographs and final concords, see below, p 224.

[12] Martin was not always first in overall precedence. He would drop in order of precedence when an earl, a bishop, or an important royal official was present. In a fine of Michaelmas 1217, for instance, Pattishall is listed third, behind William Marshal, who was essentially the regent at the time, and Hubert de Burgh, the justiciar. CAF Meekings and David Crook, *King's Bench and Common Bench in the Reign of Henry III* (Selden Society 2010) 151 (hereafter Meekings and Crook, *King's Bench and Common Bench*). From 1222, it became less common for earls and bishops to sit in the Common Bench, and Pattishall was generally ranked first in the order of precedence unless Hubert de Burgh was present. See ibid, 151–86.

[13] Alan Harding, "Pattishall, Martin of (*d.* 1229)" (ODNB, September 23, 2004) <www.oxforddnb.com/view/article/21542> accessed March 13, 2019.

Like Martin of Pattishall, William of Raleigh served a long apprenticeship as a clerk before becoming a justice. In 1235 or 1236, Raleigh referred to "Martin of Pattishall, of good memory, my sometime lord."[14] C.A.F. Meekings thought he was Martin's personal clerk from at least 1219, but we have evidence that Raleigh was serving as a clerk in the royal courts even before that, either as a subordinate clerk in Martin's employ or as another clerk directly in the employ of Martin's master, Simon.[15] Raleigh first appears as a clerk in 1214, three years before Martin became a justice, although the fact that King John had presented him to the rectory of Bratton Fleming in Raleigh's native Devon in 1212 suggests that he had done something to merit royal favor by then.[16] We know a bit more about Raleigh's family than we do about Pattishall's. His name derives from a manor in Northwest Devon, near Barnstaple. The Raleigh family, who appear to have been substantial landholders, had several branches and it is unclear whether Raleigh came from the main branch or a junior one.[17] His family connections seem to have remained important to him throughout his life. Members of various branches of the Raleigh family took advantage of his hospitality after he became bishop of Winchester.[18] It may be that he came to the royal courts through his family's influence.

Raleigh served as Martin's clerk for more than a decade, and was made a justice of the Common Bench in May of 1229, just a few months after Pattishall retired. Some of his time as a clerk must have counted as time towards his seniority, because Robert of Lexington, who had been serving on the Bench for two years already, fell below Raleigh in the order of precedence when Raleigh was promoted. In 1232, Raleigh was appointed chief justice of one of two eyre circuits and once again promoted over people who had had longer careers as justices.[19] The next year, Raleigh apparently caught up to Thomas of Moulton, who had been listed before him in precedence before that date.[20] From that

---

[14] CAF Meekings, "Martin de Pateshull of Good Memory My Sometime Lord" (1974) 47 Bulletin of the Institute of Historical Research 224, 229, reprinted in *Studies in 13th Century Justice and Administration* (Hambledon Press, 1981), item XII.

[15] CAF Meekings, "Martin Pateshull and William Raleigh" (1953) 26 Bulletin of the Institute of Historical Research 157, 160, reprinted in *Studies in 13th Century Justice and Administration* (Hambledon Press, 1981), item XI (hereafter Meekings, "Martin Pateshull and William Raleigh").

[16] David Crook, "Raleigh, William of (d. 1250)" (ODNB, September 23, 2004) <www.oxforddnb.com/view/article/23042> accessed March 13, 2019.

[17] A William of Raleigh is identified as a knight served as sheriff of Devon in the 1220s. Although there is some debate, he was probably not the same person as the future justice, but a relative. Turner, *English Judiciary* (n 3) 210.

[18] Meekings and Crook, *King's Bench and Common Bench* (n 12) 88.

[19] David Crook, *Records of the General Eyre* (Her Majesty's Stationery Office 1982) 88 (hereafter Crook, *General Eyre*).

[20] Meekings, "Martin Pateshull and William Raleigh" (n 15) 171; Meekings and Crook, *King's Bench and Common Bench* (n 12) 201, 203.

point on, he was the senior justice in the Bench, listed just behind the justiciar, Stephen of Seagrave, in the order of precedence.

Raleigh was a crafty political operator. There was political turmoil around the court in the early 1230s, and Raleigh seems to have come out of it on top. In 1232 Hubert de Burgh, the justiciar, was ousted from power by a rival group of royal councilors led by Peter des Rivaux. De Burgh's fall was rather spectacular, and he was imprisoned for a time. In 1233, Richard Marshal, Earl of Pembroke, rose up and freed de Burgh from prison.[21] The king was forced to dismiss des Rivaux's party, which included Stephen of Seagrave, who was the king's chief legal counsellor.[22] After he dismissed Seagrave from office, he turned to the chief justice of the Bench, William of Raleigh, to fill the void. Within a few days of Seagrave's dismissal, Raleigh had ridden from Westminster to Gloucester, where the king was holding a great council of the realm, and pronounced the reversal of Hubert de Burgh's outlawry.[23] The king allowed the office of chief justiciar, which had been a focal point for the troubles between de Burgh's and des Rivaux's supporters, to lapse, and instead appointed Raleigh chief justice of the court *coram rege* (before the king) or *coram ipso rege* (before the king himself).[24] A court before the king himself had existed since Henry III had achieved majority in 1227, but it is only during Raleigh's tenure on that court that the court *coram rege* attained a status equivalent to that of the Bench at Westminster.[25] In this role, Raleigh remained at the king's side as he perambulated the kingdom, hearing cases that were considered important enough to merit the king's personal attention.

Raleigh's contemporaries perceived him to be an important person. Raleigh was intimately concerned with the debates from 1234 to 1236 around the issue of bastardy. Bishop Robert Grosseteste wrote several letters to Raleigh in 1235 and 1236, during a period of conflict between the bishops and the crown over differences between canon law and the law of the king's courts.[26] Grosseteste suggests in these letters that Raleigh is the man to write to if one wants to change the law; he describes Raleigh as having been gifted with the "personal friendship of the king."[27] After receiving Raleigh's response, which unfortunately

---

[21] JR Maddicott, *Simon de Montfort* (CUP 1994) 11–14 (hereafter Maddicott, *Simon de Montfort*).

[22] BNB, vol 1, 46.

[23] CAF Meekings, "Introduction" in CRR, vol 15, xxvi–xxvii (hereafter Meekings, Introduction to CRR 15).

[24] At the same time he replaced Peter des Rivaux, who was serving as treasurer, with Hugh of Pattishall, the son of Simon of Pattishall. It is not known whether Raleigh had any connections to the son of his former master's master, but it is tempting to think that these men might have been political allies. CM, vol 3, 296.

[25] Meekings, Introduction to CRR 15 (n 23) xxiii.

[26] BNB, vol 1, 107.

[27] Robert Grosseteste, *The Letters of Robert Grosseteste, Bishop of Lincoln* (FAC Mantello and Joseph Goering trs, University of Toronto Press 2010) 122 (hereafter Grosseteste, *Letters*). "Tu, cui commissum

does not survive, Grosseteste wrote back to say that he was "not such a fool as to believe that you or anyone else can, at someone else's prompting, establish or change laws without the counsel of the king and his magnates," but that he had written to Raleigh specifically "to honour before all others you to whom I wrote before all others."[28] Raleigh did have a role in making the laws and customs of England, however. In 1236 he wrote parts of the Provisions of Merton.[29] He is credited, in one manuscript, with inventing the writs of cosinage, redisseisin, recaption, and *quare eiecit infra terminum*.[30]

Raleigh's work was not all judicial or legislative. Raleigh was an active member of the king's council during his time on the court *coram rege*. Robert Stacey thought that he was likely the primary architect of the ambitious administrative and fiscal program of the period between 1236 and 1239, which brought an additional £2,000 of revenue into the royal coffers annually.[31] He also appears to have been trusted by the king to negotiate with the clergy and the magnates of the realm on his behalf. He acted as the king's agent at several councils. In January of 1237, at a great council of the realm, "William of Raleigh, cleric and familiar of the lord king, a man [who was] indeed discerning

---

est talentum familiaritatis regiae." Robert Grosseteste, *Roberti Grosseteste Episcopis Quondam Lincolniensis Epistolae* (Henry Richards Luard ed, Longman, Green, Longman, and Roberts 1861) 94 (hereafter Grosseteste, *Epistolae*).

[28] Grosseteste, *Letters* (n 27) 124. "Nec tam idiota sum quod credam ad alicujus suggestionem te vel alium sine principis et magnatum consilio posse leges condere vel commutare," and "scripsi . . . te prae caeteris cui scripsi prae caeteris honorificandum." Grosseteste, *Epistolae* (n 27) 96.

[29] David Crook, "Raleigh, William of (d. 1250)" (ODNB, September 23, 2004) <www.oxforddnb. com/view/article/23042> accessed March 13, 2019.

[30] Elsa De Haas and GDG Hall (eds), *Early Registers of Writs* (SS 87, Bernard Quaritch 1970) xv, n 2 (hereafter De Haas and Hall, *Early Registers*). Note that the writ of cosinage was available as early as 1235, and was not, therefore, invented in 1237 as de Haas and Hall suggest. Paul Brand, *Kings, Barons, and Justices: The Making and Enforcement of Legislation in Thirteenth-Century England* (CUP 2003) 54, n 43 (hereafter Brand, *Kings, Barons, and Justices*). In a register of writs that appears to date to the 1250s, the writ of redisseisin is described as "a new writ made by W. de Ralee." Recaption and *quare eiecit infra terminum* are likewise described as writs made by Raleigh in this register. Frederic William Maitland, "The History of the Register of Original Writs" in HAL Fisher (ed), *The Collected Papers of Frederic William Maitland*, vol 2 (CUP 1911) 146–47. For the dating of this register, see De Haas and Hall, *Early Registers* (n 30) xxxiv, n 4. There is additional evidence that the writs of recaption and redisseisin were created by Raleigh. Paul Brand has argued convincingly that the authors of *Bracton* included quite a bit of draft material that William of Raleigh had prepared in his role as a legal adviser to the king. *Bracton* contains two variants of the writ of recaption, one of which does not correspond to any version known to have been used in the royal courts, and which may have been Raleigh's draft. The version of chapter three of the Provisions of Merton, which created the action of redisseisin, that appears in *Bracton* differs in some respects from all known versions of that legislation. The treatise also contains many variations on the writ of redisseisin that never seem to have been put to use in the courts. Brand thinks that these were derived from Raleigh's draft material. Paul Brand, "The Date and Authorship of Bracton: A Response" (2010) 31 *Journal of Legal History* 217, 220–21, 224–25.

[31] Robert C Stacey, *Politics, Policy, and Finance under Henry III, 1216-1245* (Clarendon Press 1987) 115–16, 131 (hereafter Stacey, *Politics, Policy, and Finance*).

and learned in the law of the land, rose up in the middle, as an intermediary between the king and the magnates of the realm, and staked out the proposition
and the will of the king in public."[32] At this council Raleigh and the queen's
uncle, William of Savoy, managed to secure a tax of one-thirtieth of the value
of all moveable goods in the realm in exchange for a confirmation of Magna
Carta and other concessions.[33] Later that year, he attended a Church council
being held by the papal legate as one of three royal representatives who were
sent to remind the council not to do anything detrimental to the king's rights.[34]
After delivering this message, his two colleagues, both laymen, withdrew, but
William of Raleigh "remained there, so as to observe it, dressed in the canonical cope and surplice . . ."[35] Matthew Paris gives us the impression that William
of Raleigh was sitting there as the king's creature, perhaps with the hint of a
passive threat, taking in the council's proceedings to report back to his master.

Grosseteste's letters may give us some hint as to Raleigh's demeanor.
Although Raleigh's letters to Grosseteste do not survive, Grosseteste occasionally describes Raleigh's responses to him and he paints them as sharp, pointed,
and mocking. Grosseteste plays the wounded (spiritual) father in his letters.
In one, in response to a letter Raleigh sent to Grosseteste to urge him to institute an underage candidate to a benefice in his diocese, Grosseteste claims
that Raleigh's letter "made me feel . . . sad and not a little anxious, because it expressed towards me, someone who loves you in the Lord with sincere affection,
an indignation that is unreasonable."[36] In his second letter to Raleigh on the
issue of legitimacy, Grosseteste chides Raleigh for a mocking play on words.
Grosseteste's original letter on the matter had been very long, and Raleigh had
apparently said that Grosseteste should not have called it a *breve*—a word that
can be both a noun for "letter" and an adjective for "brief" or "short"—but instead should have called it a *longum*.[37] Grosseteste tells him that "the fact that
you rebuke me for the length of my *breve*, and mockingly call it my '*longum*' is

---

[32] "[S]urrexit in medio Willelmus de Raele clericus ac domini regis familiaris, vir quidem discretus et
legum terrae peritus, ut quasi mediator inter regem et regni magnates regium propositum et voluntatem
in publicum propalaret." CM, vol 3, 380.

[33] David Crook, "Raleigh, William of (*d.* 1250)" (ODNB, September 23, 2004) <www.oxforddnb.
com/view/article/23042> accessed March 13, 2019.

[34] CM, vol 3, 416–17.

[35] "Et remansit ibi, ut hoc observaretur, W. de Raele, indutus capa canonicali et superpellicio . . . "
CM, vol 3, 417. The word *canonicali* is somewhat ambiguous. It is probably used here to mean that the
cope and surplice are of a kind worn by a canon, as Raleigh is described as a canon of St. Paul's Cathedral
just a few lines above this in Matthew Paris' text.

[36] Grosseteste, *Letters* (n 27) 95. "Recepimus literas dilectionis vestrae, novit Dominus dolorem et
anxietatem non modicam mihi generantes, quod erga nos, vestri dilectores caritate sincera in Domino,
vestri indignationem sine causa rationabili expresserunt." Grosseteste, *Epistolae* (n 27) 63.

[37] Grosseteste, *Epistolae* (n 27) 95.

not a very perceptive rebuke, nor is mockery proper for a wise man, since in the very composition I sent you I called it not a '*breve*', but an '*epistola*.'"[38] He goes on to say that "Because, however, I have a father's affection for you, as for a very dear son, I fully pardon the injustice of this rebuke, though with a mother's heartfelt feelings I deplore your mockery."[39]

In 1236, Raleigh made what looks very much like a play for power. He corrected a mistake by the justices in the Common Bench, after which the king sent a writ to the justices in the Bench saying that they should not make judgments in doubtful cases without the king's—read William of Raleigh's—permission.[40] Raleigh also recalled Adam Fitz William, a justice who was closely connected to him, to serve on the Common Bench and apparently to prevent his colleagues on that court from making mistakes in the future.[41] *Bracton* describes the justices of the court *coram rege* in grandiose terms, as justices who are "major, general, permanent and of greater importance" and insists that they have a duty to "correct the wrongs and errors of all others."[42] In addition to correcting the errors of the justices of the other courts, Raleigh appears to have reserved all difficult cases from the Bench or from the eyres for his own hearing.[43] Raleigh had asserted his authority over the other courts and, from 1236 until his retirement from the court in 1239, was England's senior justice.

In 1238, Richard of Cornwall, the king's brother, led an uprising against the king, which seems to have destabilized Raleigh's position. The king quickly made peace with his brother, but the price Richard exacted was influence.

[38] Ibid, 123. "Quod autem reprehendis de brevis mei longitudine, et derisorie vocas illud longum meum, non est satis perspecta reprehensio, nec conveniens viro sapienti derisio, cum scriptum tibi transmissum in eodem scripto nominaverim non breve sed epistolam." Grosseteste, *Epistolae* (n 27) 95. I have modified the translation.

[39] Ibid, 123. "Sed hujus reprehensionis injuriam paterna affectione tibi, sicut filio carissimo, plene condono; tuam autem derisionem maternis visceribus doleo." Grosseteste, *Epistolae* (n 27) 95. In his four surviving letters to Raleigh, Grosseteste professes to have a special bond of affection with Raleigh. In his first letter on the issue of legitimacy, he tells Raleigh that "you are more tied to me as a spiritual son, and by a long-standing and special affection, and by the generous bestowal of various benefits . . ." Ibid, 108. This may simply be rhetoric, but the fourth of Grosseteste's letters suggests that there may have been some genuine affection between these two men who were often opponents. In 1244 or 1245, Grosseteste wrote to Raleigh, by this point bishop of Winchester, and Walter of Cantilupe, the bishop of Worcester, simply to tell them that he had arrived safely at the papal curia, because of "the fervor of your love for me" and the "copious tears you shed for me on my departure." Ibid, 350.

[40] Turner, *English Judiciary* (n 3) 203; BNB, vol 3, 179–80 (no 1166); CR 1234–37, 348. Around the same time, a new clause began to be added to the commissions that were given to justices, usually at this time panels of four local knights, to take special assizes. The clause instructed the justices not to proceed to judgment, but rather to send the record of the proceedings to the king so judgment could be pronounced *coram rege*. CAF Meekings, Introduction to CRR 15 (n 23) xxxiv–xxxv.

[41] CAF Meekings, "Adam Fitz William (d. 1238)" (1961) 34 Bulletin of the Institute of Historical Research 1, 7, 11. Raleigh had served on more eyres with Adam than with any other justice.

[42] *Bracton*, vol 2, 307.

[43] Turner, *English Judiciary* (n 3) 198; CAF Meekings (ed), *The 1235 Surrey Eyre* (Surrey Record Society 1979) vol 1, 9.

From the spring of 1238, Richard of Cornwall was the driving force on the king's council and was probably responsible for pushing Raleigh to the margins.[44] In the summer of 1238 Raleigh's situation deteriorated even further. Peter des Roches, bishop of Winchester, died. Winchester was the wealthiest see in England and Henry III asked the cathedral chapter of Winchester to elect the queen's uncle, the same William of Savoy with whom Raleigh had appeared at the great council in Westminster just a little over a year earlier. The monks of the chapter refused to elect William of Savoy on the ground that he was a warrior cleric and told the king that they preferred Raleigh.[45] The king was furious. He wrote to the chapter of Winchester and asked them why "you refuse to elect [William of Savoy], saying that he is a man of blood, [while] you elect William of Raleigh, who has slaughtered many more with his tongue than the other has with his sword."[46]

Raleigh was not consecrated bishop at that time, but was instead elected bishop of Coventry and Lichfield, which he declined, and later bishop of Norwich, which he accepted. He resigned from the court *coram rege* and the council in the spring of 1239 to take up his see.[47] The fight over Winchester was just heating up, however. In 1241, with William of Savoy having passed away in 1239, Henry tried to secure Winchester for William's younger brother, Boniface of Savoy.[48] The monks of Winchester again elected Raleigh. Henry hired canon lawyers to take his case to the pope, among whom was Henry of Susa, a canonist in the queen's household who would become one of the greatest scholars of canon law of the Middle Ages.[49] Raleigh won his case before the pope, who confirmed him to the see in 1243. But Henry did not give up. In response, he ordered the gates of Winchester guarded against Raleigh, sent letters against him to Oxford, shut the diocese of Norwich to him, and ordered that no one give him food or shelter.[50] Raleigh skulked around London for a bit, hiding with the Augustinian canons of the church of St. Mary Overy in Southwark,

---

[44] Stacey, *Politics, Policy, and Finance* (n 31) 118, 125.

[45] Ibid, 128–29.

[46] "Rex iratus nimis procaciter respondit; 'Renuistis electum Valentinum, dicentes eum virum sanguinum, et W[illelmum] de Reale, qui multo plures lingua quam alius gladio trucidavit, elegistis.'" CM, vol 3, 494. The King refers to William of Savoy as *Valentinum* here because he was, at the time, bishop-elect of Valence in what is today Southern France.

[47] David Crook, "Raleigh, William of (d. 1250)" (ODNB, September 23, 2004) <www.oxforddnb.com/view/article/23042> accessed March 13, 2019.

[48] Boniface actually administered the diocese of Valence after William's death.

[49] He is known today as *Hostiensis* from a title he would receive in 1261, that of cardinal-bishop of Ostia, the president of the College of Cardinals. James A Brundage, *Medieval Canon Law* (Longman 1995) 214. Raleigh had the distinction of excommunicating one of Europe's most celebrated canonists for his part in keeping Raleigh from his see.

[50] CM, vol 4, 264.

a suitable location both because it was within the diocese of Winchester and was next door to the Southwark residence of the bishops of Winchester, before fleeing to the continent, where Louis IX of France offered him aid.[51] According to Matthew Paris, the French held up Raleigh's case as an example of English perfidy towards their bishops, comparing him to Anselm, Thomas Becket, and the more recent Edmund of Abingdon, all archbishops of Canterbury who had had run-ins with Henry III or his royal ancestors.[52] After intervention from the pope, for which Raleigh was rumored to have paid 8,000 marks, Henry finally relented and allowed Raleigh to return to England in April of 1244.[53] He eventually reconciled with Henry, and the king spent his Christmas courts of 1246–47 and 1249–50 at Winchester, dining in the bishop's hall on both occasions.[54] Raleigh was broke, however. While he was fighting with the king over the see of Winchester, the see and its lands had been in the king's hands and had suffered as a result. The cost of litigation had also taken a toll on Raleigh's coffers.[55] Raleigh died on the continent, in Tours, in 1250, while on a mission to raise money to rebuild his diocese.[56]

Raleigh had two clerks that we know of during his time as a justice. Roger of Thirkleby, a clerk in the Common Bench from 1230, was Raleigh's clerk from at least 1231, when Raleigh was a junior justice on that court. Thirkleby was already serving as an eyre justice in 1240, just after Raleigh retired from the court to take up his bishopric, and was promoted to justice of the Common Bench in 1242. Apart from a few breaks of a term or two, he was chief justice of the Bench from 1249 to 1260 and served as chief justice on thirty-eight eyres.[57] He seems to have been highly respected by his contemporaries. Matthew Paris calls him a "discerning man" and a "*literatus*," a term that implied that he had some Latin learning, beyond simple literacy.[58] Another chronicler said that he was incorruptible.[59] Thirkleby, it seems, made good his apprenticeship under Raleigh and was able to turn it into a lofty career as an important royal justice.

---

[51] Ibid, 285–86, 295.

[52] Ibid, 296.

[53] Ibid, 346–47, 360.

[54] Ibid, 590; vol 5, 94. The formal reconciliation occurred at a great council of the realm held at Windsor in September of 1244. Meekings and Crook, *King's Bench and Common Bench* (n 12) 72.

[55] David Crook, "Raleigh, William of (d. 1250)" (ODNB, September 23, 2004) <www.oxforddnb.com/view/article/23042> accessed March 13, 2019.

[56] CM, vol 5, 179.

[57] David Crook, "Thirkleby [Thurkilbi], Roger of (d. 1260)" (ODNB, September 23, 2004) <www.oxforddnb.com/view/article/27401> accessed March 13, 2019.

[58] CM, vol 5, 211, 317. Ralph V Turner, "The *Miles Literatus* in Twelfth- and Thirteenth-Century England. How Rare a Phenomenon?" in Ralph V Turner (ed), *Judges, Administrators, and the Common Law in Angevin England* (Hambledon Press, 1994) 122.

[59] Anthony Musson, *Medieval Law in Context: The Growth of Legal Consciousness from Magna Carta to the Peasants' Revolt* (Manchester University Press 2001) 73.

We do not know whether Thirkleby's hands touched the *Bracton* treatise. One case of "the eyre of Roger of Thirkleby in the twenty-ninth year of king Henry in the county of Nottingham" is referenced in the treatise, but otherwise he left no identifiable mark on it.[60] Another of Raleigh's clerks was involved in the writing of *Bracton*, however. Henry of Bratton is most famous today as the man who did not write *Bracton*. The treatise only bears the attribution to Henry of Bratton in manuscripts that come from a later tradition; those closest to the original bear the anonymous *ego* ("I") in the introduction.[61] We know Bratton did some work on the treatise, but just how much is an open question. We call the treatise *Bracton* today because the copyists of several of the manuscripts mistook the first "t" for a "c," an easy thing to do when reading thirteenth-century scripts. The sixteenth-century editor of the first printed edition of the treatise drew from a version that had it wrong. The man from Bratton Fleming became Henry de Bracton. Being known as the person who did not write the treatise and whose name is even misspelled on the first page is not the kind of legacy any of us would like to have. The academy, perhaps feeling a bit betrayed, has largely lost interest in Henry of Bratton since Thorne demonstrated that much of *De Legibus* must have been written before his time.[62] Bratton is an interesting figure in his own right, however. He first appears in the records in 1238 as a clerk of the court *coram rege*, of which Raleigh was the only full-time justice.[63] Bratton, like Raleigh, was from Devon. He probably came from the village of Bratton Fleming, on the Western edge of Exmoor. We know nothing of his family or his social status, which would seem to suggest that they were not among the greater families of the county. He probably owed his advancement to William of Raleigh, who was the absentee rector of Bratton Fleming and may, therefore, have become acquainted with Henry through his connection to the locality.

Bratton continued on as a clerk of the court *coram rege* for at least a few months after Raleigh retired to become bishop of Norwich. He had likely been paid out of Raleigh's own pocket while serving as a clerk—a common arrangement in this period—but by February 1240, Bratton was being paid directly

---

[60] *Bracton*, vol 4, 285. This case reference need not have been added by Thirkleby himself.
[61] *Bracton*, vol 3, li.
[62] See Brand, "Age of Bracton" (n 1) 65–90.
[63] The 1238 record is of Bratton recording an agreement he made with Stephen Fleming to hold a piece of land, which was possibly a manor, as it included among the appurtenances the advowson of the parish church, from the Fleming family. He thus appears as someone who had business before the court rather than as a clerk. There is reason to believe that he worked for the court *coram rege* at this point, however. The Bench would have been a more usual place to record such an agreement, but the court *coram rege* gave its own personnel the privilege of using that court for their own legal business. CRR 16, 51–52 (no 149F).

by the king, who authorized a retainer of forty marks a year for him. This was a large sum, equal to what junior justices would be paid later in the century.[64] He appears to have been regarded as quite senior at the time of Raleigh's retirement. But after one last mention of him in the rolls of Easter term, 1240, he disappears from the records for four years. [65] His disappearance from the records of the court, which corresponds almost exactly with Raleigh's fight with the king over the see of Winchester, possibly signals that he stood by William of Raleigh through his troubles. Bratton resurfaces in the historical record only in the fall of 1244, after Raleigh had been reconciled to the king.[66] A few months later, in April 1245, two charters were granted by Raleigh, "by the hand of Henry of Bratton, our clerk," suggesting that Bratton was part of Raleigh's episcopal household at that time.[67] In September of 1245, William of Raleigh granted him one of two papal dispensations he had received, each of which allowed a cleric to hold three benefices in plurality. These were hot commodities, and Raleigh would not have given one away lightly.[68] In the record of the dispensation recorded on the papal register, Bratton is again named as Raleigh's clerk.[69] After 1245, Bratton was a regular visitor to Raleigh's episcopal estates.[70] The two men appear to have been close.

At some point, Bratton also acquired the plea rolls of Martin of Pattishall and William of Raleigh, which were likely given to him by Raleigh. In 1247, when a litigant vouched the roll of Pattishall's Yorkshire eyre of 1226–27, Roger of Thirkleby sent a letter to the king telling him he had given one of the parties a writ addressed to William of Raleigh, by this time bishop of Winchester, "in whose custody the aforesaid rolls are."[71] The writ to Raleigh does not appear to

---

[64] There is no mention of him receiving a salary in any previous year. HG Richardson, *Bracton: The Problem of His Text* (Bernard Quaritch 1965) 2 (hereafter Richardson, *Bracton: The Problem of His Text*).

[65] CRR 16, 492–93 (no 2483).

[66] He appears in the rolls for a 1244 eyre in Devon as the creditor of Thomas of Saunton. He may not have appeared in court in person, however. Meekings and Crook, *King's Bench and Common Bench* (n 12) 82.

[67] Nicholas Vincent, "Henry of Bratton (*alias* Bracton)" in Mark Hill and RH Helmholz (eds), *Great Christian Jurists in English History* (CUP 2017) 22 (hereafter Vincent, "Henry of Bratton").

[68] The other dispensation was given to a member of Raleigh's household, presumably for loyal service. It went to Master Geoffrey Ferring, Raleigh's episcopal chancellor, who had supported Raleigh through his fight with the king. *Bracton,* vol 3, xliii; Jane E Sayers, "William of Drogheda and the English Canonists" in Peter Linehan (ed), *Proceedings of the Seventh International Congress of Medieval Canon Law* (Biblioteca Apostolica Vaticana 1988) 215. For the text of the dispensations, as recorded by the papal chancery, see Frederic William Maitland (ed), *Select Passages from the Works of Bracton and Azo* (SS vol 8, Bernard Quaritch 1895) xi.

[69] Meekings and Crook, *King's Bench and Common Bench* (n 12) 89.

[70] Raleigh's hospitality to Bratton is recorded in the Winchester pipe rolls, the financial records of the bishop of Winchester. Ibid, 88–89.

[71] "Et fecimus ei breve nostrum episcopo Wintoniensi directum, in cuius custodia predicti rotuli sunt . . ." HG Richardson and GO Sayles, *Select Cases of Procedure Without Writ Under Henry III* (SS vol 60, Bernard Quaritch, 1944) clxxxiv.

have been necessary, however, as Henry of Bratton replied to Thirkleby's letter to the king and said that he had searched the roll of Pattishall's last eyre in York, implying that the rolls were actually in Bratton's custody at that time.[72] Bratton was thought to have them still in 1258, when he was ordered to hand the rolls of Pattishall and Raleigh over to the treasury.[73] It appears, then, that Raleigh and Bratton kept an archive of old texts that included plea rolls and perhaps drafts of legislation and writs written by Pattishall and Raleigh. It is not clear exactly how this archive would have been kept. Would it have travelled with Raleigh and Bratton as they moved from place to place with the king's entourage, perhaps stored in a chest? Would it have been kept at the justice's lodgings, perhaps at one of his benefices? The fact that Bratton inherited it from Raleigh attests to a close relationship. Even if we cannot be sure exactly what his relationship to Raleigh was—scribe, senior clerk, ne'er-do-well nephew—Bratton was close enough to Raleigh to be showered with special favor and to be entrusted with his rolls, which, as we shall see, were important documents to the people in Raleigh's circle.

On account of the attribution of *Bracton* to him, Bratton has traditionally been treated as one of the great justices of the thirteenth century. More recent scholarship has demonstrated that he never quite made it to the top of the judicial ladder. He was clearly an important clerk, but his career appears to have stalled once he became a justice. A plea roll entry of 1240, when Bratton was still a clerk, describes him twice as "*domino Henrico de Bracton*" (Lord Henry of Bratton).[74] That entry has Bratton commanding two assize justices to take an assize despite a possible procedural irregularity, hinting that he was a person of substantial authority in the court *coram rege* even while he was still a clerk.[75] He seems to have returned to the royal courts after Raleigh was restored to favor, perhaps again as a senior clerk of the court *coram rege*. He served as an eyre justice in 1245.[76] On those eyres, he is named second in the order of precedence, just behind his former co-clerk, Roger of Thirkleby, who was a justice of the Common Bench.[77] More importantly Bratton, who had not yet been appointed a justice of the central royal courts, was placed above Gilbert

---

[72] Ibid, clxxxv. Richardson and Sayles argued that Thirkleby's belief that the rolls were still in Raleigh's possession was evidence that Raleigh had only recently handed them over to Bratton. At the very least, it shows that Thirkleby knew that the rolls had been in Raleigh's possession at some point, and thought he had taken them with him at his retirement.

[73] BNB, vol 1, 25.

[74] Meekings and Crook, *King's Bench and Common Bench* (n 12) 59.

[75] Ibid.

[76] Brand, "Age of Bracton" (n 1) 88.

[77] Meekings and Crook, *King's Bench and Common Bench* (n 12) 83; Crook, *General Eyre* (n 19) 105.

of Preston, who had been a justice of the Common Bench for several years and
had been chief justice of the Cornwall eyre just a year before.[78] He seems to
have been on the same track his master, Raleigh, had been on as a clerk. He
was a senior clerk who was vaulting over the heads of junior justices. But while
his career did not quite peak at this moment, it would be accurate to say that
he never reached the heights that Raleigh did. He spent two terms as a justice
of the court *coram rege*, the most important office he held, from 1247 to 1251
and from 1253 to 1257.[79] The two-year gap in his service may be explained by
Bratton's connections with Henry of Bath, the chief justice of the court *coram
rege*, who was forced to resign in 1251 amidst charges of corruption, but who
returned to the court in 1253. Most of Bratton's career as a justice was spent
on special assize commissions, which, like eyres, involved royal justices visiting the counties. Between 1248 and 1267, the year before his death, Bratton
was regularly given assize commissions for the Southwest of England. Bratton
was generally commissioned to take the assizes and to appoint two or three locals to sit with him. The only times he ever appeared as the chief justice of any
court were the times when he sat on these assize commissions.[80] Nevertheless,
Bratton was an important person. He sat on the king's council. In an ordinance
issued by the king and his council in 1256, he is listed after the royal justices
Henry of Bath and Henry de la Mare, as well as two magnates, although before
Walter of Merton, who was at the time the chancellor's right-hand man and the
prothonotary of the chancery.[81]

Just as Raleigh served the king through the troubles of the 1230s, Bratton sat
as a justice through the great political upheavals of the 1250s and 1260s. The
last ten years of Bratton's career were a period of crisis in English government,
when the king and his subjects were involved in a struggle over their respective
powers. In 1258, at a parliament at Oxford, the barons forced King Henry III to
accept rule by a council of fifteen, who would have the power to appoint, dismiss, and oversee the king's officials.[82] Open warfare between the king and the
barons broke out in 1263, and for fifteen months in 1264 and 1265, the king was
essentially a hostage of Simon de Montfort, the leader of the rebels.[83] Despite
de Montfort's death in 1265 at the battle of Evesham, fighting continued until
1267, the year before Bratton's death. We know nothing of Bratton's political
leanings, but it would appear that he successfully navigated a period of great

[78] Ibid.
[79] Brand, "Age of Bracton" (n 1) 88.
[80] BNB, vol 1, 21.
[81] Ibid, 43.
[82] Maddicott, *Simon de Montfort* (n 21) 158.
[83] Ibid, 226–28, 279–345.

turmoil, ingratiating himself with both the royalists and the Montfortians. Bratton was involved in some of the events of the period. In August 1259 the council of fifteen issued an edict restricting the justices who could sit on special assize commissions—in line with their policy of restricting the king's power to appoint his councilors and officials—to Roger of Thirkleby, Henry of Bath, Henry of Bratton, Giles of Erdington, Gilbert of Preston, William of Wilton, and John of Wyville.[84] The council not only trusted Bratton to continue his work, but also placed him third in line after the chief justices of the Common Bench and the court *coram rege*. Shortly thereafter, the council appointed Bratton to sit on one of the special eyre circuits to hear grievances against Henry's government.[85] Bratton received several advancements during the period of baronial control, from several different sources. The landed class of his native Devon showered him with gifts of land and ecclesiastical benefices, suggesting that they thought he was influential enough to want to have him on their side. He received a life estate in the manor of Tykenbrede in Cornwall from the Raleigh family, possibly relatives of his former master, in 1261.[86] He received rectories in the Southwest in 1259 and 1261, both from local landed families who held the advowsons. Early in 1264, as things were coming to a head between de Montfort and the king, he became archdeacon of Barnstaple, very close to his childhood home. Shortly thereafter, he became chancellor of Exeter Cathedral in Devon. [87]

Bratton seems to have been respected by the baronial council, but we cannot easily take this as evidence of his politics. He was also shown favor by the king in the years leading up to the baronial coup and even during the period of baronial reform. In 1253 and 1256, he was granted deer from the king's forests.[88] In 1254, the king gave him a house in London.[89] In 1260, Bratton was made the protector of the Carthusian charterhouse at Witham in Somerset. This was an important position. The austere Carthusian order was forbidden, by its own rule, to engage in lawsuits. Each Carthusian house thus needed an outside party to protect its interests. The appointment was made at a time when the council of fifteen was in control of the government. Witham was a religious establishment important to the Angevin royal house—it was built as part of

[84] BNB, vol 1, 20.
[85] Bratton was assigned to a circuit that included Gloucestershire, Worcestershire, and Herefordshire. It does not appear that this eyre circuit was ever launched. Meekings and Crook, *King's Bench and Common Bench* (n 12) 131.
[86] JH Round, "Bractoniana" (1916) 31 EHR 588, 588–89.
[87] Ibid, 589–90.
[88] BNB, vol 1, 21.
[89] Ibid.

Henry II's penance for Thomas Becket's death—and personally important to Henry III, so the king may have been given some say in the appointment.[90] Even if the king had no choice in Bratton's appointment, we know he approved of it. When, a few months later, the king recovered control of his council, he confirmed Bratton's appointment as protector of his grandfather's foundation.[91] Bratton was appointed to hear special assizes in the Southwest continuously from the 1250s to the late 1260s, by both the king's administration and the barons'. In 1267, he was placed on a special commission that was appointed to hear claims by supporters of Simon de Montfort who had lost their lands.[92] An amnesty had been declared, and the lands that the king had taken into his hand and regranted to his own faithful were being returned to the former rebels, provided they could pay a redemption fee for those lands.[93] As political fortunes rose and fell between 1258 and 1268, Bratton's career was remarkably stable. Despite all of his success, however, he never quite made it to the top of the judicial hierarchy, as his predecessors had.

## Writing *Bracton*

The most curious thing about these justices is that they spent much of their time away from the royal courts writing about their work in the royal courts. The scholarship on these justices to date has been dominated by the concerns of scholars who are interested in the *Bracton* treatise, but *Bracton* was just one of several texts produced by this group of justices. One of the major goals of this book will be to show that if we seek to understand justices like Pattishall, Raleigh, and Bratton, we need to understand *Bracton* in the context of their broader textual production. Still, *Bracton* was important to these justices. They worked on it over several decades, passing it along from justice to clerk.

*Bracton* was a massive project that appears to have taken many years to produce. The project these justices undertook was to write a great, learned tome about the work of the English royal courts, in the style of a Roman-law *summa*. After two introductions, the treatise is divided very broadly into sections on

---

[90] Richardson, *Bracton: The Problem of His Text* (n 64) 9; Colin Platt, *The Abbeys & Priories of Medieval England* (Barnes & Noble 1996) 62.

[91] Maddicott, *Simon de Montfort* (n 21) 204–05; Meekings and Crook, *King's Bench and Common Bench* (n 12) 131; CR 1259–61, 458.

[92] BNB, vol 1, 22.

[93] Alan Harding, *England in the Thirteenth Century* (CUP 1993) 295–96. For a discussion of the redemption fee and the courts that administered the process of returning the lands, see Robert C Palmer, *The Whilton Dispute, 1264-1380: A Social-Legal Study of Dispute Settlement in Medieval England* (Princeton University Press 1984) 35–46.

persons, things, and actions. This division is based on Justinian's *Institutes* and was probably borrowed from the civilian jurist Azo of Bologna's *Summa Institutionum* (*Summa on the Institutes*). Within these broad sections, the treatise is divided into tractates, some of which are on particular topics that cut across the work of the royal courts, others of which are about specific writs. In its current form, it is unfinished. The final tractate, on the writ of right, ends abruptly and there are occasional cross-references, explaining that something will be treated at greater length later, to material that does not appear in the treatise.[94]

Several hands touched it at various points, but identifying precisely whose hands they were is difficult.[95] Authors of the 1280s and 1290s would create their own recensions of *Bracton* that bear different names, names such as *Fleta* and *Thornton*. In a sense, these recensions are just a continuation of a series of three or more recensions written between about the 1220s and the 1280s. The text known today as *Bracton* is at least the third recension of the text and was probably not much older than *Fleta* or *Thornton*. One of the challenges of writing about *Bracton* is that we cannot be sure we have the full cast of characters. Historians who have examined the treatise since Thorne created his edition of the treatise have generally assumed that the base text was written primarily by William of Raleigh and a second recension was created by Henry of Bratton.[96] We can be fairly certain of the following: First, William of Raleigh and Henry of Bratton both worked on the treatise. Bratton received a recension of the treatise, in some form, probably from Raleigh. It may have been a fairly rough version of the treatise. I will refer to this recension, the text Henry of Bratton received, as the *Raleigh* treatise. Henry of Bratton then cut that text down substantially, added some of his own material, and created a second recension, which I will call *Bratton*. It was probably complete by 1256 at the latest. It existed in at least one copy, but possibly only one copy. This is not the version we know today. The version we know today is a third recension, made sometime in the second half of the thirteenth century, probably after Bratton's death in 1268. It is actually an amalgam of *Raleigh* and *Bratton*, created when a scribe who had copied *Bratton* discovered a copy—perhaps *the* copy—of *Raleigh* and

---

[94] See *Bracton*, vol 4, 183.

[95] There is a vast literature on the date and authorship of the treatise. This section attempts to synthesize that literature into a narrative. For an excellent summary of the scholarship on the date and authorship of *Bracton*, see Vincent, "Henry of Bratton" (n 67) 28–41.

[96] Ibid, 40. John Barton was the primary opponent of this view. Barton argued that the text was produced in its entirety by Henry of Bratton and was a production of the 1250s. See JL Barton, "The Mystery of Bracton" (1993) 14 Journal of Legal History 1; "The Authorship of *Bracton*: Again" (2009) 30 Journal of Legal History 117.

added material back in that had been cut by Henry of Bratton when he made his recension. We do not know, however, how many additional stages of development there may have been, or how many other hands may have touched the treatise. This is particularly true of the earlier stages in the treatise's development. There may very well have been a first recension, which we might call *Pattishall*, which was begun by Martin of Pattishall and passed on to William of Raleigh. It may be that several other people were involved in the writing and editing of the treatise before it reached Henry of Bratton's hands, both before and after Raleigh worked on it.

Work on the treatise very probably began before 1227. The evidence for the treatise's beginnings in the 1220s is compelling. Comparing the law in the treatise to the law on the plea rolls, Samuel Thorne found that the treatise often states rules that were being applied by the courts in the 1220s, but that had been abandoned or changed by the 1230s.[97] Some of the most compelling evidence of this sort comes from the many writs that were copied into the treatise. The writs that originated litigation in the royal courts had limitation dates, which barred actions that had arisen too long ago to still be justiciable. The limitation dates served a function similar to the modern statute of limitations. The writ of novel disseisin contained in the *Glanvill* treatise requires that the disseisin complained of have taken place "since my [i.e., the king's] last voyage to Normandy."[98] These limitation dates were updated periodically as the events used in the writs receded into history. Many of the limitation dates in the treatise date to before 1229. Sweeping changes were made to the limitation dates in 1237, but only one of the writs in the treatise contains a limitation date that was in force after that date.[99] These writs probably contain the limitation dates that were current at the time the treatise was written. We know that registers of writs existed in this period and were likely available in the royal courts.[100] A sitting justice, such as Pattishall, Raleigh, or Bratton, is likely to have had easy access to an up-to-date register, as well as to the actual writs that would have been returned to their courts. Additionally, William of Raleigh, as the chief justice

---

[97]  John Barton has argued that Bratton was more concerned with the authority of the justice who decided a case than with its age, and thus cited to cases that stated rules that were no longer being followed at the time of writing. I agree with Barton that the cases are cited primarily for their value as statements by great jurist-justices. There is compelling evidence, however, that the authors of the treatise updated it as the law practiced in the courts changed in the 1230s and 1240s, suggesting that they were concerned with stating the law as it was practiced in the royal courts, not just the opinions of the school of Pattishall. Barton, "Authorship of *Bracton*: Again" (n 96) 118, 119.

[98]  *Glanvill*, 167 (Book XIII, c 33).

[99]  *Bracton*, vol 3, xxviii.

[100]  Brand has persuasively argued that the Irish register of writs, the oldest surviving register, dates to 1210. Paul Brand, "Ireland and the Literature of the Early Common Law" in MCL, 453. For the text of the Irish register, see De Haas and Hall, *Early Registers* (n 30) 1–17.

of the court *coram rege* and the king's chief legal adviser is likely to have been involved in the decision-making process that led to the changes in limitation dates in 1237.

Even more compelling as evidence of an early date of composition are those passages that are not just *outdated*, but actually *updated* to reflect new rules adopted by the courts in the 1230s. In parts of the treatise, the authors appear to have attempted to update what were originally pre-1229 limitation dates in writs, to reflect current practice.[101] The treatise is also updated to reflect new rules adopted at the great council of the realm held at Merton in 1236. The first chapter of the Provisions of Merton was inserted into the text mid-sentence. The second was inserted in the middle of a long excerpt from the *Glanvill* treatise. The fourth was inserted in a place in the treatise where it contradicts the text that comes directly before it.[102] These attempts to update the treatise show us that those passages were likely written before these changes to the law were made and that the treatise's authors were looking for the current law.

This first phase of writing is likely when the treatise took its shape and most of the sections of it were begun. By 1236 there were probably several long, but possibly poorly edited, tractates in existence. The huge tractate on novel disseisin—it fills 187 pages in the modern edition—was certainly begun in this period, as was the shorter tractate on the assize *utrum*; both of these tractates contain materials that were either outdated by the late 1230s or that were revised to bring the doctrines in line with the new rules adopted at Merton.[103] The tractate on the assize of mort d'ancestor, like the tractate on novel disseisin, contains writs with limitation dates that were not in force after 1236.[104] The treatise's discussions of dower were probably written in the first phase, as well. One discussion of dower appears at the very end of the long, heavily Romanized tractate near the beginning of the treatise on acquiring dominion of things.[105] Another appears in the larger tractate on the writ of dower.[106] Both contain references to the Provisions of Merton, but in both cases they appear to be later revisions, inserted clumsily either mid-sentence or between two sentences that

---

[101] In all three cases, the attempt to update was clumsily done; the limitation dates that appear in these writs were not in use in any period. Brand, "Age of Bracton" (n 1) 68–69; Paul Brand, "The Date and Authorship of Bracton: A Response" (2010) 31 Journal of Legal History 217, 225 (hereafter Brand, "Date and Authorship"); *Bracton*, vol 3, 57, 72, 192.

[102] Bracton, vol 3, xii–xvi.

[103] *Bracton,* vol 3, xiii, xxiv; Brand, "Date and Authorship" (n 101) 219, 225–26.

[104] *Bracton,* vol 3, 249.

[105] This section runs from *Bracton*, vol 2, 42–281 in the modern edition. The discussion of dower runs from *Bracton*, vol 2, 265–81.

[106] *Bracton*, vol 3, 357–411.

look like they must have originally been contiguous.[107] Brand has argued that the writ of summons for the eyre that appears in the section of the treatise on actions is in a form that dates to before 1234, suggesting that either the author had an outdated writ in his possession or that at least parts of that tractate date to the earlier period.[108] The introduction to the section of the treatise on the law of actions also contains a reference to a type of essoin—an excuse for not appearing in court—that had been disallowed by 1236.[109] A reference to the same essoin appears in the unfinished tractate on the writ of right.[110] The tractate on exceptions, which is a subsection of the tractate on the writ of right, was probably also begun in this earlier period, since it contains a reference to the writ of *habeas corpus*, which is concerned with mesne process and is not related to our modern writ of the same name; this was no longer a regular part of court procedure by 1233.[111] If we take all of these instances of corrected or archaic law as evidence for a stage of writing that took place in the 1220s and early 1230s, then the portions of the treatise that must have been underway by 1236 at the latest include the introduction to actions and the tractates on acquiring dominion of things, pleas of the crown, novel disseisin, mort d'ancestor, utrum, dower, entry, the writ of right, and exceptions. This leaves out only the short tractates on persons and things, which owe most of their material to Roman law, the tractate on cosinage, the tractate on darrein presentment, and the tractates on essoins, default, and warranty, which are all subsections of the unfinished tractate on the writ of right. This does not mean that these seven tractates—apart from the tractate on cosinage, a writ invented in 1235—were not written in the first phase, only that we have no evidence for an early composition.

Martin of Pattishall was active in the courts until 1229, and it is certainly possible that he began the treatise before he died. Paul Brand has suggested that a royal command of 1234 to the mayor and sheriffs to proclaim "through the whole city of London" that all schools teaching law in the city were prohibited and should close without delay may have referred to a course that included instruction in both the common law and the two laws.[112] From the early thirteenth century there were lecturers in Oxford who, along with the art of

---

[107] *Bracton*, vol 3, xiii.

[108] *Bracton*, vol 2, 309–10; Brand, "Date and Authorship" (n 101) 228–30.

[109] *Bracton*, vol 2, 312; Brand, "Date and Authorship" (n 101) 232.

[110] *Bracton*, vol 4, 61; Brand, "Date and Authorship" (n 101) 232.

[111] *Bracton*, vol 4, 364–69; Brand, "Date and Authorship" (n 101) 234–36.

[112] Paul Brand, "Legal Education in England before the Inns of Court" in Jonathan A Bush and Alain Wijffels (eds), *Learning the Law: Teaching and the Transmission of English Law, 1150-1900* (Hambledon Press, 1999) 57 (hereafter Brand, "Legal Education"). My discussions with Brand have been very helpful in developing the following discussion.

letter-writing, were teaching the rudiments of procedure in both secular and ecclesiastical courts. Students likely attended such lectures to learn how to manage the affairs of the great, which would include litigation in both venues, so they could find employment as clerks or stewards. Historians often refer to these schools collectively as the "Oxford business school."[113] It is conceivable that *Bracton* was the product of a similar course of instruction in London in the 1220s and early 1230s. Although it might be more natural for a lecture course on the work of the king's courts to be offered in Westminster, where justices, clerks, lawyers, and royal officials would have lived and worked, it is possible that Martin of Pattishall would have thought to offer such a course in London. Pattishall became dean of St. Paul's Cathedral in August of 1228.[114] St. Paul's had a long tradition of education by the thirteenth century, and it was just inside the city walls, as close as one could get to Westminster while still being in London.[115] In later centuries, St. Paul's was closely connected with the law. By the late fourteenth century there is evidence that in the afternoon, after the work of the courts was done for the day, the serjeants retired to a part of St. Paul's called the "parvis" to meet with clients.[116] The association between St. Paul's and the king's courts at Westminster may have begun earlier; in 1266, the Common Bench sat in St. Paul's rather than Westminster for two terms.[117]

It is thus possible that *Bracton* began life as a course of lectures given by Pattishall. Raleigh could have continued these lectures until the prohibition of 1234; he is described as a canon of St. Paul's in a chronicle for the year 1237, and may have begun his association with St. Paul's much earlier, perhaps while his master was dean.[118] Judging from *Bracton*, this course would have been significantly more theoretical in outlook than the courses of instruction given in the Oxford business school. And where the Oxford business school seems to have been concerned with teaching the practices of the secular and the ecclesiastical courts, the *Bracton* authors do not appear to have concerned themselves

[113] HG Richardson, "The Oxford Law School under John" (1941) 57 LQR 319, 319–28; HG Richardson, "Business Training in Medieval Oxford" (1941) 46 The American Historical Review 259, 275.
[114] Alan Harding, "Pattishall, Martin of (d. 1229)" (ODNB, September 23, 2004) <www.oxforddnb.com/view/article/21542> accessed March 13, 2019.
[115] St. Paul's had a grammar school and offered some higher studies from at least the twelfth century. Nicholas Orme, *English Schools in the Middle Ages* (Methuen & Co 1973) 308–09. The chapter of St. Paul's also included several prominent English canonists at the end of the twelfth and the beginning of the thirteenth centuries, among them Peter of Blois, Benedict of Sawston, and Master John of Kent. Stephan Kuttner and Eleanor Rathbone, "Anglo-Norman Canonists of the Twelfth Century: An Introductory Study" (1949-51) 7 Traditio 279, 285, 289, 320.
[116] JH Baker, *The Order of the Serjeants at Law* (Selden Society 1984) 102–04. I would like to thank Ryan Rowberry for bringing this to my attention.
[117] Meekings and Cook, *King's Bench and Common Bench* (n 12) 294.
[118] CM, vol 3, 417.

much with canon law. They certainly knew something of canon law and occasionally cite to canons, but Roman law is cited and quoted far more often than the canons are. Additionally, and unlike the lecturers of the Oxford business school, the authors of *Bracton* did not seek to teach canon law and the law of the English courts in the same text. Indeed, *Bracton* says at one point, in the context of a discussion of the jurisdiction of secular and ecclesiastical judges that "nothing relating to the regulation of the *sacerdotium* [i.e., the kind of authority that the Church exercises through its courts] is relevant to this treatise," and then continues to discuss the jurisdiction of secular judges, implying that the treatise excludes matters that pertain solely to the ecclesiastical courts from its coverage.[119] This does not mean, however, that its authors, or others in their school, did not teach canon law separately. *Bracton* may, therefore, be evidence for a short-lived course of instruction that we might think of as the deluxe version of the courses offered at the Oxford business school.

The treatise probably came into Raleigh's hands at some point, although how much had already been written when this happened is an open question. Pattishall need not have been involved in the writing of the treatise. Raleigh had already had more than a decade of experience working in the royal courts by the mid-1220s and would have had the knowledge necessary to write such a treatise. Whoever began it, by 1236 there appears to have been at least a rough draft of the treatise. It may have still been very rough, however. The quotations from the Provisions of Merton, so clumsily worked into the text as we have it today, may have originally been written into the margin of a draft, to be incorporated later. Material that the authors wanted to add may have been written down on additional sheets of parchment, which were then stuck in-between the pages of the draft, often in the wrong place.[120] Thorne suggested that the seventeen-page discussion of partition, for instance, was inserted into the treatise in this way, which would explain why in the received text it splits what appears to be a continuous discussion of homage.[121]

Revisions and additions were made to the text sometime after 1235 or 1236. The tractate on cosinage could not have been written before Raleigh devised the writ in 1235.[122] We do not know how long after 1235 it was written, however. Brand has argued that there was likely a stage of writing that took place within a few years of 1236. The Provisions of Merton are called a *nova gratia*

---

[119] "Cum autem de regimine sacerdotii nihil pertineat ad tractatum istum . . ." *Bracton*, vol 2, 304.

[120] *Bracton*, vol 1, xxxix–xl.

[121] *Bracton*, vol 1, xlii; vol 2, 208–25. The discussion of partition is not marked as an *addicio*. It actually contains *addiciones*.

[122] Brand, *Kings, Barons, and Justices* (n 30) 53, n 43.

*et provisio* or a *nova constitutio* in two places in the treatise.[123] Brand has argued that provisions of this type were called "*nova*" for a period of just a few years after their issuance in the thirteenth century—Magna Carta, for instance, is never called a "*nova constitutio*" in the treatise—making it more probable that the person writing the references to Merton was writing within a decade of the council itself.[124] By meticulous study of the wording of the text, Brand has also made a compelling case that some of the material on the Provisions of Merton that appears in *Bracton* is actually based on preliminary drafts of the Provisions and the writs that would have accompanied it.[125] Since William of Raleigh is known to have done some of the drafting, and was credited with the drafting of the writ of redisseisin, created by the Provisions, he may have had his drafts available to incorporate into the treatise. Brand argues that it is unlikely that Raleigh would have included drafts after the Provisions were issued, since he would have had access to the final versions of the texts. This suggests that he was working on the treatise at the same time he was working on the Provisions, in the year 1236. There is much to commend this interpretation of the evidence. It is important to remember that this post-1236 material could have been added any time after 1236, however. I think it is just as likely that the draft texts were kept in some sort of archive that was later passed on to Bratton, possibly when Raleigh passed Pattishall's rolls and his own on to Bratton, and were then incorporated into the treatise by Bratton, perhaps as late as the 1250s. Bratton could have been unaware at the time he incorporated them that he was not incorporating the final version of the text.

There may, therefore, have been several earlier versions of the treatise. In addition to the recension that was complete by 1236, there may have been a second recension made around 1236, a *Raleigh II*. Or it may be that William of Raleigh or others continued to add material to the margin of *Raleigh* and slip additional pieces of parchment between its leaves until 1250. The problem of determining what was happening with the treatise between 1236 and 1250 is compounded by the fact that we do not know what, if anything, was done with the early version or versions of the treatise. Were they used to teach law to clerks of the royal courts as part of a lecture course? Were they shared with Raleigh's clerks, or his colleagues on the bench? Or did Raleigh regard these early version as drafts of a work-in-progress, to be shared at some later date when the treatise was finished?

---

[123] *Bracton*, vol 2, 276; vol 3, 398–99. This language also appears in some of the annotations to the collection of cases known as *Bracton's Note Book*. See below, p 154, n.69.
[124] Brand, "Date and Authorship" (n 101) 222–23.
[125] Ibid, 220–22, 225.

The versions written in the 1220s or 1230s were very different texts from the recension made by Henry of Bratton in the 1250s. At some point after 1252, Henry of Bratton made a new recension of the treatise, the one I call *Bratton*.[126] I suspect that Bratton created it sometime between 1252 and 1256. The reason for dating this phase of writing to after 1252 is that a case that was heard between 1252 and 1253 appears in the main text of the treatise.[127] A reference to a case in which Henry of Bratton was involved in 1255 and 1256, a case that, as we shall see, was important to Bratton, appears to be a later addition, added to the margin of Bratton's copy and only later worked into the text of the treatise.[128] Meekings and Crook thought that Bratton may have used his time away from the court *coram rege* between 1251 and 1253 to work on the treatise.[129] He may have created a fair copy, incorporating cases up through 1253, sometime shortly before he returned to the court, and then continued to add material to the margins of that copy for a number of years.

*Bratton* was quite a bit shorter than either *Raleigh* or *Bracton*. Bratton edited the treatise that had been left to him by his master. He probably inserted into the main text some passages that had originally been written into the margin, and was not always artful in doing so. He added references to some of his own cases—cases in which he was justice and, occasionally, litigant.[130] He may have updated the text to take account of the Provisions of Merton and the writ of cosinage, if those passages had not already been written into the text or margin in the 1230s. He added his name to a discussion of mistakes in writs. When Bratton's name appears in an example on the use of the incorrect title for a party named in a writ, Brand makes the tantalizing suggestion that the treatise originally used Martin of Pattishall; the example of the "correct" title is "dean," but Henry of Bratton was never a dean. Martin of Pattishall, on the other hand, was dean of St. Paul's Cathedral in London.[131] Added to the section on formed

---

[126]  *Bracton*, vol 3, xliii.

[127]  It is not marked as an *addicio*. *Bracton*, vol 4, 78; Meekings and Crook, *King's Bench and Common Bench* (n 12) 137. *Bracton* describes the case as one "in the roll of the Bench in the thirty-seventh year of king Henry in the county of Kent, between Boniface, Archbishop of Canterbury, and Robert St. John, concerning the church of Eynsford." There is an actual case between these two parties on the roll of Michaelmas term, 1253, although it is for the church of Erith and the entry does not mention that an essoin of the king's service was disallowed in the case, the point for which the case is cited in the treatise. TNA KB 26/148, m 10d. This is probably the case to which the treatise refers, however. Erith is only ten miles from Eynsford. The fact that Bratton misidentified the church implies that he was citing from memory, and he may have remembered elements of the case that did not make it into the plea roll entry. I would like to thank Paul Brand for the identification of the case.

[128]  *Bracton*, vol 2, 150.

[129]  Meekings and Crook, *King's Bench and Common Bench* (n 12) 138.

[130]  A list of those cases can be found in Meekings and Crook, *King's Bench and Common Bench* (n 12) 137.

[131]  Brand, "Age of Bracton" (n 1) 78; *Bracton*, vol 3, 79.

prohibitions—writs of prohibition drafted for exceptional circumstances and based on very specific facts—was one writ that appears to be a draft of one issued by Henry of Bratton himself in 1255.[132] Thorne thought that the articles of the eyre contained in the treatise are a copy of those given to the justices of the 1245 eyre, the one eyre on which Bratton sat as a justice.[133] Some other additions can probably be dated to this period, although they have no particular connection to Henry of Bratton. Brand argues that the passage on mesne process, which includes material about *habeas corpus*, was probably added to after the late 1240s, when grand distress, which appears after *habeas corpus* in that passage, became a common part of court proceedings.[134]

Bratton added to the text, but he also subtracted quite a lot from it. In the surviving manuscripts of *Bracton*, there are passages marked *addicio* in the margin. These appear to be material that was added to the text at some point in its history. It probably either appeared in the margins of some now-lost manuscript of the treatise or on separate slips of parchment. In the manuscripts closest to Bratton's copy, the *addiciones* all appear in the margins.[135] Thorne noticed an odd thing about these *addiciones*. Many of them contained material that was either repetitive of other material nearby or outdated by the 1250s.[136] It would have been odd to add this kind of material at a late stage of editing, to make the treatise repetitive and misleading. Thorne thought that these *addiciones* were actually material from an early draft of the treatise that Bratton deleted when he made his *Bratton* recension. He thought it had been added back into the treatise by a copyist who was copying the text of *Bratton*, but who also had access to *Raleigh*. It was common when copying texts in this period to refer to several exemplars. People who commissioned manuscripts often wanted to ensure that they had the most complete version of the text, so referring to several manuscripts made a certain amount of sense. Many of the surviving manuscripts of *Bracton*, dating to the later thirteenth century, show signs that their copyists referred to several manuscripts of the treatise when making a copy. This is one of the reasons why it is so difficult to determine the parentage of the existing manuscripts.[137] Thorne thought this copyist of *Bratton* noticed that *Raleigh* contained passages that *Bratton* did not. He

---

[132] *Bracton*, vol 4, 258–59; Brand, "Date and Authorship" (n 101) 228.

[133] Thorne argues that Bratton or some other editor later came back to these articles and made some changes to take account of the changes in the articles given to the justices in the visitations of 1246 to 1249 and 1250 to 1251. *Bracton*, vol 2, 329, n 3.

[134] Brand, "Date and Authorship" (n 101) 234–36.

[135] *Bracton*, vol 3, xliv, xlviii–xlix.

[136] *Bracton*, vol 3, xliv–xlvii.

[137] *Bracton*, vol 3, xlix.

copied these into the margins. When later scribes copied that manuscript, they moved those marginal passages into the main text, but marked them with the word *addicio*. Not all of the *addiciones* can be explained this way. Some include later material that was added in the 1250s. Those *addiciones* may have been in the margin of the *Bratton* recension and been copied into the margin of the new, combined copy, where they would have appeared with all of the material copied from *Raleigh*.[138]

*Bratton* appears to have been a shorter, more tightly edited treatise than *Raleigh*, although parts were still incomplete and there were numerous errors in the text. *Bratton* cut out repetitions. He cut cases of the 1220s and 1230s, probably because he considered them to be out-of-date. He cut some of the Roman law material, although he added some Romanisms of his own.[139] If we accept H.G. Richardson's dating of William of Drogheda's *Summa Aurea*—a manual of Romano-canonical procedure by an Oxford scholar—as 1239 at the earliest and his estimate of the dates when Raymond de Peñafort's *Summa de Matrimonio* could have arrived in England at around 1235 to 1240, then Henry of Bratton becomes a more likely candidate for the author of those sections of the treatise that rely on Drogheda and Peñafort than William of Raleigh.[140] Raleigh may have been keeping up with the latest in civilian learning, even while he was a clerk and justice of the courts, and he may have still been working on the treatise after 1236. We do not know when he turned the treatise over to Bratton. On the other hand, the later a passage was written, the more likely it is that it was written by Bratton. The core of the treatise was there when Bratton made his recension, but Bratton himself did quite a bit to it.

[138] One *addicio*, for instance, recounts a case decided by the King's council in 1262. *Bracton*, vol 2, 447; Meekings and Crook, *King's Bench and Common Bench* (n 12) 137. One way to explain this particular *addicio* is that the copyist found it in the margin of the *Bratton* recension. If Bratton had completed that recension by 1256, he may have added this case, for which he was probably present, to the margin of his treatise. The copyist, may, then, have simply left it in the margin, where the additional material from *Raleigh* also appeared. It then would have been marked as an *addicio* when it was taken into the main text along with the archaic material.

[139] *Bracton*, vol 3, xlv.

[140] HG Richardson, "Azo, Drogheda, and Bracton" (1944) 59 EHR 22, 23–26. The *Summa Aurea* may have been available in earlier drafts, but probably not much earlier. It contains numerous references to events and works of the 1230s. A case used in the treatise is dated to 1239 in many of the manuscripts. The treatise also cites to the constitutions of the legatine council held in London in 1237. It contains citations to Roffredus of Benevento's *Libelli de Iure Civile*, which was likely only available from 1235, and to the *Decretals of Gregory IX*, available from 1234. Jane E Sayers, "William of Drogheda and the English Canonists" in Peter Linehan (ed), *Proceedings of the Seventh International Congress of Medieval Canon Law* (Biblioteca Apostolica Vaticana 1988) 206.

Schulz thought that *Bracton* also relied upon William of Sacrobosco's *Computus Ecclesiasticus*, which he dates to 1236. Fritz Schulz, "Bracton as a Computist" (1945) 3 Traditio 265, 279.

Unfortunately, in most cases it is difficult to assign an author to a particular part of the treatise. The cases of the 1240s and 1250s that were added to the treatise are mostly connected to Henry of Bratton, so we can be fairly sure he was working on it in the 1250s. We do not know how much earlier he might have been working on it, however. Material that we can date before 1236 probably was not written by Bratton, since he first appears in the records of the courts in 1238, although we cannot be entirely sure even of this, as Bratton may have been working for Raleigh for several years before he appeared in the record. Raleigh might have handed the treatise over to Bratton on his retirement from the court in 1239 or continued to work on it for several years. He lived until 1250 and probably would have had the free time to do so during his exile. There is a great deal of material—including the tractate on cosinage and the updates to bring the treatise into line with the Provisions of Merton—that was added sometime after 1236, but we cannot be sure when or by whom. I will, therefore, often refer to "the author" of a particular passage, although in places where there is evidence pointing to one author in particular, I will note that.

## An In-House Text?

We do not know what was done with *Raleigh*, but *Bratton* was likely shared, in some way, with the justices and clerks of the royal courts. The treatises known as *Hengham Magna* and *Fet Asaver* rely, in part, on one of the versions of *Bracton*.[141] A third text, *Casus et Judicia*, was probably the work of someone who knew *Bracton*, and will be treated in greater detail in Chapter 7. It is not entirely clear how these authors knew of it, but all three of these texts were likely written during Henry of Bratton's lifetime.[142] Perhaps Bratton loaned the treatise out to clerks such as John Blundel, the senior clerk and contemporary of Bratton who probably wrote *Hengham Magna*.[143] It is also possible that Bratton and others were giving a lecture course based on the treatise in the 1250s. There is good evidence that oral instruction in the law of the king's courts existed in the 1250s and 1260s, and we are certain it existed in the 1270s. That instruction would have been quite different from the instruction one would have received

---

[141] Thomas J McSweeney, "Creating a Literature for the King's Courts in the Later Thirteenth Century: Hengham Magna, Fet Asaver, and Bracton" (2016) 37 Journal of Legal History 41, 50–51, 61–65 (hereafter McSweeney, "Creating a Literature").

[142] Paul Brand, "*Hengham Magna*: A Thirteenth-Century English Common Law Treatise and Its Composition," in MCL 389 (hereafter Brand, "*Hengham Magna*"); McSweeney, "Creating a Literature" (n 141) 57.

[143] Brand, "*Hengham Magna*" (n 142) 386–91; McSweeney, "Creating a Literature" (n 141) 45–47.

from a lecturer working from *Bracton*, however. It seems to have been delivered mostly, although not exclusively, in French and been for the benefit of people who wished to practice as serjeants or attorneys in the royal courts.[144] *Bracton*, on the other hand, appears to have been primarily an in-house text. Its authors appear to have imagined the ideal reader of the text as a clerk or a junior justice of the central royal courts.[145] *Bracton* addresses itself specifically to the justices and clerks of the royal courts. Indeed, justices and clerks are the only groups specifically addressed in the treatise. As we have seen, the introduction to the treatise tells us that the laws and customs of England "are often dragged into misuse by men of little wisdom and small learning who ascend the judgment seat before they have learned the laws, and stand amid doubts and a confusion of opinions, and are frequently subverted by the greater men (*maiores*) who decide cases according to their own will rather than the authority of the laws."[146] To remedy this problem, the author tells us, "I [have written this treatise] to instruct the *minores*, if no one else . . ."[147] By this he probably means the clerks and junior justices of the royal courts; the word *minores* is used to refer to junior justices and clerks elsewhere in the treatise.[148] As we have seen, the three justices with the closest links to the treatise served as judicial clerks for long periods of time before they became justices. That was their route to the bench. The author of this passage is addressing people like him.

---

[144] Brand, "Legal Education" (n 112) 58–61; John S Beckerman, "Law-Writing and Law Teaching: Treatise Evidence of the Formal Teaching of English Law in the Late Thirteenth Century" in Jonathan A Bush and Alain Wijffels (eds), *Learning the Law: Teaching and the Transmission of Law in England, 1150-1900* (Hambledon Press 1999) 33–50. The collection known as *Casus Placitorum*, which exists in a number of manuscripts, may have been made as a collection of notes from a course given in the 1250s or shortly thereafter, as it cites to several justices, none of whom were on the bench after 1260. Brand, "Legal Education" (n 112) 60. The text known as *Brevia Placitata* at one point uses the second person to say "You should make a similar defense," hinting that it was originally given as lectures. The year 1260 appears in writs in the treatise, and this may be the date of the lectures. Ibid, 59. Brand also identified a manuscript of French lectures given between 1276 and 1278, along with a second, revised version of those lectures. Paul Brand, "Courtroom and Schoolroom: The Education of Lawyers in England Prior to 1400" in MCL, 62–64 (hereafter Brand, "Courtroom and Schoolroom").

[145] *Brevia Placitata* seems to assume an audience of pleaders, since it gives specimen counts and instructs people in how they should make them.

[146] *Bracton*, vol 2, 19.

[147] *Bracton*, vol 2, 19.

[148] In the tractate on essoins, the author says that "for the instruction of the *minores*, something must be said of the manner of enrolment." *Bracton*, vol 4, 99; see also vol 3, 364; vol 4, 77, 101. Enrolling entries was the responsibility of clerks. The treatise also alludes to making marginal notations in the roll and to searching the rolls, tasks that would have been performed by clerks. *Bracton*, vol 4, 101–02; Meekings and Crook, *King's Bench and Common Bench* (n 12) 16.

At times, *minores* and *maiores* are used to refer to certain types of justices. The justices of the court *coram rege* are referred to as *maiores* at one point in the treatise. *Bracton*, vol 2, 307. Here they are not specifically contrasted with *minores*, but the text implies that the justices of the Common Bench, of the eyres, and of special assize commissions are not as great as those of the court *coram rege*. Ibid. The

This becomes clearer just a little beyond the discussion above, on what is the treatise's second page in Thorne's edition. One of the authors copies passages from texts of Roman and canon law, but modifies them in telling ways.[149] He demonstrates his focus on the justices and clerks of the royal courts by changing references to jurists found in his sources into references to judges. In the *Summa Institutionum*, Azo tells us that the utility of the knowledge of law is that

it ennobles apprentices, furnishes offices, and doubles their honors and profits, and (so that I may acknowledge truth in all things) enables professors of law to rule solemnly throughout the whole world and to sit in the imperial chamber, judging tribes and nations, plaintiffs and defendants, in lordly order.[150]

In *Bracton*, the professors who sit in the imperial chamber become the justices of the English king:

The utility [of this work] is that is ennobles apprentices and doubles the honors and profits and enables them to rule in the realm and sit in the royal chamber, on the very seat of the king, on the throne of God, so to speak, judging tribes and nations, plaintiffs and defendants, in lordly order, in the place of the king, as though in the place of Jesus Christ, since the king is God's vicar.[151]

Azo imagines his readers to be preparing to rule "throughout the whole world," while *Bracton* imagines them to be preparing to rule simply in the

tractate on exceptions, in a discussion of the king's delegation of his judicial authority, refers to the jurisdiction of "the greater and lesser justices," although it is not exactly clear what the author means by this. *Bracton*, vol 4, 281.

---

[149] Although this passage comes very shortly after the passage discussed above and is still part of the introduction to the treatise, the two may have been the work of different authors. In the printed editions of *Bracton* the introduction is divided into two parts, the *introductio* and the *prohemium auctoris*. These divisions do not appear in the manuscripts. They may or may not be the work of two different authors. There are stylistic differences that hint that the *introductio* and the *prohemium* were written by different people with different aims. The problems of the introduction will be discussed in greater detail in Chapter 6.

[150] "Haec si velut almisca dominatrix nobilitat addiscentes, exhibet magistratus, et honores conduplicat et profectus, et (ut vera per omnia fatear) iuris professores per orbem terrarum fecit solemniter principari, et sedere in imperiali aula, tribus, et nationes, actores et reos ordine dominabili iudicantes." Azo, *Summae*, 1043.

[151] "Utilitas autem est quia nobilitat addiscentes et honores conduplicat et profectus et facit eos principari in regno et sedere in aula regia et in sede ipsius regis quasi in throno dei, tribus et nationes, actores et reos, ordine dominabili iudicantes, vice regis quasi vice Ihesu Christi, cum rex sit vicarius dei." *Bracton*, vol 2, 20.

"realm," probably referring specifically to the realm of England. Those apprentices are preparing for different things, as well. The professors of law, a term that was used at the time to refer to university-educated jurists, disappear in Bracton's version.[152] Azo presents the work's ability to find promotion for its reader as a knowing aside, perhaps with an implicit wink. Civilians and canonists were a bit ashamed of their fields' lucrative nature. Popes, bishops, and councils sought to restrict the study of Roman law, in particular, because students, lured by the money and advancement it could bring, preferred it to canon law and theology, which were important for the Church's mission of saving souls.[153] Azo's treatise is preparing its reader to sit as a judge, but Azo only tells us that the study of civil law can lead to such advancement because he must "acknowledge truth in all things." The author of the passage in Bracton shows no such shame. His treatise is for people who already work in the royal courts. The imperial chamber becomes the royal chamber, and the people to whom this treatise is addressed are being prepared to exercise the king's God-given power of judgment.

The author of this passage makes it clear that the people he is addressing are not just junior justices, but also clerks who wish to become justices, when he says that his intention is, in part, to teach "the [art] of preparing records and enrolments according to what is alleged and denied," a task performed by clerks.[154] Once again, the author intentionally changed his source to refer to the work of people in the royal courts. This passage draws from the *prohemium* of William of Drogheda's *Summa Aurea*. The sentence that comes immediately after this one in Bracton, "The general intention is to treat of law that the

---

[152] The term *legum professor* was used in the thirteenth century to refer to people who were actually teaching law and may have broadened in meaning by the time *Bracton* was written to mean anyone who had taken a degree in law, whether teaching or not. R Feenstra, "'Legum doctor', 'legum professor', et 'magister' comme termes pour designer des juristes au moyen âge" in Olga Weijers (ed), *Actes du colloque terminologie de la vie intellectuelle au moyen âge* (Brepols 1988) 73, 75–76. Phrases such as *legum professor* and *iuris civilis professor* appear in the *Digest* and the *Codex* in contexts where they clearly refer to teachers of the law. Sometimes they are contrasted with students. See D.Const. Omnem.9–11; D.Const. Tanta.22; D.50.13.1.5; *Digest of Justinian*, vol 4, 443; C.1.17.2.22; C.12.15.

[153] Numerous provincial synods and Church councils banned monks and even secular clergy from going to universities to study Roman law or medicine, the *scientiae lucrativae*. James A Brundage, *The Medieval Origins of the Legal Profession: Canonists, Civilians, and Courts* (University of Chicago Press 2008) 124 (hereafter Brundage, *Medieval Origins*); X.3.50.3; *Corpus Iuris Canonici*, vol 2, 658; RW Hunt, "The Preface to the *Speculum Ecclesiae* of Giraldus Cambrensis" (1977) 8 Viator 189, 198. During the thirteenth century, there was a concerted move against Roman law. In his decree *Super Specula* of 1219, Pope Honorius III extended the bans on the study of civil law and medicine to priests who held benefices with cure of souls and banned the teaching of Roman law at the University of Paris in order to bring more students—who, he complained, preferred Roman law for the wealth it could bring them—into the faculties of theology and canon law. Brundage, *Medieval Origins* (n 153) 231–32. Gerald of Wales, writing in England around 1220, echoed *Super Specula*'s concern about the lucrative fields. Hunt, "*Speculum Ecclesiae*" (n 153) 198, 206.

[154] *Bracton*, vol 2, 20.

unskilled may be made expert, the expert more expert, the bad good and the good better," comes from Drogheda with few changes, and none substantive.[155] This sentence, on the other hand, has been changed significantly. Drogheda has, instead, that the *materia* of his work will be the "art of interpreting and of preparing impetrations, citations, records, and all other instruments pertaining to cases, sureties and the like, distinctions, altercations, and contumacy."[156] All of this becomes "records and enrolments" in *Bracton*, emphasizing the work of the judicial clerk, who kept his master's roll. The treatise does not disappoint in its promise to provide sample enrolments. There are numerous examples throughout the treatise, usually introduced with words such as "let the enrolment be made thus" (*tunc fiat irrotulatio sic*) and once with "for the instruction of the *minores* something must be said of enrolment."[157]

*Bracton* is also notable for whom it excludes. Drogheda tells us that his goal is to make the reader of his text the "best orator" and "most prudent advocate," focusing on the lawyer, not the court functionary, as his main audience.[158] One would never know from *Bracton*, however, that there were people, even by the 1220s, who were working as semi-professional pleaders in the royal courts. In contrast to the number of sample enrolments given in the treatise, there are only a few sample counts—the statement of the case that the litigant or his pleader would have made—in the treatise, and most, but not all, are written in the third person, as a count delivered by a professional pleader would have been.[159] The authors of the treatise obviously knew of the existence of these people, but chose not to explicitly mention them.

*Bracton* also seems to assume that its reader will have direct access to the plea rolls, the records of the courts. As I will discuss in more detail in Chapter 4,

---

[155] "Item communis intentio est de iure scribere ut rudes efficiantur subtiles, subtiles subtiliores, et homines mali efficiantur boni et boni meliores . . ." *Bracton*, vol 2, 20. Drogheda has, "Utilitas vel finis est, quod rudes efficiantur subtiles, balbutientes loquentes, subtiles subtiliores boni meliores et inter omnes alios nobiliores et prudentes, et quod mali fiant boni." William of Drogheda, *Die Summa Aurea Des Wilhelmus De Drokeda* (Ludwig Wahrmund ed, Wagner 1914) 2 (hereafter William of Drogheda, *Summa Aurea*).

[156] "Item ars interpretandi et conficiendi impetrationes, citationes, acta et omnia alia instrumenta ad causas pertinentia, cautelae et similia, distinctiones, altercationes et contumaciae." William of Drogheda, *Summa Aurea* (n 155) 2.

[157] See *Bracton*, vol 4, 209 and vol 4, 99. For other sample enrolments, see *Bracton* vol 2, 414; vol 3, 332, 333, 345, 364, 398; vol 4, 32, 77, 100, 101, 102, 103, 109, 113, 116, 117, 118, 122, 127, 136, 140, 148, 150, 153, 167, 175, 186, 187, 201, 206, 207, 208, 212, 364, 365, 367, 369, 370, 371, 373, 374.

[158] "[E]t optimus fiet orator, advocatus tutissimus." William of Drogheda, *Summa Aurea* (n 155) 2. Drogheda himself was a successful advocate, just as Raleigh and Bratton were judges.

[159] Brand, *Legal Profession* (n 2) 54. Six passages in the treatise contain specimen counts. Some of them contain multiple counts. In two of those passages, the counts are given in the first person, as a litigant speaking on his own behalf would deliver the count. *Bracton*, vol 4, 25, 274. In the other four, the counts are given in the third person, as a serjeant speaking on a client's behalf would give the count. *Bracton*, vol 3, 319, 358, 406; vol 4, 169. Brand also points out that two of those counts include a Latin phrase, "*hoc vobis ostendit*," a word-for-word translation of the French phrase "*ceo vous mustre*," which

each justice kept his own roll. As far as we know, there was no concerted effort to create a central archive of rolls until 1258. Until then, many rolls remained in the custody of the justices themselves.[160] The treatise cites to the rolls of Pattishall and Raleigh. Of course, citations are not always meant primarily to allow the reader to find the author's sources. They can serve many other purposes, such as giving the reader, even if he does not know how to use the citation, a sense that what the author says has a greater authority behind it.[161] There is some evidence that the authors of *Bracton* anticipated that their reader would be able to go to the roll to look up the case, however. *Bracton* will often tell the reader where on the roll the case can be found, "around the end of the roll," "at the end of the roll," or "at the beginning of the roll."[162] Only the justices and their clerks would have had regular and easy access to these rolls.

The authors also appear to have imagined their ideal reader as having some training in Roman and canon law. The treatise contains a number of citations to texts of Roman and canon law given in the usual format of the time.[163] Citations to the *Digest, Codex, Institutes,* and *Decretum* in this period were very difficult to navigate unless one had memorized large parts of Roman and canon law. Citations to Justinian's *Digest,* for instance, included the name of the title— the 400 titles constituting one form of subdivision in the *Digest*—followed by the first few words of the individual *lex.* During the Renaissance, civilians and canonists created alphabetical tables of the titles and *leges* to help a reader find a reference, but in the thirteenth century these were still several centuries in the future. Civilians and canonists had to memorize the names of the titles and the first few words of the most important *leges* unless they wanted to go through the laborious process of searching a large chunk of the *Digest* every time they wanted to look up a citation. Some Roman-law quotations in the text are even

---

appears in specimen counts in texts of the 1260s on. The phrase would have been a further way of indicating that the person speaking was speaking on behalf of someone else. *Bracton,* vol 3, 358; vol 4, 169; Brand, *Legal Profession* (n 2) 181, n 44.

[160] Some rolls were probably left in official custody before 1258. Meekings and Crook think it likely that William of Raleigh left his rolls from the years 1227 to his retirement in 1239 with the court when he retired from the court *coram rege.* That may explain their survival. Meekings and Crook, *King's Bench and Common Bench* (n 12) 87. Of course, it is also possible that he simply left them with Henry of Bratton. It may not have been clear whether Raleigh was leaving the rolls with Bratton in his capacity as an official of the court or as his protégé, friend, and supporter. Many pre-1258 rolls survive apart from those that were called in to the treasury in 1258, suggesting that some justices either left their rolls with the treasury or the court or that they were brought in at some later date.

[161] See Anthony Grafton, *The Footnote: A Curious History* (Harvard University Press 1997) 5–6, 13.

[162] *Bracton,* vol 2, 52, 55, 93, 153, 249, 432, 448; vol 3, 107, 187, 226, 231, 267, 281, 304, 316, 330, 335, 381, 395, 403, 405; vol 4, 32, 78, 102, 105, 121, 168, 177, 189, 193, 199, 211, 225, 229, 232, 346, 361, 368.

[163] For roughly thirty citations to texts of Roman and canon law in *Bracton,* see above, p 5 n.15. For a description of the citation format for Justinian's *Digest,* see below, p 180.

left incomplete, apparently on the assumption that the reader will be able to fill in the rest from memory. In a passage that has been discussed at length by scholars interested in *Bracton's* political theory, one of the authors says that the king "can do nothing save what he can do *de jure*, despite the statement that the will of the prince has the force of law, because there follows at the end of the *lex* the words 'since by the *lex regia*, which was made with respect to his sovereignty.'"[164] The author of this passage is taking pains to demonstrate that the king's power is not unlimited. But the words, "since by the *lex regia*, which was made with respect to his sovereignty," do not, by themselves, prove that the king's power is limited. The words are actually a quotation; they can be found in both the *Digest* and the *Institutes*.[165] As Fritz Schulz demonstrated, we must read these quoted words together with the words that immediately follow them in the *Digest* and the *Institutes* before the author's purpose in quoting them becomes clear: he wants to demonstrate that the phrase "that which pleases the prince has the force of law" does not mean that the king's power is unlimited. To understand that, we must read the passage in its entirety, which, in the *Institutes*, appears in this form:

> That which pleases the prince also has the force of law because, by the *lex regia*, which was made with respect to his sovereignty, the people conferred on him its whole sovereignty and authority. If the emperor decides a question in a written reply, or if he hears a case and gives judgment, or if he ordains something by edict, his utterance is law. These are called constitutions.[166]

In both the *Institutes* and the *Digest*, this passage appears as part of a larger discussion of the sources of law. If the reader knew the full passage and the context in which it appears, it would be obvious to him how the words "since by the *lex regia*, which was made with respect to his sovereignty" support the thesis that the king's power is not unlimited; the phrase "that which pleases the prince has the force of law" refers only to the prince's legislative power, which

---

[164] "Nihil enim aliud potest rex in terris, cum sit dei minister et vicarius, nisi id solum quod de iure potest, nec obstat quod dicitur quod principi placet legis habet vigorem, quia sequitur in fine legis cum lege regia quæ de imperio eius lata est." *Bracton*, vol 2, 305.

[165] Inst.1.2.6; D.1.4.1.pr.

[166] "Sed et quod principi placuit, leges habet vigorem, cum lege regia, quae de imperio eius lata est, populous ei et in eum omne suum imperium et potestatem concessit. Quodcumque igitur imperator per epistulam constituit vel cognoscens decrevit vel edicto praecepit, legem esse constat: haec sunt, quae constitutiones appellantur." Inst.1.2.6. The provision in the *Digest* is nearly identical. I have based my translation partly on Birks' and McLeod's, but have made some changes to show where the authors of *Bracton* borrowed from this text. *Justinian's Institutes*, 38.

was actually conferred on him by the people. If he did not know this context, the words would be meaningless.[167] The author of this passage has abbreviated the text for a reader whom he assumes to know the relevant texts by heart. This was, as Brian Tierney has observed, "a quite normal way of citing familiar legal maxims in the Middle Ages."[168]

The circle of people who would have been able to make full use of *Bracton* is thus very small. The treatise assumes both access to the plea rolls and knowledge of Roman and canon law. This is not to say that the authors of *Bracton* necessarily meant to exclude other audiences; they may have had multiple audiences in mind when they wrote the text. Even if addressed primarily to clerks of the court, the treatise could be of use to, say, pleaders in the royal courts who may have had limited access to the plea rolls and little to no knowledge of Roman law. It might be that the authors of *Bracton* hoped that it would circulate widely. It certainly did become popular, for reasons that are still not well understood, in the last decades of the thirteenth century, when much of the material contained in it was out of date. But overall, the text gives the impression of being an in-house text, written for a small group of people who were very much like its authors. The authors' sense of their primary audience probably included thirty to forty people, justices and clerks, working full-time in the royal courts. If the treatise had its origin in a lecture course, it was a lecture course that was narrowly conceived. In fact, it may not have circulated much beyond the justices and clerks of the courts before Henry of Bratton's death. There is no evidence that any version of *Bracton* circulated beyond the circles of justices and clerks before the 1270s. The earliest texts that rely or appear to rely upon it, *Casus et Judicia*, *Hengham Magna*, and *Fet Asaver*, all likely written during Bratton's life, are consistent with this

---

[167] Fritz Schulz, "Bracton on Kingship" (1945) 60 EHR 136, 154–56 (hereafter Schulz, "Bracton on Kingship").

[168] Brian Tierney, "Bracton on Government" (1963) 38 Speculum 295, 297. The authors of the treatise do the same with Biblical quotations. Just before this quotation from the *Institutes* or *Digest*, in fact, the author of this passage says that the king "ought to have no peer, much less a superior, especially in the doing of justice, that it may be truly said of him, 'Great is our lord and great is his virtue etc.'" *Bracton*, vol 2, 305. This is a reference to verse five of Psalm 146: "Great is our Lord, and great is his power: and of his wisdom there is no number." In the tractate on the assize of novel disseisin, when speaking of a tenant's right to resist someone who is trying to disseise him by force, one of the authors says "To him who will use his strength there will be strength to resist, with arms or without, according to this, 'When a strong man armed, etcetera.'" *Bracton*, vol 3, 21. "When a strong man armed" are the first words of the twenty-first verse of the eleventh chapter of the Gospel of Luke: "When a strong man armed keepeth his court, those things are in peace which he possesseth." Luke 11:21. Schulz, "Bracton on Kingship" (n 167) 155, n 3. In this case, the author clearly expected the reader to be able to produce the rest of the verse from memory, without any accompanying citation, as the quotation does not make much sense without it.

view. *Hengham* and *Casus et Judicia* were almost certainly written by clerks of the courts and *Fet Asaver* may have been, as well.[169] The fact that there are no surviving manuscripts of the *Bratton* and *Raleigh* recensions of the text is likewise consistent with a limited circulation. Indeed, all of the surviving manuscripts of the *Bracton* recension appear to descend from a single archetype. *Bratton* may have existed in only one manuscript, and that manuscript may have been the one that was mentioned in a loan document in 1278. In that year Robert of Scarborough, a chancery official, said that he had borrowed the "book which Lord Henry of Bratton composed" from Master Thomas Bek, a former chancellor of the University of Oxford who was at the time the king's keeper of the wardrobe and archdeacon of Dorset.[170] Thomas was acting as agent for Robert Burnell, who was at the time both chancellor of England and bishop of Bath and Wells.[171] Burnell's possession of the treatise may be explained by the fact that Henry of Bratton had been a canon of Wells Cathedral. He may have left his manuscript of the treatise there at his death.[172] Burnell may have had access to that manuscript or a copy of it. This loan document is the earliest explicit reference to the treatise, and the earliest known attribution to Henry of Bratton. It may well be that it refers to Bratton's own copy of his recension of the treatise.

It is not clear when or by whom the final recension, the one that combined *Raleigh* and *Bratton* into *Bracton*, was made. Sometime after *Bratton* was completed, someone compared it to *Raleigh* and re-inserted the passages that Henry of Bratton had cut out, placing them in the margins, which already appear to have contained some notes on cases that Bratton had heard or heard of after he finished the *Bratton* recension.[173] When scribes made further copies of the text, they sometimes left these *addiciones* in the margins, but eventually started to work them into the text.[174] This version of the text, the version known from at least the 1290s as *Bracton*, circulated much more widely than either *Raleigh* or *Bratton*. Pleaders were reading it—or were at least expected to read it—by the end of the century. Chief Justice Mettingham, who, like Pattishall, Raleigh, and Bratton, had risen to the bench through service as a judicial clerk, hinted that he expected lawyers practicing before him to know their *Bracton* when,

[169] McSweeney, "Creating a Literature" (n 141) 55–56.
[170] Barton, "Authorship of *Bracton*" (n 2) 173.
[171] Ibid.
[172] Brand, "Age of Bracton" (n 1) 74.
[173] *Bracton*, vol 3, xliv.
[174] *Bracton*, vol 1, xi.

in 1294, he told a serjeant who was unsure about a point of law to "go to your *Bracton*, and it will teach you."[175] The *Bracton* to which Justice Mettingham was referring, however, was not a text that was known to William of Raleigh and Henry of Bratton. It is merely our best evidence for a process of writing and rewriting that took place over half a century.

---

[175] *"Alez a vostre Bruton' e yl vous ensegnera."* Lincoln's Inn MS Misc 738 fo 121v, quoted in Brand, *Legal Profession* (n 2) 113; Brand, "Courtroom and Schoolroom" (n 144) 73.

# 2

# Law as Text

We know from the *Bracton* treatise that its authors were well-versed in Roman law and had some knowledge of canon law. Training in Roman or canon law would have led these future clerks and justices of the royal courts to think about law in new ways. The king's courts were increasingly relying on texts in the thirteenth century. Litigation in the central royal courts was governed by writs. Eyre justices and jurors received written instructions. But still in the thirteenth century, a great deal of the law practiced in England's courts was contained in the collective memory of the jurors or the suitors of the court. Texts were not as central to the practice of law in the county courts or even the central royal courts as they were in the schools of Roman and canon law. By the time *Bracton* was being written Roman and canon law had established themselves as academic disciplines, and they were academic disciplines built around the study of particular texts. The study of those texts produced yet more texts. Through their study of Roman and canon law, the authors of *Bracton* would have learned to think of law as a textual practice. As we will see in the next few chapters, this appears to have influenced the way they approached the texts produced by the royal courts.

## Higher Studies in the Thirteenth Century

In the thirteenth century, it was common for members of that group of substantial freeholders who would later come to be called the gentry to send their children to school for a period of time. Greater administrative burdens were being placed on this group of people, who filled offices such as sheriff, under-sheriff, coroner, regarder, and eyre juror. It was important for landholders of substance to have some formal education so they could participate in the government of the county. The opportunities available to men with some learning were impelling people of humbler status to send their children to school, as well. The central administration of the Church and the crown were making much greater use of written procedures by the year 1200 than they had before. Officials at all levels of the royal and ecclesiastical administration required clerks. Many

*Priests of the Law.* Thomas J. McSweeney, Oxford University Press (2019). © Thomas J. McSweeney.
DOI: 10.1093/oso/9780198845454.003.0003

of the higher officers of the crown began their careers as clerks of one kind or another, producing the documents upon which the royal administration depended. In addition to the Church and crown, many of the realm's great magnates were hiring learned men as stewards, to manage their estates and to hold their courts. Merchants, tradesmen, and prosperous peasants, as well as the more substantial landholders, might send their children to song schools, where they would have learned the basics of reading, and grammar schools, where they would have learned to read Latin and perhaps learned the *ars dictaminis*, the art of composing and writing letters.[1] The "Oxford business school" mentioned in the last chapter was designed to teach the kinds of practical skills one would need to obtain a position as a steward or a clerk. The Walters Art Gallery in Baltimore holds a manuscript, probably used at Oxford to teach these kind of practical skills, that contains a manual of Romano-canonical procedure along with forms for documents that would be useful in both ecclesiastical and secular affairs. It contains forms of documents for the appointment of a rector to a parish church, stages of litigation in an ecclesiastical court, deeds, mortgages, and settlements of disputes in both secular and ecclesiastical courts. This type of training appears to have continued in Oxford, unconnected to the university, throughout the middle ages.[2]

Many of the justices of the thirteenth century rose to the judiciary of the central royal courts through service as estate stewards or as officials in the counties, and would have had such an elementary education. The authors of *Bracton*, however, appear to have had a somewhat deeper education; they were, to put it mildly, well-read. At least one of the authors of *Bracton* had done some reading in the field of ecclesiastical *computus*—the science of calculating the dates of moveable feasts—and applied that learning to the problem how to determine the year for legal purposes in a leap year.[3] They also appear to have known their Bible very well.[4] And we know that they had read widely in Roman law and perhaps a little less widely in canon law. They were keeping up with the latest works in the field. A single short passage in the tractate on actions draws from Justinian's *Institutes* (with its gloss), *Digest*, and *Codex*, Azo's *Summa Codicis* and his *Summa Institutionum*, the Bible, Gratian's *Decretum*,

---

[1] Nicholas Orme, *Medieval Schools: From Roman Britain to Renaissance England* (Yale University Press 2006) 68–71.

[2] HG Richardson, "Business Training in Medieval Oxford" (1941) 46 The American Historical Review 259, 275.

[3] Fritz Schulz thought that the authors of *Bracton* had access to William of Sacrobosco's *Computus Ecclesiasticus*, which he dates to 1236. There are similarities in language between the two texts. Fritz Schulz, "Bracton as a Computist" (1945) 3 Traditio 265, 279–80.

[4] See above, p 27 and p 65, n.168.

the *Glanvill* treatise, John of Salisbury's *Policraticus*, and the *Leges Anglorum*, a text on law and royal power made in London sometime around 1200, likely to criticize King John, that contains, among other things, accounts of King Arthur as a lawgiver, both genuine legal texts of the Anglo-Saxon period and spurious ones, and pronouncements of the Norman and Angevin kings.[5]

Because it can be so difficult to ascribe individual passages in the treatise to a particular author, we cannot be sure which authors had read which texts. We can be sure, however, that several of the authors had knowledge of Roman law. While some historians have tried to separate *Bracton* into its "Roman" and "English" portions, this dichotomy is misleading.[6] Roman law pervades the treatise and must have been there from the very beginning. Quotations drawn from the texts of Roman law appear throughout the treatise, but even parts that do not contain direct quotations use Roman-law concepts and terminology. No part of the treatise is wholly devoid of Roman law. Thorne thought that Bratton cut a great deal of Roman law from the treatise when he made his recension, but this does not indicate that Bratton had no interest in Roman law: the passages that make some of the most sophisticated use of Roman law were almost certainly added by Bratton.[7]

We cannot say for certain where and how the authors acquired this education. It is possible that they were self-taught. One need not necessarily attend university classes to learn law. The depth of their learning and the breadth of texts they knew would suggest that they had had some formal training in law, however. In chapters three, four, and five, we will see that at least some of the authors of *Bracton* were adept at the methods of textual manipulation and analysis that were being taught in the schools of Roman and canon law. The *Bracton* authors did not simply quote and cite texts of Roman and canon law; as we will see in Chapter 5, they also applied the schools' dialectical method of argument to these texts. The methods of Roman and canon law would have been easier to learn through classroom exercises than through texts.[8] Moreover, the authors' deep knowledge of and commitment to Roman law makes it likely that some of them had formal instruction in law at some place of higher studies, not simply a grammar school or a school of *ars dictaminis*. The courts seem to

---

[5] *Bracton*, vol 2, 305–06. For the *Leges Anglorum*, see "Leges Anglorum Londoniis collectae (Leges Angl)" (Early English Laws 2019) <www.earlyenglishlaws.ac.uk/laws/texts/leges-angl/> accessed March 11, 2019. I would like to thank Charlie Donahue for suggesting this passage as an example.

[6] Both Kantorowicz and Richardson thought that certain parts of the treatise consisted of "Roman learning added to a work complete without it." *Bracton*, vol 1, xxxii.

[7] See below, pp 173–79.

[8] It is also possible that they learned these methods by studying something other than law. Beryl Smalley noted that Biblical scholars used methods of argumentation very similar to those used in the schools of law. Beryl Smalley, *The Study of the Bible in the Middle Ages* (Basil Blackwell 1952) 52–62.

have been recruiting men of leaning in the early thirteenth century. Even some of the nameless clerks of the royal courts, who we know only from their rolls, appear to have been men of substantial learning. The clerk who, on a 1204 plea roll of the king's court, mocked the complicated procedures of the bishop of Durham's court by ending the entry with a quotation from Horace's epistles—"And thus with what knot may I hold Proteus, shifting his visage?"—likely had some advanced training in the arts, beyond what was strictly necessary to keep a plea roll or understand a writ.[9]

The authors of *Bracton* likely acquired their knowledge of Roman law from some formal course of study in a university or cathedral school. A university education was a path to advancement. In the middle ages, most of England's bishops came out of the schools.[10] In some English dioceses around the year 1200, as many as a third to half of the men who were installed as cathedral canons were accorded the title master (*magister*).[11] From at least the middle of the twelfth century, *magister* was used as a rank in England, to denote that one had been licensed by a school of higher learning.[12] The royal and ecclesiastical administrations required men who could read and write, but they were also looking for more advanced skills.[13] The study of law, in particular, was lucrative. There were concerns as early as the twelfth century that law was eclipsing the study of theology and the arts—more elevated, but less lucrative, fields of study—in the schools and that the higher offices of the Church and crown were going to men who had studied the law. Peter of Blois, a twelfth-century scholar who studied Roman law before turning to the study of theology, wrote

[9] "Et ita quo teneam nodo mutantem Prothea vultus." CRR, vol 3, 110; CT Flower, *Introduction to the Curia Regis Rolls, 1199-1230 A.D.* (SS vol 62, Bernard Quaritch 1944) 7–9. This unknown clerk appears to have enjoyed making jokes in his rolls. He occasionally changed the names of parties, such as when he transformed William de Sancta Fide ("of holy faith") to William Sine Fide ("without faith"). For more on this clerk, see CRR, vol 4, vii.

[10] Alan B Cobban, *The Medieval English Universities: Oxford and Cambridge to c. 1500* (University of California Press 1988) 394 (hereafter Cobban, *Medieval English Universities*).

[11] Julia Barrow, "The Education and Recruitment of Cathedral Canons in England and Germany 1100-1225" (1989) 20 Viator 117, 134, 138 (hereafter Barrow, "Cathedral Canons").

[12] Ibid, 118–19. The terms "master" and "doctor" were synonymous at this point in the history of higher education, indicating that the holder of the title had mastered the subject (hence "*magister*") and now had a license to teach it (*licentia docendi*, hence "doctor"). In spite of the title's modern connection with the medical profession, it was probably the lawyers who were the original "doctors." The terms *legum doctor* and *iuris doctor* appear in Justinian's *Codex*. The fact that they are found in the primary sources of Roman law may have encouraged teachers of Justinian's texts to appropriate the title for themselves. R Feenstra, "'Legum doctor', 'legum professor', et 'magister'" comme termes pour designer des juristes au moyen âge" in Olga Weijers (ed), *Actes Du Colloque Terminologie De La Vie Intellectuelle Au Moyen Âge* (Brepols 1988) 72, 72–73 (hereafter Feenstra, "Legum doctor"). There is some evidence that the title *magister* was preferred to *doctor* in France for those who had completed a course of study in Roman or canon law, and this may have been true in England, as well. Ibid, 76.

[13] Indeed, cathedral canons were often episcopal or royal servants who had been installed as canons through the patronage of their masters. Barrow, "Cathedral Canons" (n 11) 132–33.

that "There are two things which drive men strongly to the study of law, ambition for honors and vain appetite for glory."[14] Richard the Lionheart's confessor complained that "the dignities and goods of the Church go to the jurists (*iurisperitos*)."[15] Daniel of Morley, who went to Spain to study Arabic texts in the 1180s, complained upon his return to England that the study of the arts was being neglected in favor of the study of law.[16] Gerald of Wales, writing in England in the 1220s, lamented that in former times, emperors and princes bestowed honors and rewards on philosophers and poets, but today the "Sibyll's prophecy" once made by Abelard's student Master Mainerius, that "The days will come, and with force, in which the laws will obliterate the knowledge of letters," has actually come to pass.[17] Roger Bacon, an English scholar of the middle decades of the thirteenth century who is celebrated as one of the great scientists of the middle ages, complained that "the civil lawyers have so bewitched prelates and princes that they receive nearly all of the rewards and benefices; so all the best people, even those with the most aptitude for theology and philosophy, dash off to study civil law, because they see the jurists enriched."[18]

English dioceses were especially in need of people who had a good knowledge of canon law. Parts of the Church's work were becoming judicialized in the twelfth and thirteenth centuries. Excommunications, which previously could simply be pronounced by a bishop, required a judicial process by 1200.[19] The Church had jurisdiction over marriages, land held in free alms (i.e., land held by the Church, free from any secular services), and the probate of wills of moveables, among other things. The law of the Church was becoming complex in the early thirteenth century and, with an appeal to Rome always a possibility, clerics who held courts in England had to be familiar with the proper procedure, the *ordo judiciarius*. This opened up a whole range of new positions within the ecclesiastical administration for those with training in law. Bishops and even some of those below them in the diocesan hierarchy, such

---

[14] Quoted in Ralph V Turner, "Clerical Judges in the English Secular Courts: The Ideal Versus the Reality" in Ralph V Turner, *Judges, Administrators, and the Common Law in Angevin England* (Hambledon Press 1994) 176 (hereafter Turner, "Clerical Judges").

[15] "Videmus ad iurisperitos dignitates et bona transire ecclesiae." Quoted in CR Cheney, *From Becket to Langton* (Manchester University Press 1956) 16.

[16] HG Richardson, "The Schools of Northampton in the Twelfth Century" (1941) 56 EHR 595, 601 (hereafter Richardson, "Schools of Northampton").

[17] "Venient dies, [et] vhe illis, quibus leges obliterbunt scientiam litterarum." RW Hunt, "The Preface to the *Speculum Ecclesiae* of Giraldus Cambrensis" (1977) 8 Viator 189, 193, 204–05 (hereafter Hunt, "*Speculum Ecclesiae*").

[18] Quoted in Jean Dunbabin, "Careers and Vocations" in JI Catto (ed), *The History of the University of Oxford, Volume I: The Early Oxford Schools* (Clarendon Press 1984) 565, 574 (hereafter Dunbabin, "Careers and Vocations").

[19] RH Helmholz, *The Oxford History of the Laws of England, Volume I: The Canon Law and Ecclesiastical Jurisdiction from 597 to the 1640s* (OUP 2004) 127.

as archdeacons, employed subordinate officials who were often university-educated canonists.[20] Additionally, new expectations were being placed on those lower down in the hierarchy of the Church. Although in the twelfth century papal judges delegate were mostly selected from among bishops and abbots, in the thirteenth the papacy began to reach lower and lower down in the ecclesiastical hierarchy in selecting judges. It is tempting to think of service as a judge delegate as analogous to service as one of the king's justices in eyre or as a justice commissioned to hear a single special assize, exercising the king's delegated authority to do justice in the counties, far away from the king's court. A better analogy would probably be to jury duty, however. Appointment as a judge delegate appears to have been more of an obligation than an honor. Just as the wealthy and powerful purchased exemptions from jury duty from the king, important clerics purchased exemptions from hearing cases as judges delegate from the pope.[21] This meant that the burdens of delegation fell on people further down the ecclesiastical ladder. Rural deans, who oversaw groups of parishes, regularly served as judges delegate; there is evidence that one dean owned a complete set of the texts of Roman and canon law sometime around 1200.[22] Even some of the humbler members of the parish clergy, such as vicars and chaplains, could be appointed as subdelegates to act in place of one of the judges commissioned by the pope.[23] As the papacy shifted the burden of delegation onto lesser clerics, it essentially obligated these men to have some knowledge of canon law.

The king and secular lords also needed the counsel of people trained in canon law, as they often ended up in ecclesiastical courts. The famous legal battle between Mabel of Francheville and Richard of Anstey over the inheritance of the lands of William of Sackville went back and forth between ecclesiastical and secular courts because it involved both inheritance of land, a secular matter, and the question of whether William's marriage was valid—and thus whether his daughter was legitimate—a matter solely within the cognizance of the ecclesiastical courts. Richard drew up an account of his expenses for this litigation, which lasted from 1158 to 1167, and it included payments to canon lawyers resident in England.[24] Canonists could rise high in royal service.

---

[20] Jane E Sayers, *Papal Judges Delegate in the Province of Canterbury, 1198-1254: A Study in Ecclesiastical Jurisdiction and Administration* (OUP 1971) 127 (hereafter Sayers, *Judges Delegate*).

[21] Ibid, 113, 143–47, 161.

[22] Ibid, 128–29.

[23] Ibid, 139.

[24] Patricia M Barnes, "The Anstey Case" in Patricia M Barnes and CF Slade (eds), *A Medieval Miscellany for Doris Mary Stenton* (Pipe Roll Society 1962) 10, n 6; Paul Brand, *The Origins of the English Legal Profession* (Blackwell 1992) 2 (hereafter Brand, *Origins*). Professional canon lawyers continued to practice

William of Kilkenny, who was an Oxford master from at least 1221 and who was described by Matthew Paris as "expert in civil and canon law," was retained as a king's clerk from 1234 and handled a good deal of Henry III's business with the papacy.[25] He received an annual retainer of 60 marks for his services, an income that would have supported a knightly family. He received several benefices from the king, and, just a few years before his death, was elected bishop of Ely and was invested by the king with the responsibilities, although not the title, of the chancellor.[26]

It is not difficult to see why people flocked to the schools to study canon law. The benefits of an education in Roman law are less obvious. No court in England applied the substantive law of Rome as a positive law in this period. Roman law was seen as a source of universal legal principles, however. As we saw in the introduction, Roman law was regarded by many of its scholars and practitioners as "written reason," a sort of ideal form of law that approached the perfection of natural and divine law. This legal reason could be applied to work in any court, whether that court used Roman law as a positive law or not. Study of Roman law was also essential to an understanding of canon law.[27] The surviving evidence suggests that the two laws were taught together at Oxford in the twelfth and thirteenth centuries.[28] Moreover, an education in Roman law could impart more generalizable skills, skills that one would not necessarily acquire in the study of the arts, theology, or even canon law. As Jean Dunbabin

---

in the English courts into the thirteenth century and beyond. Brand, *Origins*, 145–54. A Church council held by the Papal Legate Otto in London in 1237 stated that justice "is greatly impeded by the quibbles and cunning of advocates," lawyers who argued on behalf of clients in the ecclesiastical courts. The council decreed that any advocate who wished to practice would henceforth be required to take an oath before his bishop to the effect that he would make his argument faithfully and not "delay or snatch away the justice of any party." Matthew Paris, *Matthew Paris's English History*, 3 vols (JA Giles tr, Henry G Bohn, 1852-54) vol 1, 91–92; CM, vol 3, 439–40; James A Brundage, *The Medieval Origins of the Legal Profession: Canonists, Civilians and Courts* (University of Chicago Press 2008) 299 (hereafter Brundage, *Medieval Origins*).

[25] Jane E Sayers, "William of Drogheda and the English Canonists" in Peter Linehan (ed), *Proceedings of the Seventh International Congress of Medieval Canon Law* (Biblioteca Apostolica Vaticana 1988) 205, 221 (hereafter Sayers, "William of Drogheda"); Robert C Stacey, "Kilkenny, William of (d. 1256)" (ODNB, September 23, 2004) <www.oxforddnb.com/view/article/15527> accessed March 13, 2019; CM, vol 5, 130.

[26] Robert C Stacey, "Kilkenny, William of (d. 1256)" (ODNB, September 23, 2004) <www.oxforddnb.com/view/article/15527> accessed March 13, 2019.

[27] See Kenneth Pennington, "*Legista sine canonibus parum valet, canonista sine legibus nihil*" (2017) 34 Bulletin of Medieval Canon Law 249, 249–50.

[28] Leonard Boyle thought that the schools at Oxford taught a combined law curriculum that included both Gratian's *Decretum*, the basic textbook of canon law, and the *Liber Pauperum*, a textbook of Roman law written by England's first teacher of Roman law, Master Vacarius. He noted that this curriculum may have survived up until the 1230s. Leonard Boyle, "Canon Law Before 1380" in JI Catto (ed), *The History of the University of Oxford, Volume 1: The Early Oxford Schools* (OUP 1984) 532, 534. Boyle thought that canon law and civil law became distinct faculties at Oxford in the 1230s, in response to the promulgation of the *Decretals of Gregory IX*, but that the teaching of the two laws remained intertwined. As Boyle points

has observed, the study of Roman law involved the application of abstract principles to concrete situations.[29] Secular rulers could use people with those kinds of skills in both legal and non-legal capacities.

Secular rulers may have had other reasons for turning to civil lawyers. In the face of an assertive Church that was increasingly speaking in the language of law to affirm its rights, the crown may have felt the need to lawyer up. The Becket conflict of the 1160s and 1170s was probably responsible for some of the drive to bring learned men, particularly men learned in Roman law, into the royal administration. The conflict between Henry II and his archbishop of Canterbury, Thomas Becket, over the rights of the crown and rights of the Church sparked a propaganda war in which both sides employed scholars in canon law, civil law, and theology. When the Church used the language of law to assert its rights, the crown felt the need to fire back in the same language.[30]

By 1200, there were good reasons for a young man who had the requisite time and financial resources to continue beyond the grammar school and study law. Education in either Roman or canon law could, along with patronage or family connections, open up opportunities in the administration of the Church or the crown. It is not, therefore, terribly surprising to find justices and clerks in the royal courts who had studied Roman and canon law.

## A Different Kind of Law

In the schools, a young scholar would have encountered a cosmopolitan law that connected him with contemporary jurists throughout Latin Christendom and with jurists of the ancient Roman past. He would have been taught to understand that law as a universal law in some sense. Historians often refer to Roman and canon law collectively as the *ius commune*—literally the "common law"—to reflect the fact that jurists of the twelfth and thirteenth centuries regarded Roman and canon law together as constituting the universal law of

---

out, some of the early statutes of the university made it a requirement for the doctorate in civil law that the aspiring doctor have participated in several *quaestiones* in the canon law faculty and that students taking degrees in the canon law faculty have at least three years of study in the civil law faculty. Ibid, 535–39.

[29] Dunbabin, "Careers and Vocations" (n 18) 574.

[30] See Beryl Smalley, *The Becket Conflict and the Schools: A Study of Intellectuals in Politics in the Twelfth Century* (Basil Blackwell 1973); Anne J Duggan, "Roman, Canon and Common Law in Twelfth-Century England: The Council of Northampton (1164) Re-Examined" (2010) 83 Historical Research 379; John Hudson, *Oxford History of the Laws of England, Volume II, 871-1216* (OUP 2012) 498, 532 (hereafter Hudson, *Oxford History*).

Christendom. I will generally avoid the term, however. The phrase *ius commune* was, at times, used by people in the early thirteenth century to refer collectively to Roman and canon law and to differentiate them from the *ius proprium*, the laws of specific kingdoms.[31] This was not the only sense in which the term was used in the thirteenth century, and it was not necessarily the most common sense of the phrase. The *Bracton* authors use the phrase *ius commune* to mean the law that applies in the absence of a private agreement, a usage Ada Kuskowski has labelled the "comparative use" of the term.[32] They may have been following canonist sources. Canonists of the twelfth and thirteenth centuries sometimes used the term in contrast to a special privilege.[33] It is not entirely clear from the text of *Bracton* what Raleigh and Bratton were envisioning when they used the term. In contrasting *ius commune* with an agreement, they only tell us what it is not. Was *ius commune*, for them, synonymous with natural law, as it was for some civilians and canonists of the early thirteenth century?[34] Or did the authors *of Bracton* mean something more specific, such as the common law of England? All they tell us is that it is the law that applies when there is no agreement to the contrary.

The ambiguity inherent in the terminology raises a caveat about the two laws: although the people who taught and administered the two laws often spoke in universal terms—as if *ius commune*, or whatever they called it, was a monolith—the two laws were actually a culture or a discourse that manifested itself differently in different times and places. There were institutions

---

[31] Laurent Mayali, "Ius Civile et Ius Commune dans la tradition juridique médiévale" in Jacques Krynen (ed), *Droit Romain, Jus Civile, et Droit Français* (Presses de l'Université des Sciences Sociales de Toulouse 1999) 213–15; James A Brundage, "Universities and the "*Ius Commune*" in Medieval Europe" (2000) 11 Rivista internazionale di diritto comune 237, 239 (hereafter Brundage, "*Ius Commune*").

[32] *Bracton* vol 2, 68, 73, 148, 149; vol 3, 232, vol 4, 84, 273; Ada Maria Kuskowski, "The Birth of Common Law and the Invention of Legal Traditions," British Legal History Conference, University College London, July 7, 2017.

[33] Brundage, "*Ius Commune*" (n 31) 238; John Hudson, *The Formation of the English Common Law* (2nd edn, Routledge, 2018) 14; Frederick Pollock and Frederic William Maitland, *The History of English Law before the Time of Edward I*, 2 vols (2nd edn, CUP 1898) vol 1, 176–78. The phrase *ius commune* was also used as a synonym for the law of nature (*ius naturale*) or the law common to all peoples (*ius gentium*), as well as to mean the Roman civil law contained in the *Institutes, Codex,* and *Digest*. Brundage, "*Ius Commune*" (n 31) 238.

[34] Brundage, "*Ius Commune*" (n 31) 238–39. It is, of course, impossible to avoid all anachronistic uses of language and it can, at times, be useful for historians to use terms in ways that the people they study would not have used them. I am keen to avoid the term *ius commune*, however, because that phrase carries a great deal of historiographical baggage. In the literature on European law it often takes on a transhistorical quality. Manlio Bellomo, for instance, frames the history of European law from 1000 to 1800 in terms of the changing relationship between the *ius commune* and the *ius proprium*. Manlio Bellomo, *The Common Legal Past of Europe, 1000-1800* (Lydia G Cochrane tr, Catholic University of America Press 1995). For my own purposes, which are to reconstruct the ways in which a particular group of people working in the middle decades of the thirteenth century might have perceived the relationship between the two laws and the work they were doing in the royal courts, I think the term *ius commune* is likely to distort more than it clarifies.

and networks that encouraged uniformity throughout Latin Christendom, but there was variation between regions, locales, and even individuals in how the two laws were understood. Indeed, understandings of the two laws were changing rapidly in this period; Laurent Mayali has argued that the term *ius commune* itself was shifting in its meaning in the late twelfth century, so that a reference to the *ius commune* in 1150 and a reference to it in 1200 probably meant different things.[35] The *ius commune* was a universal, but it was a universal experienced in particular times and places.

We must, therefore, examine how a person learning Roman and canon law in England would have perceived the two laws. Fortunately, we know something of the way that law was taught in the schools of higher learning in the late twelfth and early thirteenth centuries. An Italian doctor of Roman law named Vacarius arrived in England in the 1140s to work in the household of Theobald, Archbishop of Canterbury.[36] We do not know where and when he taught, but it is certain that he taught Roman law somewhere in England; Vacarius wrote a book called the *Liber Pauperum* (*The Book for Poor Men*), which excerpted the most important parts, in Vacarius' view, of the *Digest* and *Codex* for poor students who could not afford to purchase their own copies of the two books, a sort of "Justinian's greatest hits."[37] Vacarius' disciples were known as *pauperistae*, after the *Liber Pauperum*, and were regarded as a peculiarly English school of civilians. The *Liber Pauperum* survives, as do several other texts that appear to be products of this school.[38]

Although we do not find the authors of *Bracton* using *ius commune* to refer collectively to Roman and canon law, it is fairly clear that they and their contemporaries in the English schools understood Roman and canon law as part of a single system of law. Vacarius and his students treated Roman and canon law as a collective; the *pauperistae* learned both Roman and canon law. The first known foreign students at Oxford, the German brothers Emo and Addo, are said to have divided the night between them "copying out, studying, and glossing the *Decretum*, the decretals, and the *Liber Pauperum*, as well as other

---

[35] Mayali, "Ius Civile" (n 31).

[36] Jason Taliadoros, *Law and Theology in Twelfth-Century England: The Works of Master Vacarius* (Brepols 2006) 3 (hereafter, Taliadoros, *Law and Theology*).

[37] Francis De Zulueta (ed), *The Liber Pauperum of Vacarius* (SS vol 44, Bernard Quaritch 1927) (hereafter De Zulueta (ed), *Liber Pauperum*).

[38] In addition to the *Liber Pauperum*, there is a surviving set of lectures on the *Institutes*, probably given around 1200 by someone associated with the *Pauperistae*. They are edited and translated in Francis De Zulueta and Peter Stein (eds), *The Teaching of Roman Law in England around 1200* (Selden Society 1990) lxxxi (hereafter De Zulueta and Stein (eds), *Teaching of Roman Law*). Two *Brocardicae*, a type of teaching text, survive from this school, as well. They will be discussed in more detail in Chapter 5.

books of canon and civil law."[39] There were terms, other than *ius commune*, that English scholars could and did use to refer to the two laws collectively. The phrase *utrumque ius* was in common use in the thirteenth century to describe Roman and canon law. The phrase does not translate neatly into English; the adjective *utrumque* is generally attached to a singular noun, such as *ius*, but has a plural meaning. It is sometimes translated as "both laws" or "the two laws." Although it does not appear in *Bracton*, this phrase might have had some currency for the treatise's authors. In the prologue to the *Liber Pauperum*, Vacarius speaks of the "way of both laws" (*utriusque legis viam*).[40]

Students learning Roman and canon law in England had a sense that they were part of a community of scholars that spanned Latin Christendom. Vacarius and his students perceived themselves as engaged in debates over the meaning of Roman law with people throughout the Christian West; one of the glosses to the *Liber Pauperum* pits an opinion of Vacarius against the opinion of "the Bolognese."[41] The debates over Roman and canon law spanned the Christian West because the law itself was perceived as universal. It is easy for us to see how contemporaries could have perceived canon law as a universal law; it was the law of a Church that was perceived as a universal institution. The texts that these scholars would have studied were produced by the Church fathers, the early councils, and, increasingly, the popes.[42]

Roman law could also be perceived as a universal law, however. Some treated it as the secular equivalent of canon law. It had a sort of sacred status as the law of the Roman Empire, which was considered, in some circles, the universal secular power of Christendom, the Church's secular counterpart. Where the pope held the *sacerdotium*, the priestly power, the emperor held the *imperium*, the secular power. The two powers complemented each other and should come to each other's aid.[43] The students of Martinus Gosia, a Bolognese jurist of the twelfth century, referred to canon law as "divine law" (*lex divina*), but also

---

[39] Quoted in Boyle, "Canon Law before 1380" (n 28) 532. A text known as the *Brocardica Dunelmensia*, discussed in more detail below at pp 167–68, supports the view that Vacarius and his students treated Roman law and canon law as intertwined and of similar authority. The *Brocardica*, which was produced by *pauperistae* in the 1190s, contains 128 general statements of law, each one followed by citations to texts that either support or contradict the statement. Although the vast majority of the citations are to texts of Roman law, often by way of the *Liber Pauperum*, there are a few citations to Gratian's *Decretum* and to papal decretals. Hans van de Wouw, "*Brocardica Dunelmensia*" (1991) 108 Zeitschrift der Savigny-Stiftung für Rechtsgeschichte: Romanistische Abteilung 235, 242.

[40] De Zulueta (ed), *Liber Pauperum* (n 37) 2.

[41] De Zulueta and Stein (eds), *Teaching of Roman Law* (n 38) lxxxi.

[42] D. 19 *dicta ante* c.1, D.19 c.1; Gratian, *The Treatise on Laws with the Ordinary Gloss* (Augustine Thompson and Katherine Christensen trs, Catholic University of America Press 1993) 76–77 (hereafter Gratian, *Treatise on Laws*); *Corpus Iuris Canonici*, vol 1, 58–59.

[43] Kings could also perceive themselves as the successors to the Roman emperors within their own territories, and their *regnum* as the secular equivalent of the *sacerdotium*. Both *Glanvill* and *Bracton* borrow from the introduction to Justinian's Institutes, but replace the emperor with the king and the *imperium* with the *regnum*. *Glanvill*, 1; *Bracton*, vol 2, 19. For a discussion of *sacerdotium* and *regnum* or

referred to Roman law as "sacred law" (*lex sacra*), implying that both laws came from God. Vacarius echoed Martinus in the prologue to the *Liber Pauperum* when he referred to "the sacred laws and books from which this compendium descends," the *Digest* and the *Codex*.[44]

As we saw in the introduction, Roman law also represented natural reason. As the most rational form of law humans had produced, Roman law approached the natural law. A set of lectures on Justinian's *Institutes* given by one of the *pauperistae* around the year 1200 survives. In those lectures, the lecturer makes it clear to his students that the law laid out in that text is a timeless and universal law. He tells us that the *Institutes* is also known as the "elements" by way of analogy from the four natural elements, earth, water, fire, and air, "because in this volume are four books containing all the foundations of all legal science."[45] He says that the *Institutes* "treats of the [five] sources from which all law is derived," and then lists the five sources, all of which are specific to Roman law.[46] Roman law was thus a model for what secular law should be. To many of its students, it had normative value. The laws of their own realms should, ideally, reflect its universal glory.

Education would have revolved primarily around lectures. The lectures were based on and organized around the authoritative legal texts, Vacarius' "sacred laws and books."[47] The focus on texts differentiated the practice of Roman and canon law from practice in England's secular courts. Abbot Samson of the great Benedictine house of Bury St. Edmunds illustrates the differences between the discourses of law current in the schools and the ecclesiastical courts, on the one hand, and England's secular courts, on the other. When Samson was elected abbott in 1182, "a horde of new relatives hastened to him, wishing to be taken into his service."[48] Samson turned all of them down, except for "one knight,

---

*imperium*, see Jacques Le Goff, *Medieval Civilization, 400-1500* (Julia Barrow tr, Barnes & Noble Books 2000) 264–68.

---

[44] "[S]acrarum legum et librorum, ex quibus hoc descendit compendium." De Zulueta (ed), *Liber Pauperum* (n 37) 1. Martinus may have actually been one of Vacarius' teachers in Bologna. Taliadoros, *Law and Theology* (n 36) 45. The idea that Roman law was holy or sacred appears in other texts that were being read or produced in the twelfth and thirteenth centuries. In a fragment that appears in Justinian's *Digest*, the jurist Ulpian also said that "knowledge of civil law is indeed a most hallowed (*sanctissima*) thing ..." D.50.13.1.4; *Digest of Justinian*, vol 4, 443. The Emperor Frederick Barbarossa's edict granting privileges to the jurists of Bologna, the *Authentica Habita* of 1155, called the teachers of Roman law *sacrarum legum professores*. R Feenstra, "Legum doctor" (n 12) 73.

[45] "Quia in hoc volumine sunt iiii. Libri, in quibus continentur universa principia totius legittime scientie." De Zulueta and Stein (eds), *Teaching of Roman Law* (n 38) 2.

[46] "Agit enim de iii. a quibus universum ius derivatur." The editors of the text assumed that "iii." was a copying error, as the manuscript continues on to list five sources. Ibid.

[47] De Zulueta (ed), *Liber Pauperum* (n 37) 1.

[48] Jocelin of Brakelond, *Chronicle of the Abbey of Bury St. Edmunds* (Diana Greenway and Jane Sayers trs, OUP 1989) 22 (hereafter Jocelin, *Bury St. Edmunds*); MT Clanchy, *From Memory to Written Record* (3rd edn, Wiley-Blackwell 2013) 250–52 (hereafter Clanchy, *Memory*).

who was eloquent and had knowledge of the law, not so much on account of his blood relationship, but because his experience in worldly affairs would be useful."[49] Samson admitted that he was "ignorant of such matters" and that "before he became abbot he had never been in a place where securities were given", i.e., a secular court, such as the county court or royal court.[50] This knight thus served as Samson's "assistant in secular disputes."[51] After a time, Samson "became quite experienced in secular cases, and his precise mind was admired by everyone." The under-sheriff, Osbert Fitz Hervey, said of him "This abbot is a natural [debater] (*disputator*), and if he continues as he started, he will blind every one of us with his knowledge."[52] Jocelin tells us that "having gained a favorable reputation in cases of this kind, he was made an itinerant justice" in the king's courts.[53]

Samson lacked knowledge of secular law. He acquired that knowledge not through texts, but through experience. When Jocelin discusses the kinds of skills Samson needed to acquire for the secular courts, he emphasizes the spoken word. Samson's knightly adviser is described as "eloquent," and Samson himself becomes a good "debater." Roman and canon law required a different set of skills, exemplified by Jocelin's very different story about Abbot Samson's initiation into the mysteries of canon law. Shortly after his election, Samson "was surprised to receive from the pope a mandate appointing him a judge delegate to hear certain cases."[54] Samson had studied the arts and theology in the schools, but apparently had as little knowledge of canon law as he did of secular law at his election. As he did with the knight who served as an adviser in secular law, "he invited two clerks with legal training to be his companions, and used their advice in ecclesiastical matters."[55] But he acquired his knowledge of ecclesiastical law in a very different manner from which he had acquired a knowledge of secular law. Samson "gave his attention to the *Decretum* and to decretal letters," so that, eventually, "partly by the study of books and partly by hearing cases, he came to be considered a discerning judge who followed law and procedure closely."[56] Samson did rely on advisers and experience gained in the courtroom, but he also turned to texts, something he did not do, and probably could not do, to learn the law of the county and central royal courts.

---

[49] Jocelin, *Bury St. Edmunds* (n 48) 22.
[50] Ibid, 22–23.
[51] Ibid, 23.
[52] Ibid, 31; Clanchy, *Memory* (n 48) 250–52.
[53] Jocelin, *Bury St. Edmunds* (n 48) 31.
[54] Ibid; Sayers, *Judges Delegate* (n 20) 119.
[55] Jocelin, *Bury St. Edmunds* (n 48) 31.
[56] Ibid.

Jocelin emphasizes the differences between the law applied in the secular courts and that applied in the courts of the Church. Those differences were probably less stark by the early thirteenth century than they had been previously, since texts were becoming more important to the practice of law in the secular courts. Written records were becoming ubiquitous, not only in the royal courts, but even in the courts of the county and the manor.[57] In the secular courts of England, however, texts did not play the same kind of role that they played in Roman and canon law. Both types of courts kept records of their proceedings, but in the ecclesiastical courts, the substantive law was contained in texts, decretal letters, which would be cited for their authority. This was not true of the secular courts. Where the secular courts used writing, in the ecclesiastical courts one could and did actually cite to authoritative texts as sources of law.

Texts were thus central to the study of Roman and canon law. Roman and canon law were often referred to as *ius scriptum*. According to the *Institutes*, one of the fundamental distinctions in law is between written law (*ius ex scripto*) and unwritten law (*ius ex non scripto*).[58] Among written law, the *Institutes* includes *leges*, imperial decrees, and the *responsa* of jurists, the texts that are included in the *Digest* and *Codex*, the raw material of medieval Roman law.[59] The integrity of the text was important. Two of the three imperial constitutions that preface the *Digest*, the *Constitutio Omnem* and the *Constitutio Tanta*, contain prohibitions on abridging the work. An abridged version is not the law and cannot be cited in court.[60] Because of these prohibitions, Vacarius felt the need to defend his abridgement of the *Digest* and *Codex* in the introduction to his *Liber Pauperum*.[61] The author of *Bracton's introductio* makes this distinction between written and unwritten law when he tells us that "Though in almost all regions use is made of the *leges* and the *ius scriptum*, England alone uses unwritten law and custom."[62]

Educational exercises revolved around these texts. Lectures would be given on the major texts of the legal *corpus*, the *libri legales* as some jurists of civil and

---

[57] Hudson, *Oxford History* (n 30) 553–54, 561–62; Zvi Razi and RM Smith, "The Origins of the English Manorial Court Rolls as a Written Record: A Puzzle", in Zvi Razi and RM Smith (eds), *Medieval Society and the Manor Court* (OUP 1996) 39–40, 48.

[58] Inst.1.2.3.; *Justinian's Institutes*, 37.

[59] Ibid.

[60] D.*Constitutio Omnem*.8; D.*Constitutio Tanta*.22.

[61] De Zulueta (ed), *Liber Pauperum* (n 37) xliv–xlv, 2.

[62] "Cum autem fere in omnibus regionibus utatur legibus et iure scripto, sola Anglia usa est in suis finibus iure non scripto et consuetudine." *Bracton*, vol 2, 19. This may be an intentional echo of words found in the prologue to the *Liber Pauperum*. Vacarius refers to his English readers as people "who do not use those laws" (*qui legibus istis non utuntur*) meaning the laws of the *Digest* and *Codex*. De Zulueta (ed), *Liber Pauperum* (n 37) 2. For further discussion of this language in *Bracton* and similar language indicating that English law is unwritten law in the *Glanvill* treatise, see below, pp 107–11.

canon law would call them. In civil law Justinian's *Institutes, Digest,* and *Codex* would have been on the list. In canon law, Gratian's *Decretum,* the text that had essentially established canon law as an academic discipline at Bologna, was still a proper subject for lectures at the beginning of the thirteenth century, but it was being supplemented by the *ius novum*—the "new law"—of the papal decretals. Decretals were essentially papal *consilia,* in which the pope gave a legal decision in response to a question from a judge or litigant in a particular case. The decretal was designed to be of use in that case, but decretals were also important to jurists, judges, and lawyers as a source of law. Indeed, Gratian himself had said that "Decretal letters are thus legally equivalent to the canons of councils," and thus were a type of binding canon law, similar to legislation.[63] English bishops made collections of papal decretals in the twelfth century, and there were a number of important collections, later known as the *Quinque Compilationes Antiquae,* made in Italy between 1190 and the 1220s that circulated widely throughout Latin Christendom.[64] In 1234, the decretals were compiled by Raymond of Peñafort into an official collection known as the *Decretals of Gregory IX* or the *Liber Extra,* which superseded all earlier collections in its authority.[65]

Lectures on these texts would be virtuoso performances, in which the lecturer would expound the various senses of sentences and even individual words, explaining their meaning, comparing them to other texts within the corpus with which they might come into conflict, and explaining the opinions of various doctors on the meaning of the text. The great canonist Hostiensis, who we encountered in Chapter 1 as one of Henry III's canon lawyers in his dispute with William of Raleigh over the diocese of Winchester, wrote about his ideal lecture in his *summa* on the decretals in the 1250s:

And how he ought to teach. First by putting the case [with which this legal text was meant to deal] or discussing the sense of the text. Second, by reading the text and expounding it and also construing it, if it appears to be difficult. Third, by introducing similar texts. Fourth, by introducing contrary texts, and solving them, and distinguishing them. Fifth, by asking questions and settling them. Sixth, by discussing noteworthy parts of the text, to which, and

[63] D.20 dict. ante c.1; *Corpus Iuris Canonici,* 65; Gratian, *Treatise on Laws* (n 42) 85.
[64] Charles Duggan, *Twelfth-Century Decretal Collections and Their Importance in English History* (Athlone Press 1963) (hereafter Duggan, *Decretal Collections*); Harry Dondorp and Eltjo JH Schrage, "The Sources of Medieval Learned Law" in John W Cairns and Paul J du Plessis (eds), *The Creation of the Ius Commune: From Casus to Regula* (Edinburgh University Press, 2010) 40–41 (hereafter Dondorp and Schrage, "Sources"); Boyle, "Canon Law before 1380" (n 28) 535.
[65] Dondorp and Schrage, "Sources" (n 64) 43–44.

how he ought to introduce the decretals . . . There are, however, those who
read the gloss just as the text, which pleases idiots . . .[66]

For Hostiensis, the lecture is, above all, the explication of the text (*litera*). The
text is a starting point for further discussion, for the exploration of other texts,
and for the consideration of particular problems and questions. And it is not
just any text that counts. While reading the gloss may please idiots, the gloss is
not of the same status as the text of the decretal, which is the authoritative text.

The doctor would move through a text book-by-book and line-by-line, expounding the text in order as the term went on. The surviving lectures on the
*Institutes* given at Oxford follow this pattern, as do Azo of Bologna's *Summae*
on the *Institutes* and the *Codex*, which were probably produced out of Azo's
ordinary lectures on those texts. The texts themselves would have been available to both master and student in the classroom. In medieval images of the
classroom, the master is usually depicted with an open book in front of him.[67]
The students would sit on benches, and might have desks in front of them, as
well.[68] On his desk—or his lap, if he had none—the student would likely have
a copy of the text being discussed. The lectures on the *Institutes* from Oxford
assume that the student can follow along in the *Institutes* as the doctor lectures
on the text. The lectures would not be of much use without a copy of the text itself, as they constantly refer to individual words within it.[69] Vacarius wrote the
*Liber Pauperum* because the texts of Roman law were prohibitively expensive
for many students.

The idea that law was a textual practice would have been reinforced by
the plethora of subsidiary texts produced as part of this education. Glosses
were added to the margins of the authoritative texts to explain the meanings
of words, point out other texts on the same subject, and acquaint the reader
with the opinions of various jurists on the text. Indeed, the earliest scholars
of Roman law at Bologna were known as the glossators. Many texts acquired

[66] "Et qualiter debeat docere. Primo ponendo casum, sive dicendo sensum literae. Secundo, legendo
literam, et exponendo, et etiam construendo, si difficulis appareat. Tertio, inducendo similia. Quarto,
inducendo contraria, et solvendo, et distinguendo. Quinto, quaestiones faciendo, et determinando.
Sexto, dicendo notabilia, ad quae, et qualiter induci debeat decretalis: non tamen haec omnia semper
per ordinem servari possunt, vel quia oblivioni traditur, vel quia non plene providetur. Sunt etiam
qui glossam legunt sicut textum, quod idiotis placet." Henricus a Segusio, *Aurea Summa* (Cologne
1612) 1343–44; Brundage, *Medieval Origins* (n 24) 253.
[67] MT Clanchy, *Abelard: A Medieval Life* (Blackwell 1999) 89 (hereafter Clanchy, *Abelard*); Susan
L'Engle and Robert Gibbs, *Illuminating the Law: Legal Manuscripts in Cambridge Collections* (Harvey
Miller 2001) 86, 213.
[68] JI Catto, "Citizens, Scholars, and Masters" in JI Catto (ed), *The History of the University of Oxford,
Volume I: The Early Oxford Schools* (Clarendon Press 1984) 187.
[69] De Zulueta and Stein (eds), *Teaching of Roman Law* (n 38) xliv.

their own ordinary gloss, a standard gloss that would accompany any copy of the text itself.[70] The text could almost not be considered complete without its ordinary gloss. Not everyone was as negative about reading the gloss at lectures as Hostiensis was: the earliest statutes of Oxford order the lecturer to read the gloss along with the text.[71] The *Liber Pauperum* actually contained two glosses, a primary gloss that was probably completed by Vacarius himself and a secondary gloss created by his students.[72] These glosses were likely built up over decades of teaching from the text. Some of them present solutions to apparent contradictions in the text, citing to the *Decretum* and decretals and to the opinions of Bolognese jurists such as Placentinus, Martinus, Irnerius, Bulgarus, and Johannes Bassianus, alongside the opinions of Vacarius himself.[73] We have a set of lectures on the *Institutes* because it was common for both masters and students to reduce lectures to writing; several *reportationes* of lectures on Roman and canon law survive from the early thirteenth century.[74] Records were made of disputations, as well. These exercises involved quite a bit more interaction than the lectures. Medieval scholars often distinguished between the Socratic and Ciceronian methods of instruction. Cicero was a master of the comprehensive survey of a field of knowledge, which he delivered via lecture. Socrates, on the other hand, was the master of the discussion, in which master and students sought to find truth through discourse.[75] Scholars in the medieval universities learned in both ways. In the disputation, a doctor would set a topic and doctors and senior students would debate it, using texts from the authoritative volumes of law. This oral exercise was, therefore, based on texts, just as the lecture was. After hearing both sides, the presiding doctor would propose a solution, which would take account of all texts cited, reconciling them to each other and demonstrating that the texts of law were in harmony with each other and produced one, correct answer. These exercises were not popular at Oxford and did not take place often, but were required for those who wished

---

[70] The *glossa ordinaria* to the *Institutes*, *Digest*, and *Codex* is often called the Accursian gloss after Accursius, the student of Azo who created it. The earliest version of the gloss on the *Digestum Vetus* was in circulation by 1235. Dondorp and Schrage, "Sources" (n 64) 24–25. The *glossa ordinaria* to Gratian's *Decretum* was originally assembled by Johannes Teutonicus and finished in 1217. It was later updated by Bartholomew of Brescia to take account of the issuance of the *Decretals of Gregory IX* in 1234. Ibid, 41.

[71] John Barton, "The Study of Civil Law before 1380" in JI Catto (ed), *The History of the University of Oxford, Volume I: The Early Oxford Schools* (Clarendon Press 1984) 525 (hereafter Barton, "Civil Law before 1380"). Apparently the masters of Oxford were happy to please idiots.

[72] De Zulueta (ed), *Liber Pauperum* (n 37) xxvi.

[73] Ibid, xxxii, xxxiii.

[74] De Zulueta and Stein (eds), *Teaching of Roman Law* (n 38) 531.

[75] Clanchy, *Abelard* (n 67) 85.

to advance to the doctorate by the early fourteenth century.[76] At Bologna, a transcript was made during the disputation and would be sent to the university stationer for copying.[77] Thus, even the oral elements of a legal education, of explicating the primary texts through lecture and discussion, would eventually become textual.

Students may have had writing implements with them in the classroom to take notes, but they also would have spent some time memorizing the texts that were being expounded. Memory was much more highly prized in the thirteenth century than it is today. Memorization and the process of recalling things from the memory were seen as creative processes, by which someone drew upon established knowledge and applied authoritative texts in new and interesting ways. When medieval people praised the great theologian Thomas Aquinas, they did not praise him for his originality; they praised him for his memory. It was his memory and the new uses he was able to make of the authoritative texts he had stored in his mind that allowed him to create the *Summa Theologica*.[78] There were doctors of law who had memorized large parts of the *Digest* or the decretals.[79] When *Bracton* introduces the distinction (*divisio*) between people in their own power and people in the power of another, the text quotes Azo's praise of teaching by *divisiones*, "for by *divisiones* learning is more easily imparted. A partition or division of a subject arouses the attention of the reader, prepares the mind for understanding [and] strengthens the memory by art."[80] Indeed, the *Bracton* authors were probably working from memory at least some of the time when they quoted the texts of civil and canon law in *Bracton*. The slight variations in wording that we find in the treatise, different in particulars but not in sense from the surviving manuscript copies of the texts, hint that they did not have those texts in front of them at times.[81]

---

[76] Brundage, *Medieval Origins* (n 24) 255. According to the early statutes of the university, a student who wished to take the doctorate in either the faculty of civil or of canon law was required to object and respond at one public disputation held by each regent doctor in the faculty of canon law. Leonard Boyle, "The Curriculum of the Faculty of Canon Law at Oxford in the First Half of the Fourteenth Century" in *Oxford Studies Presented to Daniel Callus* (Clarendon Press 1964) 152 (hereafter Boyle, "Curriculum"); Boyle, "Canon Law Before 1380" (n 28) 539. Unfortunately these statutes are difficult to date, and may or may not reflect practice in the first half of the thirteenth century.

[77] Brundage, *Medieval Origins* (n 24) 255; Boyle, "Curriculum" (n 76) 152; Boyle, "Canon Law Before 1380" (n 28) 539.

[78] Mary Carruthers, *The Book of Memory: A Study of Memory in Medieval Culture* (2nd edn, CUP 2008) 2–5.

[79] Ibid, 127.

[80] "[U]t per divisiones facilius tradatur doctrina, partito enim sive divisio animum legentis incitat, mentem intelligentiae praeparat, memoriam artificiose reformat." *Bracton*, vol 2, 33–34.

[81] *Bracton*, vol 1, xxxv; John L Barton, *Roman Law in England* (Ius Romanum Medii Aevi, Pars V, 13a, Typis Giuffrè 1971) 18.

In the schools, students would have engaged in these practices of reading, writing, and interpreting texts. They would have learned to apply and interpret the authoritative texts of the law, those texts that contained the law itself. They might have produced their own texts, such as reports of lectures or disputations. They would have engaged with the intellectual life of Bologna through the texts produced by its jurists; where Azo's *Summae* may have started life as oral lectures, by the time they arrived in England, they were texts. Students in the schools would have learned to see law as something that happens in writing.

## The *Bracton* Authors and the Schools

The authors of *Bracton* certainly knew something of Roman and canon law. They knew quite a bit of the substantive law and, as we shall see in later chapters, engaged in the same kinds of textual practices that were taught in the schools. Unfortunately, we have little evidence to connect the justices who were likely involved in the *Bracton* project with the schools. This is, in part, because we know very little about most royal justices before they entered royal service. From 1268, the justices of the royal courts become three-dimensional figures. We can hear their voices through the texts known as law reports, which often purport to be verbatim records of what was said in court.[82] Our sources for the period before 1268 are much more limited. We do not even know when Martin of Pattishall, William of Raleigh, or Henry of Bratton were born, for instance. Matthew Paris knew some of these justices and included them occasionally in his *Chronica Majora*, one of our best sources for the reign of King Henry III. Matthew had his own axe to grind, however, and even he does not discuss any of the justices at great length. We get little snippets of information when one of the justices enters the story of the high politics of the realm, Matthew's primary interest.

What we do know about the justices is mostly drawn from the administrative records of the crown and the Church. There were no birth or baptism registers in this period, so it was only later in life that most justices entered the written record. Occasionally we find a future justice or clerk engaged in a land transaction. Many only enter the record once they are already working for the king. Even then, they had few opportunities to enter the historical record until

---

[82] For an early example of a justice speaking directly in a law report, see Paul Brand (ed), *The Earliest English Law Reports, Volume I: Common Bench Reports to 1284* (SS vol 111, Selden Society 1996) 9–10, entry 1270.2. This is a report of a case heard in 1270.

they became justices. Even though they were the people who produced the texts that kept the king's government running, clerks in the royal administration only rarely appear in those texts. Clerks in the courts did not sign the writs they produced until 1292, and they did not sign their plea rolls until 1305.[83] Most were not paid out of the treasury, which kept records of payments. They may have been paid something by the justices they served, but also probably earned a large part of their income from fees paid by people who had business before the court.[84] Some chance records survive of these justices from the period before they were justices. William of Raleigh first appears in 1212, when a record was made on the chancery's patent roll that King John had presented him to the bishop of Exeter to be rector of a church in Devon.[85] Henry of Bratton first appears in the records of the courts in 1238, and then it was because he was recording an agreement in the court *coram rege*, appearing as a party, not a clerk.[86] He was probably a clerk of that court at the time, although the record does not tell us one way or the other. He may have already been a man of mature years in 1238; at his next appearance in the historical record, in 1240, he already appears to be a senior clerk.[87] Even once they became justices, the dry and formulaic records of Church and crown cannot tell us much about who these men were. They can tell us how much land and how many benefices they held, where they were at particular times, and whether they enjoyed royal favor.

Although we cannot say anything very definite about the education of Martin of Pattishall, William of Raleigh, or Henry of Bratton—the three people most closely connected with the treatise—we can say something about the kind of learning reflected in the treatise itself. There are signs that at least one of the authors of *Bracton* followed the teachings of the *Pauperistae*. In places, *Bracton* adopts the interpretations of the civilian texts, some of them idiosyncratic, that had been adopted by Vacarius and his students.[88] The relationship we find

---

[83] Paul Brand, "The Clerks of the King's Courts in the Reign of Edward I" in MCL, 170, 171 (hereafter Brand, "Clerks").

[84] By the late thirteenth century, clerks were certainly collecting fees to produce certain types of documents, such as chirographs, writs, and articles of the eyre. Ibid, 183. We have some evidence for this practice earlier in the thirteenth century. For payments the clerks received for copying the articles of the eyre, for instance, see Richardson and Sayles, *Procedure without Writ* (n 7) ciii; CAF Meekings (ed), *The 1235 Surrey Eyre*, 3 vols (Surrey Record Society 1979) vol 1, 95. Litigants also regularly assigned some proportion of their recovery to the clerks of the court. Brand, "Clerks" (n 83) 184.

[85] BNB, vol 1, 14; RLP, vol 1, 93b.

[86] CRR, vol 16, 51–52, no 149F.

[87] CAF Meekings and David Crook, *King's Bench and Common Bench in the Reign of Henry III* (Selden Society 2010) 59 (hereafter Meekings and Crook, *King's Bench and Common Bench*).

[88] In one passage where the *Bracton* treatise follows Azo closely, it abruptly diverts from Azo's interpretation of a passage in the *Institutes* and appears instead to adopt an idiosyncratic view adopted by both Vacarius and by the *pauperista* who was lecturing on the *Institutes* around 1200. JL Barton,

between Roman and canon law in the treatise could itself have been inspired by the thought of Vacarius and his students. The emphasis in the treatise is clearly on Roman law. Justinian's corpus is cited far more often than the decretals or Gratian's *Decretum* are. This may reflect the fact that the authors were writing a text on the workings of the secular courts and Roman law, as a secular law, was simply more relevant to them. As I noted in the introduction, the treatise notes that "nothing relating to the regulation of the *sacerdotium* is relevant to this treatise."[89] But the focus on Roman law may reflect the fact that the *Pauperistae* gave pride of place to Roman law. Vacarius famously said that "ecclesiastical laws take dissonant meanings and varying forms," and ridiculed those "who toil in vain to recall the discord of contradictions into concord," a clear reference to the foundational text of canon law, Gratian's *Harmony of Discordant Canons*.[90] Peter Stein suggests that Vacarius and his successors gave primacy to Roman law. They saw civil law as the law that represented written reason. It provided a system for solving problems in any field of inquiry.[91] Vacarius did not doubt that canon law was a binding positive law, but he does seem to have doubted that canon law represented written reason in the same way Roman law did. The *Bracton* authors' commitment to demonstrating that English law could be explained using the terms of Roman law in particular may, therefore, owe something to the Vacarian idea that Roman law constituted a more coherent system than canon law.

There are echoes of the Vacarian school in the treatise, but there are also many references to the texts that would have superseded the *Liber Pauperum* in the early decades of the thirteenth century, such as Azo's *Summae* and the Oxford scholar William of Drogheda's *Summa Aurea*. It would seem that at least some of the authors were connected to networks that gave them access to the most recent works coming out of Bologna and Oxford. It is impossible to know who worked these materials into the treatise. We do not know, for instance, whether Martin of Pattishall ever worked on the treatise and, if he did,

---

"Bracton as a Civilian" (1967-68) 42 Tulane Law Review 555, 580; De Zulueta and Stein (eds), *Teaching of Roman Law* (n 38) lxv. Vacarius and his students also held custom in high regard, taking the extreme position, against that of most civilians and canonists of the time, that custom (*consuetudo*) could abrogate written law (*lex*) even when the custom was contrary to reason. Ibid, lix–lx. This is in line with the treatise's identification of English law with custom.

---

[89] "Cum autem de regimine sacerdotii nihil pertineat ad tractatum istum . . ." *Bracton*, vol 2, 304.
[90] Peter Stein, "Vacarius and the Civil Law" in CNL Brooke and others (eds), *Church and Government in the Middle Ages: Essays Presented to C.R. Cheney on His 70th Birthday* (CUP 1976) 134 (hereafter Stein, "Vacarius and the Civil Law"). Taliadoros, *Law and Theology* (n 36) 85.
[91] Stein, "Vacarius and the Civil Law" (n 90) 135–36. Jason Taliadoros has demonstrated that Vacarius made extensive use of legal analogies, drawn from Justinian's texts, in his theological writings. Taliadoros, *Law and Theology* (n 36) 293.

what he might have added. We do not know whether there were people in addition to Pattishall, Raleigh, and Bratton who may have worked on the treatise and if so, who they were.

There are ways in which the civilian and canonist learning we find in the treatise might fit into the careers of Pattishall, Raleigh, and Bratton. What evidence we do have for the education of these three justices is negative. Although some royal justices are accorded the title *magister* in the records of the royal courts of the thirteenth century, none of the three justices associated with *Bracton* is ever addressed as *magister* in those records.[92] If any of these men had incepted as a master in one of England's schools, we might expect the title to appear on the plea rolls, but it does not.

The fact that Pattishall, Raleigh, and Bratton are never called masters does not necessarily indicate that they had short academic careers, however.[93] One could spend a great deal of time in the schools without ever incepting as a master. By the time the earliest statutes for Oxford's civil law faculty were written sometime between 1230 and about 1300, a course of study leading to a degree had been laid down. A student could only be licensed to lecture after six years of study. At that point he would be regarded as a bachelor of law. Then he would be required to prepare and give a series of lectures that would lead to the doctorate, and these might take several years to give.[94] Even if one did study for the requisite period of time, there were other bars to incepting as a master. We know that in later centuries, the student who wished to take a degree had to pay fees and throw a feast, which could be quite expensive.[95] Incepted masters or doctors in civil law were required to teach for at least a year after taking their degrees, which may have imposed a burden that some scholars, eager to take

[92] Ralph V Turner, *The English Judiciary in the Age of Glanvill and Bracton, c. 1176-1239* (CUP 1985) 150, 211, 226 (hereafter Turner, *English Judiciary*).

[93] Nicholas Vincent has additionally noted that Ralph Niger made a comment around 1190 that teachers of Roman law in England were eschewing the titles of master and doctor in favor of "lord." Nicholas Vincent, "Henry of Bratton (*alias* Bracton)" in Mark Hill and RH Helmholz (eds), *Great Christian Jurists in English History* (CUP 2017) 20 (hereafter Vincent, "Henry of Bratton"). Pattishall, Raleigh, and Bratton were certainly styled "lord" (*dominus*) at times, although this does not appear to have been unusual for people of their status within the court. It opens up the possibility, however, that Pattishall, Raleigh, and Bratton did incept as masters or doctors in the schools.

[94] Barton, "Civil Law before 1380" (n 71) 525–26. Gerald of Wales suggested that one could incept as a master of the arts in far less time, three or four years, in a text he wrote in the 1220s. We should take this with a grain of salt, however. Gerald was near the end of his life and was complaining about the state of learning in the 1220s. He claims that, in his time, people would study for twenty years before attempting to teach. This has the feel of a hyperbolic, "when-I-was-a-kid" story. Hunt, "*Speculum Ecclesiae*" (n 17) 194, 206.

[95] For costs at Bologna, see Brundage, *Medieval Origins* (n 24) 260–62. For evidence of costs at Oxford and Cambridge in later centuries, see Alan B Cobban, *English University Life in the Middle Ages* (Ohio State University Press 1999) 223 (hereafter Cobban, *English University Life*).

up positions won through patronage, were unwilling to accept.[96] A period of study that did not lead to a degree would still have been valuable to the justice, both for its educational value and for its value to his future career. Formularies of letters were circulating in Oxford as early as the beginning of the thirteenth century. Along with the proper forms for a letter home to mom or dad asking for more money, many contained a form for a letter attesting that the student, although he had not taken a degree, had studied at the university.[97] A future justice therefore could have studied for several years in the schools, gaining an intimate knowledge of Roman and canon law, without ever incepting as a master. Even a period of study that did not culminate in the awarding of the title *magister* could have given the future justice some experience in giving lectures, experience he may have used in a lecture course on the law of the royal courts later in his career.

*Bracton* itself provides us with some evidence that its authors studied law in the schools, and there were certainly opportunities for Martin of Pattishall, William of Raleigh, and Henry of Bratton to obtain an education in Roman law. Students usually went on to higher studies between the ages of fourteen and seventeen.[98] It was always possible for men of more mature years to attend a cathedral school or a university, however. Bishops would occasionally send clerks in their households to pursue higher studies.[99] A clerk in the royal courts could potentially have been allowed to leave for a time to further his education. But if we assume that Pattishall, Raleigh, and Bratton attended the schools prior to their service in the royal courts, we can get a sense of when they attended school and what it might have been like, as higher education was changing rapidly around the turn of the thirteenth century.

Martin of Pattishall died in 1229. We might place his birth around the 1160s or 1170s. That would place the higher stages of Pattishall's education sometime between the 1170s and 1190s. English students in that period could go fairly far afield, to Paris or the center of legal studies par excellence at Bologna.[100]

---

[96] Barton, "Civil Law before 1380" (n 71) 525. The earliest evidence we have for the pay received by regent masters hints that it was rather low and probably would have required the master to seek other means of support in addition to teaching. Catto, "Citizens, Scholars, and Masters" (n 68) 190.

[97] Cobban, *English University Life* (n 95) 24.

[98] Catto, "Citizens, Scholars, and Masters" (n 68) 170.

[99] See Frank Barlow, *Thomas Becket* (Phoenix Press 1986) 37.

[100] Ralph V Turner, "Roman Law in England Before the Time of Bracton" in *Judges, Administrators, and the Common Law in Angevin England* (Hambledon Press 1994) 51–54 (hereafter Turner, "Roman Law in England"). The bull *Super Specula*, which forbade the University of Paris to grant degrees in civil law, but not in canon law, was not issued until 1219. Even then, Roman law was taught at Paris as part of the canon law course. Brundage, *Medieval Origins* (n 24) 231–33. In the 1150s, Thomas Becket was sent to Bologna to study law for one year while he was a cleric in Archbishop Theobald's household. Barlow, *Thomas Becket* (n 99) 37.

By 1174, the community of English students in Bologna was substantial enough to endow an altar dedicated to the newly canonized St. Thomas Becket in one of the city's churches.[101] By the early thirteenth century, they had dedicated a chapel to him there.[102] Pattishall could have made the voyage to one of these centers of learning. Higher learning was available closer to home, however. In the second half of the twelfth century, several of England's cathedrals had schools attached to them that had attracted prominent scholars, some with reputations that crossed the English Channel. Study in the cathedral schools usually focused on the seven liberal arts. Law came into the program as part of the study of rhetoric, but might also be taught on its own.[103] Hereford Cathedral is known to have had some of the most recent works of the civilian jurists of Bologna in its library around 1200 and there is evidence for the teaching of law there in the late 1190s.[104] Lincoln Cathedral had a flourishing school up until about 1225.[105] But if Pattishall did study law in a school, the most likely location would have been Northampton. There was a thriving school in Northampton in Pattishall's day, a center that had such a reputation that it could easily have developed into England's third university.[106] Vacarius may have taught there for a time in the 1170s or 1180s.[107] The formulary held by the Walters Art Gallery mentioned above, which contained information relevant to practice in both ecclesiastical and secular courts, was probably begun in Northampton in the 1190s, as it contains numerous references to that town and places near it.[108] Northampton is a mere seven miles from Martin of Pattishall's home village, and this connection may help to explain why such a small village produced two major royal justices of the early thirteenth century, Simon of Pattishall and Martin of Pattishall.

---

[101] Brundage, *Medieval Origins* (n 24) 224.

[102] Turner, "Roman Law in England" (n 100) 54.

[103] Ibid, 55.

[104] Ibid, 52; Cobban, *Medieval English Universities* (n 10) 27.

[105] Cobban, *Medieval English Universities* (n 10) 27. Cobban's note that Peter of Blois ranked Lincoln along with Bologna, Paris, and Oxford as a center for law is a bit misleading. Peter does not say that Lincoln and these three other cities were particularly good places for the study of law. He lists those four cities as places where ecclesiastical courts were held. RW Southern, "From Schools to University" in JI Catto (ed), *The History of the University of Oxford, Volume I: The Early Oxford Schools* (Clarendon Press 1984) 12 (hereafter Southern, "Schools to University").

[106] Turner, "Roman Law in England" (n 100) 55. Richardson, "Schools of Northampton" (n 16).

[107] Stein, "Vacarius and the Civil Law" (n 90) 132. The reference in one of Vacarius' letters to being in Northampton "*causa studendi*" is, admittedly, ambiguous. It seems unlikely he was in Northampton as a student, as he was already a learned civilian by the time he came to England. It is possible that he was there to brush up his learning in some other field of study, however. Ibid.

[108] See above, p 69; HG Richardson, "The Oxford Law School under John" (1941) 57 LQR 319, 325–28.

William of Raleigh and Henry of Bratton were men of different generations than Pattishall's, however. William of Raleigh seems to have begun his royal service by 1212, when the king presented him to the church of Bratton Fleming. If we assume he was at least in his early twenties by this time, he would likely have been born around the 1180s.[109] That would place Raleigh's higher education around 1200. By then the educational scene in England had changed quite a bit. Education outside of England was still a possibility. Thomas of Marlborough, a scholar and monk of the abbey of Evesham, studied at Bologna for six months sometime between 1202 and 1205, while in Italy to present a case to the pope on behalf of his abbey.[110] Cathedral schools in England would also have been a possibility. In Raleigh and Bratton's native Devon, Exeter's cathedral school had been known as an important center of learning in the middle of the twelfth century.[111] Bartholomew, its bishop from 1164 to 1181, was highly regarded as a canonist and was appointed regularly as a judge delegate by the pope, often in difficult cases.[112] Baldwin of Totnes, a canonist trained at Bologna who was a collector of decretals and a future archbishop of Canterbury, was teaching

[109] In theory, Raleigh should have been at least twenty-four when he was instituted to the rectory of Bratton Fleming. A rectory was a benefice with what was called the "cure of souls" (*cura animarum*). The rector was the chief priest of the parish and had duties towards the people of the parish, primarily to say mass and hear confession. Because these duties required the rector to be ordained as a priest, rectors of churches were required, under canon law, to be ordained as priests within a year of their institution, and the canonical age for ordination as a priest was thirty, although ordinations could take place at the age of twenty-five in cases of necessity. Kathleen Edwards, *The English Secular Cathedrals in the Middle Ages: A Constitutional Study with Special Reference to the Fourteenth Century* (Manchester University Press 1967) 253 (hereafter Edwards, *Secular Cathedrals*); D.78 c.4-c.5; *Corpus Iuris Canonici* vol 1, 275–76. His institution to the rectory of Bratton Fleming is not a reliable guide to his age, however, because Raleigh could have sought a dispensation that would allow him to take up the benefice despite the fact that he was underage. Michael Burger, *Bishops, Priests, and Diocesan Governance in Thirteenth-Century England: Reward and Punishment* (CUP 2014) 24 (hereafter Burger, *Diocesan Governance*). Children were, at times, instituted to rectories. John RH Moorman, *Church Life in England in the Thirteenth Century* (CUP 1946) 34–35. Later in his career, William of Raleigh actually exchanged a series of letters with Bishop Robert Grosseteste to try to induce Grosseteste to institute a young man who had royal patronage to a rectory in the diocese of Lincoln. Grosseteste refused on the ground that "he is a minor and not sufficiently educated, still a boy, in fact, who thinks Ovid the greatest letter-writer!" Robert Grosseteste, *The Letters of Robert Grosseteste, Bishop of Lincoln* (FAC Mantello and Joseph Goering trs, University of Toronto Press 2010) 95.
It was the pope who granted dispensations, but clergy usually did not have to petition the pope directly to acquire them. English bishops were often delegated the power, called a faculty, to dispense a certain number of clerics for holding benefices in plurality, and sometimes also received the delegated power to dispense underage clerics and nonresident clerics. Burger, *Diocesan Governance* (n 109) 119. Raleigh almost certainly acquired a dispensation to excuse his non-residency at his parish, since he was likely working as a clerk in the courts at the time and could not have visited his parish regularly. He could have acquired a dispensation for being underage at the same time. He is not likely to have been beyond his thirties in 1212, however, as he died in 1250.
[110] Jane E Sayers, "Marlborough, Thomas of (d. 1236)" (ODNB, September 23, 2004) <www.oxforddnb.com/view/article/18077> accessed March 13, 2019.
[111] A charter made in 1160 lists ten scholars as witnesses. Nicholas Orme, *Education in the West of England, 1066-1548* (Exeter University Press 1976) 52 (hereafter Orme, *West of England*).
[112] Duggan, *Decretal Collections* (n 64) 211.

in Exeter's cathedral school in the 1160s.[113] We know little about Exeter's reputation at the beginning of the thirteenth century, however, and it seems to have been declining.[114] After about 1190 legal study at Lincoln seems to have dropped off in favor of theology.[115] Salisbury Cathedral may have had a school of some renown in the thirteenth century where one could learn law.[116] Richardson thought that there was probably a migration of scholars from Northampton to Oxford sometime in the 1190s, but Northampton's schools maintained some renown throughout the thirteenth century.[117] In 1260 a group of Oxford masters migrated with their students to Northampton, pre-sumably because there was already a *studium* there.[118] King Henry III was even willing to recognize Northampton as the third English university in 1261, al-though it would not retain its university status for long.[119] Indeed, a period of study at Northampton could explain how William of Raleigh, a Devonian, came to the attention of Martin of Pattishall.

By the 1190s, however, these other schools were being eclipsed by the new center at Oxford, which some were referring to already in the 1190s as a *studium commune*, a term that connoted something more exalted than a typical cath-edral school.[120] More English scholars were staying in England for their study

---

[113] Ibid, 111–12.

[114] It had been thought that Thomas of Marlborough taught civil and canon law at Exeter at some point in his career, but this is based on what was probably a copying mistake in a manuscript. Jane E Sayers, "Marlborough, Thomas of (d. 1236)" (ODNB, September 23, 2004) <www.oxforddnb.com/view/article/18077> accessed March 13, 2019. There is some evidence for the teaching of theology at Exeter around 1200. Orme, *West of England* (n 111) 52. The next solid evidence for the teaching of higher studies at the cathedral comes from 1283, when the bishop laid down new statutes requiring the chancellor to be qualified to lecture in either theology or canon law and to lecture regularly in one or the other subject, although these lectures were probably intended for the clergy of the diocese. Ibid, 53.

[115] Frans Van Liere, "The Study of Canon Law and the Eclipse of the Lincoln Schools, 1175-1225" (2003) 18 (1) History of Universities 1, 4–5, 10.

[116] Edwards, *Secular Cathedrals* (n 109) 191. The college model, which would become so influential on the organization of the Universities of Oxford and Cambridge, actually began at Salisbury with the founding of de Vaux College in 1262. Ibid, 191–92.

[117] The legal formulary examined by Richardson appears to have been begun at Northampton, as many of the sample forms contained in it refer to places near Northampton. It also appears to have been completed in Oxford sometime early in John's reign, however. Other evidence hints at the possibility of a migration, such as a reference to local officials in Northampton harassing scholars. Richardson, "Schools of Northampton" (n 16) 603.

[118] Ibid, 596.

[119] In 1265, while the government was held by the rebel barons led by Simon de Montfort, parliament responded to a plea from the borough of Oxford to suppress the new school. Royal letters were issued suppressing the university and expelling the scholars from the town. CH Lawrence, "The University in State and Church" in JI Catto (ed), *The History of the University of Oxford, Volume I: The Early Oxford Schools* (Clarendon Press 1984) 127.

[120] Cobban, *Medieval English Universities* (n 10) 40–41. The term *studium commune* or *studium generale* could imply several different things. First, it often meant that a school drew students from beyond the boundaries of the kingdom in which it was located. Second, it usually implied that the school offered studies in one of the higher faculties, and not just in the arts. Third, the phrase was associated with the *ius ubique docendi*, the right of the school's graduates to teach at any other school without further examin-ation. Ibid; Patrick Zutshi, "When Did Cambridge Become a *Studium Generale*?" in Kenneth Pennington

and Oxford seems to have been the new institution of choice. From 1193, when war with France made the journey to foreign universities more perilous, clerks who received royal patronage to study were sent exclusively to Oxford.[121]

If William of Raleigh attended Oxford before he entered royal service, he likely would have had to do so before 1209. In that year, an Oxford student murdered his mistress. The student fled the town, but the mayor was able to get his hands on two of his housemates, and the citizens of Oxford summarily hanged them. In protest, the masters and students of Oxford abandoned the town. The schools at Oxford did not reopen until 1214, after Raleigh had received his benefice from the king and was likely in royal service.[122] If he did attend the schools at Oxford in this period, his education probably would have been influenced by the *pauperistae*. Within a generation of Vacarius' death, they appear to have been centered at Oxford. Gerald of Wales, writing around 1220, associated the *pauperistae* specifically with Oxford, speaking of a time, probably in the 1190s, when the *Liber Pauperum* "stood in high regard" in Oxford, and when the scholars of Oxford who had learned from it felt that they could best a scholar of Bologna in debate.[123]

Henry of Bratton was a man of a later generation, and likely would have encountered a somewhat different approach to Roman law if he attended Oxford in the 1220s or 1230s, before he entered royal service. By the time Bratton would have been of an age to attend a school of higher studies, Oxford had become even more likely as a location for his study of civil and canon law. The *studium* at Cambridge had acquired some recognition by this time. The first reference to a chancellor of the schools at Cambridge, which presupposes some kind of central organization, dates to 1225 or 1226, and both Oxford and Cambridge received some important privileges from the crown in 1231.[124] The schools of Cambridge, like those of Oxford, may have risen to prominence because Cambridge was a town where ecclesiastical courts met, suggesting that legal studies were important from the very beginning. But while the masters

---

and Melodie Harris Eichbauer (eds), *Law as Profession and Practice in Medieval Europe: Essays in Honor of James A. Brundage* (Routledge 2011) 155–60 (hereafter Zutshi, "*Studium Generale*").

[121] Cobban, *Medieval English Universities* (n 10) 33.

[122] Southern, "From Schools to University" (n 105) 26–27.

[123] "[D]um Pauperum scilicet li[ber il]le sic dictus in precio stetit . . ." Hunt, "*Speculum Ecclesiae*" (n 17) 194, 205. Gerald did not think much of the *pauperistae*. In the story he recounts, the Bologna-trained jurist, Master Martin, chides the *pauperistae* for moving straight from the study of basic Latin grammar to the study of the *Digest*, *Codex*, and *Institutes*, skipping over the study of the arts. Ibid. Gerald uses the pejorative term *superseminati*, which he claims to have borrowed from Master Mainerius, one of Abelard's students, to refer to scholars who skip over the study of grammar and rhetoric so they can move directly to dialectic and law. Ibid, 197.

[124] Zutshi, "*Studium Generale*" (n 120) 161, 62.

of Cambridge appear to have taught canon law in the early decades of the thirteenth century, there is no evidence for the teaching of Roman law there until the second half of the thirteenth century, long after Bratton would have left the schools for the courts.[125] There are also a few bits of evidence that link *Bracton* to Oxford; the use that the *Bracton* authors made of the Oxford jurist William of Drogheda's *Summa Aurea* may indicate an Oxford connection.[126] William was a rough contemporary of Henry of Bratton, and Raleigh and Bratton may have become familiar with his work through an Oxford connection.

It is not clear whether the Vacarian school would have still been a major force in Oxford in the 1220s and 1230s. Leonard Boyle has suggested that when teaching resumed at Oxford in 1214, the *pauperistae* may no longer have been a coherent school.[127] Whether 1214 was a turning point or not, by the 1230s or so the teaching of the *pauperistae* seems to have given way to teaching based on more recent Roman-law texts, brought back by masters trained in Bologna, such as Azo's *summae* on the *Institutes* and the *Codex*, which were probably completed around 1210. Although the *Liber Pauperum* was still being copied in the second half of the thirteenth century, William of Drogheda's *Summa Aurea* of 1239 does not appear to owe anything to Vacarius' text or the work of the *pauperistae*. This would suggest that he either was not taught in the pauperist tradition or that he rejected it.[128] William had likely been studying and teaching at Oxford since the early 1230s. Boyle also thought a major reorganization may have taken place in 1234 and 1235, where the scholars of law were separated into two faculties of civil law and canon law, suggesting that the scholars of Oxford were putting a bit more distance between the disciplines than the *pauperistae* had.[129] Bratton would likely have learned from a different set of texts from Raleigh, and it is even possible that it was Bratton who worked portions of civilian and canonist texts of the 1220s and 1230s into the treatise.

## A Different Kind of Justice

The authors of *Bracton* were different from other justices in the royal courts in that they had studied Roman and canon law and had been introduced to a new way of thinking about law, one that they likely would not have shared with

---

[125] Ibid, 160.
[126] See, for example, pp 62–63, pp 176–77.
[127] Boyle, "Canon Law before 1380" (n 28) 533.
[128] Sayers, "William of Drogheda" (n 25) 208.
[129] Boyle, "Canon Law before 1380" (n 28) 535–36.

justices who had come up through the administration of law in the counties. The authors of *Bracton*, in their study of Roman law, would have learned to think of law as a practice that was carried out largely through texts. To be clear, sheriffs and eyre jurors worked with texts, so justices who spent their early careers in the administration of the counties would be familiar with government through texts. Some of those texts were even texts of authority. Writs and articles of the eyre gave authoritative instructions to their recipients. But the idea that the substance of the law was contained in texts, and that the practice of law should revolve around the reconciliation and exposition of authoritative texts, often by producing other texts, was something new.

This divide, between justices who had learned Roman and canon law and those who had not, was probably more important than another divide that has received quite a bit of scholarly attention: that between clerics and laymen. In the past, historians have made much of the fact that a substantial proportion of the justices of the English royal courts before 1300 were clerics. Their clerical status does not appear to have affected their outlook very much, however. The clerical/lay divide appears to have been more about how a justice was paid than about his fundamental outlook. Pattishall, Raleigh, and Bratton may have begun to identify as clerics fairly early in their careers. Students at Oxford had clerical status from at least 1214. They were probably tonsured, meaning that the hair was shaved from the crown of the head to indicate clerical status.[130] Some scholars might even have been ordained to the minor orders of acolyte, lector, porter, or exorcist. Minor orders would have given our future justice certain advantages. He could hold an ecclesiastical benefice, for instance, and members of the royal administration were often rewarded with benefices.

Pattishall, Raleigh, and Bratton were clerics. All held office within the Church by the time they were senior clerks. William of Raleigh and Henry of Bratton both acquired their first benefices before they were justices. King John himself held the advowson of Bratton Fleming when Raleigh was instituted as rector in 1212, while he was still a judicial clerk.[131] It seems probable that someone in the royal courts was instrumental in bringing him to the king's attention. Martin of Pattishall seems to have recommended Raleigh for promotion to many of the benefices he held later in his career. From 1220, Raleigh was rector of Blatherwycke in Northamptonshire, Pattishall's home county.[132] He was also a canon of St. Paul's Cathedral in London, where his master had briefly

---

[130] Catto, "Citizens, Scholars, and Masters" (n 68) 155.
[131] Meekings and Crook, *King's Bench and Common Bench* (n 87) 60.
[132] Turner, *English Judiciary* (n 92) 199.

been dean, from at least 1237, but possibly earlier.[133] The rectory of King's Somborne in Hampshire almost certainly came to him through Pattishall's influence, since Pattishall had been rector of the parish before Raleigh. Perhaps Patishall had resigned from it in Raleigh's favor upon his retirement from the bench.[134] The holder of the benefice therefore might be able to exercise patronage to the benefice through access to his own patron. This kind of patronage does not seem to have been uncommon. Another justice, William of York, resigned the rectory at King's Ripton in Huntingdonshire and managed to secure it for one of his relatives, a poor scholar, through the influence of his own patron, the chancellor, who had probably presented William to the living in the first place.[135]

Despite the efforts of the reforming party within the Church to clearly separate the sacred from the secular and the clerical from the lay, the line was actually still permeable in the thirteenth century. Taking minor orders allowed a young scholar or clerk to hold a benefice, but also left his options open.[136] If no benefice was forthcoming or the rewards of a secular life—such as a good marriage to a landed widow or heiress—were greater than those of the clerical, a man in minor orders could give up the clerical life for the lay. The minor orders, although ordained orders of clergy, were not of the same character as the major orders of bishop, priest, deacon, and subdeacon; they did not prevent the ordinand from later marrying, for instance.[137] Henry III's steward, John of Lexington, was clearly a layman, but was said to be learned in Roman and canon law, suggesting that he had some formal schooling.[138] John of Lexington may have identified as a cleric while he was at school. Some clerics, like Raleigh's clerk Roger of Thirkleby, did indeed abandon their clerical status later in life to marry, surrendering several benefices, which were apparently

---

[133] CM, vol 3, 417.

[134] CAF Meekings, "Martin de Pateshull of Good Memory my Sometime Lord" (1974) 47 Bulletin of the Institute of Historical Research 224, 227–29, reprinted in Studies in 13th Century Justice and Administration (London: Hambledon Press 1981), item XII.

[135] CAF Meekings, "Six Letters Concerning the Eyres of 1226-8" (1950) 65 EHR 492, 501–502.

[136] Even rectors, who had cure of souls, could obtain dispensations to remain in minor orders. One survey of institutions to rectories in the diocese of Lincoln found that, of the clerics instituted to rectories between 1209 and 1235, only about a quarter were listed as priests. Of 104 clerics instituted in the diocese's archdeaconry of Oxford in that period, forty-five were listed as subdeacons, considered to be a major order by some and a minor order by others, and twenty were listed as being either acolytes or clerici, probably indicating that they were in minor orders. Moorman, Church Life (n 109) 34.

[137] Jean Dunbabin, "From Clerk to Knight: Changing Orders" in C Harper-Bill and R Harvey (eds), The Ideals and Practice of Medieval Knighthood II: Papers from the Third Strawberry Hill Conference (Boydell Press 1988) 28.

[138] Ralph V Turner, "The Miles Literatus in Twelfth- and Thirteenth-Century England. How Rare a Phenomenon?" in Ralph V Turner, Judges, Administrators, and the Common Law in Angevin England (Hambledon Press 1994) 119, 123.

not as lucrative as his new wife's lands, in the process.[139] The justice Stephen of Seagrave, a contemporary of Raleigh who is mentioned several times in *Bracton*, may have been in orders as a young man. Matthew Paris tells us that when he and his political allies fell from royal favor, Stephen fled to the abbey of St Mary des Prés near Leicester, where "he who had earlier fled from clergy to knighthood through arrogance . . . regained the crown [i.e., the tonsure], which he had abandoned without consulting the bishop."[140]

Apart from the fact that they could abandon it without much trouble, there is also evidence that these justices were not overly committed to the clerical life. Conflicts regularly arose between the role of cleric and the role of justice and these justices appear to have resolved them in favor of the latter. Clerics were not allowed to participate in the pronouncement of a sentence of death, a prohibition that was confirmed in the canons of the Fourth Lateran Council of 1215 and in English provincial and diocesan legislation immediately following the council.[141] This does not seem to have bothered Pattishall, Raleigh, or Bratton enough to lead them to resign from the court. Henry III's statement that William of Raleigh had "slaughtered many more with his tongue than [William of Savoy] has with his sword" was clearly hyperbolic, but seems to imply that Raleigh participated in blood judgments.[142] Robert Grosseteste complained that Robert of Lexington, another clerical justice, not only heard capital cases, but heard them on Sundays.[143] Several English dioceses had diocesan statutes that prohibited clerics from serving in any kind of secular administration, and some specifically included the office of justice among those proscribed. Indeed, once he was a bishop, William of Raleigh himself issued statutes that contained very specific prohibitions against royal service and service as a secular justice.[144] Perhaps this nagged at him a bit during his nearly

[139] Thirkleby was a senior clerk at the time. David Crook, "Thirkleby [Thurkilbi], Roger of (*d.* 1260)" (ODNB, September 23, 2004) <www.oxforddnb.com/view/article/27401> accessed March 13, 2019. Another example is John of Gaddesden, Queen Eleanor's chamberlain, who gave up his clerical status and his ecclesiastical benefices to marry a wealthy woman. Clanchy, *Memory* (n 48) 244.

[140] "Stephanas vero de Segrave in ecclesia Sanctae Marias in abbatia Canonicorum apud Legrecestriam delituit; et qui prius a clericatu ad militiam per arrogantiam confugerat, ad clericatus officium reversus, coronam, quam reliquerat inconsulto episcopo, revocavit." CM, vol 3, 293; William Hunt, "Seagrave, Sir Stephen of (*d.* 1241)" (Paul Brand rev, ODNB, September 23, 2004) <www.oxforddnb.com/view/article/25041> accessed March 13, 2019.

[141] Turner, "Clerical Judges" (n 14) 162–63.

[142] "Rex iratus nimis procaciter respondit; 'Renuistis electum Valentinum, dicentes eum virum sanguinum, et W[illelmum] de Reale, qui multo plures lingua quam alius gladio trucidavit, elegistis.' " CM, vol 3, 494. Henry was responding to the objections of the monks of the Winchester Cathedral chapter, who refused to elect the king's candidate, William of Savoy, because he was a "man of blood." Henry's response implies that William of Raleigh was also a man of blood. See above, p 40.

[143] Turner, *English Judiciary* (n 92) 266.

[144] Turner, "Clerical Judges" (n 14) 164.

three decades as a clerk and justice in the king's courts, but it did not bother him enough to drive him to resign.

The primary divide between justices on the courts was probably less between clerical and lay than it was between those who had been trained in Roman and canon law and those who had not. These two groups would have viewed law in very different ways. The authors *of Bracton* had been exposed to the schools' ways of thinking about law. Not all of their colleagues would have this background. Others had risen to the bench not through higher education followed by service as a clerk, but through service in the counties. A young man who wished to become a bailiff, estate steward, or under-sheriff might leave the schools after acquiring a bit of Latin grammar and skill at writing. He might attend one of the schools Richardson described in Northampton or Oxford, which would teach him how to compose letters and give him a bit of rudimentary education in the procedure of the king's and ecclesiastical courts. He would then return home, possibly to learn the knightly arts and be knighted sometime in his late teens or early twenties. Several of the *Bracton* authors' colleagues and contemporaries followed this kind of path. Henry of Bath, who was chief justice of the court *coram rege* when Henry of Bratton was sitting on that court, had begun his career in the 1220s as a manorial bailiff working under his kinsman Hugh, who was the keeper of the royal honor of Berkhamstead. After serving as a bailiff, he continued on to become an under-sheriff, sheriff, and eventually a royal justice.[145] Henry de la Mare, another *coram rege* justice, served as steward to William Longespée, who was earl of Salisbury in all but name. He retired from the court in 1249 so he could return to William's service, to manage his estates while he was on crusade.[146]

Justices who took this route to the bench probably would have come to the bench with a very different understanding of law from that possessed by Pattishall, Raleigh, and Bratton. They would have spent their careers in the courts of the honor, manor, hundred, and county, where the law was contained in the memory of the collected suitors and legal practice was primarily oral, not written. Stewards often attended the county court in place of their lords and thus served as the suitors, or judges, of that court. Service as a steward, bailiff, or sheriff probably would have influenced the future justice's perception of judicial work in other ways, as well. The steward usually presided over the

---

[145] David Crook, "Bath, Henry of (*d.* 1260)" (ODNB, January 3, 2008) <www.oxforddnb.com/view/article/1686> accessed March 13, 2019.

[146] CAF Meekings, "Henry de Bracton, Canon of Wells" (1951-54) 26 N. & Q. for Somerset and Dorset 141, reprinted in *Studies in 13th Century Justice and Administration* (Hambledon Press 1981), item VII.

lord's manor courts, held for the lord's villeins and less exalted tenants, travelling from manor to manor to hold court. Indeed, by the late thirteenth century, this appears to have been the central feature of a steward's work.[147] The steward also looked after the lord's interests. The manor court certainly heard disputes between the lord's tenants, but it was also designed to protect the lord's rights from his tenants and his officials. Stewards had oversight of the lesser officials, the bailiffs who managed individual manors and the reeves, often unfree tenants, who were responsible for accounting to the lord for the agricultural management of those manors. The steward was generally responsible for ensuring that the lord's bailiffs and reeves were not cheating him. He might hear the annual accounts of the reeves, which were still given orally on all but the largest estates in the first half of the thirteenth century.[148] He was responsible for looking after the lord's rights and liberties, defending them from encroachment by his tenants in the manor court, or from others in the county court and royal court.

Men who came to the royal courts from service as a bailiff or a steward might have understood their service in the courts through that lens. The parallels between service as a baronial steward and service as a royal justice must have been obvious to any justice who had previously served as a steward. In addition to the fact that both offices required the holder to judge cases, there were similarities in the ways stewards and justices were expected to look after their lords' interests.[149] The king's justices in eyre, in addition to punishing felons and hearing disputes between the king's subjects, also looked into the conduct of the king's bailiffs and made sure that the king's rights in the county were not being encroached upon. The eyre justice was, in his duties, very similar to a steward. He should do good justice in his lord's name, just as any baronial steward should, but at the same time, his primary job was to protect the king's interests and to collect the revenues that belonged to him. Many people in England appear to have understood the royal justice's role in this way. Those who were subject to the eyre visitations had no trouble viewing the royal justice as someone whose primary job was to collect revenue for the king and look

[147] There is one example of a steward of the 1280s who claimed that he had been hired only to hold the lord's courts and defend his liberties. Paul Brand, "Stewards, Bailiffs and the Emerging Legal Profession in Later Thirteenth-Century England", in Ralph Evans (ed), *Lordship and Learning: Studies in Memory of Trevor Aston* (Boydell Press 2004) 139, 146, 148.

[148] PDA Harvey, "The Manorial Reeve in Twelfth-Century England", in Ralph Evans (ed), *Lordship and Learning: Studies in Memory of Trevor Aston* (Boydell Press 2004) 125, 135.

[149] Sheriffs, likewise, were responsible both for presiding over the county court and for taking custody of lands that had escheated to the king, for instance. John Sabapathy, *Officers and Accountability in Medieval England 1170-1300* (OUP 2014) 84–85, 102.

after his interests.[150] The idea that the justice was someone who looked after the king's interest was also part of the official discourse. Henry II's Assize of Northampton of 1176 exhorts the king's justices to "apply themselves to the utmost to act in the advantage (*commodum*) of the lord king."[151] This language makes an appearance in *Bracton*. The treatise describes the oath that itinerant justices are to take before they go on eyre, which includes promises to "do right justice to the best of their ability to rich and poor alike, and that they will observe the assise according to the articles set out, to be expounded below, and that they will execute all that is right and just in matters pertaining to the crown of the lord king."[152] After the justice swears this oath, however, he is to be "instructed to promote, to the best of his ability, the advantage of the lord king."[153] The justices themselves, at times, showed signs that they understood their work in this way. During the eyre visitation of 1246 to 1249, the justices made some changes to procedure that seem to have been designed primarily to raise more revenue for the king.[154]

A justice who had spent a significant amount of time learning Roman and canon law in the schools would likely have understood this vision of the justice's role, but he would have had an alternative view at his disposal, in which law was a system and his role was to bring harmony to it. He was to do this through the production of particular types of texts. When he arrived in the courts, as a clerk, he would have found a community that was focused on the production of texts, although these texts were very different from the types of texts he had read and produced in the schools. Still, these justices seem to have drawn parallels between the textual production of the schools and the textual production of the courts. When they brought this textual view of the law to bear on their work in the king's courts, it affected the way they thought about that law and about themselves. They were not simply servants of the king. They were priests of the law.

---

[150] See the discussion in CAF Meekings (ed), *Crown Pleas of the Wiltshire Eyre, 1249* (Wiltshire Archaeological and Natural History Society 1961) 7; see also Turner, *English Judiciary* (n 92) 269.

[151] David C Douglas and George W Greenaway (eds), *English Historical Documents, Volume II: 1042-1189* (Eyre & Spottiswoode 1953) 412 (c.7). "Intendant tamen pro posse suo ad commodam domini regis faciendum." William Stubbs, *Select Charters and Other Illustrations of English Constitutional History* (9th edn, Clarendon Press 1913) vol 1, 180 (c 7).

[152] "Iurabit quilibet post alium quod rectam iustitiam facient pro posse suo in comitatibus in quibus fuerint itineraturi, tam pauperibus quam divitibus, et quod assisam servabunt secundum capitula subscripta et inferius exprimanda, et quod facient omnes rectitudines et iustitias spectantes ad coronam domini regis." *Bracton*, vol 2, 309.

[153] "Et post suum sacramentum dicatur eis expresse quod pro posse suo intendant ad faciendum commodum domini regis." Ibid.

[154] JR Maddicott, "Magna Carta and the Local Community" (1984) 102 Past & Present 25, 47.

# 3

# Thinking About Law

While they were learning Roman law, the authors of *Bracton* would have learned to think of themselves as part of a community that was defined by its texts. *Bracton* is, in a sense, a text that is meant to create a bridge between what these men had learned in their study of Roman law and what they encountered in the royal courts. The influence of the schools on the treatise is readily apparent: *Bracton* is a text on the practices of the royal courts, but it is written in the style of a civilian *summa*. *Bracton* invites its reader into a world where the work that the justices and clerks of the royal courts were doing as part of their daily routine was part of the world of the two laws. Descriptions of English writs are punctuated by hypothetical cases about Titius and Sempronius.[1] Citations to the *Digest* and *Codex* sit alongside citations to cases decided by English justices.

The aim of this chapter will be to explain the role Roman and canon law play in the treatise. The main focus of this chapter will be on Roman law. The authors of the treatise knew something of canon law and even had access to some of the most recent texts coming out of the continental schools.[2] They cite canon law for general principles just as they do Roman law.[3] That said, Roman law plays a much larger role in the treatise than canon law. The authors of *Bracton* had certainly learned something of both Roman and canon law, but they appear to have been Romanists first and canonists second.[4]

---

[1] Once Titius even appears in a writ, as a hypothetical chief justice of the eyre. *Bracton*, vol 3, 201.

[2] The authors of the treatise relied on works of Raymond de Peñafort written in the 1220s and the 1230s. HG Richardson, "Tancred, Raymond, and Bracton" (1944) 59 EHR 376; Naomi D Hurnard, *The King's Pardon for Homicide before A.D. 1307* (Clarendon Press 1969) 70 (hereafter Hurnard, *King's Pardon*).

[3] In their discussion of homicide, the *Bracton* authors try to work canon-law principles on state of mind into their text, and even attempt to reconcile them with Roman-law principles of criminal responsibility. Hurnard, *King's Pardon* (n 2) 71–74.

[4] In doing so, they may have simply been following the predominant teaching in England. In the *Brocardica Dunelmensia*, a product of the Vacarian school, Gratian's *Decretum* and papal decretals are cited together with provisions of the *Digest, Codex*, and *Institutes* to prove general legal principles, suggesting that the author of that text thought that the primary texts of canon law were sources of general legal principles just as the texts of Roman law were. The texts of canon law are cited far less often than texts of Roman law in the *Brocardica*, however, even when the matter at hand appears to be ecclesiastical in nature, suggesting that the teachers and students who used it were primarily concerned with Roman law. Hans van de Wouw, "*Brocardica Dunelmensia*" (1991) 108 Zeitschrift der Savigny-Stiftung für Rechtsgeschichte: Romanistische Abteilung 235, 236, 241–42. See above, p 78n.39, and below, pp 167–68.

*Priests of the Law.* Thomas J. McSweeney, Oxford University Press (2019). © Thomas J. McSweeney. DOI: 10.1093/oso/9780198845454.003.0004

*Bracton*'s Roman borrowings have long been recognized. Maitland thought that the author of *Bracton* was "a poor, an uninstructed Romanist."[5] Since Maitland wrote, however, scholars have developed a much higher opinion of the Roman material in the treatise. It appears that the authors had significant training in Roman law. Woodbine pointed to the tractate on acquiring dominion of things, and demonstrated that the author of this tractate was incorporating Roman law in very sophisticated ways. He had multiple sources in front of him; at one point he copies Azo into the tractate, finds a citation to the *Digest* in Azo, looks up the citation, and adds material from the *Digest* that is not found in Azo.[6] Brian Tierney has argued that we can often make better sense of *Bracton* when we assume that its author was a good Romanist rather than a bad one, and John Barton has demonstrated that in many cases, the treatise's critics knew their civilian sources less well than the authors of *Bracton* did.[7]

Civilian and canonist ideas and concepts permeate the treatise, and must have been part of it from the beginning. There was certainly a great deal of Roman law in the treatise by the time the post-1236 changes were made to it.[8] Azo of Bologna's *Summa Codicis* and *Summa Institutionum* supply the framework for much of the treatise. The works of other famous civilians and canonists can be found throughout. Texts on Romano-canonical procedure make frequent appearances. Although many of the citations and quotations to the primary sources of Roman and canon law—the *Digest, Codex, Institutes, Decretum,* and decretals—are quoted through the secondary sources, not all of them are. The authors of *Bracton* had direct access to these texts. In some cases, they may have worked from memory to reproduce citations and quotations, as civilians and canonists often did.

---

Alternatively, the authors of *Bracton* may have simply thought that Roman law was more relevant than canon law in the context of a treatise on secular law. As we saw above, at p 89, one author said that "nothing relating to the regulation of the *sacerdotium* is relevant to this treatise." *Bracton*, vol 2, 304. *Bracton* does not cover the workings of the ecclesiastical courts and it is logical that its authors would only turn to canon law when it provided general principles that applied in the secular courts, as well. Hurnard, *King's Pardon* (n 2) 71–74.

---

[5] Frederic William Maitland (ed), *Select Passages from the Works of Bracton and Azo* (SS vol 8, Bernard Quaritch 1895) xviii (hereafter Maitland (ed), *Bracton and Azo*).

[6] George E Woodbine, "The Roman Element in Bracton's De Adquirendo Rerum Dominio" (1922) 31 Yale Law Journal 827, 834.

[7] Brian Tierney, "Bracton on Government" (1963) 38 Speculum 295; JL Barton, "Bracton as a Civilian" (1967-68) 42 Tulane Law Review 555.

[8] In the middle of a passage of the tractate on acquiring dominion over things, one of the most Roman parts of the treatise, we find a passage from the Provisions of Merton inserted in the middle of some text taken from the *Glanvill* treatise, an obvious update added in an awkward way. Roman-law quotations surround this passage. *Bracton*, vol 2, 179.

Roman and canon law appear to have been central enough to the authors' project that they continued to add civilian and canonist material to the text as new scholarship became available to them. Many of the civilian and canonist texts used in the treatise would not have been available until the later stages of writing. The version of the *Summa Aurea* the authors of the treatise used was probably not available before 1239 at the earliest.[9] Tancred's *Ordo* would not have been available when Raleigh would most likely have been in the schools, as it was completed in 1216, nor would Raymond of Peñafort's *Summa de Casibus*, a text of the 1220s.[10] Even Azo's *Summae*, which must have been part of the treatise from the earliest phases of writing, were probably not available when Raleigh would most likely have been in the schools; they were likely completed between 1208 and 1210, but are not known to have circulated before 1211.[11] Either Raleigh was keeping abreast of the latest literature or Bratton brought much of this Roman learning with him.

So significant are the civilian borrowings that Sir Henry Maine, as we saw in the introduction, claimed that *Bracton* "put off on his countrymen as a compendium of pure English law a treatise of which the entire form and a third of the contents were directly borrowed from the Corpus Iuris."[12] Maitland, no great admirer of Maine, said that this was a "stupendous exaggeration" and that "The amount of matter that Bracton directly borrowed from the Corpus Iuris is not one-third, is not a thirtieth part of the book."[13] Maitland admitted that the amount of matter borrowed from Azo of Bologna's two *summae* is larger, but pointed out that it is still a small fraction of the treatise. It is not clear, however, that the Roman- and canon-law influence on the treatise should be measured in terms of the proportion of the treatise that is directly borrowed from the texts of the two laws, because the two laws play an important role in framing much of the treatise.

But why did the authors of *Bracton* make the two laws so central to their project on the laws and customs of England? Maitland thought that the authors of the treatise used the two laws primarily as gap-fillers, to provide law in areas where the royal courts had none.[14] Other scholars have argued that

---

[9] There are references to events of the late 1230s in the *Summa*, the latest of which dates to 1239. The version used in the treatise is probably a post-1239 version of the *Summa* that contains an additional prefatory letter. HG Richardson, "Azo, Drogheda, and Bracton" (1944) 59 EHR 22, 39.

[10] Nicholas Vincent, "Henry of Bratton (*alias* Bracton)" in Mark Hill and RH Helmholz (eds), *Great Christian Jurists in English History* (CUP 2017) 33.

[11] André Gouron, "Introduction" in Azo, *Summae*, xii–xiii; Jane E Sayers, "William of Drogheda and the English Canonists" in Peter Linehan (ed), *Proceedings of the Seventh International Congress of Medieval Canon Law* (Biblioteca Apostolica Vaticana 1988) 208.

[12] Henry Sumner Maine, *Ancient Law* (16th edn, John Murray 1897) 82.

[13] Maitland (ed), *Bracton and Azo* (n 5) xiv.

[14] Ibid, xx; *Bracton*, vol 1, xxxii.

the authors of *Bracton* were reformers who wanted to change the rules of English law to be more in line with the written reason of Roman law.[15] These explanations do have something to commend them. Occasionally the authors do borrow directly from texts of Roman law to fill gaps in English law. Naomi Hurnard demonstrated that the authors of *Bracton* attempted to flesh out the English law of homicide by turning to texts of Roman and canon law, for instance.[16] Occasionally the application of a Roman-law doctrine will lead the authors to state a rule of law or a distinction that does not appear to have been in contemporary use in the royal courts.[17] These are not the primary uses to which Raleigh and Bratton put Roman law, however. The *Bracton* authors were not on a mission to change the way English law works. Their relationship to Roman law was more interesting and more subtle. As Plucknett pointed out, the treatise would not have been of much use to the practitioner if its authors had Romanized too much of their procedure.[18] When the practices of the courts conflicted with what they knew of Roman and canon law, the authors of *Bracton* generally did not distort the practices of the courts. They seem to have taken the work they were doing in the royal courts as a given. When they did run into situations where the practices of the courts flatly contradicted the rules laid out in the *Institutes, Digest, Codex, Decretum*, or decretals, they saw that as a problem. One possible response would have been to say that the English practice was wrong and should be reformed to bring it into line with the rule of the two laws. The authors of the treatise did not take this tack, however. Instead, they sought to reconcile the English practice with the rules they learned in their study of Roman law, to demonstrate that the rules were actually in accord with each other. *Bracton* is thus an attempt to reconcile the work the justices were already doing in the courts of the English king with the law they

[15] Paul Hyams, *King, Lords, and Peasants in Medieval England: The Common Law of Villeinage in the Twelfth and Thirteenth Centuries* (Clarendon Press 1980) 84.

[16] Hurnard, *King's Pardon* (n 2) 68–75. Hurnard points out that the authors of *Bracton* were not very successful in this instance, as Roman and canon law had different standards and they tried to incorporate both. The short sections at the beginning of the treatise on the law of persons and of things could also be described as gap-fillers. Likewise, the discussion of "imaginary gifts" that will be discussed in Chapter 7 could be understood as an attempt to apply a rule of Roman law where the English courts had not yet established any law one way or the other.

[17] *Bracton* makes a distinction between being "in seisin" and being "seised," a distinction derived from the *Digest*. There is no evidence that this distinction was used in the English courts. *Bracton*, vol 3, 124–25; D.41.2.10.1; John Hudson, *Oxford History of the Laws of England, Volume II, 871-1216* (OUP 2012) 672 (hereafter Hudson, *Oxford History*).

[18] TFT Plucknett, *Early English Legal Literature* (CUP 1958) 59. It is important to note that Plucknett's practitioners were the serjeants and attorneys of the royal courts, for whom he thought the treatise was written. As I explain above at p 59, I doubt that they were the intended audience, but the point still holds. The treatise would not have been of much use to a justice or clerk if it did not correctly state the law of the royal courts.

had learned in the universities, to show that one was a constituent part of the other, despite the apparent conflicts between the two. The authors often had to resort to complex circumlocutions to make the two fit, and even then the results were often disastrous. Roman law and English law were not all that closely related; if they were cousins, they certainly weren't first cousins. The fact that *Bracton's* authors persevered, despite the difficulty, only demonstrates their commitment to the project. The Roman law in the treatise was not intended as a reform program for English law, but neither was it mere window-dressing. It was central to the authors' project. Their goal was not to reform English law along the lines of the two laws, but rather to show that English law *already was* in accord with the two laws.

## Different Categories of Law

Raleigh and Bratton faced a fundamental problem when trying to demonstrate the harmony of the practices of their courts with the rules of Roman law: many of the rules followed by the royal courts actually conflicted with the rules of Roman law. The authors used various methods to demonstrate that the conflicts were more imagined than real. A reader opening the *Bracton* treatise will first find a few sentences about how both arms and laws are necessary to the king. This introduction, lifted from the *Glanvill* treatise, would also have been familiar to the authors of *Bracton* from another source: it is an obvious reworking of the introductory words of Justinian's *Institutes*.[19] *Glanvill's* source would have been difficult for them to miss, and in this case we have direct evidence that the author of this passage in *Bracton* knew whence it came. He went to Azo's *summa* on the *Institutes* and drew some additional material from Azo's exposition of this passage of the *Institutes*.[20] The author also modifies the text of the *Institutes* for the English context. Where the *Institutes* talk about the "Roman *princeps*" and "imperial majesty," the *Bracton* authors inserted "the king who wishes to rule rightly."[21] *Bracton* signals right away that this treatise will be placing the law of the English king on par with the law of the Roman emperor.

It goes on to say, "Though in almost all regions use is made of the *leges* and written law (*ius scriptum*), England alone uses unwritten law (*ius non scriptum*)

---

[19] *Glanvill*, 1–2; Inst.pr.; *Justinian's Institutes*, 33.
[20] *Bracton*, vol 2, 19.
[21] *Bracton*, vol 2, 19; Inst.pr.; *Justinian's Institutes*, 33. *Bracton's* formulation differs slightly from that found in *Glanvill*. *Glanvill*, 1.

and custom within its boundaries. There law derives from nothing written [but] from what usage has approved."[22] This language, which appears to be original to *Bracton*, complicates the relationship between English law and Roman law hinted at in the first few sentences. The term *lex*, the singular of *leges*, is used throughout the treatise, sometimes in a general sense, to mean either law in general (usually indicated by the Latin term *ius*, not *lex*, in the texts of the two laws) or a specific provision of law (the word's usual meaning in the texts of the two laws). Often, however, it is used in a much more specific sense. The authors of *Bracton* sometimes use the word *lex* to refer to a particular provision of *Roman* law.[23] Indeed, later in the treatise, one of the authors tells us that, if a felon gives land to someone after he commits the felony, the gift is valid until the felon is condemned, and that in this case, "*lex* agrees with English custom," and then immediately gives a citation to the relevant *lex*, an excerpt from the writings of the jurist Marcian preserved in the *Digest*, "where it is said that gifts made after the commission of a capital crime are valid unless condemnation follows."[24] *Ius scriptum*, or written law, is a term that the author of this passage would have encountered in many of the texts he read in the schools. It was often used to refer to the authoritative texts of Roman and canon law. According to the *Institutes*, *ius scriptum* includes *leges*, pronouncements of the emperor, and the *responsa* of jurists. In other words, it includes those things that are contained in the *Codex* and the *Digest*.[25] When he says that almost all other regions use *leges* and *ius scriptum*, the author of the *introductio* seems to be imagining a written culture of law, modeled on the culture of Roman law, that exists everywhere in Latin Christendom except in England. Of course, the claim that all other regions used *leges* and *ius scriptum* in a way that is different from the way they were used in England was not a terribly plausible one. If the author of this passage refers

---

[22] "Cum autem fere in omnibus regionibus utatur legibus et iure scripto, sola Anglia usa est in suis finibus iure non scripto et consuetudine." *Bracton*, vol 2, 19.

[23] The word *lex* could be used to refer to legislation in Roman and canon law. Two sources with which the *Bracton* authors were undoubtedly familiar, Gratian's *Decretum* and Isidore of Seville's popular *Etymologiae*, a universal encyclopedia, contain the sentence "Lex est constitutio scripta" ("*lex* is a written constitution."). *Constitutio* was used in texts of Roman and canon law to refer to the decrees of Roman emperors and of popes. In his third distinction, Gratian explains that ecclesiastical constitutions are called canons, which include, among other things, papal decrees. D.3 p.1; D.3 p.2; *Corpus Iuris Canonici*, vol 1, 4, 5; Gratian, *The Treatise on Laws with the Ordinary Gloss* (Augustine Thompson and Katherine Christensen trs, Catholic University of America Press 1993) 10, 11 (hereafter Gratian, *Treatise on Laws*). Individual provisions of the Digest, Codex, and Institutes were referred to as *leges* and were cited as such. The "l." in the citation format stood for "*lex*." The *Bracton* authors were aware of this usage and referred to provisions of those texts as *leges*. *Bracton*, vol 2, 53.

[24] "Et quod numquam ante condemnationem, vel donec felonia convincatur, possit terra felonis esse eschæta domini capitalis, convenit lex cum consuetudine Anglicana, ff. de donationibus l. post contractum [a citation to D. 39.5.15], ubi dicitur quod post contractum capitale crimen donationes factæ valent nisi condemnatio subsecuta sit." *Bracton*, vol 2, 101.

[25] *Inst*.1.2.3; *Justinian's Institutes*, 38.

to legislation, English kings used legislation no less than their counterparts in France or Spain, although perhaps less than the Italian communes, some of which had their own written laws.[26] If he refers to Roman and canon law specifically, again, the courts of the King of France were no more or less heavily influenced by the legal learning of the schools than those in England.[27] But the authors of *Bracton* seem to have perceived England as an outlier.

There is an important tension in the sentence "Though in almost all regions use is made of the *leges* and *ius scriptum*, England alone uses *ius non scriptum* and custom."[28] This sentence clearly distinguishes what is done in England from the *ius scriptum* of Roman and canon law. At the same time, it places English law firmly within the traditions of Roman and canon law. England may eschew *leges* and written law in favor of unwritten laws and customs, but custom itself is a recognized category within Roman and canon law. When the author of the *introductio* wrote this sentence, he may have had the first few distinctions of Gratian's *Decretum*, perhaps remembered from lectures heard in the schools, in mind. He may have even been thinking back to a text that he could easily have encountered in his grammar school days, Isidore of Seville's *Etymologiae*. Both discuss custom (*consuetudo*). Indeed, Gratian, in a passage that would have appeared on the first folio of many manuscripts of the *Decretum*, reproduced Isidore's definition of custom. Isidore and Gratian associate custom with unwritten law. Isidore says that "Custom is a sort of law established by usages and recognized as *lex* when *lex* is lacking."[29] Gratian tells us in his commentary on Isidore that although "custom is partly reduced to writing," the term custom is also used as a general term for "that which is not reduced to writing."[30] Gratian tells us later that "when custom is shown to

[26] Manlio Bellomo, *The Common Legal Past of Europe, 1000-1800* (Lydia G Cochrane tr, Catholic University of America Press 1995) 84–85.
[27] The Parlement of Paris did adopt a version of Romano-canonical procedure over the course of the thirteenth century. Peter Stein, *Roman Law in European History* (CUP 1999) 59. But the kings of France occasionally reaffirmed that, at least in the Northern part of the kingdom, the *pays de droit coutumier*, Roman law was not a formal source of law. Paul Ourliac and Jean-Louis Gazzaniga, *Histoire du Droit Privé Français de l'an Mil au Code Civil* (Albin Michel 1985) 78–79. In 1278, King Philip III issued an *ordonnance* forbidding citation to Roman law in the parlement if the case before the court came from the *pays de droit coutumier*. RC Van Caenegem, *An Historical Introduction to Private Law* (DEL Johnston tr, CUP 1992) 81. Although Roman and canon law did exert influence over the customary law of France as it was written down, there is nothing to suggest that the Northern French used the *leges* and the *ius scriptum* more than the English did.
[28] *Bracton*, vol 2, 23.
[29] Gratian, *Treatise on Laws* (n 23) 5. "Consuetudo autem est ius quoddam moribus institutum, quod pro lege suscipitur, cum deficit lex." D. 1 c.5; *Corpus Iuris Canonici* vol 1, 1. I have modified the translation.
[30] Gratian, *Treatise on Laws* (n 23) 6. "[Q]uod consuetudo partim est redacta in scriptis, partim moribus tantum utentium est reservata. Quae in scriptis redacta est, constitutio sive ius vocatur; quae vero in scriptis redacta non est, generali nomine, consuetudo videlicet, appellatur." D. 1 dict. post c.5; *Corpus Iuris Canonici*, vol 1, 1.

contradict neither the sacred canons nor human laws (*legibus*), it should be observed undisturbed."[31] Custom is thus a part of the world of the two laws. It fits
into a world of *ius scriptum* and *leges*, as a source of law that can act, and that
can even be regarded as *lex*, when it is not contrary to them.

The author of *Bracton's introductio* presents custom as part of the framework
of Roman and canon law at the same time that he emphasizes its difference
from it. Custom is *lex* and is not *lex* at the same time. Returning to *Glanvill*
to borrow a line, he says "Nevertheless, it will not be absurd to call English
laws 'laws' (*leges Anglicanas . . . leges appellare*) though they are unwritten, since
whatever has been rightly decided and approved with the counsel and consent
of the magnates and the general agreement of the *res publica*, the authority of
the king or prince having first been added thereto, has the force of law."[32] In
this passage, England's unwritten law and custom become *leges Anglicanas*, as
the author informs us that, despite the fact that they are founded upon custom
and *ius non scriptum*, they can still be considered *leges*, a term usually used for
written law.[33] The author of this passage first fits English law into the two laws'
framework by assimilating it to the civilian and canonist concept of custom,
and then makes the fit even tighter, by transforming English custom into *lex*.

Custom was not necessarily the firmest ground upon which to base the law
of the royal courts. There had been debates between canonists and royal par-
tisans in England over the role of custom in the decades before Raleigh and
Bratton had entered the courts, and the canonists made strong arguments
against its normativity, at least in the face of a contrary provision of canon law.
In 1164, Henry II issued the Constitutions of Clarendon, a text which pur-
ported to be a record of the "customs and liberties and dignities of [Henry's] ancestors . . . which ought to be observed and held in our kingdom" regarding the

---

[31] Gratian, *Treatise on Laws* (n 23) 38. "Cum vero nec sacris canonibus, nec humanis legibus
consuetudo obviare monstratur, inconcussa servanda est." D. 11 c. 4 p. 2; *Corpus Iuris Canonici*, vol
1, 23. For a discussion of custom and writing, see chapter two of Ada Maria Kuskowski, *Law in the
Vernacular: Composing Customary Law in Thirteenth Century France* (forthcoming).

[32] "Sed non erit absurdum leges Anglicanas licet non scriptas leges appellare, cum legis vigorem
habeat quidquid de consilio et consensu magnatum et rei publicæ communi sponsione, auctoritate
regis sive principis præcedente, iuste fuerit definitum et approbatum." *Bracton*, vol 2, 19. Maitland
noted that this passage actually looks like it may have been influenced by the definition of a *lex* found
in book one of the *Digest*: "a *lex* is a communal directive, a resolution of wise men, a forcible reaction to
offenses committed either voluntarily or in ignorance, a communal covenant of the *res publica*." There
are some important similarities. The phrase "general agreement of the *res publica*" (*rei publicæ communi
sponsione*) in *Bracton* is almost identical to a phrase used in the *Digest* (*communis rei publicae sponsio*).
*Bracton's* mention of the "counsel and consent of the magnates" (*consilio et consensu magnatum*) may be
an echo of the *Digest's* mention the "agreement of wise men" (*virorum prudentium consultum*). Maitland
(ed), *Bracton and Azo* (n 5) 13; D.1.3.1; *Digest of Justinian*, 11.

[33] This fits fairly well with Isidore's statement noted above, that custom is "recognized as *lex* when
*lex* is lacking." D. 1 c.5, 1; *Corpus Iuris Canonici*, vol 1, 1; Gratian, *Treatise on Laws* (n 23) 5 (translation
modified by author).

relationship between the crown and the English Church.[34] The canonists who supported the Church were fond of quoting Pope Gregory the Great's maxim that "The Lord is never found to have said 'I am custom.' But he did say 'I am the truth.'"[35] The canonists argued that English custom should give way to the truth and reason of enacted canon law. The *Codex* similarly states that "the authority of custom and long usage is not slight, but only avails insofar as it does not overcome reason or *lex*."[36] Thus, if the *Bracton* authors distinguish English law from Roman and canon law on the ground that English law is custom and Roman and canon law are *lex*, then English law should, theoretically, give way to Roman and canon law when the two contradict each other.

This was not the only way one could think about the validity of custom, however. Vacarius and his students appear to have accorded a great deal of authority to custom. An English lecturer on the *Institutes*, one of the *pauperistae*, held that a custom that was in accord with reason could fully abrogate a contradictory *lex*, "For the force of *lex*, like the force of custom, is the will of the people."[37] Legislation and customary law have the same force, since the emperor's authority to legislate was given to him by the people, the same people who make custom through their usages. The *Codex* says that custom cannot "overcome reason or *lex*," but, according to the lecturer, "overcome" is not synonymous with "abrogate."[38] A custom contrary to reason will still apply in the cases where it is used, but will not be applied to similar cases by analogy.[39] A custom that is in accord with reason, on the other hand, can be applied by analogy to other, similar cases, just like a *lex*. The author of the introduction to *Bracton* may, therefore, have been echoing a mainstream opinion about custom within civilian circles in England when he wrote that English law was based on unwritten law and custom, contrasting English custom with Roman *lex* while, at the same time, presenting the two as being of similar authority.

---

[34] "[C]onsuetudinum et libertatum et dignitatum antecessorum suorum . . . quae observari et teneri debent in regno." William Stubbs, *Select Charters and Other Illustrations of English Constitutional History* (9th edn, Clarendon Press 1913) 163.

[35] This version of Pope Gregory's quotation comes from the writings of William FitzStephen, who was a legal adviser to Thomas Becket. Beryl Smalley, *The Becket Conflict and the Schools: A Study of Intellectuals in Politics in the Twelfth Century* (Basil Blackwell 1973) 128. This letter, from Gregory to the bishop of Aversa, appears in the *Decretum*, as well. D. 8 c.5 p. 26; *Corpus Iuris Canonici*, vol 1, 14; Gratian, *Treatise on Laws* (n 23) 26.

[36] "Consuetudinis ususque longaevi non vilis auctoritas est, verum non usque adeo sui valitura momento, ut aut rationem vincat aut legem." C.8.52.2; Francis De Zulueta and Peter Stein (eds), *The Teaching of Roman Law in England around 1200* (Selden Society 1990) 11 (hereafter De Zulueta and Stein (eds), *Teaching of Roman Law*).

[37] "Vigor enim legis sicut et consuetudinis est voluntas populi." De Zulueta and Stein (eds), *Teaching of Roman Law* (n 36) 12.

[38] Ibid.

[39] Ibid, lx, 12.

The authors of *Bracton* found other ways of explaining apparent contradictions while staying within the framework provided by Roman and canon law. In the tractate on acquiring dominion over things, one of the *Bracton* authors follows Azo in explaining that "wild beasts, birds and fish, that is, all the creatures born on the earth, in the sea, or in the heavens" are "owned by no one" and therefore may be reduced to ownership by the first person to take possession, "no matter where they may be taken."[40] This was not true in England, as anyone living in that kingdom in the thirteenth century would have been aware. One of the most contentious political issues of the thirteenth century was the royal forest, those parts of the realm in which the king had special hunting rights over particular types of animals and a special set of courts designed to protect his hunting rights.[41] For a hunter to slay a deer in the royal forest, which may have covered as much as a third of England when this part of the treatise was written, was an offense against the forest law. The Charter of the Forest, issued along with Magna Carta in 1217 and, in revised form, in 1225, guaranteed that English people would no longer suffer the dire consequences that poaching carried in the early thirteenth century—the loss of eyes and testicles along with a fine of one ox—but severe fines still awaited those who committed "crimes against the venison."[42]

The *Bracton* authors did qualify the *Institutes'* insistence that wild beasts belonged to no one and were ripe for the taking by including Azo's language, which appears throughout his commentary on acquiring dominion, that this is true, "unless custom rules to the contrary."[43] Their Roman-law source itself includes an exception for local custom. The *Bracton* authors' primary solution to this problem, however, was to assign the English rule and the *Institutes'* rule to different kinds of law. The *Institutes* begin with a series of distinctions between natural law (*ius naturale*), the law of nations (*ius gentium*), and civil law

---

[40] *Bracton*, vol 2, 42.

[41] The king reserved exclusive hunting rights over deer and boar in the royal forest, although he could license others to hunt in his forest and granted licenses to others to establish parks and chases where they could hunt deer. The king regulated the taking of hares and other small animals even outside of the royal forest, granting rights of warren to some of his subjects, which allowed them to hunt such animals. Charles R Young, *The Royal Forests of Medieval England* (University of Pennsylvania Press 1979) 45–46. The taking of birds and fish required no special grant, so the rules regarding those animals seem to have been roughly in line with the rules of Roman law. Major disputes over the extent and administration of the royal forest arose during Henry III's minority. See DA Carpenter, *The Minority of Henry III* (University of California Press 1990) 89–91, 168–69, 276–78.

[42] JC Holt, *Magna Carta* (3rd edn, CUP 2015) 431 (1225 version, c 10); "1217 Carta de Foresta (Charter of the Forest)," in Daniel Barstow Magraw, Andrea Martinez, and Roy E Brownell (eds), *Magna Carta and the Rule of Law* (American Bar Association, 2014) 422.

[43] The *Bracton* authors extend this to "unless custom *or privilege* rules to the contrary." *Bracton*, vol 2, 42.

(*ius civile*).[44] The *Institutes'* position on natural law is difficult to discern. In places, the text implies that a provision of civil law or the law of nations that is in conflict with natural law is null.[45] In others, the text implies that natural law is simply a descriptive label. It is the law that applies in the state of nature, and can be modified by the civil law or the law of nations.[46] Civilians and canonists did have ways of reconciling these positions. The *glossa ordinaria* to the *Decretum*, for instance, tells us that the word "nature" can be used in different ways, some of which imply that the law of nature is a firm command that cannot be abrogated and others of which imply that it may be abrogated by civil law.[47] The *Bracton* authors, like Azo, treat the provisions on wild beasts as rules of the law of nature that can be abrogated by some other form of law. Later in *Bracton's* tractate on acquiring dominion, the author explains that the king has certain "privileges by virtue of the law of nations" which means that "things which by the natural law ought to be the property of the finder, as treasure trove, wreck, great fish, sturgeon, waif, things said to belong to no one" actually belong to the king in England.[48] He later includes wild beasts in this list.[49] Indeed, at the beginning of the tractate on acquiring dominion over things, the author begins by saying that his subject is "things that are owned by no one," but then qualifies this by adding, "and now belong to the king by civil law."[50] Where the rules laid out in the *Institutes* are the rules of the natural law, the rules followed in England are the rules of either the law of nations or the civil

[44] Inst.1.1–1.2.

[45] Inst. 1.2.11 says that "The law of nature, which is observed uniformly by all peoples, is sanctioned by divine providence and lasts for ever, strong and unchangeable." *Justinian's Institutes*, 39. Gratian likewise says that "whatever has been either received in usages or set down in writing is to be held null and void if it is contrary to natural law." D.8 dict. ante c.2; *Corpus Iuris Canonici*, vol 1, 13; Gratian, *Treatise on Laws* (n 23) 25.

[46] Inst.1.2.2 says that "People were captured and made slaves, contrary to the law of nature. By the law of nature all men were initially born free." *Justinian's Institutes*, 38. Inst. 1.3.2 uses even stronger language indicating that slavery constitutes an abrogation of the natural law: "Slavery on the other hand is an institution of the *ius gentium*; it makes a man the property of another, contrary to the law of nature." *Justinian's Institutes*, 39. The *Decretum* contains similar texts, such as Gratian's explanation that "by natural law all things are common to all people," but "in contrast, by customary and enacted law, one thing is called 'mine' and something else 'another's.'" D.8 dict. ante c.1; *Corpus Iuris Canonici*, vol 1, 12; Gratian, *Treatise on Laws* (n 23) 24.

[47] Gratian, *Treatise on Laws* (n 23) 6.

[48] "Habet etiam præ ceteris omnibus in regno suo privilegia de iure gentium propria, quæ de iure naturali esse deberent inventoris sicut thesaurus, wreccum, grassus piscis, sturgio, wayvium, quæ in nullius bonis esse dicuntur." *Bracton*, vol 2, 166–67. See also vol 2, 293.

[49] *Bracton*, vol 2, 167.

[50] *Bracton*, vol 2, 42. The words "and now belong to the king by civil law" were identified by Thorne as an interpolation, and they seem to have been garbled by the scribes. Some manuscripts read "and now belong to the king by the civil law, and are not common as before." Others read "and do not now belong to the king by the civil law, and are in common as before." *Bracton*, vol 2, 42, fns 39, 40. Either reading is possible. All that matters for our purposes is that this shows us that the authors of the treatise thought that the civil law modified the natural law on the issue of wild beasts.

law, both recognized categories of law in the discourse of Roman law, and both of which are given exposition in the *Institutes*. English practice can therefore fit neatly into the *Institutes'* framework despite the fact that it plainly contradicts the actual doctrines of the *Institutes*.

## Possession That Has Nothing of Possession

Some of the best illustrations of the role that Roman law plays in *Bracton* appear in the context of the law related to the holding of land.[51] Much of *Bracton* is concerned with what the Romans would have called the law of things, and what today we would call property law. Most of the writs of the early common law were concerned with rights in land or its appurtenances. Throughout the treatise, we see its authors going to extraordinary lengths to devise a way of discussing these writs using the Roman language of property. This was more difficult to do than it might initially seem. The authors of *Bracton* made desperate attempts to describe the English courts' procedures concerning land using both the terms and the methods of Roman-law analysis. The result was disastrous. Internal contradictions accumulated in the text as the authors tried to transform the multi-tiered hierarchies of English writs into Roman binaries and to explain English procedures in terms of a Roman substantive law driven by abstract rights. The authors appear to have retained their commitment to Roman law despite the fact that it was probably obvious even to them that they had not fully succeeded in creating a single scheme for thinking about the rights in property protected by the English writs.

Roman jurists thought primarily in terms of abstract interests. Justinian's *Institutes* states that all law is divided into the law of persons, things, and actions.[52] The law of things (*res* in both the singular and plural) encompasses every kind of right a person might have, including property rights, but also including rights arising from obligations created by contract and by delict, the field we would call tort law today.[53] These "things" take up most of the text of the *Institutes*, encompassing all of books two and three, as well as the first few chapters of book four. For the remainder of book four, the final book of

---

[51] This subsection and the three following it are derived from Thomas J McSweeney, "Property before Property: Romanizing the English Law of Land" (2012) 60 Buffalo Law Review 1139.

[52] Inst.1.2.12.

[53] In book II, where the section on things begins, the *Institutes* first discusses corporeal things and then moves on to incorporeal things, which "consist of legal rights—inheritance, usufruct, obligations however contracted." Inst.2.2.2.; *Justinian's Institutes*, 61; Robin Evans-Jones and Geoffrey MacCormack, "Obligations" in Ernest Metzger (ed), *A Companion to Justinian's Institutes* (Cornell University Press 1998) 127.

the *Institutes*, the text turns to the law of actions.[54] The student reading the *Institutes*, or hearing lectures on them in an English schoolroom, would have learned about abstract interests, the *res*, before he learned about the actions used to enforce those abstract interests. This is not an accident of organization. Roman jurists thought of things as being conceptually prior to actions. The *Institutes* describes an action as "nothing but the right to go to court to get one's due."[55] That "due" is defined by the law of things. The English lecturer on the *Institutes* devoted a good deal of space in his lectures to the definition of actions, noting that the language in the *Institutes* suggests that they "arise from obligations."[56] The English lecturer also notes, however, that the *Institutes* gives too narrow a definition of actions, because they arise from more than just obligations; property rights also give rise to actions, and they are not properly classified as obligations.[57] In other words, anything that constitutes a "thing" can give rise to an action. The *Bracton* authors took this relationship between the action and the underlying right to heart when they drew upon Azo in the introduction to the section on actions. They borrow from Azo when they tell us that "it is clear that actions are born of obligations, just as a daughter is born from a mother."[58]

To a justice trained in Roman law, an action is simply what enforces an abstract right. By the time *Bracton* was written, the English were already beginning to think in this way. In the Northern French world, it was common in the twelfth and thirteenth centuries to refer to an abstract "right" (*ius, droit*) in one's land. The grand assize, a process by which a party elected to put the question of right to a jury, asked who had the "greater right" in a piece of land.[59] The English had other ways of talking about land that were more concrete than abstract, however. Although twelfth- and early thirteenth-century English landholders did refer to holding a fee (*feodum* in Latin), by which they were referring to a heritable interest in land, feoffors were more likely to state in their

---

[54] Inst.4.6.

[55] "Actio autem nihil aliud est, quam ius persequendi iudicio quod sibi debetur." Inst.4.6.pr.; *Justinian's Institutes*, 129.

[56] De Zulueta and Stein (eds), *Teaching of Roman Law* (n 36) 110.

[57] Ibid, 111. The *Institutes* later recognize this, in book four, when they state that actions may arise from disputes about things. Inst.4.6.1; *Justinian's Institutes*, 129.

[58] "Et sciendum quod ex obligationibus præcedentibus tamquam a matre filia." *Bracton*, vol 2, 283.

[59] In the twelfth-century French epic *Raoul de Cambrai*, the title character is told by his mother that his family's hereditary patch of land, which the emperor refuses to give to Raoul, is "your right (*ton droit*)." *Droit* appears several other times in reference to the dispute over this land. William Kibler (ed), *Raoul De Cambrai* (Sarah Kay tr, Livre de Poche 1996) 74, 78, 92. *Dreit* was the more common form of the word in the Anglo-Norman dialect of French. For the grand assize, see Elsa De Haas and GDG Hall (eds), *Early Registers of Writs* (SS vol 87, Bernard Quaritch 1970) 7 (no 17) (hereafter De Haas and Hall (eds), *Early Registers*).

charters that they were granting land "in fee" and the assize of mort d'ancestor referred to holding "as of fee."[60] These latter two usages imply that the holder of the land does not hold an abstract interest in the land called a fee, but rather he holds the *land* in a fee-like way (meaning that he holds it in a such a way that it can be passed to his heirs). The authors of *Bracton* usually, but not always, preferred to think in terms of abstract interests, however, and to find Roman equivalents for English terms.

Already in the *Glanvill* treatise, written by someone working in the royal courts at the very end of Henry II's reign, the Anglo-French concepts of right and seisin are treated as abstract interests equivalent to the Roman interests called *proprietas* (ownership) and *possessio* (possession). The author of *Glanvill* simply maintained the Roman binary, treating the concepts of right and seisin as interests in land equivalent to the Roman interests. Early in the treatise, he distinguishes between pleas that "concern solely claims to the ownership in the disputed subject-matter" and pleas where "the claim is based on possession."[61] On the possession side of the line, he places all those pleas "which are determined by recognitions," meaning primarily those assizes that historians of English law know so well—novel disseisin, mort d'ancestor, utrum, and darrein presentment—and tells us that these "will be discussed later in their proper place."[62] When he gets to the proper place, book XIII on recognitions, he does not use the Roman division between possession and ownership that he used in the introduction to his work. Instead, he says that he has dealt with "pleas about right" (*placita de recto*) and is now turning to recognitions, which are concerned "with seisins only."[63] The Romanist language of possession and ownership that the author began with has morphed into the language of seisin and right.[64] The author of *Glanvill* thus transforms the Roman binary into an English binary. The *Bracton* authors experiment with this equation of seisin with possession and right with ownership. In a discussion of succession to land, one of the authors seems to follow *Glanvill*, saying "if seisin or possession sometimes turns aside so that it does not follow the pure right, in the end it will

---

[60] De Haas and Hall (eds), *Early Registers* (n 59) 3 (no 8).

[61] *Glanvill*, 4.

[62] Ibid.

[63] Ibid, 148. I have modified Hall's translation. Hall translates this phrase as "with seisin only," but the Latin word he translates as "seisin," *saisinis*, is plural. I would like to thank John Hudson for pointing this out to me.

[64] This is not the only place in the treatise that the author makes it clear that he equates the Roman *possessio* with the Anglo-French *seisin* and the Roman *ownership* with the Anglo-French *right*. He also speaks of pleas brought "on the question of ownership by means of a writ of right (*breve de recto*)" which he parallels later with the phrase "except on the question of right (*recto*) by . . . a writ of right." Ibid, 6, 10.

revert to the ownership."[65] The author of this passage appears to equate seisin with possession and right with ownership.

At some point, however, the authors of *Bracton* appear to have noticed that the seisin-possession and right-ownership binary was of only limited use in explaining the ways English writs operated. The binary breaks down, for instance, when, at the beginning of the tractate on writs of entry, one of authors says

> We have spoken above of the *causa* of possession, which is determined by assises and recognitions. Now we must speak of the *causa* of ownership (*proprietas*), which is determined by a jury on the testimony and proof of those who can prove of their own sight and hearing, where, that is, one claims seisin, his own or that of some ancestor, of a thing which he willingly demised to another for a term of years or a term of life, and which at the conclusion of the term ought to return to him . . .[66]

The author of this passage echoes *Glanvill* in dividing writs into writs of ownership and possession, placing the writs of entry on the ownership side of the line. They are writs based not on right, however, but on seisin. Seisin, therefore, is not equivalent to possession in this passage. The criteria for deciding whether a writ is a writ of seisin are different from those for deciding whether it is a writ of possession, and a writ can be one and not the other.

Even more troubling for the authors was the fact that Roman law used a two-tiered hierarchy of procedures to recover land. There were actions based on ownership and interdicts based on possession. Possession was a lesser interest than ownership. Indeed, Roman jurists treated possession as if it was not an interest at all; while ownership was an abstract right, possession was a mere fact.[67] A less rigorous procedure was, therefore, warranted for the recovery of

---

[65] "Et si seisina sive possessio aliquando exorbitet ita quod ius merum non sequitur, in fine tamen ad proprietatem revertetur si sit heres qui petat." *Bracton*, vol 2, 184.

[66] "Dictum est supra de causa possessionis quæ per assisas et recognitiones terminatur. Nunc autem dicendum de causa proprietatis quæ terminatur per iuratam ex testimonio et probatione eorum qui probare possunt de visu suo proprio et audito, ubi quis scilicet seisinam suam propriam petierit vel alicuius antecessoris sui quam de voluntate sua de aliqua re ad terminum annorum vel ad terminum vitæ aliis dimisit, et quæ post terminum præteritum ad ipsum reverti debeat . . ." *Bracton*, vol 4, 21.

[67] Although possession was treated as a mere fact, it could become fairly abstract in certain cases. To acquire possession of land, one had to do so both *animo*, by mind, and *corpore*, by body. This meant that one had to physically take possession of the land—a difficult concept to get one's head around, as land cannot be handed over or held in one's hands as moveables can be—and also have the intent to take possession. Once possession was acquired *animo et corpore*, it could only be lost *animo et corpore*. That means that a person who is not physically in control of the land may be considered a possessor. In a fragment contained in the *Digest*, the jurist Ulpian tells us that "if someone had gone away from his field or his house leaving none of his household there, and on his return either was prevented from entering the premises themselves or was detained in mid-journey by someone who took possession himself, he is held to have been forcibly ejected.

possession. If a person was ejected from land of which he was in possession, he could bring an interdict *unde vi* to recover his possession. Interdicts were simple procedures because they dealt solely with facts, and with fairly simple facts, not with the determination of abstract rights.[68] All the plaintiff had to show to recover possession by the interdict *unde vi* was that he had been in possession of the land and that the defendant had ejected him by force.[69] The court hearing a case brought under the interdict *unde vi* did not need to delve into the more abstract and mysterious question of who owned the land in question; the jurists made it clear that "ownership has nothing in common with possession."[70] The *rei vindicatio*, the action by which the owner of a thing attempted to recover it from a possessor, required the plaintiff to produce proof of his ownership.[71] That could be a heavy burden. In a fragment contained in the *Digest*'s sixth book, on the *rei vindicatio*, the jurist Gaius recommends that "anyone contemplating suing for a thing ought to consider whether he can obtain possession of it by some interdict. For it is far more convenient for him to be in possession himself and put the burden of being plaintiff on his opponent than for him to sue with his opponent in possession."[72]

In this passage, Gaius points to another element of the Roman distinction between interdicts for possession and actions for ownership: the two existed in a sort of hierarchy. The interdict was always the preferred way of moving forward. If Titius could recover his land without having to resort to the *rei vindicatio*, he might as well do it and save himself time, trouble, and expense. If he failed to prove the elements of the interdict *unde vi*, he could always bring the *rei vindicatio* afterwards and try to prove his ownership. This hierarchy of procedures for ownership and possession is sometimes referred to as the dual process.[73]

For you have deprived him of the possession of what he was holding *animo* if not *corpore*. I have learned that Proculus used to give as an example the common saying that we hold our possessions of summer and winter pastures *animo*. For the same applies to all property in land from which we have withdrawn without the intention of abandoning their possession." D.43.16.1.24–25; *Digest of Justinian*, vol 4, 98.

---

[68] For the proposition that interdicts deal with facts, while actions deal with rights, see D.8.5.2.3.
[69] See generally D.43.16; *Digest of Justinian*, vol 4, 96–102.
[70] "Nihil commune habet proprietas cum possessio." D.41.2.12.
[71] Adolf Berger, *Encyclopedic Dictionary of Roman Law* (American Philosophical Society 1953) 672, "rei vindicatio."
[72] "Is qui destinavit rem petere animadvertere debet, an aliquo interdicto possit nancisci possessionem, quia longe commodius est ipsum possidere et adversarium ad onera petitoris compellere quam alio possidente petere." D.6.1.24; *Digest of Justinian*, vol 1, 205.
[73] Frederic Joüon Des Longrais, "La portée politique des réformes d'Henry II en matière de saisine" (1936) 15 Revue historique de droit français et étranger, 4th Series 540, 547–55. Joüon des Longrais thought that Roman and canon law had probably influenced the development of the petty assizes under Henry II, but only in broad outline, not in the specifics. He thought Henry and his counsellors had taken the idea of a dual process from the two laws when they created their assizes, but not much more than that. Ibid, 555.

The *Bracton* authors state the Roman distinction several times in the introduction to the section on actions. They tell us that "of actions *in rem*, some are founded on possession, others on ownership" and "that possession rather than ownership must first be dealt with and that a possessory action must be brought first, though in the end ownership must prevail, may clearly be seen."[74] The authors clearly have the dual process in mind. So far, they are simply doing what the author of *Glanvill* had done; they are using the model of a dual process of procedures on the possession and on the ownership. They also present us with a different model, however. Where Roman actions and interests existed in a two-tiered hierarchy, the English courts developed a multi-tiered hierarchy of writs. In the introduction to actions, the *Bracton* authors also present us with this hierarchy; elsewhere in the introduction to actions, they tell us that if a litigant

> has withdrawn from an assize of novel disseisin he may at once have recourse to the assize of mort d'ancestor, if that is available to him, after that to the writ of entry, and finally to the writ of right . . . But he may not proceed by descending in the contrary order, for from the writ of right descent is never made to other lesser writs . . . nor after he has once brought an action on the seisin of an ancestor [by the assize of mort d'ancestor] may he sue on his own seisin by the assize [of novel disseisin].[75]

The *Bracton* authors are describing something like the dual process, by which one can move up the list but not down. The only problem is that the process is actually a four-fold process, with multiple levels of writs.

It is difficult to see how these two systems can be reconciled. The section of the treatise on civil actions is partly organized around this hierarchy, moving from novel disseisin, to mort d'ancestor, to entry, and finally to right.[76] The section on civil actions is, therefore, largely organized around the concerns of the royal courts. But the authors start this section with the basic distinction

---

[74] *Bracton*, vol 2, 294, 320.

[75] "Si enim ab assisa novæ disseisinæ recessum fuerit, statim habeatur recursus ad assisam mortis antecessoris si competat, et postea breve de ingressu, et ad ultimum ad breve de recto, et ita ascendendo de possessione usque ad proprietatem. Sed non e contrario descendendo, quia numquam de brevi de recto fit descensus ad alia brevia inferiora, quia qui semel egerit per breve de recto totum ius tam super possessione quam super proprietate deducit in iudicium, secundum quod videri poterit infra ubi tractatur de brevi de recto. Numquam enim a causa proprietatis fit descensus ad causam possessionis, nec postquam semel actum fuerit de seisina antecessoris non poterit quis agere de seisina propria per assisam." *Bracton*, vol 2, 297.

[76] Although the authors inserted tractates on the assizes having to do with the Church—darrein presentment and *utrum*—as well as one on dower, topics that do not fit neatly into this hierarchy because they deal with different types of rights, in-between these other tractates.

between actions on possession and actions on ownership. Their goal is to demonstrate that this binary can be reconciled to the hierarchy of writs that dominates the organization of this part of the treatise. These tractates show us that the authors of *Bracton* clearly knew of the tradition of equating right with ownership and seisin with possession, but also understood the problems inherent in a straight equation between the Roman and Anglo-French terms that the *Glanvill* author had used. The *Bracton* authors knew enough about Roman law and the practice of the English royal courts to see that this one-to-one equation would not work. Although writs that used the word *seisin* and writs that used the word *right* might be equivalent to Roman actions on the possession and the ownership to the limited extent that both systems used something like a dual process, once the *Bracton* authors explored the substantive law of Roman possession and ownership more deeply, they found that reconciling the two systems would require a much more complex scheme. Both, however, had to be correct as far as the justices were concerned. They could not stray too far from the rules they themselves applied in the English courts, but Roman law was a universal law. They maintained their investment in demonstrating equivalence between English and Roman law even as it must have become apparent to them that this would not work. In the process, they created several schemes for understanding landholding that fit possession and property together with seisin and right in increasingly contradictory and absurdly complex ways.

## The *Causae* of Possession

The authors take a stab at this problem in the introduction to the section on actions. In a passage on actions *in rem*, one of the authors begins by telling us that "some are founded on the possession, others on ownership," employing the Roman-law binary.[77] He then describes a number of Roman actions and attempts to produce English analogues. For ownership he gives us the *rei vindicatio* along with the *actio confessoria* and the *actio negatoria*, all three of them Roman actions that did not exist in English law, but, as we shall see, had arguable analogues.[78] When the author of this passage turns to discuss actions founded on possession, he employs a Roman distinction between different types of actions on possession to explain the English hierarchy of writs. The

---

[77] "Item earum quae sunt in rem, quaedam proditae sunt super ipsa possessione, et quaedam super propriatate." *Bracton*, vol 2, 294.

[78] *Bracton*, vol 2, 294.

*Institutes* and *Digest* both distinguish between actions for recovering possession, for obtaining possession, and for retaining possession. The action for recovery of possession would, at Roman law, be the interdict *unde vi*, but the
author of this passage adds the explanatory note, "that is, of one's own seisin
formerly held, by the assize of novel disseisin."[79] The lost possession suddenly
becomes a lost seisin, and where we would expect to find the interdict *unde vi*,
the author of this passage has provided us with the assize of novel disseisin.
He makes the equation explicit when he says, shortly thereafter, that the action on one's own possession "is called the action *unde vi* and can be called the
assize of novel disseisin."[80] At the same time he explicitly equates the Roman
action *quorum bonorum* with the assize of mort d'ancestor, telling us that "the
*hereditatis petitio possessoria* [lies] on the possession of some ancestor, for
a thing of which the ancestor died seised as of fee, [and] is called the action
*quorum bonorum* or the assize of mort d'ancestor."[81] The authors are thus able
to fit the English hierarchy of writs into the Roman dual process by saying that
several of the writs in the hierarchy are writs of possession; they are simply different types of writs of possession.

The authors' schemes for reconciling the Roman binary and the English
hierarchy become more complicated at other points in the treatise. In the tractate on acquiring dominion over things, one author discusses a gift made by
someone who has no right in the thing he is giving (i.e., what happens when
William gives away land that actually belongs to Ranulf?).[82] As part of this discussion, the author presents us with a new scheme for thinking about the relationship between the Roman law of property and English court practice. He
tells us that, "A thing may be entirely and in every way another's, with respect to
the right and the ownership, the fee and the free tenement, the usufruct and the
bare use."[83] This scheme represents a very different way of thinking about land
law than what we saw in the introduction to actions. In that introduction, the
author translated the multi-tiered hierarchy of writs into the Roman binary of

---

[79] "Recuperandae, hoc est seisinæ propriæ prius habitae per assisam novae disseisinae." *Bracton*, vol
2, 294.

[80] "[D]icitur actio unde vi. . . et dici poterit assisa novae disseisinae." *Bracton*, vol 2, 295.

[81] "Item dicitur possessoria petitio de possessione aliena, sicut alicuius antecessoris, de aliquo de quo
antecessor obiit seisitus ut de feodo, quæ dicitur actio quorum bonorum sive assisa mortis antecessoris."
*Bracton*, vol 2, 295.

[82] There are several references to the Provisions of Merton of 1236 in this tractate, but they appear to
be later additions to bring the text up to date. One is placed in the middle of a long excerpt from *Glanvill*
and another between two sentences that appear to have been consecutive at one point, indicating that
the main text was written before 1236 and needed to be updated. *Bracton*, vol 2, 179, 276; vol 3, xii.
These all point towards an early date for this tractate.

[83] "Poterit quidem res esse aliena omnino et ex toto quantum ad ius et proprietatem, feodum et liberum tenementum, usumfructum et nudum usum." *Bracton*, vol 2, 101.

possession and ownership by discussing several writs as if they were different types of Roman actions on possession. Possession and ownership are essentially the abstract interests. The assizes of novel disseisin and mort d'ancestor are the actions that arise out of those interests in different situations. In the tractate on acquiring dominion, however, the author is not talking about actions. He's talking solely in terms of interests. Elsewhere in the tractate on acquiring dominion, he provides similar lists and calls these things the *causae possidendi* ("causes of possessing") or *causae possessionis* ("causes of possession").[84] This particular use of the word *causa*, as the legal basis for a person's possession, comes from Roman law.[85] By calling these *causae possidendi*, or *causae possessionis*, the author seems to be indicating that possession is a fact and that each of these six things is the interest that justifies or legitimates that possession. He's thinking in a very Roman way, in terms of interests, but he's not using the Roman binary of ownership and possession. Instead, he has created a hierarchy of interests that seem to line up with different writs a person could bring.

These six interests—right, ownership, fee, free tenement, usufruct, and bare use—add up to the greatest power one can have over a piece of land, since they make the land "entirely and in every way" the other person's land.[86] This is a curious list because it combines Roman and English terms. Three terms come from Roman law. Ownership (*proprietas*) was the highest right that one could have in land in Roman law. It had three constituent elements: the *usus*, or right to use the land, the *fructus*, the right to take and enjoy the fruits of the land, and the *abusus*, the right to dispose of the land.[87] The *usufruct* was a lesser right that included only the *usus* and the *fructus*. The bare use (*nudus usus*) was the *usus* without the *fructus* or the *abusus*. Raleigh combines these with three terms that do not come from Roman law. Right (*ius* in this instance) is probably derived from English practice, as are fee and free tenement, which appear in contemporary English charters and in the assizes of mort d'ancestor and novel disseisin, respectively.

This looks like an attempt to fit the Roman language of ownership and possession into the multi-tiered hierarchy of English writs. Right is at the top. Fee, the term that appears in the assize of mort d'ancestor, comes beneath it. Free

---

[84] *Bracton*, vol 2, 104, 140.

[85] A *lex* in the *Digest* illustrates this use of the term *causa*. In a discussion of possession, the jurist Paul said that "The earlier jurists further laid down that no one can for himself change the *causa* by which he possesses something." D.41.2.3.19; *Digest of Justinian*, vol 4, 20.

[86] *Bracton*, vol 2, 101.

[87] DL Carey Miller, "Property," in Ernest Metzger (ed), *A Companion to Justinian's Institutes* (Cornell University Press 1998) 42, 49 (hereafter Miller, "Property").

tenement, the term that appears in the assize of novel disseisin, is below that. That is the correct order in the hierarchy. A writ of right will preclude a writ of mort d'ancestor on the same facts because the writ of right decides more than the writ of mort d'ancestor. Likewise, a writ of mort d'ancestor will preclude an assize of novel disseisin. Notice that instead of discussing the writs, this author draws particular words out of the writs, words that he thinks of as characterizing those writs, and turns those words into abstract interests protected by the writs. The Roman terms, which do not correspond to any writ, appear to have been thrown in because the author thought they should be. He is combining two different ways of speaking about the relationship between human beings and land into one set of interests.

The author of this passage is doing something rather extraordinary. Where the *Glanvill* treatise used *writs* to create its organizational framework—sections of the treatise tend to focus on the procedures surrounding a particular writ—this author is using *interests*. Where the *Glanvill* author would focus on the assize of novel disseisin and the assize of mort d'ancestor, this author is focusing his discussion on the meanings of the words *fee* and *free tenement*. So, for instance, where he could have said that the assize of novel disseisin was available to a doweress or a widower holding by curtsey, but not to a guardian or termor, he instead gives us the phrase *free tenement*, which is contained in the writ, and defines it as an interest that only extends to the end of the holder's life, what modern lawyers would call a life estate. This is what a doweress or widower holding by curtsey would have.[88] To say that the free tenement is held for life is equivalent to saying that the assize applies only to estates held for life or longer. It is the fact that the author of this passage discusses these matters using abstract concepts rather than concrete writs that is really interesting. He is thinking like the authors of the *Institutes*, who placed things prior to actions, concepts prior to the procedures that put them into practice.

There is a real danger of over-systematizing the *Bracton* authors' writing on the *causae possidendi*. The authors, possibly writing different passages at different times, are inconsistent in the content of the list of *causae* itself, sometimes leaving out terms and sometimes replacing them with others.[89] Many of the lists we find in the treatise omit the bare use.[90] Once we see the usufruct and the bare use replaced with *seisin*.[91] The authors are least consistent when they

---

[88] Donald Sutherland, *The Assize of Novel Disseisin* (Clarendon Press 1973) 13.
[89] For additional examples of the *Bracton* authors' use of the *causae*, see *Bracton*, vol 2, 123, 127; vol 3, 132; vol 4, 41, 43.
[90] *Bracton*, vol 2, 127.
[91] "[T]he right and the ownership, the fee and the free tenement and seisin." *Bracton*, vol 2, 123.

discuss *right* and *ownership*. Where the terms *usufruct, free tenement*, and *fee* are fairly stable, appearing in most of the versions of the list we find in the treatise, the terms at the top of the list change regularly. In one version of the list, they become the "pure right and the ownership."[92] In another, they are called the "*dominium* and *proprietas*," two Roman-law terms for "ownership."[93] Even stranger is the fact that *dominium* plays a different role immediately before this passage. On what would be the same folio in most manuscripts, the author tells us that the *dominium* of an estate is composed of "the pure right and the ownership, the fee and the free tenement and the usufruct."[94] In this list, ownership is a part of a larger right called *dominium*, which includes all of the *causae*. In the other list, *dominium* and *proprietas* are separate *causae*.[95] The authors of *Bracton* do not appear to have fully worked this out.

## The Two Rights

Recall that actions on ownership and possession existed in a binary at Roman law. The *causae possidendi* scheme is not a binary. It does not do a good job of reconciling the dual process of Roman law with the practice of the English courts. Where the *Glanvill* author had treated *right* and *ownership* as synonyms, the authors of the *causae* of possession scheme in *Bracton* imagined them to be separate, if ill-defined, *causae*. Other parts of the treatise present us with a view of the relationship between *right, property*, and *possession* that contradicts both of these views, however. Near the beginning of the treatise, an author presents us with two kinds of right:

> For there is a right of possession (*ius possessionis*) and a right of ownership (*ius proprietatis*): the right of possession, as of fee, where the assise of mort d'ancestor is applicable; and as of free tenement, as where one holds only for life, no matter in what way. The right of ownership is termed the pure right.

---

[92] *Bracton*, vol 2, 127.

[93] *Bracton*, vol 2, 128.

[94] "[M]erum ius et proprietatem, feodum et liberum tenementum, et usumfructum." *Bracton*, vol 2, 127.

[95] *Dominium* could mean two things to an English justice with Roman law training. On the one hand, it could be a synonym for *proprietas*. On the other hand, it was the Latin translation for *demesne*, the land which the person at issue held and worked personally (or by unfree tenants, who did not count in the eyes of the law), rather than holding through a free tenant. Perhaps it means *demesne* here, since one who had held by all of these *causae* would, by definition, be working the land himself. One could hold in demesne without having the fee, the ownership, or the right, however. A woman holding in dower would hold only a free tenement, but could be said to hold in demesne.

Thus one may well have both. The right of ownership may sometimes be sep-arated from the right of possession, for immediately after the death of his an-cestor the ownership descends to the nearer heir, whether he is a minor or of full age, a male or a female, a madman or a fool, as an idiot, one who is deaf and dumb, present or absent, ignorant of the matter or apprised of it. Possession, however, is not at once acquired by such persons, though posses-sion and the right of possession ought always to follow the ownership.[96]

In this passage, the author bifurcates the concept of *right* into a right of posses-sion (*ius possessionis*) and a right of ownership (*ius proprietatis*). In doing so, he follows earlier treatises to an extent. Like *Glanvill*, he uses the binary of pleas of possession and pleas of ownership, and places the assizes of novel disseisin and mort d'ancestor on the side of possession. Unlike *Glanvill*, he does not equate *possession* with *seisin* and *ownership* with *right*. In this scheme, both writs of possession and writs of ownership implicate right.[97] The author of this passage may not be following *Glanvill*, but he follows the Roman law of possession and ownership very closely. The right of ownership descends automatically to the heir at death because taking ownership requires no act or intention. The right of possession, however, does not pass automatically because, at Roman law, one had to take possession both *corpore* and *animo*, by body and by mind. The author lists several classes of people who would be unable to take possession

[96] "Quia est ius proprietatis et ius possessionis. Item ius possessionis sicut feodum, et unde locum habet assisa mortis antecessoris. Item ius possessionis sicut liberum tenementum, si quis tenuerit tantum ad vitam quacumque ratione. Item ius proprietatis quod dicitur ius merum. Et unde poterit quis habere utrumque. Et dividi poterit quandoque ius proprietatis a iure possessionis. Quia proprietas statim post mortem antecessoris descendit heredi propinquiori, minori et maiori, masculo et feminæ, furioso et stulto sicut fatuo, surdo et muto, præsenti et absenti, et ignoranti sicut scienti. Sed tamen non statim adquiritur talibus possessio, licet possessio et ius possessionis semper sequi debeat proprietatem." *Bracton*, vol 2, 24. Thorne calls these two rights *possessory right* and *proprietary right*, but in the Latin, *possessionis* and *proprietatis* are genitive nouns, not adjectives. This passage is found in a section of the treatise most likely written in the early stages of the writing. Even if these words were written by Bratton, however, the idea of separating right into a right of possession and a right of ownership must have come from one of the earlier authors, since it appears throughout the treatise, and in parts that Raleigh is almost certain to have written. A notable example occurs in the tractate on acquiring dominion over things, very close to two passages that are updated to reflect the Provisions of Merton of 1236, indicating that the primary text was written before that date. *Bracton*, vol 2, 189.
[97] It is, of course, possible that the author of this passage is using the word *right* (*ius*) in a different sense than the *Glanvill* author does. *Ius* was a word that could have many meanings. The *Glanvill* author was using the term in the same manner as the grand assize, which asked who had the "greater right" (*maius ius*) in the land. But *ius* was also used in a general way in Roman-law texts to mean any right. In the *causae* of possession scheme and in the "quantum of right" scheme, which we will examine next, Bratton and Raleigh appear to use the word *ius* in the same way the grand assize and the *Glanvill* author used it. Shortly after the section quoted above, the treatise tells us that when the right of ownership is split, one person will have the "greater right" (*maius ius*), language drawn directly from the grand as-size, indicating that he was thinking about the grand assize when he wrote the text that contains the two rights scheme. *Bracton*, vol 2, 25.

**Table 3.1** *Causae* of Possession and Two Rights Compared

| The *Causae* of Possession | | The Two Rights | | |
|---|---|---|---|---|
| RIGHT | | Writ of Right | OWNERSHIP | |
| OWNERSHIP | *Causae* of POSSESSION | Fee/ Mort d'an. | | RIGHT |
| Fee | | | | |
| Free Tenement | | | POSSESSION | |
| Usufruct | | Free ten/ Nov. dis. | | |
| Bare Use | | | | |

*animo* because they lacked the mental capacity to do so. He is making another valiant effort to work the writs he administered in the courts into the frame of Roman property law.

This scheme of the two rights conflicts with the *causae* scheme in some significant respects, however. If we look at the list that gives the *causae* as "the right and the ownership, the fee and the free tenement, the usufruct and the bare use" we can see that it does not sit neatly with a bifurcated scheme that separates right into a right of possession and a right of ownership.[98] In the *causae*, right and ownership are often listed as two separate *causae*, two separate reasons for possessing the land. Possession is what the landholder has, and right or ownership is his reason for having it, a reason which also determines the temporal scope of the landholding (whether it is hereditary, for life, for a term, etc.). In the *causae* scheme, right and ownership are comparable terms, both essentially *causae*. Possession is not a *causa* and is not comparable to these two other terms. In the scheme of the two rights, it is possession and ownership that are the comparable terms. They are two attributes a right may have. So the words *right, possession,* and *ownership* play very different roles in these two schemes, as can be seen in Table 3.1.

The two schemes also differ greatly in their treatment of the substantive law of possession. In the *causae possidendi*, possession appears to be a fact. The list of *causae* is a list of underlying interests that make that possession legitimate. They are abstract rights in the land that allow that land to be possessed in a certain way. In the bifurcated right scheme, the word *possession* is doing different work. I discussed earlier possession's tendency to become an abstract right. That is what has happened here. It has become a *right of possession,* a lesser right than the right of ownership. Gone is the *Digest*'s insistence, repeated elsewhere

---

[98] *Bracton*, vol 2, 101.

in *Bracton*, that possession and ownership have nothing in common.[99] Here they exist on the same continuum.

## A Quantum of Right

In the two rights scheme, the treatise associated the writ of right, the assize of mort d'ancestor, and the assize of novel disseisin with the concept of right, despite the fact that *Glanvill* associated only the writ of right with right and associated the two lower writs, mort d'ancestor and novel disseisin, with seisin. The idea that right exists even in some of the writs at the lower end of the scale is central to a third scheme employed by the authors of the treatise, which I call the "quantum of right" scheme. In the tractate on acquiring dominion over things, very close to several of the accounts of the *causae possidendi* we have already seen, one of the authors presents us with the following:

[1] There is possession which has nothing of right but something of possession, as where one is in possession by intrusion. [2] There is another kind that has something of possession but nothing of right, as where one is in possession as guardian or creditor and the like. [3] There is another that has much of possession [but] little of right, as the possession of an ancestor, [recovered] in a possessory action, where another has the pure right and the ancestor the fee and free tenement. [4] And another that has a great deal of possession and something of right, where it is changed into a proprietary *causa*, as where one holds for a term of life or years. [5] There is also possession that has much of possession and much of right, as where in some thing one has the pure right and the ownership, the fee and the free tenement with seisin.[100]

<hr/>

[99] *Bracton*, vol 2, 321; vol 3, 25.
[100] "Item est quædam quæ nihil iuris habet sed aliquid possessionis, ut si quis fuerit in possessione per intrusionem. Est et alia possessio quæ aliquid habet possessionis, sed nihil iuris, ut si quis fuerit in possessione ut custos vel creditor, et huiusmodi. Est et alia quæ multum habet possessionis et parum iuris, sicut est possessio antecessoris in causa possessionis ubi alius habet ius merum et antecessor feodum et liberum tenementum. Est et alia possessio quæ plurimum habet possessionis et aliquid iuris, ubi vertitur causa proprietatis, ut si quis tenuerit ad terminum vitæ vel annorum. Est etiam possessio quæ multum habet possessionis et multum iuris, sicut illa ubi quis habet in re aliqua ius merum et proprietatem, feodum et liberum tenementum cum seisina." *Bracton*, vol 2, 122–23. I have modified the translation slightly from Thorne's. For situation [3], Thorne has a "good deal of possession" but the Latin is *"multum . . . possessionis,"* the same phrase he translates as "much of possession" for situation [5]. There is a second version of the quantum of right scheme in the treatise, in the introduction to the section of the treatise on civil actions. This version has six tiers. *Bracton*, vol 3, 13.

The author places various types of land arrangements on a continuum based on how much possession and how much right each one contains. Right increases fairly steadily from [1] to [5]. Possession generally increases as right increases, but this is not universally so. Situations [1] and [2] have something of possession, [3] has much of possession, [4] has a great deal of possession, and [5] reverts to much of possession. Possession and right appear to be independent of each other.

In one way, this list fits with the *causae* of possession very well. Apart from number [5], these are all cases where the holder of the land holds by one *causa*, but not by another. In number [3], for instance, the author has imagined a case where the possessor holds by fee, but not by right. He is thus finding ways to separate and distinguish categories of landholding. In other ways, however, the quantum of right conflicts directly with the *causae possidendi* and two rights schemes. In the *causae possidendi*, right and ownership were comparable terms, of the same order. In the two rights scheme, possession and ownership were comparable. In the quantum of right scheme, possession and right are the comparable terms. The author is taking the Roman binary between possession and ownership, which the author of *Glanvill* applied to the Anglo-French terms *seisin* and *right*, and hybridizing it into a binary between possession and right. This was not altogether new. One of the authors of the *Très Ancien Coutumier de Normandie* had used the same distinction, as had William of Raleigh in a 1231 case recorded on his roll.[101] This binary continued to be used by later generations of lawyers; David Seipp has shown that the possession-right dichotomy was also used in the law reports of the late thirteenth century to describe writs.[102]

---

[101] See Ernest Joseph Tardif (ed), *Coutumiers De Normandie* (Espérance Cagniard 1881) vol 1, 23. In the 1231 case, Raleigh said "[T]o be lord and heir pertains to right and not to possession . . ." ("[E]sse dominum et heredem spectat ad ius et non ad possessionem . . ."). BNB, vol 2, 435, 437 (no 564).

[102] Seipp has shown that in the year books, the possession-right dichotomy was used in two, inconsistent, ways, one absolute and the other relative. See David J Seipp, "Roman Legal Categories in the Early Common Law" in Thomas G Watkin (ed), *Legal Record and Historical Reality: Proceedings of the Eighth British Legal History Conference* (Hambledon Press 1989) 9, 26. First, it was used to create two, entirely separate categories of writs. All writs of possession shared certain procedures, and all writs of right shared a different set of procedures. Ibid, 22. Second, it was used to describe writs in a relative way. Ibid, 25. When faced with a situation in which a plaintiff had already brought a writ that was alleged to be higher in the hierarchy than the one he was currently trying to use, the lawyers of the late thirteenth century would often refer to the higher writ as a writ of right and the lower writ as a writ of possession. Thus, when a person had sued on a writ of entry and later sued on a writ of right, the writ of right would be, unsurprisingly, denominated a writ on the right and the writ of entry a writ on the possession, because it is lower. But if the plaintiff had sued on a writ of mort d'ancestor and later wanted to sue on a writ of entry, the writ of entry would be denominated a writ on the right, because, of the two writs, it is the higher in the hierarchy. Whether a writ was on the possession or the right was thus situational, based on the writ to which it was being compared. Ibid, 25–26.

Possession and ownership, according to the conventional interpretations of Roman law, did not come in amounts. One could not have greater ownership than another.[103] Although it would describe Roman law actions poorly, the quantum of right scheme actually describes English writs rather well because it does not require a binary classification. A writ such as mort d'ancestor, which is higher in the hierarchy of writs than novel disseisin, but lower than the writ of right, can be both a writ of possession and a writ of right. Situation [3] describes an assize of mort d'ancestor, or another writ of the mort d'ancestor family, which has "much of possession" and also a "little of right."[104] So the assize of mort d'ancestor is primarily possessory, but also has some of the aspects of an action on right or ownership.

The quantum of right scheme causes at least as many problems as it solves, however. Situation [4], where the possessory *causa* turns into a proprietary one, shows some of the contradictions inherent in the author's thinking.[105] The author is thinking about possession in two different ways: he uses the possession/right distinction of the quantum of right scheme, but also the possession/ownership distinction of the two rights scheme. So, in this situation, the plaintiff's *causa* "is changed to a proprietary *causa*."[106] The plaintiff's cause of action, or his writ, has crossed a line from a writ of possession to a writ of ownership. The author clearly thinks that one may have more or less of possession and right when thinking in terms of the quantum of right scheme, since he says this person has a great deal of possession and something of right. In the two rights scheme, however, there are no amounts of possession and ownership. An action is *either* possessory *or* proprietary. And yet an action that has crossed the line from possession to ownership still has "a great deal of possession" and, strangely, only "something of right."

Indeed, in this passage, the author combines all three of the schemes. In situation [5], which is greatest of the five in right and possession, he combines the quantum of right scheme with the *causae possidendi* scheme. A person in this situation holds the land under all of the *causae possidendi* except, perhaps, the usufruct and bare use: "the pure right and the ownership, the fee and the free tenement with seisin."[107] This sounds like absolute ownership, since the person has pure right and ownership in the land, but even a person who holds in this manner is only said to have "much of right" and "much of possession."[108]

---

[103]  Miller, "Property" (n 87) 45.
[104]  *Bracton*, vol 2, 122.
[105]  *Bracton*, vol 2, 123.
[106]  *Bracton*, vol 2, 123.
[107]  *Bracton*, vol 2, 122–23.
[108]  *Bracton*, vol 2, 122–23.

The author, in combining these schemes, uses the word *right* in two different ways. It is part of his hybrid binary of possession and right, but it is also a *causa possidendi*. One who has the purest right one can have has "much right" in the land. In the *causae possidendi* scheme, right is something one has or does not have and, in this case, represents the highest and purest type of interest one can have in land. In the two rights scheme, right is bifurcated, but it is still something one has or does not. In the quantum of right scheme, it is something one can have more or less of. The author of this passage was able to combine all of the various schemes into one, but only at the cost of using the same words in different ways within a single paragraph.

## The Writ of Nuisance and the Law of Servitudes

The conflicts between Roman law and English practice, and the authors' attempts to resolve those conflicts, demonstrate that the authors of the treatise were deeply committed to the notion that the practices of the English courts were in line with Roman law. Roman law and English practice did not always conflict, however. Sometimes the authors thought that Roman law could, in fact, explain some of the peculiarities of English law. In the tractate on the assize of novel disseisin, one of the authors uses Roman law to explain why the royal courts grouped certain writs together. From the late twelfth century, the assize of nuisance was treated as a subcategory of the assize of novel disseisin. Although Roman law is unlikely to have influenced the decision to group these writs together, this author used the Roman law of servitudes to supply a logical and substantive reason for the grouping of the assize of nuisance together with the assize of novel disseisin.

Recall that the overarching organization of the treatise is borrowed from Justinian's *Institutes*. It is divided into three large sections on the law of persons, the law of things, and the law of actions. The tractate on the assize of novel disseisin is found within the section on actions. That section of the treatise is largely organized by writ. This is not quite how the *Institutes*' section on actions is organized. The *Institutes* discusses particular topics in the law of actions, such as the distinction between real and personal actions, the particular problems of bringing litigation through an agent, procedural steps such as exception and replication, and the penalties that may accrue to a plaintiff who brings a baseless suit.[109] The decision to organize *Bracton*'s section on actions by writ

---

[109]   See Inst.4.6, 4.10, 4.13, 4.14, 4.16.

was likely dictated not by Justinian, but by the authors' experience in the royal courts. Early texts produced within the royal courts show us that the people who worked in those courts tended to group writs into families, and that the families were probably pretty well established by the time *Bracton* was written.

The organization within the tractate on the assize of novel disseisin was probably dictated by the practices of the English courts, as well. The *Bracton* treatise groups together several variants of the assize, first discussing the form of the writ of novel disseisin for a free tenement and then moving to particular forms, including the assize of novel disseisin for common of pasture and forms of the writ of novel disseisin for nuisance.[110] This method of treating writs for disseisin of free tenement and of common of pasture together with the writ of nuisance had a long pedigree by the time the authors of *Bracton* sat down to write the tractate. The Irish register, which probably dates to 1210, groups the assize of novel disseisin for a free tenement together with the assize of novel disseisin for common of pasture and the assize of novel disseisin for the diversion of a watercourse.[111] The *Glanvill* treatise, written between 1187 and 1189, does something similar, providing the writ of novel disseisin for a free tenement, then several forms for nuisance—a category that would have included the diversion of a watercourse—and finally a form for disseisin of common of pasture.[112] There are some striking similarities between the writs. Indeed, what historians call the assize of nuisance was usually considered a variant of the assize of novel disseisin in the twelfth and thirteenth centuries; "assize of nuisance" was not a title used by contemporaries.[113] The assize of novel disseisin for a free tenement reads "N. has complained to me that R. has unjustly and without a judgment disseised him of his free tenement . . ."[114] The assize of nuisance simply substitutes a few words: "N. has complained to me that R. unjustly and without a judgment has raised up (or knocked down) a bank . . . to the nuisance of N.'s free tenement . . ."[115] Both used the same assize procedure, with a jury summoned to answer a simple question before royal justices visiting the county in which the land was situated. The writs shared a relatively

---

[110] *Bracton*, vol 3, 162–93.

[111] De Haas and Hall (eds), *Early Registers* (n 59) 2–3. The register opens with letters patent that claim to have been issued by Henry III in 1227, ordering his courts in Ireland to use the writs contained in the register. Ibid, 1. For a persuasive argument that the register actually dates to 1210, see Paul Brand, "Ireland and the Literature of the Early Common Law" in MCL, 450–56. Either way, this register probably either predates *Bracton* or dates to the period when the first work was being done on the treatise.

[112] *Glanvill*, 167–69 (XII, c 32–37).

[113] Janet Loengard, "The Assize of Nuisance: The Origins of an Action at Common Law" (1978) 37 Cambridge Law Journal 144, 158 (hereafter Loengard, "Assize of Nuisance").

[114] *Glanvill*, 167 (XIII, c 33).

[115] *Glanvill*, 168 (XIII, c 36).

short limitation period, so they could only be used to remedy acts that had happened fairly recently. There is also a sense in which the wrongs complained of in the assize of novel disseisin and the assize of nuisance existed on a continuum. Novel disseisin dealt with cases in which the plaintiff had essentially been—although I hesitate to use the Roman term—dispossessed of his land. The assize of nuisance dealt with cases in which the defendant interfered with the plaintiff's use of his land. There was a gray area where interference with use might overlap with disseisin.[116] There was at least one important difference, however, which made the assize of nuisance sit uncomfortably in the novel disseisin family. The writs for novel disseisin of a free tenement or of common of pasture both refer to the wrong complained of as a disseisin; the writ of nuisance speaks of an act committed "to the nuisance" of a free tenement, with no mention of a disseisin at all. It was not, therefore, a foregone conclusion that the assize of nuisance should be considered an assize of novel *disseisin*. Indeed, although there is still quite a bit of uncertainty about the origins of the assize of novel disseisin, Janet Loengard has argued that the two writs were created by the same enactment in 1166, and the primary reason for grouping these writs together may have been that they were created at the same time.[117]

Whatever the reason for grouping the assize of novel disseisin and the assize of nuisance together, by the time *Bracton* was written justices and clerks clearly thought of them as belonging to a single novel disseisin family, and it is therefore unsurprising that the *Bracton* authors would place them both in the tractate on novel disseisin. The *Bracton* authors went to some pain to show that the writ of nuisance actually was concerned with a disseisin, however. It was not the disseisin of a free tenement or a common right, but the disseisin of a servitude, a type of property right that they drew from their study of Roman law. The author of the tractate thus uses Roman law to explain *why* the writ of nuisance should be classed along with the assize of novel disseisin for a free tenement or for common of pasture.

The tractate on the assize of novel disseisin starts with the most basic form of the writ, which is the version in which the plaintiff uses the assize to reclaim his free tenement. About three-quarters of the way through the tractate, the author turns to some special cases, such as the use of the assize by a widower holding by curtsey, by a bastard, and by a termor.[118] The author then tells the reader that he is switching gears. He has already explained "how the ownership of corporeal

---

[116] I would like to thank Paul Brand for this suggestion.
[117] Loengard, "Assize of Nuisance" (n 113) 159, 64.
[118] *Bracton*, vol 3, 151–62.

things is acquired and the acquisition of possession" and how "possession may be restored" to someone who has been ejected from his tenement by the assize of novel disseisin. Now he is going to turn to "how one is restored who has been wrongfully ejected from things appurtenant to a free tenement."[119] This sub-section begins with a long analytical discussion that attempts to synthesize the Roman concept of servitudes with English court practice. The *Bracton* treatise was the first attempt to import the Roman law of servitudes to English law.[120] It exerted an important influence on the later English law of servitudes; when English lawyers were developing the law of easements in the seventeenth century, they often turned to *Bracton*, which was available in two printed editions by that time.[121] *Bracton* was therefore used to systematize the substantive law of servitudes (although American lawyers may balk at calling the modern law of servitudes "systematic"). The author of this passage fuses together the English concept of appurtenances—those rights that accompany a piece of land, which might include the advowson of the local parish church, the right to administer the local hundred court, or a right-of-way across a neighbor's land—with the Roman concept of praedial servitudes.

*Bracton* explains why the writs for nuisance and common of pasture, in particular, are of the same kind, and does so by making a rather ingenious argument from the Roman law of servitudes. Common of pasture is a type of appurtenance. It gives the tenant of tenement A a right to pasture animals on tenement B. It is fairly easy to see how writs remedying the disseisin of an appurtenance such as common of pasture could be assimilated to the Roman law of servitudes. They both have to do with use of the land of another. This required a leap of the imagination, but not a large one. The author's stroke of genius was to explain the writ of nuisance as a writ about servitudes, as well. The connection between servitudes and nuisance is not obvious, but the author of this passage explains it this way: the things that are protected by the writ of nuisance are use-rights in another's land. They are simply use-rights created by law rather than by some agreement between the landowners. To take

---

[119] "Dictum est supra qualiter rerum corporalium dominia adquiruntur et de adquirenda possessione, et quale remedium competit ei qui a tenemento suo eiectus fuerit, et qualiter restituatur ei possessio, libertas et pax si possessio perturbetur. Nunc autem dicendum qualiter quis restituatur si fuerit eiectus iniuste de iis quæ pertinent ad liberum tenementum." *Bracton*, vol 3, 162.

[120] For a detailed discussion of the ways in which *Bracton* discusses the law of nuisance and its relation to servitude law, see Joshua Getzler, *A History of Water Rights at Common Law* (OUP 2004) 55–71 (hereafter Getzler, *Water Rights*).

[121] Ian Williams, "A Medieval Book and Early-Modern Law: Bracton's Authority and Application in the Common Law C.1550-1640" (2011) 79 Tijdschrift voor Rechtsgeschiedenis/Legal History Review 47, 67–68; DEC Yale, "'Of No Mean Authority': Some Later Uses of Bracton" in Morris S Arnold and others (eds), *On the Laws and Customs of England: Essays in Honor of Samuel E. Thorne* (University of North Carolina Press 1981) 388.

an example, there was a writ of nuisance that dealt with the situation where the tenant of tenement B had raised the level of his mill pond so that it flooded part of tenement A. The tenant of tenement A could sue in nuisance. We can conceive of the tenant of A's ability to prevent the tenant of B from raising the mill pond as a property right that the tenant of A has in tenement B. That right is a servitude. *Bracton* explains that servitudes of this type are "imposed by law, not by man or by use," and are fairly extensive, explaining that servitudes imposed by law provide that "no one can do anything on his own land by which damage or nuisance accrues to a neighbor."[122] This form of analysis, which treats nuisance and servitudes as two sides of the same coin, actually has some resonance in the modern world; it is employed in the most widely assigned property casebook in American law schools.[123]

The author of this passage does not appear to have gotten the idea that a nuisance is a servitude imposed by law from his Roman sources. He built upon the Roman law of servitudes, but, as Joshua Getzler notes, he extended the concept of a servitude well beyond its boundaries in Roman law.[124] Book eight of the *Digest* does contain a discussion of something that sounds like nuisance law. Its fifth title is on actions regarding servitudes, and includes a long fragment from the jurist Ulpian in which he recounts that the jurist Aristo "does not think that smoke can lawfully be discharged from a cheese shop onto the buildings above it, unless they are subject to a servitude to this effect" and thinks that it is unlawful "to discharge water or any other substance from the upper onto the lower property, as a man is only permitted to carry out operations on his own premises to this effect, that he discharge nothing onto those of another."[125] Aristo is saying that there are certain things that an owner of land cannot do if they interfere with his neighbor's use of his land. This looks very similar to the kind of thinking behind the assize of nuisance, which prevents A from using his land in a way that interferes with B's use of his land. According to Aristo, the owner of the property that is harmed by the smoke or the water can bring either an *in rem* action, for interference with his ownership of the land, or the interdict *uti possidetis*, which protects a possessor of land from potential interference with his possession.[126] The authors of *Bracton* may have known title

---

[122] "Et eodem modo imponitur qunadoque a iure et nec ab homine nec ab usu, scilicet ne quis faciat in proprio per quod damnum vel nocumentum eveniat vicino." *Bracton*, vol 3, 163–64. See also *Bracton*, vol 3, 189–90.

[123] Jesse Dukeminier and others, *Property* (7th edn, Aspen 2010) 729; see Guido Calabresi and A Douglas Melamed, "Property Rules, Liability Rules, and Inalienability: One View of the Cathedral" (1972) 85 Harvard Law Review 1089, 1105.

[124] Getzler, *Water Rights* (n 120) 70–71.

[125] D.8.5.8.5; *Digest of Justinian*, vol 1, 269–70.

[126] Ibid.

five of book eight of the *Digest*; there are several phrases in *Bracton* that may have been pulled from book eight, including one maxim that appears in title five.[127] But it is important to note that Ulpian never implies, in the example of A's smoke or water making its way onto B's land, that B's right to recover from A constitutes a servitude over A's land, a servitude to prevent him from emitting smoke. This text is included in the section of the *Digest* on servitudes, but it is included there because it discusses what an owner cannot do *in the absence of a servitude*. In other words, Aristo says that A cannot release smoke or water *unless he has a servitude over B's land*.[128]

When it came to the law of nuisance, then, the Roman texts were probably not driving *Bracton*'s organization or discussion. The author of this passage placed the assize of nuisance and the assize of common of pasture under the heading of the assize of novel disseisin, just as his forebears had been doing for several decades. He used the law of servitudes to explain this organization in a new way, however. By giving a name to the thing the plaintiff had lost on account of that nuisance—namely, a servitude—this author could explain how a nuisance was a disseisin.[129] He took a procedure that was designed to proscribe a particular bad act, the raising of a nuisance, and explained why it should actually be understood as a part of the law of property, an action that protects an abstract interest called a servitude. He thus used the *Digest* and the *Institutes* to create a substantive law for a particular procedure.

## Conclusion

In the *Bracton* authors' organization and discussions of various substantive areas of law, we can see them trying to work out a way to describe the practices of the king's courts as entirely consistent with Roman law. They did not always succeed. Their failures actually show us the nature of their commitment. They do not seem to have seen, in their commitment to Roman law, a need to make English law more like Roman law. *Bracton* was, therefore, an attempt to demonstrate that the work of the justices was very similar to the work of the jurists. As it appears to have been written primarily for a small group of people

---

[127] *Bracton*, vol 2, 239 (D. 8.3.3.3); vol 2, 305 (D. 8.5.15); vol 3, 152 (D. 8.6.11.pr); vol 3, 91 (D. 8.2.28); vol 4, 244 (D. 8.5.15 again).

[128] See WW Buckland and Arnold D McNair, *Roman Law and Common Law: A Comparison in Outline* (Revised edn, FH Lawson rev, CUP 1974) 139.

[129] He explicitly uses the language of disseisin of a servitude when discussing common of pasture. See *Bracton*, vol 3, 170.

working in the courts, it would seem that the authors were mostly trying to convince themselves of this fact, to create a text that would give them and their clerks, who aspired to be justices themselves someday, a sense that the enterprise in which they were engaged was not just another branch of administration or royal service. It was part of the culture of the two laws.

# 4

# From Classroom to Courtroom

We saw in the previous chapter that the authors of *Bracton* made the case that the work they were already doing in the royal courts could be understood as part of the cosmopolitan culture of the learned laws. By reconciling the rules of the courts with the rules of Roman and canon law, they were trying to show that English law could be fit into the framework of the two laws. In the following chapters, we will see how these justices made the case that the practices of textual production that justices and clerks engaged in were analogous to the textual practices of Roman and canon law. Writing a treatise modeled on a civilian *summa* was itself a way of making this claim. The process of writing *Bracton* was clearly a textual practice designed to emulate the textual practices of the great civilians and canonists. It is only the most obvious example of such practices in the circle of Raleigh and Bratton, however. The plea rolls, the administrative records of the king's courts, did not look much like the erudite commentaries on the *Institutes* and *Codex* that Raleigh and Bratton had read in the schools, but these justices asserted—through new reading and writing practices that transformed the plea roll into a learned text—that the everyday, mundane administrative work of the royal courts was very much like the work of a jurist of the learned laws.

In this chapter we will look at one particular practice of this circle of justices. During the same span of decades in which they produced *Bracton*, these same justices created several collections of cases drawn from their plea rolls. They committed a great deal of time to producing these texts. In later chapters, we will see that the authors of the *Bracton* treatise analogized cases decided in the king's courts to genres of texts they had encountered in the schools. In *Bracton*, they cited to English cases and provisions of the *Digest* and *Codex* side-by-side, applying the same methods of dialectical reasoning to both. The authors also treated the judgments of royal justices, found in the plea rolls, as if they were the *consilia* and *responsa* of jurists. In this chapter we will see how the justices and clerks in the circle of Pattishall, Raleigh, and Bratton worked to transform the plea roll entry itself into a different type of text. They removed it from its original context as an administrative record and placed it in a new context that was reminiscent of the legal texts they had encountered in the schools.

*Priests of the Law.* Thomas J. McSweeney, Oxford University Press (2019). © Thomas J. McSweeney.
DOI: 10.1093/oso/9780198845454.003.0005

## Clerks and Writing

In October of 1226, William of York wrote to his patron, the Chancellor Ralph Nevill, to ask "whether you want me to go on eyre with Martin of Pattishall farther than to Yorkshire."[1] William complained that "it will be a great nuisance, because of the heavy expense and enormous labor, for the aforesaid Lord Martin is so vigorous and painstaking and set in his ways in his work that he has already rendered all his associates, especially Lord William of Raleigh and myself, weary through exhausting labors. Nor is it a wonder, because he begins to work each day at the rising of the sun and does not cease until nightfall."[2]

A few months earlier, in May and June, letters close issued from the royal chancery to the sheriffs of twelve counties informing them that the king's justices would soon visit their counties as the first stage of an eyre *ad omnia placita* (for all pleas).[3] The eyre was initially divided into two circuits staffed by different groups of justices. A third was added later.[4] As the justices completed their visitations of the twelve counties named in the initial proclamation of the eyre, a second stage was added, and later a third, to take in counties that had not been included in the first.[5] In October of 1226, William of Raleigh was travelling on one such eyre circuit with his master, Martin of Pattishall, and his fellow clerk, William of York. Before the first stage of this eyre was over, Martin and the two Williams would visit five counties over about six months, spending

---

[1] "[S]upplico, quatenus mihi vestro penitus consilium vestrum per latorem praesentium significare velitis, si consulatis et velitis ut ulterius itinerem cum domino M[artino] de Pateshulle, quam in partibus Eboracensibus." Walter Waddington Shirley (ed), *Royal and Other Historical Letters Illustrative of the Reign of Henry III, Vol. 1: 1216-1235* (London 1862) 342 (no. 281) (hereafter Shirley, *Royal Letters*); CAF Meekings, "Six Letters Concerning the Eyres of 1226-8" (1950) 65 EHR 492, 495, reprinted in *Studies in 13th Century Justice and Administration* (Hambledon Press 1981), item V (hereafter Meekings, "Six Letters").

[2] "[P]ro certo scientes, quod si ulterius cum eo itinerem, valde tediosum erit mihi, tum propter graves expensas, cum propter laborem immoderatum. Dictus enim dominus M[artinus] fortis est, et in labore suo ita sedulus et assuetus, quod omnes socios suos, et maxime dominum W[illelmum] de Ralege et me, labore tediosissimo jam reddidit affectos. Nec mirum, quia incipit in ortu solis quotidie laborare, nec cessat usque ad noctem." Shirley (ed), *Royal Letters* (n 1) 342 (no. 281); Meekings, "Six Letters" (n 1) 495. I have modified Meekings' rather free translation of the letter here. The eyre began in Lincoln, where it sat from September 9th to October 13th, before moving on to Yorkshire, arriving at Doncaster on October 20th. David Crook, *Records of the General Eyre* (Her Majesty's Stationery Office, 1982) 79 (hereafter Crook, *General Eyre*). The letter seems to suggest that the eyre was not yet in Yorkshire. This letter was, therefore, probably written in Lincoln or between Lincoln and Doncaster, the eyre's first stop in Yorkshire. If William was telling the truth about Martin of Pattishall's habits, and not simply being hyperbolic, he was indeed working long days: the period from sunrise to nightfall would have been a little less than eleven hours in Lincolnshire at this time of year.

[3] RLC, vol 2, 151; Crook, *General Eyre* (n 2) 1, 78. For the types of letters patent and close that issued from the chancery to initiate a general eyre, see CAF Meekings (ed), *The 1235 Surrey Eyre*, 3 vols (Surrey Record Society 1979) vol 1, 17-20 (hereafter Meekings (ed), *1235 Surrey Eyre*).

[4] Crook, *General Eyre* (n 2) 78.

[5] Ibid, 78-79.

anywhere from less than a week to two months in one place, hearing cases and the returns of the eyre jurors.[6]

What was it that kept Martin of Pattishall's clerks busy from the rising of the sun until nightfall? For the most part, it was the production of documents. The royal administration, by the 1220s, largely operated on small slips of parchment, and clerks such as William of Raleigh and William of York were tasked with creating and maintaining the texts through which the king's government was sustained. Clerks would have been responsible for receiving and filing the original writs that initiated litigation, for writing judicial writs, for making copies of the articles of the eyre for the eyre jurors, for drafting chirographs, and for making rolls of the fines and amercements levied by the eyre.[7] Most importantly for our purposes, the justice's clerks would have been responsible for writing that justice's plea rolls. Each justice of the king's courts kept his own roll of the business done before that court.[8] That roll was compiled by his clerk or clerks. The clerk would take down formulaic summaries of each of the cases

[6] Ibid, 79–80.
[7] For writ files, in which original writs returned to the court were kept, see MT Clanchy, *The Roll and Writ File of the Berkshire Eyre of 1248* (SS vol 90, Selden Society 1973) lx; CT Flower, *Introduction to the Curia Regis Rolls, 1199-1230 A.D.* (SS vol 62, Barnard Quaritch 1944) 347 (hereafter Flower, *Curia Regis Rolls*); Crook, *General Eyre* (n 2) 37–38. The eyre justices could, in certain circumstances, issue their own original writs. *Bracton* gives an example of a writ of novel disseisin issued by an eyre justice. The treatise indicates that this would be appropriate when the defendant committed the disseisin during the eyre. If that was the case, the plaintiff need not go all the way to Westminster to acquire a writ and then come back to his native county, where the eyre justices were already sitting. He could instead obtain that writ from the eyre justices themselves. *Bracton*, vol 3, 201. There is also evidence that, if the wrong complained of occurred during the eyre, the justices could hear the case even without a writ. HG Richardson and GO Sayles (ed), *Select Cases of Procedure without Writ under Henry III* (SS vol 60, Selden Society 1941) xl–xli (hereafter Richardson and Sayles, *Procedure without Writ*). For judicial writs, see Elsa de Haas and GDG Hall (eds), *Early Registers of Writs* (SS vol 87, Bernard Quaritch 1970) lxx (hereafter De Haas and Hall (eds), *Early Registers*); Meekings (ed), *1235 Surrey Eyre* (n 3) vol 1, 29–33. For the copying of the articles of the eyre, and the payments which the clerks received for it, see Richardson and Sayles, *Procedure without Writ* (n 7) ciii; Meekings (ed), *1235 Surrey Eyre* (n 3) vol 1, 95; SR, vol 1, 33; Paul Brand, "The Clerks of the King's Courts in the Reign of Edward I" in MCL, 183 (hereafter Brand, "Clerks of the King's Courts"). For chirographs, see John Hudson, *Oxford History of the Laws of England, Volume II, 871-1216* (OUP 2012) 523 (hereafter Hudson, *Oxford History*); Paul Brand, "'Multis Vigiliis Excogitatam et Inventam': Henry II and the Creation of the English Common Law" in MCL, 87 (hereafter Brand, "Henry II"); MT Clanchy, *From Memory to Written Record: England 1066-1307* (3rd edn, Wiley-Blackwell 2013) 70, 89–90 (hereafter Clanchy, *Memory*). On the taxing session of the eyre, and the recording of fines and amercements, see Meekings (ed), *1235 Surrey Eyre* (n 3) vol 1, 128–30.
[8] Flower, *Curia Regis Rolls* (n 7) 10. A letter sent from the royal chancery to the king's justiciar in Ireland in 1221 explained that this was to ensure that no single justice had the only record of what had transpired in court, "because in one roll alone, danger can threaten" (*eo quod in uno solo rotulo periculum iminere posset*). Presumably this meant that if one roll was lost or tampered with, there would be others to check. Up to this point, there had only been a single itinerant justice operating in Ireland. The letter ordered that that justice henceforth associate himself with two other justices, one layman and one cleric. Crook, *General Eyre* (n 2) 14; RLC vol 1, 451; Paul Brand, "The Birth and Early Development of a Colonial Judiciary: The Judges of the Lordship of Ireland, 1210-1377" in WN Osborough (ed), *Explorations in Law and History: Irish Legal History Society Discourses, 1988-1994* (Irish Academic Press 1995) 6–7. The association of justices with particular rolls was made clear in the 1256 Shropshire eyre, in which Peter Percy was added to the eyre as a justice and instructed to keep the "third roll of the eyre."

heard before the justices. It was important that the rolls be complete; litigants could "vouch the roll" in future litigation.[9] We do not know exactly how these rolls were made. *Bracton* suggests that the rolls of the justices in the Bench and on the eyres were derived from the roll kept by the *prenotarius* (prothonotary) of the court, probably equivalent to the office known later as the keeper of the rolls and writs, a roll which the treatise refers to as the "first roll."[10] Just how they were derived from this roll is difficult to tease out for the first half of the thirteenth century, however. All of the current theories have some objections that cannot be answered, suggesting that there may have been several methods current for constructing a plea roll. In his analysis of the rolls of the Common Bench for Trinity and Michaelmas terms, 1225, G.D.G. Hall noted that there were some similarities between the rolls that we would only expect to see if they were based upon a common source. Rolls will often contain the same scribal errors, as when all three surviving rolls for Michaelmas term, 1225, accidentally supply a plural verb with a singular subject.[11] This could not be a mere coincidence; some copying must have taken place. There are also major differences between the rolls, however. The Michaelmas 1225 rolls do not have the cases in the same order. That could hardly have happened if one clerk was copying another's roll. Hall's theory was that one clerk wrote a first draft of the entries on scraps or sheets of parchment, possibly even while he was sitting in court. Those scraps or sheets were circulated and copied, perhaps with some of the parchment out of order, into a final copy by each clerk.[12] Additional recording duties fell on the clerk of the senior professional justice of the eyre; we find "process marks" in the margins of the senior justice's roll, which tell

Crook, *General Eyre* (n 2) 121. There is some ambiguity as to whether every justice kept a roll. It may be that some justices did not keep rolls. Crook, *General Eyre* (n 2) 13, 15.

[9] Hudson, *Oxford History* (n 7) 535, 542; CAF Meekings and David Crook, *King's Bench and Common Bench in the Reign of Henry III* (Selden Society 2010) 84 (hereafter Meekings and Crook, *King's Bench and Common Bench*). For examples of situations in which a party vouches the roll, see BNB, vol 2, 256 (no 307). See also Robert C Palmer, *The Whilton Dispute, 1264-1380: A Socio-Legal Study of Dispute in Medieval England* (Princeton University Press 1984) 69, 74, 94, 98.

[10] The passage in *Bracton* is less clear than one might hope. *Bracton* states that, if there is a discrepancy between the rolls of the Bench or of an eyre as to a date, "the day must always be presumed to be that given in the first roll, that is, the roll of the prothonotary, whose enrolment all the other subsequent rolls ought to follow and whence they ought to take their origin and authority." *Bracton*, vol 4, 113. When the author of this passage says these other rolls "follow" and "take their origin" from the first roll, he may be referring to direct copying, but could also be referring to the kinds of practices described by G.D.G. Hall. In 1253, the priority was changed by royal command. The keeper of the rolls and writs in the Common Bench was ordered to hand the "first roll" over to the chief justice, Roger of Thirkleby. From that point on, the roll kept by the keeper of the rolls and writs was considered the second roll of the court. CR 1251-53, 374.

[11] CRR, vol 12, 156 (no 755), 248 (no 1218); GDG Hall, Review of *Curia Regis Rolls of the Reign of Henry III: 9-10 Henry III* (1959) 74 EHR 107, 109 (hereafter Hall, "Review of CRR 12").

[12] Hall, "Review of CRR 12" (n 11) 108.

us things like whether an amercement had been copied into the estreat roll or whether a pardon was granted in a particular case.[13] The senior justice and his clerk thus seem to have been responsible for making sure that the court's orders and judgments had been carried out.

The clerk's life would have been one of writing. That was what made him valuable to the king, his ability to produce the texts of a royal government that was becoming increasingly text-driven. But by the time William of York and William of Raleigh went North on eyre with Martin of Pattishall, they may not have been doing much of their own writing. Both were senior clerks who would shortly become justices, and they were likely supervising junior clerks. Martin of Pattishall's correspondence and rolls before 1225 all seem to be written in the same hand, which C.A.F. Meekings thought was probably the hand of William of Raleigh.[14] Starting in 1225, however, Pattishall's rolls and correspondence are written in a different hand and Raleigh's hand seems to make appearances only to correct the rolls.[15] William of York actually worked for the chancery, although he appears to have spent his entire career in the king's courts. He was probably the first in the line of senior clerks styled the *prenotarii* by *Bracton* and later known as the keepers of the rolls and writs of the Common Bench.[16] This clerk was always employed by the chancellor, but actually worked in the courts, maintaining their records.[17] William had been serving in this role since at least 1219, and possibly earlier.[18] He may have been serving in the same capacity on the 1226 eyre. By the time he was sent on eyre as a clerk in 1226, he had already sat as a justice; beginning in 1225 he was occasionally commissioned as a justice to take special assizes.[19] The year after he wrote his letter complaining of the hardship of working for Martin of Pattishall as an eyre clerk, William was commissioned as an eyre justice himself, serving in the Cumberland eyre, and can be found once again complaining about it to his patron, since Cumberland "disagrees with my constitution."[20] He was probably a wealthy man by this time. Even as a clerk he held several ecclesiastical benefices; in the letter in which he complains about going to Yorkshire, he also asks his master how he should go

---

[13] Crook, *General Eyre* (n 2) 32; Meekings and Crook, *King's Bench and Common Bench* (n 9) 8.

[14] Flower, *Curia Regis Rolls* (n 7) 8–10, 32, 271; CAF Meekings, "Martin Pateshull and William Raleigh" (1953) 26 Bulletin of the Institute of Historical Research 157, 178, reprinted in *Studies in 13th Century Justice and Administration* (Hambledon Press 1981), item XI.

[15] Meekings, "Martin Pateshull and William Raleigh" (n 14) 177.

[16] Brand, "Clerks of the King's Courts" (n 7) 173.

[17] Ibid, 173, n 16; Meekings and Crook, *King's Bench and Common Bench* (n 9) 63.

[18] David Crook, "York, William of (d. 1256)" (ODNB, January 3, 2008) <www.oxforddnb.com/view/article/29479> accessed March 13, 2019.

[19] Ibid.

[20] Crook, *General Eyre* (n 2) 82; Meekings, "Six Letters" (n 1) 497; Shirley, *Royal Letters* (n 1) 222.

about obtaining a dispensation to hold multiple ecclesiastical benefices with cure of souls. He apparently had a decent home in London by this time, as well, as he mentions in the same letter that he has three casks of wine stored away in his lodgings there.[21] He may have been whiny, but William of York was successful and prosperous in 1226.

Whether they were supervising or writing, both of these senior clerks would have been concerned with the plea rolls. According to *Bracton*, the *prenotarius* of the eyre was responsible for creating the most authoritative roll of the eyre, one that was separate from the roll of the senior justice.[22] If William of York was functioning as *prenotarius* on this eyre, as he was at the Bench in 1226, he was probably responsible for keeping his own roll. In 1226, William of Raleigh was serving as a clerk to Pattishall and, in the minds of some, was closely connected with Pattishall's rolls. The rolls of the junior justices of the Bench for Hilary term, 1223, and Michaelmas term, 1228, refer to the roll of Martin of Pattishall, as "the roll of W. de Raleigh."[23] Raleigh also appears to have had custody of Pattishall's rolls. He probably held onto them after his master's retirement before passing them on to his own clerk, Henry of Bratton.[24] Just a few years after the eyre of 1226, around the time of Pattishall's retirement and Raleigh's elevation to the judicial bench in 1229, Raleigh began to use these rolls in a new way, elevating them from administrative record to a type of legal literature.

## Writing the Plea Roll Entry

By the time Martin of Pattishall or William of Raleigh began writing *Bracton* in the 1220s, the royal courts had been keeping plea rolls for at least forty years.[25] They were designed to be administrative records and were very formulaic. A typical example drawn from a roll, probably Martin of Pattishall's, illustrates the form of the plea roll entry:

---

[21] Meekings, "Six Letters" (n 1) 497; Shirley, *Royal Letters* (n 1) 222.

[22] *Bracton*, vol 4, 113. There is also a mention of a "roll of the treasury" (*rotulo de thesauro*) in a case from the Common Bench in 1219. This may refer to the roll of the *prenotarius*. CRR, vol 8, 114; Hudson, *Oxford History* (n 7) 548, n 86.

[23] Flower, *Curia Regis Rolls* (n 7) 9; Meekings, "Martin Pateshull and William Raleigh" (n 14) 169.

[24] BNB, vol 1, 25.

[25] Portions of this subsection have been adapted from Thomas McSweeney, "English Judges and Roman Jurists: The Civilian Learning Behind England's First Case Law" (2012) 84 Temple Law Review 827, 836–37. A copy of a plea roll entry from 1181 exists in a roll from 1207, confirming that plea rolls existed at least from that date. There is evidence that they may have been kept as early as 1176. Brand, "Henry II" (n 7) 95.

Lincolnshire—Hugh Malebisse, through his attorney, seeks against Alan de Cheveremunt two bovates of land with appurtenances in Cheveremunt as his right, into which he [i.e., Alan] had no entry except for a term which has passed: and Alan comes and seeks the view. Let him have it. A day is given to them, during the quindene of Saint Martin: and meanwhile etc.; and then Alan should have his charter, because he claims that he has that land in fee.[26]

This entry, from the Common Bench's Michaelmas, 1223 term, records the opening stages of litigation. It records, in the margin, the county in which the dispute arose. It gives us the names of the parties, and lets us know that one of them, Hugh, did not appear personally, but through an attorney.[27] It was important for the court to know when one of the principals in a case had appointed an attorney, since that attorney acted as the principal's agent and had full power to bind him for better or for worse. The rolls are thus replete with entries that record nothing more than that one party appointed an attorney:

Leicester—The Abbot of Croxton appoints in his place Brother Hamo, his canon, etc., in the suit which is between him and Robert le Butyller concerning a plea of land etc.; and he removes Brother Richard and Brother Paganus, whom he first appointed.[28]

Apparently Hugh Malebisse had already appointed his attorney, possibly when he had acquired the writ initiating his litigation from the royal chancery. After

---

[26] "Linc'.—Hugo Malebisse per attornatum suum petit versus Alanum de Cheveremunt duas bovatas terre cum pertinentiis in Cheveremunt ut ius suum, in quas non habet ingressum nisi ad terminum qui preteriit: et Alanus venit et petit inde visum. Habeat. Dies datus est eis a die sancti Martini in xv. dies: et interim etc; et tunc habeat Alanus cartam suam, quia dicit quod habet terram illam in feodo." CRR, vol 11, 136 (no 682).

[27] Attorneys were not necessarily professionals or even proto-professionals. The attorney might simply be a friend or relative who was going to London on business and agreed to travel to Westminster Hall to act as Hugh's agent. Professional attorneys, in the sense of people who spent much of their time acting as attorneys and acquired much of their income in this way, are only observable in the records of the king's courts from the late 1250s, although they may have acted in them before that. By the 1220s, some people were doing this work regularly enough that we could consider them semi-professionals. Paul Brand, *The Origins of the English Legal Profession* (Blackwell 1992) 50–51, 65–67 (hereafter Brand, *Legal Profession*). Some judicial clerks worked as attorneys on the side. Richard Duket, one of the justices who served on the 1226 Yorkshire eyre with William of Raleigh and William of York, had worked for various clients as an attorney while serving as a clerk to the justiciars Geoffrey FitzPeter and Hubert de Burgh. Doris M Stenton, *Pleas before the King or His Justices, 1198-1212, Volume 3* (SS vol 83, Bernard Quaritch 1966) cccxi–cccxiii. Duket's responsibilities as a clerk would have been only partly judicial, as the justiciar, more like a prime minister than a judge, had many non-judicial responsibilities. For more on judicial clerks working as attorneys, see Frank Pegues, "The Clericus in the Legal Administration of Thirteenth-Century England" (1956) 71 EHR 529; Brand, *Legal Profession* (n 27) 89–90.

[28] "Leyc'—Abbas de Crocston' ponit suo fratrem Hamonem canonicum suum etc. in loquela que est inter eum et Robertum le Butyller de placito terre etc.; et ammovet fratrem Ricardum et fratrem Paganum, quos prius posuerat." CRR, vol 11, 121 (no 619).

the mention of the attorney, our entry tells us what is at issue. In this case it is two bovates of land, each of which would be roughly the amount of land it would take one ox (*bos, bovis* in Latin) to plough in one season. This was not an unusual way to describe the quantity of land being claimed. In the rolls, land is measured in terms of bovates, virgates (an amount of land that could be ploughed by two oxen) and carucates (an amount that could be ploughed by a team of eight oxen). It might also be denominated in terms of acres or hides, or in terms of the amount of rent the land generated per year. The clerk would have taken these descriptions of the land from the writ or the plaintiff's oral narration of his case, but we can see in *Bracton* that the justices who wrote that treatise, who had spent part of their youth in the schools learning the rules of Roman and canon law, had also picked up quite a bit of knowledge about the management of an agricultural estate along the way. When local people are appointed "extenders" to make the valuation of an inheritance, the authors explain that the extenders are to determine "how many acres or virgates of arable land (*terra arabilis*) [the estate has] and the annual value of each acre or virgate. Also how many acres there are in pasture (*pastura*) and what each is worth per annum. Also what and how much lies in waste (*vastum*). Also how many acres of meadow (*pratum*) and in what year they may be mowed and in what year not. Also how many acres of wood (*boscus*) and how much they are worth a year, with the pannage [the right to allow one's livestock to roam free in the forest to forage for food] and without it."[29] Land is not just land. The clerks are careful to designate land according to its use in the agricultural economy, as *terra, pastura, vastum, pratum*, and *boscus*.

Although the clerk took quite a bit of the information in the entry from things the parties to the case had said in court, the entry is not a transcript of what was said by any means. Plea roll entries do not record the direct speech of the parties. They often contain indirect speech, or language that alludes to speech that took place in court, as when "Alan comes and seeks the view" in the entry above. The parties' pleading and the jury's verdict will often be represented in indirect speech, as well. Even when we do have this speech in the entry, however, it is mediated through the clerk who is writing the entry. The parties are unlikely to have spoken Latin in court. The pleadings and most of the rest of the courtroom discussion were likely conducted in French, although some English may have been spoken as well.[30] The parties' vernacular speech is thus translated into the Latin of the roll and presented indirectly.

[29] *Bracton*, vol 2, 219.
[30] Paul Brand, "The Languages of the Law in Later Medieval England" in DA Trotter (ed), *Multilingualism in Later Medieval Britain* (DS Brewer 2000) 63, 63–66.

A clerk would have been able to tell from most entries what writ the plaintiff had acquired from the chancery to initiate the litigation.[31] The magic words in this entry are "into which he had no entry except for a term which has passed," indicating that this is a writ of entry *ad terminum qui preteriit*, a type of writ that a lessor could use to eject a lessee who stayed on the land after his lease had ended.[32] The type of writ would have been important to the judge and his clerks; different writs asked different questions, so the choice of the writ would determine what kind of claim the plaintiff could make and what kinds of defenses the defendant could make. The different writs also had different procedures associated with them. Some did not allow essoins (excuses for non-appearance), for instance.[33] The first of the procedural steps is given to us in the entry: Alan requests the view of the land.[34] By the time this entry was written, plea roll entries had become standard enough that not every piece of information had to be written out in full. The entry therefore tells us simply "and meanwhile, etc." in place of the words, "and meanwhile, let the view be had," words that would have been understood by a clerk or justice reading the roll.

The clerk then records a return day, in this case the quindene of Martinmas, which begins on the fifteenth day after the feast of St. Martin of Tours, a feast that falls on November 11th. The parties would have to make their next appearance during the return day, which was not a single day, but a range of days; the quindene of Martinmas ran from November 25th to December 1st.[35] The entry ends with a procedural reminder, that Alan should bring his charter as evidence for his claim. Entries contained a bit of information about the parties and their claim, but they were primarily about the procedures taken in court.

---

[31] Hall pointed out, however, that plea roll entries often fail to distinguish between writs of right and writs of entry, and between different kinds of writs of entry. GDG Hall, Review of *Curia Regis Rolls of the Reign of Henry III. Vol. xiii: 11-14 Henry III* (1962) 77 EHR 103, 105.

[32] For an example of this writ from a register of the early fourteenth century, see de Haas and Hall (eds), *Early Registers* (n 7) 288.

[33] Meekings, *1235 Surrey Eyre* (n 3) vol 1, 36–37. One of the advantages to the plaintiff of an assize of novel disseisin was that it did not allow the defendant to make any essoins. Ibid, vol 1, 70.

[34] The view was a procedure in which the defendant requested that he be allowed to go, along with a number of knights, to be shown which land was at issue in the case. The *Glanvill* treatise treats this as a dilatory tactic, since it causes the case to be adjourned while the view is being made. The court would set a new date for the hearing of the case and the defendant would be allowed to cast essoins from that date, allowing him to push the litigation out even further, potentially for more than a year. *Glanvill*, 22 (Book II, c 1). Jurors were also sent to view the land before they gave their verdict in both the grand assize and the petty assizes.

[35] CR Cheney and Michael Jones, *A Handbook of Dates for Students of British History* (Revised edn, CUP 2000) 100.

## Plea Roll Collections

In 1226, when William of Raleigh was serving as Martin of Pattishall's clerk on the eyre of Lincolnshire and Yorkshire, work on the *Bracton* treatise had probably already begun.[36] While he was part of Martin of Pattishall's household, William of Raleigh was thus involved in the production of two very different types of texts: plea rolls and the *Bracton summa*. Within a few years, Raleigh would be producing texts that bridged the gap between the two. Raleigh was probably the mover behind several collections of cases, drawn from the plea rolls, that were made over the next fifteen to twenty years.

British Library MS Add 12669, which Maitland dubbed *Bracton's Note Book*, is a collection of about 2,000 cases decided in the king's courts between 1217 and 1240. It is a large work. It is composed of twenty-four quires—sheets of parchment that have been sewn together into booklets—most of which have twenty-four sides, for a total of 574 manuscript pages. That figure alone does not give an accurate picture of the scale of the work, however, as more text could be fit onto the average medieval manuscript page than the modern printed page. Maitland's edition of the text runs to a full 1,442 pages. The 2,000 cases were copied from more than fifty rolls of the eyre circuits, the Common Bench, and the court *coram rege*.

*Bracton's Note Book* was created in the same circle as the *Bracton* treatise. The vast majority of the cases contained in it are drawn from the rolls of either Martin of Pattishall or William of Raleigh. The *Note Book*, like *Bracton*, was a major production. It, too, was probably created by working "long into the night watches."[37] The historian John C. Fox estimated, based on conversations with legal stationers working in the 1920s, that it took approximately eight hours to produce one copy of Magna Carta.[38] The *Note Book* is about one hundred times the length of Magna Carta.[39] The cursive hand of the *Note Book* is not quite as fine as the cursive engrossing hand of copies of Magna Carta, but even so, the copying of the *Note Book* alone must have taken several hundred man-hours, not to mention the work that went into selecting cases for inclusion.

---

[36] *Bracton*, vol 3, xxvii; Paul Brand, "The Date and Authorship of *Bracton*: A Response" (2010) 31 Journal of Legal History 217, 225 (hereafter Brand, "Date and Authorship").

[37] *Bracton*, vol 2, 19.

[38] John C Fox, "The Originals of the Great Charter of 1215" (1924) 39 EHR 321, 333; David Carpenter, *Magna Carta* (Penguin Books 2015) 11.

[39] Modern texts of Magna Carta generally fill somewhere between ten and fifteen pages. Carpenter, *Magna Carta* (n 38) 36–69; JC Holt, *Magna Carta* (3rd edn, CUP 2015) 378–98. Both of the books cited include facing-page Latin and English versions of the charter.

It probably represents even more work than all that. The *Note Book* is the only surviving example of several case collections created within the circle of Raleigh and Bratton. It copies from a number of prior case collections that were made at various points during Raleigh's and Bratton's careers.[40] The *Note Book* jumps back and forth a bit chronologically, but there are discrete sections of the *Note Book* that can be separated into units of cases drawn from the periods 1218 to 1228, 1229 to 1232, 1233 to 1234, and 1234 to 1240, along with a section of miscellaneous terms that were missed when the earlier collections were made and a section of cases drawn from Martin of Pattishall's eyres of the 1220s. I argue in the appendix that these units were likely independent collections that were later copied into the *Note Book*. The *Note Book* itself contains evidence for their existence. There are physical breaks in the manuscript that correspond to these units of text. They also correspond to the various stages of Raleigh's career. The first unit is composed of cases from Martin of Pattishall's rolls, and ends at his retirement. It may have been made by Raleigh and his clerks upon Pattishall's retirement, when Raleigh became a justice of the Common Bench. The second unit may have been made shortly after Raleigh received his first appointment as chief justice of an eyre in 1232, and the third on his transfer to become the chief justice of the newly reconstituted court *coram rege* in 1234. The unit running from 1234 to 1240 corresponds to his period as chief justice of the court *coram rege*. I think it likely that each of these collections was made shortly after the major event to which it corresponds.[41] The *Note Book* itself was probably compiled by Bratton from the earlier collections sometime between 1240 and 1256.[42] It appears to have remained in his hands, as it contains marginal references to cases Bratton himself decided in the 1250s.[43]

Case collecting was not altogether new in William of Raleigh's time. The exchequer official Richard FitzNigel, writing in the late 1170s, mentions that he wrote a history of England in three columns, one of which was composed of "various public and private matters, including judgments of the court."[44]

[40] *Bracton*, vol 3, xxxvii–xxxviii.

[41] See Appendix.

[42] The *Note Book* is unlikely to postdate 1256 since it contains an addition that discusses the problem of the leap year. A defendant who made an essoin of bed-sickness, an excuse for non-appearance due to a serious illness, could delay his case a year and a day. The courts had to decide what to do when the year was a leap year. In 1256, the king mandated that the defendant should receive the benefit of the extra day. CR 1254–56, 414–15. A note that was added to a blank space on one folio of the *Note Book*, sometime after its completion, says that he should not receive the benefit. Henry of Bratton witnessed the mandate that adopted the opposite rule, and it is unlikely he would have added this note to the *Note Book* after 1256. BNB, vol 1, 42; vol 3, 299–301 (no 1291). The *Note Book* was, therefore, probably complete by 1256.

[43] BNB, vol 3, 664 (next to entry 1884).

[44] "In tertia vero de pluribus negociis tam publicis quam familiaribus, necnon et curie iudiciis agitur." Emilie Amt and SD Church (eds) *Dialogus de Scaccario and Constitutio Domus Regis: The Dialogue of*

Whether Richard drew the stories of these cases from the plea rolls—which appear to have existed as early as 1181, and possibly earlier—is unclear.[45] There was also a Norman case-collecting tradition by the later thirteenth century, and it may have had earlier antecedents.[46] Even at the time Raleigh and Bratton were collecting cases from Pattishall's rolls, others who had access to the rolls of Pattishall were likely doing the same thing. When Maitland was working on the *Note Book*, he turned to the plea rolls to find the original case records. Maitland found odd markings in some of those rolls, next to the very cases that had been excerpted into the *Note Book*. Someone had sidelined certain cases with a "firm heavy line, in colour a dark rusty brown." [47] Other cases had the word "*volo*" ("I want this") written next to them. Others had subject headings, such as "of novel disseisin" or "of essoins" placed above them.[48] A few rolls had very elaborate markings, with sidelines that end in the letter "N", for "*nota*." These are combined with subject headings and the words "*visus est*" ("it has been seen") at the top of each side of the folio.[49] Maitland believed that these notes were all related, and had been made by Henry of Bratton as notes for the scribes who would copy the cases into the *Note Book*.[50] Samuel Thorne cast serious doubt on this part of Maitland's thesis when he produced his translation of *Bracton*, demonstrating that cases marked with *volo* and the subject headings often did not end up in the *Note Book*. Thorne offered the theory that "a number of men, working independently, seem to have been collecting cases for their own purposes during the years covered by the *Note Book*, each with his own method of marking the roll."[51] The straight-line scoring and the elaborate markings, with the "N" and "*visus est*," were likely used by the people who created the *Note Book* and its predecessor collections.[52] *Volo* is still a mystery, however. This annotator looked at some of the same rolls that Raleigh and Bratton had looked at and marked many of the same cases, but also marked

the *Exchequer and the Establishment of the Royal Household* (Clarendon Press 2007) xviii–xix, 40–41 (hereafter Amt and Church (eds), *Dialogus*).

---

[45] Brand, "Henry II" (n 7) 95. John Hudson thought it possible that the third column of the work was composed of records, as many contemporary chronicles were. John Hudson, "Administration, Family, and Perceptions of the Past in Late Twelfth-Century England: Richard FitzNigel and the Dialogue of the Exchequer" in Paul Magdalino (ed), *The Perception of the Past in Twelfth-Century* Europe (Hambledon Press 1992) 79–80.

[46] SR Packard (ed), "Miscellaneous Records of the Norman Exchequer" (1927) 12 Smith College Studies in History 1.

[47] BNB, vol 1, 66–67.

[48] Ibid, 65–69.

[49] Ibid, 68.

[50] Ibid, 68.

[51] *Bracton*, vol 3, xxxiv–xxxvi.

[52] See Appendix.

some that they had skipped. We have no way of knowing when he was working; it is impossible to know who marked the roll first. The rolls that contain *volos* tend to be chronologically earlier—all belong to Pattishall—which may suggest that *Volo* was working sometime in the 1220s.[53] This person was probably associated in some way with Pattishall, as Pattishall's rolls would not have been widely accessible in the thirteenth century. Raleigh and Bratton seem to have had custody of them until 1258, when they were presumably transferred to the treasury in accord with a royal command.[54] Thus, *volo* is likely someone who was granted access to the rolls by Pattishall, Raleigh, or Bratton and who had permission to mark them, or at least thought he could get away with returning the rolls with his markings on them. Circles of justices and clerks overlapped, and Raleigh or Bratton may have granted access to the rolls of the great Martin of Pattishall to another member of the judicial establishment who wanted to copy cases of the master. *Volo* was, therefore, likely someone who was close to the people who wrote *Bracton*.

Raleigh, Bratton, and *Volo* also had contemporaries who were copying from rolls of other justices. Three rolls, those of the Common Bench for Trinity 1222 and Hilary and Michaelmas 1223, bear a different set of markings altogether. The annotator's method is complex and difficult to decipher. Some cases contain a single capital A next to them. Others contain two A's. Others contain a circle with either a horizontal line, a vertical line, or both running through it.[55] These symbols appear in combination with each other. Although Martin of Pattishall sat on these terms of the court, we can be fairly certain that these are not his rolls. Another roll survives for Michaelmas 1223 that is marked with sidelines and seems to have been used for the collection that later formed the first half of the *Note Book*. These rolls of 1222 and 1223 were, therefore, likely the rolls of one of Pattishall's colleagues on the bench. Stephen of Seagrave, Ralph Hareng, Thomas of Heyden, and Robert of Lexington all sat during all of these terms of the Common Bench along with Pattishall.[56] Another roll, a roll of special assizes taken by the king's justices in Norwich in 1209, contains markings against fourteen cases. These markings are different from any of the others, consisting of two parallel, vertical lines with a slash through them.[57]

---

[53] The latest roll to contain the *volo* markings is a roll of 1221. Doris M Stenton, *Rolls of the Justice in Eyre for Lincolnshire 1218-9 and Worcestershire 1221* (SS vol 53, Selden Society 1934) lxxv–lxxxiii (hereafter Stenton, *Lincolnshire and Worcestershire*).

[54] BNB, vol 1, 25.

[55] Curia Regis Rolls 81, 82A, and 84.

[56] Meekings and Crook, *King's Bench and Common Bench* (n 9) 166, 168, 170.

[57] Doris M Stenton, *Pleas before the King or His Justices, 1198-1212, Volume 3* (SS vol 83, Bernard Quaritch 1966) cccxx (hereafter Stenton, *Pleas 3*). The roll is reproduced in Doris M Stenton, *Pleas before the King or His Justices, 1198-1212, Volume 4* (SS vol 84, Bernard Quaritch 1967) 168–282.

These markings may or may not have been made in anticipation of a collection of cases. The markings could simply be some kind of complex process markings, made for administrative purposes. But the cases so marked are more interesting than the average plea roll case.[58]

Why were people collecting cases from the rolls in the early thirteenth century, and why did the circle of Raleigh and Bratton go to so much trouble to create these texts? The *Note Book* itself doesn't tell us why it was made. The work contains no linking material and no commentary apart from marginal glosses. If it ever contained an introduction, it was lost long ago. The *Note Book* does not appear to have been given a binding in the early years of its existence, and was instead left as a series of loose quires. At some point, the outer sheet of parchment of the first quire was lost, not an uncommon occurrence when quires circulate without a binding, as the outer sheet of the quire often takes quite a bit of wear. That sheet would have contained the first two pages of the *Note Book*. If anyone ever wrote an introduction to it, it would have been there. We are therefore left to guess the *Note Book*'s utility from the structure and content of the text itself.

We do not know what the *Notebook*'s predecessor collections looked like, but the *Note Book*, as a material object, gives us some clues as to what its creators intended for it. The creators of the *Note Book* differentiated this text in various ways from the rolls that served as its source. The plea rolls, like most of the royal courts' administrative records, were rolls. The plea rolls were admittedly more codex-like than the rolls of the chancery. They were not sewn end-to-end and rolled up for storage as the chancery's rolls were. Instead, individual membranes—which were sometimes individually referred to as rolls (*rotuli*)— were sewn together at the head into a collection that looked something like a modern legal pad. That collection of individual membranes was, confusingly, also referred to as a roll.[59] When they copied from those rolls, however, the *Note Book*'s creators copied the entries onto quires. Quires formed the building blocks of codices, books in the modern sense, which were considered more appropriate for works of learning than rolls were. The *Note Book* was meant to be an impressive text. It is written in the same script—called *cursiva Anglicana* by paleographers—used by clerks of the royal courts when they copied the plea rolls. In the *Note Book*, however, that documentary script has been elevated to a

---

[58] Stenton, *Pleas* 3 (n 57) cccxx.
[59] RF Hunnisett, "What is a Plea Roll?" (1988) 9 Journal of the Society of Archivists 109, 111.

fine book script, very neat and tidy.[60] The manuscript is also well-lined. It looks more like a schools text than an administrative record.

Maitland argued that the *Note Book* was created in preparation for the *Bracton* treatise. *Bracton* contains more than 500 references to cases decided in the king's courts and Maitland thought that, to organize all of this material, Bratton, who Maitland believed to be the author of the treatise, had created this *Note Book* and possibly several others.[61] Thorne cast serious doubt on the thesis that the *Note Book* was created in preparation for the treatise, demonstrating that the *Note Book* was not likely to have been the primary source for most of the cases in the treatise.[62] Sometimes the treatise will contain information about a case that is on the roll, but not in the *Note Book*, and it will often tell the reader where on the roll a particular case can be found, information the author could only have gotten by looking at the roll itself, not by reading the *Note Book*.[63]

If it wasn't made as preparatory work for the *Bracton* treatise, to serve William of Raleigh's literary aspirations, could it have been created to serve some administrative purpose? Works of administrative memory were occasionally written in the codex format in this period. Domesday Book, William the Conqueror's 1086 land survey, was copied into two codices. The Red Book of the Exchequer, a compilation of records taken from various rolls of that royal office, was made, in codex format, sometime in the 1230s.[64] These texts could be useful as references to important administrative acts that needed to be remembered. The *Note Book* would not have been very useful as an administrative reference, however. Information that would have been crucial to an administrator, such as the names of parties, is often abbreviated to "a certain person" in the *Note Book*. Thorne suggested a slightly different purpose, but still an administrative one. He thought that the earliest collections of plea roll entries, those of the 1220s, were made to give junior judicial clerks practice in copying plea roll entries and perhaps to provide them with a form-book for making future entries.[65] This is possible, but if true, things had changed by the time the

---

[60] Albert DeRolez, *The Paleography of Gothic Manuscript Books from the Twelfth to the Sixteenth Century* (CUP 2003) 134–35; MB Parkes, *English Cursive Book Hands 1250-1500* (OUP 1969).

[61] See Paul Brand, "The Age of Bracton" in John Hudson (ed), *The History of English Law: Centenary Essays on "Pollock and Maitland"* (OUP 1996) 80 (hereafter Brand, "Age of Bracton").

[62] *Bracton*, vol 3, xxxiv–xxxvi. G.D.G. Hall made similar observations in his review of the printed edition of the *Curia Regis Rolls* for the years 1221 to 1224 and 1230 to 1232. GDG Hall, review of *Curia Regis Rolls of the Reign of Henry III: 5-6 Henry III and 7-9 Henry III* (London: H.M.S.O., 1949, 1955) (1958) 73 EHR 481, 483–84; Hall, Review of *Curia Regis Rolls of the Reign of Henry III, vol. xiv: 14-17 Henry III* (1964) 79 EHR 155, 155–56.

[63] *Bracton*, vol 3, xxxiv–xxxvi.

[64] Clanchy, *Memory* (n 7) 103; Amt and Church (eds), *Dialogus* (n 44) xi–xii; Robert C Stacey, *Politics, Policy, and Finance under Henry III, 1216-1245* (Clarendon Press 1987) 41.

[65] *Bracton*, vol 3, xxxviii.

*Note Book* was created in the 1240s or 1250s. The *Note Book* itself is clearly not a mere copying exercise. One would think that if the justices or senior clerks wanted to give their junior clerks practice copying plea roll entries, they would have chosen something other than quires of high-quality parchment to do so. The *Note Book* also provides evidence that cuts against Thorne's thesis that the case collections of the 1220s were made as reference texts junior clerks could turn to when looking for the proper format for an entry. Neither the *Note Book* nor its predecessors were organized to be useful for such a purpose. The *Note Book* is organized by term of court. A clerk who needed an example of an entry related to a case brought by the assize of novel disseisin would have no way to find it other than to read through the entire text until he found such a case.

Moreover, although Thorne is correct that we do find some mundane entries in the earlier parts of the *Note Book*, it is dominated by cases that are longer, less typical, and more interesting than the average plea roll entry. Pattishall's rolls for Michaelmas 1219 and Michaelmas 1223 both survive and were likely used in creating the *Note Book*. To give a sense of how selective the compilers of the *Note Book* were, there are 798 entries on the Michaelmas, 1223, roll; only forty-four of them, or a little more than five percent, made it into the *Note Book*.[66] The proportion is roughly the same for the Michaelmas, 1219, roll; only forty-three out of 750 entries made it into the *Note Book*.[67] I have sampled the first 100 cases on each roll. Between the two of them, there were twenty-seven entries (thirteen and a half percent of the total) that just recorded appointments of attorneys. None of them were copied into the *Note Book*. None of the eleven entries recording licenses to concord made it into the *Note Book*. None of the sixteen entries that record a new day being given to the parties because the jury failed to show up—and these actually outnumber the cases where the jury did show up to give a verdict—made it into the *Note Book*. These were the bread and butter of the royal courts, the kinds of things clerks would have had to record on the plea rolls on a regular basis. If the *Note Book* or its predecessors were created as practice for the clerks or as a formulary book that would give

---

[66] I selected these two rolls because we can be fairly certain that the surviving rolls for those terms were Pattishall's own rolls, and almost certainly the ones used in the creation of the *Note Book*. See Stenton, *Lincolnshire and Worcestershire* (n 53) lxxv, lxxxvi. I would like to thank my research assistant, Evan Steiner, for his assistance in compiling information about these rolls and the cases excerpted from them into the *Note Book*.

[67] Some of these are conjectural. Cases from this term would probably have been on one of the missing folios of the *Note Book*. Maitland examined Curia Regis Roll 71, which contains copyist's marks, and guessed that an additional eight cases, marked on the rolls but not contained in the *Note Book*, were probably contained on that missing folio. BNB, vol 3, 717–23; Stenton, *Lincolnshire and Worcestershire* (n 53) lxxv.

them examples of the different kinds of enrolments they would be required to make, one would expect to see this routine business in the *Note Book*.

Instead, the *Note Book* copies the most interesting cases. The *Note Book* was part of a process of constituting the plea roll entry as a new genre of legal literature. No longer simply an administrative record, the plea roll entry as constituted in the *Note Book* was a text that could be read for the legal principles it contained. The *Note Book* is not merely a collection of plea roll entries; it is a collection of plea roll entries that have been selected because they fit within a certain set of parameters set by its creator. The entries chosen are longer and more involved than the average entry. The first 100 entries on the Michaelmas, 1223 roll average eleven printed lines per entry in the *Curia Regis Rolls* edition. The fourteen cases out of those first 100 that were excerpted for the *Note Book* average twenty-one. Four of the six cases out of these 100 that ended in a final judgment are recorded in the *Note Book*.

The cases selected for the *Note Book* appear to have been chosen because they illustrate important points of law. Occasionally the creator of the *Note Book* even supplied a deep meaning to an entry that did not appear on its face to have one. An entry from the rolls of the Common Bench in 1220 reads:

> Reginald Carpenter, through his attorney, seeks against Alice de Medham half a virgate of land with appurtenances in Medham as his right etc. And as of that which she etc. And she comes and says that she claims nothing except her dower and thence calls to warrant Hugh Sanzaver, who was present and warranted her. And he sought the view. He shall have it.
>
> He sought in the same way and through the same words against Hugh Sanzaver one virgate of land with appurtenances in Medham as his right and Hugh comes and seeks the view concerning both lands. He shall have it. A day is given etc. And meanwhile etc. And Alice may remain.[68]

This is a fairly simple case. Reginald claims land against Alice. Alice says the land is her dower. Upon her death, a widow's dower lands would pass to her husband's heir. That heir was required to warrant the land, meaning that he would defend any case brought against the widow for the land and, if he lost,

---

[68] "Reginaldus Carpentarius per attornatum suum petit uersus Aliciam de Medham dimidiam uirgatam terre cum pertinenciis in Medham ut ius suum etc. et ut illam unde etc. et ipsa uenit et dicit quod nichil clamat nisi dotem suam et uocat inde ad warantum Hugonem Sanzau' qui presens fuit et ei warentizauit et petit inde uisum, habeat.
    Idem petit eodem modo et per eadem uerba uersus Hugonem Sanzau' i. uirgatam terre cum pertinenciis in Medham ut ius suum et Hugo uenit et de utraque terra petit uisum, habeat. Dies datus est etc. et interim etc. et Alicia remaneat." BNB, vol 2, 106 (no 119).

replace those lands with equivalent ones by a process known as *escambium*, or exchange. Therefore, when Alice is sued by Reginald for her dower lands, Alice calls Hugh, her husband's heir, to warrant. He does so and requests the view. The court orders that the view be made and assigns a return date to the parties for the next stage of their case. The copyist omits this return date, since it would not be necessary for a reader of the *Note Book* to know, replacing the "three weeks after Trinity" that is found on the roll with an "*etc.*"

There isn't much to this case, but the creators of the *Note Book* were able to produce some gold from this dross. The *Note Book* contains many marginal glosses, some of which may have been in the predecessor collections and others of which were added later, probably by Henry of Bratton. Raleigh and Bratton would have been familiar with the glossing of texts from their time in the schools. Texts of Roman and canon law were heavily glossed, to the extent that, when the text of, say, the *Digest* or the *Decretum* was copied into a manuscript, the scribe would generally leave large blank spaces in the margins for the gloss to be added. The *Note Book* is glossed much more lightly than these schools texts. Many pages contain no annotations at all. Bratton may have considered the glosses a continuing work, however. The glosses seem to have been added to the *Note Book* over a period of many years.[69] Some simply tell us the subject of the case, usually which writ it concerns.[70] Some summarize the case.[71] Many tell us what principle the case is meant to stand for. Most of them are posed in procedural terms—"the view lies for [an action of] *de proparte*" or "that the

---

[69] Most of the annotations were made by the same person, a person who also wrote a few of the headings in the main text. BNB, vol 1, 64; vol 2, 14, 193, 249; BL MS Add 12669 fos 3, 35, 45. Maitland thought, since the annotator added those headings, that he was probably the person who oversaw the construction of the text. That seems a reasonable conjecture. Several of the glosses refer to cases that were decided by Henry of Bratton. These glosses demonstrate both that Bratton was probably the person who oversaw the construction of the *Note Book* and that at least some of the glosses were written in the 1250s or 1260s, as several of them refer to cases that were heard in those decades. BNB, vol 1, 83, 94–102. This would hint at a later date for the glosses, and possibly for the *Note Book* as well. On the other hand, some of the marginal glosses hint at an early date for both the *Note Book* and the glosses themselves. One gloss refers to the Provisions of Merton as a "*nova gracia,*" or a "new grace." BNB, vol 3, 362 (no 1409); BL MS Add 12669, fo 210. Paul Brand has argued that acts of lawmaking were only referred to as "new" for a maximum period of about five years after their issuance. Brand, "Date and Authorship" (n 36) 223. It is worth noting that this language also appears in parts of *Bracton* in relation to the Provisions of Merton, which may suggest that the annotations in the *Note Book* were written around the same time as those parts of the treatise. See above, p 54.

There are several ways to reconcile this seemingly contradictory evidence. The glosses may have been made over a long period of time. Another possibility is that the gloss that refers to Merton as a *nova gracia* was originally written in the margin of the *Note Book*'s predecessor collection sometime close to 1236 and simply copied into the *Note Book* when it was made. Brand, "Age of Bracton" (n 61) 79. This gloss is not in Bratton's hand. It is in the hand of another annotator who Maitland refers to as the "occasional annotator." BNB, vol 1, 64.

[70] See BNB, vol 2, 67 (no 75), 70 (nos 77, 78), 82 (no 91), 94 (no 103), 98 (nos 108, 109), 103 (no 114).

[71] BNB, vol 2, 105 (nos 117, 118).

parson of the church will not answer in a plea of advowson."[72] Some are placed in substantive terms, however, such as "Note that a free man can do villein customs by reason of a villein tenement, but he will not be a villein on account of this, because he can relinquish the tenement" and "Note that a gift without seisin has no force where the donor died seised."[73] In Reginald and Alice's case, the annotator wrote "Note that the view is conceded to the warrantor after he has warranted concerning the land which he has warranted."[74] Alice and Reginald's case thus illustrates a point of procedural law, that the view comes after warranty.

More complex cases could lead to deeper discussions of the law. Records of certifications are popular in the *Note Book*.[75] The certification procedure was the closest thing one could find to an appeal in thirteenth-century English law. Writs with titles such as *de habendo recordo et processu* ("of having the record and process") and, famous today because of its present use in appeals to the Supreme Court of the United States, *certiorari* ("to be informed") were used when one court needed to know what had happened in another court.[76] Thus, if a defendant before the Bench at Westminster claimed that the action should not proceed because he had been sued on the same writ and the same facts before the eyre in his home county, the Bench might send a writ to the justices of the eyre asking them to appear and make their record orally or to send their plea rolls to confirm that the case had been heard already. Sometimes these procedures were used to clarify what had happened in the previous court. For instance, if a litigant thought that the jurors' verdict had been too vague at the initial trial, they could ask a justice to call the jurors back to clarify their verdict.[77] Certification writs could also be used, however, when one of

---

[72] BNB, vol 2, 8 (no 8), 80 (no 89).
[73] BNB, vol 2, 62–3 (no 70), 120 (no 144).
[74] "Nota quod visus conceditur waranto postquam warantizavit de terra quam warantizavit." BNB, vol 2, 106 (no 119).
[75] BNB, vol 2, 56 (no 63), 233 (no 281), 306 (no 371), 315 (no 382), 435 (no 564), 459 (no 595), 588 (no 751), 638 (no 829); vol 3, 82 (no 1083), 221 (no 1209), 225 (no 1211), 242 (no 1226), 275 (no 1265), 290 (no 1281), 294 (no 1285), 538 (no 1691), 690 (no 1928).
[76] The analytical index to de Haas and Hall's *Early Register of Writs* shows the wide variety of writs that used the *certiorari* or *de habendo recordo et processu* language. De Haas and Hall (eds), *Early Registers* (n 7) 380–81. Both kinds of language often appear in the same writ. For instance, a writ recorded in an early fourteenth-century register is titled "De recordo et processu assise nove disseisine," but contains the formula "volumus certiorari." Ibid, 265 (no 679). This type of writ could also be used to acquire information that was unrelated to litigation. A writ in the same early fourteenth-century register uses the *certiorari* language to order an escheator to send the king information about how particular lands had come into the king's hand. Ibid, 288 (no 765).
[77] The author of a section of *Bracton*'s tractate on the assize *utrum*, probably Henry of Bratton himself, distinguishes clearly between certification and conviction by attaint. An attaint is a procedure in which the justices call a jury of twenty-four to convict the jury of twelve of swearing a false oath, and is only appropriate in cases where the jury "wittingly swears otherwise than the matter in truth is." *Bracton*, vol

the litigants felt that the justices had made the wrong decision in the earlier case.[78]

Because certifications involved discussions of what had been done incorrectly in the first instance, and usually contained detailed exposition of the facts of the case and the steps the court took to reach its decision, they could serve as teaching tools. In a 1231 certification that appears in the *Note Book*, for instance, we see a group of justices who have to explain what, in the first instance, may have appeared as the historian's bane—the general verdict—on the rolls. In a general verdict, the jury was only asked the final, dispositive question for the case: "did A disseise B?" We often do not even get their answer, but only hear the court's conclusion from it: "it is considered that B have his seisin and A is in mercy," does not tell us what facts led the jury to the conclusion that A had disseised B. It need not tell us who had input in the decision. Did the jury debate the matter? Did the justices ask specific questions to lead the jury through the issue of whether there was a disseisin or not? S.F.C. Milsom effectively demonstrated that the general verdict could hide the real issues in the case.[79] The certification gives us some insight into the jurors' reasoning, as they are summoned to certify, or provide information, to the justices of the higher court, who question them on the specifics. Even more interesting is the fact that one group that is never questioned in other plea roll entries, the justices themselves, are occasionally forced to argue on their own behalf that they did not make a mistake in the original case. Some certifications thus contain one set of justices acting as justices and another set of justices acting as defendants.[80] The original roll may have told us only that the jurors said that Oliver de Gladefen was the next heir of Roger Gernon, who was seised in demesne as of fee on the day he died. The certification, however, shows us that the case was far more complicated, that there was argument over fine points of law, and that

---

3, 337. A certification is a procedure in which the justices call the original jury back to clarify their oath, and is appropriate where the jurors are "led astray by reasonable error." *Bracton*, vol 3, 338.

---

[78] One example from a register of writs of the early fourteenth century implies that there was error on someone's part in the earlier proceedings: "The king to R., greeting. Since for certain [reasons we wish to be informed as to the record and process of the assize of novel disseisin concerning a tenement in N. which was summoned and taken at N. by our writ between A., who was the wife of C., and B., the son of C., before you and your fellows, our justices assigned to the aforesaid assize] . . . we command you to send the record etc. and this writ, that, having inspected the aforesaid record and process, we may cause to be done to the parties . . . whatever *ought to be done by right and according to the law and custom of our realm*. Witness." De Haas and Hall, *Early Registers* (n 7) 265–66 (no 680) (emphasis mine). In place of the words that appear in brackets in the quotation above, the register actually has the words "etc. as above up to" referring the reader to the writ that comes immediately before it in the register. I have supplied the missing words from that prior writ. Ibid, 266.

[79] SFC Milsom, *The Legal Framework of English Feudalism* (CUP 1976) 5.

[80] See BNB, vol 3, 221 (no 1209).

the justices were making decisions about the law that affected the outcome of the case.[81]

The parties to the original suit in the 1231 entry were Oliver de Gladefen, the demandant, and the prior of Lees, a house of Augustinian canons in Essex. The prior was tenant of half a carucate of land and another parcel that produced forty shillings of rent per year. Oliver brought an assize of mort d'ancestor claiming that the land had belonged to Oliver's now deceased brother, Roger. The writ of mort d'ancestor asked the jury two simple questions: "whether [the deceased] was seised [of the land in question] in his demesne as of fee on the day he died" and "whether [the complainant] is his nearer (*propinquior*) heir," meaning that he is first in line of inheritance.[82] Thus, if Oliver could show that his brother had been seised on the day he died and that he, Oliver, was next in line of succession after his brother, he would take the land. In the initial case, Oliver had won and the prior was ordered to return the land to him. The prior, however, complained to the king's court that "the assize was taken unjustly and against the custom of the realm of England" and asked that "he have the aforesaid Oliver and the bodies of the recognitors [i.e., the jurors] to hear the record of the same assize to certify it."[83]

We have several parties already—Oliver, the prior, the jurors—but the scribe writing the entry makes it clear that the main parties to the certification are the four justices who heard the original case, who are ordered by name to appear "before the justices" of the Common Bench at Westminster.[84] The suit had originally been heard by a special assize commission composed of four knights of the county, local men who were not active in the central courts. These justices from the original case stood before the justices at Westminster and told their

[81] BNB, vol 2, 435 (no 564).

[82] This example comes from the *Glanvill* treatise: "Si O. pater predicti G. fuit saisitus in dominico suo sicut de feodo suo de una virgata terre in illa villa die qua obiit . . . et si ille G. propinquior heres eius sit." *Glanvill*, 150 (Book XIII, c 3) . The writ asks a third question that is not at issue in this case, "whether he died after my first coronation." Ibid. This is the limitation date for the writ, barring actions that happened too long ago to be justiciable. The limitation date for the assize of mort d'ancestor was later changed to the first coronation of King Richard I. De Haas and Hall, *Early Registers* (n 7) 23 (no 16). In 1237 it was changed to King John's last return from Ireland, although within a few years officials in the royal courts believed that the change had been made at the council of Merton of 1236. SR 1, Statutes Section, 3; *Bracton*, vol 3, 249; Brand, "Date and Authorship" (n 36) 223. The writ was also limited in one other way, in that it was only available to someone who claimed to be the next heir of a parent, sibling, aunt, or uncle.

[83] "Prior queritur quod assisa illa iniuste et contra consuetudinem Anglie capta fuit etc., et quod haberet predictum Oliverum ad audiendum recordum illud et corpora recognitorum eiusdem assise ad certificandum etc." BNB, vol 2, 435 (no 564).

[84] "Preceptum fuit vicecomiti quod venire faceret coram iusticiariis Rogerum filium Osberti, Radulphum de Muncy, Robertum de Colevilla, et Michaelem de Bauent iusticiarios constitutos ad assisam mortis antecessoris capiendam inter Oliverum de Gladefen petentem et Willelmum Priorem de Legha tenentem . . ." Ibid.

superiors that the prior called a man named Ralph to warrant the priory's claim to the land. Ralph was another brother of Oliver and Roger, and was older than both. As we learn later in the record, Ralph had inherited the obligation to do warranty from his father, Osbert, who had originally granted the land to the prior and who had included in his charter an obligation to do warranty that would be binding on his heirs. If the prior lost, Ralph would have to give him equivalent land in *escambium*. But Ralph had not shown up to warrant the priory. The justices said that they took the assize in his absence and the jury determined that Roger had died seised and Oliver was his next heir. Oliver recovered his seisin and the prior was placed in mercy.[85]

After questioning the four knights who had sat as justices in the case, the justices at Westminster turned to the jury and asked if they agreed with the record those justices had made. The jurors now told a somewhat different story. Apparently when the jurors heard that Oliver's elder brother had been called to warrant the land, they "doubted whether that Oliver was the nearer heir or not."[86] They knew if there was an elder brother, namely Ralph, then the younger brother was not the nearer heir: the assize of mort d'ancestor followed the rule of primogeniture. An elder brother would completely exclude a younger one as heir. In other words, Ralph, who had been called to warrant, not Oliver, should be the heir of their brother Roger.

They also knew, however, that Ralph was the lord of that land, a fact that should disqualify him from inheriting the land from Roger. The royal courts, by this period, had developed the "lord and heir" rule, meaning that one could not be both lord and heir with respect to the same piece of land. When Roger had died, Ralph, as lord, could not inherit it.[87] The jurors actually knew some of the history of this land. It had been given to the prior by Osbert, the father of Ralph, Roger, and Oliver, when he had become a monk. When he entered religion, Osbert suffered civil death, and his lordship and duty to warrant the land passed to Ralph, his eldest son. Indeed, the jurors knew of an earlier case concerning the land, in which Ralph himself had brought an assize of mort d'ancestor to try to take the land from the prior, claiming it as his inheritance from Osbert. The court in that case determined that, since Osbert had entered into religion, Ralph had inherited his duty to warrant. Since Ralph was bound to warrant the land, he could not bring the assize.[88]

[85] Ibid.
[86] "Dubitaverunt utrum ipse Oliverus esset propinquior heres vel non ..." BNB, vol 2, 436 (no 564).
[87] Hudson, *Oxford History* (n 7) 651.
[88] BNB, vol 2, 436 (no 564).

The jurors were thus confused as to whether Oliver could be said to be the nearer heir. Ralph would have possessed a superior claim to Oliver, but Ralph was barred from claiming the land because he was lord. Should the jury then treat Ralph as if he did not exist and count Oliver as the nearer heir? Or should they decide that Oliver was not the nearer heir simply because Ralph existed, even if Ralph was unable to claim the land? The jurors were not sure and the four local knights who were sitting as justices seem to have left them in doubt. At Westminster, these justices tried to defend themselves. They contradicted the jurors and "denied this [that they knew that Oliver had an elder brother at the time of the trial] at first and afterwards admitted that the aforesaid jurors had said that that Oliver had a certain first-born brother."[89] Indeed they admitted that the prior had tried to call Ralph to warrant and that the justices had refused to require his appearance because Ralph had offered the king a goshawk to have the case delayed. The justices surely knew of Ralph's existence at the time of the case.[90]

Within the genre of the plea roll entry, the certification format provided room for more people to speak and at greater length than was permitted in other types of entries. The general verdict gave little room for the justices, the parties, or even the jurors to speak. In the certification, however, several groups of people are required to speak. The justices in the original case must explain why the case came out the way it did. The jury must tell us whether they agree with the record those justices made. If the justices at Westminster think the case was decided wrongly, we might be lucky enough to hear them speaking *ex cathedra* on the correct solution to the case, something we do not generally see in ordinary plea roll entries. That is precisely what the justices at Westminster did in this case. They held for the prior, throwing out Oliver's case. They explained that "to be lord and heir certainly looks to the right and not to the possession or to the assize of mort d'ancestor."[91] By this they meant that the issue of whether Ralph should be cut out of the picture—the question that confused the jury—is not one for the assize of mort d'ancestor. The assize of mort d'ancestor only asks whether the person suing is the nearer heir. The answer to that question is no, Oliver is not the nearer heir because Ralph exists, even if he is barred from inheriting the land because he is lord. Thus, if Oliver is going to cut Ralph out of the running for this parcel of land, he must sue by a different writ—the

---

[89] "Et predicti iusticiarii hoc primo dedixerunt et postea cognoverunt quod predicti iuratores dixerant quod idem Oliverus habuit quemdam fratrem primogenitum." BNB, vol 2, 436 (no 564).

[90] Ibid.

[91] "Et hoc scilicet esse dominum et heredum spectat ad ius et non ad possessionem vel assisam mortis antecessoris." BNB, vol 2, 437 (no 564).

writ of right—in which the jury is asked a broader question than they are asked in the assize of mort d'ancestor. A jury hearing a case brought by writ of right would be asked who, of the parties involved, has the greater right to the land, a more open-ended question under the umbrella of which they could consider the issue of the lord and heir.

The case was probably attractive to the creators of the *Note Book* because it demonstrated the operation of the lord-and-heir rule and even contained a pithy statement of the reason for the justices' decision in the case: "To be lord and heir certainly looks to the right and not to the possession or to the assize of mort d'ancestor" is a general statement that can be applied to other cases. The creators of the *Note Book* were not content to let the plea roll entry speak for itself, however. A long gloss of the case was included in the margin. The glossator tells us to

> Note that the assize of mort d'ancestor does not lie between a younger brother claiming on account of the death of his brother and any other person; since it was the elder brother who was the lord—although he could not be lord and heir, because this pertains much more to the right and not to the seisin— because the first seisin pertains to the elder and therefore the assize does not lie. But when the elder shall have had seisin, then the younger could seek his seisin from the aforesaid elder for this reason: because the elder is always the nearer heir, but right will expel him.[92]

The compilers of the *Note Book* were interested in the legal point this case illustrated. They were not interested in what happened to Oliver, Ralph, and the prior. In this entry, the court never gets to the merits of this case: did the monastery have the better claim to the land? The question asked was much more preliminary—did Oliver even satisfy the "nearer heir" test that would get him to the other issues in the assize of mort d'ancestor, such as whether his elder brother was actually seised of the land when he died, a contention that the priory was sure to contest. This case and the marginal note appended to it are all about a very complicated preliminary question, not about the outcome of the case.

---

[92] "Nota quod non iacet assisa mortis antecessoris inter fratrem iuniorem petentem de morte fratris sui et quemlibet alium, cum fuerit frater antenate qui dominus est, licet non posit esse dominus et heres, quia hoc pertinet tantum ad ius et non ad seisinam, quia ad antenatum pertinet prima seisina et ideo non iacet assisa. Set cum antenatus seisinam habuerit tunc poterit postnatus petere seisinam suam ab antenato predicta racione quia antenatus semper est propinquior heres set ius eum eiciet." BNB, vol 2, 437 (no 564).

In a few entries, what appear to have originally been marginal annotations have been taken directly into the text. It is not clear how, when, or why this happened. In those cases where the marginal note has been taken into the entry itself, however, the entry certainly looks more like a text about the law than a text about an individual case. One entry, for instance, begins:

> Concerning Augustine and Geoffrey of Baddeleye that if he who was impleaded by one person upon the right and by another person concerning the same land upon the possession through the assize of mort d'ancestor, the action on the ownership will be delayed until such time as the action on the possession will have been pleaded, because Augustine sought land against Geoffrey . . .[93]

This entry does not begin like a plea roll entry. It does not contain the formulaic language indicating the parties, the place, and the type of writ used to bring the action before the king's justices. It starts off by saying that this case concerns two real-life parties—"Concerning Augustine and Geoffrey de Baddelegha"—but it quickly switches style to inform us about a general rule of law: if someone is impleaded in two actions, one on the right and one on the possession, the action on the possession will be heard first, followed by the action on the right. This was likely a marginal notation that was contained in one of the prior collections upon which the *Note Book* was based. The two cases before it both appear to be marginal notations, without their associated cases, that were copied into the text itself.[94] After these first few sentences, however, the entry takes the form of an administrative record, telling us that a day was given for the case to be heard, just as one would find on a plea roll.[95] An annotator placed a note in the margin that highlighted the case's usefulness for the legal rule contained in it: "note that first possession should be heard, then ownership."[96] This dispute between two real people over a real plot of land was reduced to a pithy,

---

[93] "De Augustino et Gaufrido de Baddelegha quod si quis implacitatus fuerit ab uno super recto et ab alio de eadem terra super possessione per assisam mortis antecessoris, differtur accio super proprietate quousque discussum fuerit super possessione quia Augustinus petiit terram versus Galfridum." BNB, vol 2, 193 (no 240).

[94] BNB, vol 2, 192–93 (nos 238 and 239). Entry 239 is out of place. It is actually a note to entry no 226. BNB, vol 2, 181–82 (no 226).

[95] Ibid. There is one other indication in this entry that its author might have perceived it as something different from a plea roll entry. He uses the pluperfect tense, "a day had been given", rather than the perfect "a day was given" when he recounts the court's adjournment of the case.

[96] "Nota quod prius cognoscendum est de possessione quam proprietate." BNB, vol 2, 193 (no 240). Note also that the author of this entry and the gloss upon it appear to have equated right with ownership and seisin with possession.

abstract statement of law, in which the players are possession and ownership, not Augustine and Geoffrey.

Augustine and Geoffrey's case is one of the most dramatic examples of this kind of tampering with cases, but it is not unique. The creators of the *Note Book* regularly signal that they are less interested in the parties and their dispute than in the plea rolls as texts that can tell us something about the law by expunging information specific to the parties from the entry. When there are multiple plaintiffs listed on the roll in a single case, for instance, the name of the first plaintiff usually appears in the *Note Book*, but the text will replace the names of the rest with "and others." The names of jurors are similarly abbreviated. Specific dates that appear on the roll are transformed to "such a day."[97] We sometimes find more significant cuts. A case from the Michaelmas 1223 roll of the Common Bench, brought by a writ of customs and services, describes the customs at issue in detail.[98] The *Note Book* omits them. The omission was deliberate. This entry is marked for copying on the roll and also contains the notation "he is to speak with me concerning this chapter" ("*loquatur mecum de hoc capitulo.*")[99] This section of the *Note Book* comes near the end of the collection and may have been created specifically for the *Note Book*, not copied from some earlier collection. It contains cases from miscellaneous terms of court that were, for some reason, left out of earlier parts of the *Note Book*. Henry of Bratton, who was probably the person who commissioned and oversaw the construction of the *Note Book*, was probably also responsible for selecting the cases that went into this part of it. Bratton appears to have decided that he wanted to cut the customs and services. In his edition of the *Note Book*, Maitland drops a footnote that says "the note-book does not describe the services, but they are so interesting that I supply them from the roll within brackets."[100] He then goes on to include a substantial selection, about a third of a very long entry, that describes these customs in detail. The part that was of interest to Maitland, the historian, and presumably also to the lord who was claiming his customs, was of absolutely no interest to Bratton. There is no marginal note next to this case in the *Note Book* to explain to us why it is there, but it is an interesting case procedurally. A group of tenants of the prior of Merton claim that they are free and hold in free tenure, while the prior claims they are villeins. The abbot vouches the record and claims that two of the men were

---

[97] BNB, vol 1, 68. For some examples, see BNB, vol 2, 193 (no 240), 544 (no 705), 549 (no 716), 552 (no 720), 553 (nos 721, 722), 707 (no 920), 710 (no 925), 711 (no 927), 717 (no 937).

[98] BNB, vol 3, 509 (no 1661).

[99] Ibid.

[100] Ibid.

found to be villeins in the king's court in prior litigation. The villeins then pay for an inquisition to look into the customs of the manor, which would include the kinds of payments and services that the tenants owed to the abbot and would presumably give some clue as to whether they were villeins or not, because villeins traditionally owed certain types of services. These are the kinds of things that would be interesting to a justice—or to a clerk who wanted to become a justice—who was trying to learn the finer points of the procedures of the English courts. What is the justice to do when someone claims to be free? The case also contains some clever pleading by the prior, who uses the imagery, current in thirteenth-century canon law and ecclesiology, of a corporate body as an actual human body.[101] The prior pleads that the "manor of Ewell, the members of which are such lands which the aforesaid men hold, is a villeinage, and they know this, whence he asks judgment whether the members can be more free than the head."[102] The prior's phrase was clever enough for the clerk to record it on the roll. It may have been this clever phrase that made the case interesting enough to copy into the *Note Book*.

## Conclusion

In both the schools and the courts, the future justice's life would have revolved around texts. They were different types of texts, but it appears that Raleigh and Bratton could see parallels. The creators of the *Note Book* and its predecessors were taking the plea roll entry out of its original context as an administrative record and turning it into a different type of text altogether, removing the facts so important to them in their role as administrators, but retaining the law so important to them in their role as jurists.

There is a tantalizing parallel between the processes of collecting plea roll entries and of collecting papal decretals. Several of the decretal collections of the early thirteenth century were compiled directly from the papal registers, the administrative texts that recorded papal correspondence.[103] It is possible that the *Bracton* authors knew of this practice of removing decretals from the

---

[101] For a recent discussion of the imagery of the body politic in the twelfth and thirteenth centuries, see Robin Chapman Stacey, *Law and the Imagination in Medieval Wales* (University of Pennsylvania Press 2018) 91–93.

[102] "[Q]uia manerium de Ewell cuius membra sunt tales terre quas predicti homines tenent est villenagium, et ipsi hoc cognoscunt, unde petit iudicium si membra possint esse liberiora quam capud..." BNB, vol 3, 511 (no 1661).

[103] Edward Andrew Reno III, "The Authoritative Text: Raymond of Penyafort's editing of the Decretals of Gregory IX (1234)" (PhD dissertation, Columbia University 2011) 33, 36, 39 (hereafter Reno, *Authoritative Text*).

administrative context and placing them in a legal context. The decretal collection known as *Compilatio Tertia*, made between 1209 and 1210 by Peter of Benevento, begins with a bull, *Devotioni Vestrae*, in which Pope Innocent III confirmed that the decretals contained in the collection were authentic and could be regarded as authorities. That bull references the registers. It says that the text contains "the decretal letters compiled faithfully by our beloved son master Peter, our subdeacon and notary, and collected under relevant titles, contained in our registers up to the twelfth year . . ."[104] *Compilatio Tertia* had received official sanction from the papacy in 1210 and would have been available in England in the early thirteenth century.[105] Decretal collectors often modified the decretals to remove certain information specific to the case, just as the compilers of the *Note Book* removed names, dates, and details that were not related to the law.[106] Indeed, the decretalists occasionally edited their decretals more extensively, sometimes even changing the meaning to bring them into line with current law.[107] There are certainly differences between the *Note Book* and the decretal collections. By the time Raleigh was collecting cases from the plea rolls, the latest decretal collections, which were likely known to the authors, were organized into titles, by subject. The *Note Book* is arranged chronologically. But the decretal collections of the early thirteenth century may have provided some general inspiration for the *Note Book* and its predecessor collections.[108]

Raleigh and Bratton were certainly committed to this project. It would have taken a clerk hundreds of hours just to copy the material found in the *Note Book*. When we add to this the amount of time it would have taken to copy

---

[104] "Decretales epistolas a dilecto filio magistro P. subdiacono et notario nostro compilatas fideliter, et sub competentibus titulis collocatas, in nostris usque ad XII annum contineri registris . . ." Emil Friedburg (ed), *Quinque Compilationes Antiquae* (Tauchnitz 1882) 105.

[105] Harry Dondorp and Eltjo JH Schrage, "The Sources of Medieval Learned Law" in John W Cairns and Paul J du Plessis (eds), *The Creation of the Ius Commune: From Casus to Regula* (Edinburgh University Press 2010) 40.

[106] Charles Duggan, *Twelfth-Century Decretal Collections and Their Importance in English History* (Athlone Press 1963) 55, 60–61 (hereafter Duggan, *Decretal Collections*). The decretalist Bernard of Compostella was actually thought to have over-edited some of the decretals he included in his *Compilatio Romana*. The desire to provide more complete texts of those decretals may have been part of Peter of Benevento's impulse to create *Compilatio Tertia*. Reno, *Authoritative Text* (n 103) 39.

[107] Reno, *Authoritative Text* (n 103) 40.

[108] It seems likely that, if the authors of *Bracton* were keeping up with the latest literature on Roman and canon law and were sophisticated enough consumers of canon law to look up Tancred's canon-law sources, as one of them does in the tractate on pleas of the crown, they almost certainly knew of at least some of the *Quinque Compilationes Antiquae* and, by the late 1230s, of the *Decretals of Gregory IX*, which were organized by subject-matter. *Bracton*, vol 2, 404. Not all decretal collections were arranged systematically, however. Before the *Quinque Compilationes*, decretal collections were generally not organized by subject matter. It is possible that the authors knew of the less systematic collections of decretals that were made in England in the 1170s, 1180s, and 1190s, and that these might have served as an inspiration for the *Note Book*. See Duggan, *Decretal Collections* (n 106) 66–118, *passim*.

out each of its predecessor collections, to select the cases for inclusion in these collections, and to compose the *Bracton* treatise, it becomes clear that William of Raleigh, Henry of Bratton, and their clerks must have regularly spent their night watches and vacations from the bench producing texts that were not directly related to their duties in the royal courts. We don't know where case collections such as the *Note Book* would have been kept. We don't know how, or even if, they were ever used. The text itself is the primary source of information on what it was created to do and the function its creator intended it to serve as a material object. It could certainly function as a teaching tool, and contains elements, such as explanatory glosses, that hint that it was intended to be used that way. Fortunately, the justices did leave us some hints as to why plea roll entries were important to them. The *Bracton* treatise contains over 500 references to cases decided in the royal courts. In *Bracton*, Raleigh and Bratton assimilate the plea roll entry to the kinds of legal literature produced by jurists in Bologna. By reading *Bracton* and the *Note Book* together, we can shed light on the way these justices sought to understand their work in the king's courts through the lens of the schools.

# 5

# Cases and the Dialectic

In the previous chapter, we saw that the authors of *Bracton* were, at the same time they were writing the treatise, excerpting cases from the plea rolls and placing them in separate collections. In this chapter we will see that the authors of *Bracton* took the processes we see in the *Note Book* a step further in *Bracton*.[1] In the *Note Book* and its predecessors, Raleigh and Bratton began the process of turning the case into a statement of abstract legal principle by turning places, dates, and people into the abstract, "a certain place," "a certain day," and "others." They glossed the *Note Book*, and probably also its predecessor collections, to demonstrate that a case could stand for a general statement of law. In *Bracton*, plea roll entries become even more abstract: they become citations. *Bracton* contains over 500 citations to cases on the plea rolls. The treatise sometimes gives us the facts of the case, but often just uses the case citation to support some rule, doctrine, or principle outlined in the text.

In *Bracton* it becomes clear that a case decided in the royal courts was not merely an illustration of legal principle for William of Raleigh and Henry of Bratton. Rather, that case, as recorded on the plea roll, was a text that could be relied on to provide authority for the rule. The plea roll entry was treated as an authoritative text not so different from the authoritative texts of Roman and canon law, the imperial constitutions and jurists' opinions found in the *Codex* and *Digest* and the papal decretals found in texts such as the *Quinque Compilationes Antiquae* and the *Decretals of Gregory IX*. The authors of *Bracton* treat plea roll entries and the authoritative texts of Roman and canon law as if they are part of a single universe of legal authorities. They cite to them using very similar styles. Passages in the treatise will often include citations to both the texts of the schools and the texts of the king's courts. The authors even apply dialectical reasoning—a type of reasoning used in the schools to reconcile conflicting authorities—to these records of cases. In *Bracton*, William of Raleigh and Henry of Bratton reconstitute the plea roll entry as an authoritative text of the kind they had encountered in the schools.

---

[1] Much of this chapter is adapted from Thomas McSweeney, "English Judges and Roman Jurists: The Civilian Learning Behind England's First Case Law" (2012) 84 Temple Law Review 827.

*Priests of the Law.* Thomas J. McSweeney, Oxford University Press (2019). © Thomas J. McSweeney.
DOI: 10.1093/oso/9780198845454.003.0006

# Harmony and Authority

There is a text of the late twelfth century that Hans van de Wouw has dubbed the *Brocardica Dunelmensia,* because it resides in the library of Durham Cathedral.[2] The *Brocardica Dunelmensia* was undoubtedly created in England; van de Wouw has demonstrated that it relies heavily on Vacarius' *Liber Pauperum.* It was probably used to teach law in England sometime in the 1190s.[3] It presents 128 legal rules or maxims, known to medieval jurists as *generalia* or *brocarda,* each of which is followed by a number of citations to provisions from Justinian's *Digest, Codex,* and *Institutes,* and even occasionally to papal decretals and Gratian's *Decretum.*[4] In most cases, the maxim is followed only by texts that support it, but a number of brocards are followed by some texts that support the maxim and others that contradict it. This for-and-against format may have given the *brocardica* genre its name: it has been suggested that *brocardica* is a bastardization of *pro-contra.*[5]

To take an example of how the text works, the twenty-third brocard reads "From the want of one an action is given against another."[6] This very general statement is followed by citations to four texts, two to Justinian's *Digest,* given in the standard scholastic form for such citations, and two to glosses to provisions of the *Digest,* which van de Wouw identifies as glosses to Vacarius' *Liber Pauperum.*[7] These four all support the proposition. One of the citations is to a provision of the *Digest* that states that if A's beast causes loss to B because of C's fraud or malice, and A is insolvent, then B can recover against C.[8] Thus, on

---

[2] Durham, Dean and Chapter Muniments, Fragment 30; Hans van de Wouw, "*Brocardica Dunelmensia*" (1991) 108 Zeitschrift der Savigny-Stiftung für Rechtsgeschichte: Romanistische Abteilung 235–78.

[3] The *Brocardica* follows the organization of the *Liber Pauperum,* probably derives most of its citations to the primary texts of Roman law from the *Liber Pauperum,* and cites to glosses in the *Liber Pauperum.* Van de Wouw, "*Brocardica Dunelmensia*" (n 2) 236–40, 242.

[4] Peter Stein, "The Vacarian School" (1992) 13 Journal of Legal History 23, 27–28 (hereafter Stein, "Vacarian School").

[5] Kantorowicz suggests that *brocarda* or *procarda* may have been students' slang. Hermann Kantorowicz, "The Quaestiones Disputatae of the Glossators" (1937-38) 16 Tijdschrift voor Rechtsgeschiedenis 4; Stephan Kuttner, "Réflections sur les Brocards des Glossateurs" in *Gratian and the Schools of Law, 1140-1234* (Variorum Reprints 1983) 768 (hereafter Kuttner, "Brocards"). Van de Wouw doubted that the word *brocardum* was derived from pro-contra, given that so many of the brocards in the *Brocardica Dunelmensia* do not contain any texts that are "contra." The text itself refers to the maxims in it as brocards, citing to itself with the abbreviation "*Bro.*" Van de Wouw, "*Brocardica Dunelmensia*" (n 2) 236. Another suggestion is that the word derives from *broccus,* a protruding tooth, emphasizing the sharp nature of the arguments that ensued when students tried to reconcile the conflicting texts. Francis De Zulueta and Peter Stein (eds), *The Teaching of Roman Law in England around 1200* (Selden Society, 1990) xxxix.

[6] "Ex inopia unius in alium datur accio." Van de Wouw, "*Brocardica Dunelmensia*" (n 2) 250.

[7] Ibid

[8] D.4.3.7.6; *Digest of Justinian,* vol 1, 121.

account of A's inability to pay, an action is given against another, C. These four citations are followed by the word "*contra*," and then a further citation to a text of the *Institutes* that appears to contradict the statement.[9] The citation is to a discussion of novation. The *Institutes* state that when A owes a debt to B, and then a third party, C, enters into a contract with B to pay A's debt to B, A's obligation to B merges with C's obligation. C's is the only obligation remaining to B, and A's is extinguished. But what if C's obligation is unenforceable because C is a minor and did not have his guardian's permission to bind himself contractually? C's obligation is null. That fact does not reinstate A's obligation, however. As the *Institutes* put it, "the right is lost," and B cannot recover from A or C.[10] Thus, this is an instance in which the want of one possible defendant does not grant an action against another. How do we reconcile the maxim and the texts supporting it with this text that appears to contradict it? The *Brocardica* provides no solution to this conundrum. But texts such as the *Brocardica Dunelmensia* were intended to spur the reader to find solutions to these apparent contradictions.[11] They were meant to be teaching texts. The *Brocardica* leaves it to the teacher or student to work through these texts and to find a way to reconcile them.

The *Brocardica Dunelmensia* is a text that challenges its reader to reconcile texts that appear to contradict each other. It is only one example of a broader phenomenon in twelfth- and thirteenth-century education. The reconciliation of authoritative texts would have been one of the major emphases of a scholastic education in any field. The twelfth and thirteenth centuries were a time of rapid change in education in Europe; new methods of argumentation were being taught in the cathedral schools and, later, in Europe's first universities. Starting in the twelfth century, scholars began to organize knowledge into systems that were internally coherent.[12] Alex Novikoff has argued recently that the practices of disputing in the medieval universities were part of a broader medieval culture of disputation.[13] Harmonization was just as important to the universities as disputation, however. Harmony could be described as an aesthetic in multiple fields of life in the twelfth and thirteenth centuries. Masters in the schools were devising harmonious systems of knowledge out of authoritative texts at

---

[9] Inst.3.29.3; *Justinian's Institutes*, 120–121.

[10] "Quo casu res ammititur." Ibid.

[11] Only one of the brocards in this collection contains a *solutio*. Van de Wouw, "*Brocardica Dunelmensia*" (n 2) 236.

[12] Charles M Radding and William W Clark, *Medieval Architecture, Medieval Learning: Builders and Masters in the Age of Romanesque and Gothic* (Yale University Press 1992) 204–07 (hereafter Radding and Clark, *Medieval Architecture*).

[13] Alex J Novikoff, *The Medieval Culture of Disputation: Pedagogy, Practice, and Performance* (University of Pennsylvania Press 2013).

the same time master builders were taking a more comprehensive approach to the design of cathedrals, designing buildings where every element was intended to be part of a harmonious whole based on divine ratios.[14] The act of creating harmony out of dissonance could even be envisioned as an act of faith. Discord was the result of original sin; harmony was a mark of the divine.[15]

Harmony was important partly because certain texts were thought to be texts of authority. Different texts acquired this authoritative status in different fields. In theology, the Bible, obviously, but also the writings of the Church fathers and the *Sentences* of Peter Lombard had acquired the status of authoritative texts by the early thirteenth century.[16] In Canon law, Gratian collected various texts of popes, councils, and the fathers of the Church, texts which he deemed to be authoritative, into the *Decretum* in the middle decades of the twelfth century, and particular collections of papal decretals would acquire authoritative status by the beginning of the thirteenth century.[17] In Roman law, it was Justinian's monumental collections: the *Institutes*, the *Codex*, and especially the *Digest*.[18] To masters in the schools authoritative texts should, ideally, not conflict with each other, so scholars in all of the faculties emphasized the harmony of authorities. It was a commonplace among medieval theologians that the opinions of the Church fathers were "diverse, but not adverse."[19] Thus, when the teachings of, say, Augustine and Jerome appeared to conflict, there had to be a way to reconcile them. The book that established canon law as an academic discipline in the universities, Gratian's *Decretum*, was titled, in full, *The Harmony of Discordant Canons (Concordia Discordantium Canonum).*[20] Gratian took seemingly contradictory texts and not only placed them beside each other, but also offered solutions to the contradictions.[21] Gratian's method

[14] Radding and Clark, *Medieval Architecture* (n 12) 80, 140–41; MT Clanchy, *Abelard: A Medieval Life* (Blackwell, 1999) 29–30 (hereafter Clanchy, *Abelard*).
[15] Jacques Le Goff, *Medieval Civilization, 400-1500* (Julia Barrow tr, Barnes & Noble Books 2000) 279.
[16] John Marenbon, *Medieval Philosophy: An Historical and Philosophical Introduction* (Routledge 2007) 213–14.
[17] Anders Winroth, *The Making of Gratian's Decretum* (CUP 2000) 1–2. Gratian drew upon papal letters and stated that papal decretals were authoritative texts. See generally D. 19; *Corpus Iuris Canonici*, vol 1, 58–63; Gratian, *The Treatise on Laws with the Ordinary Gloss* (Augustine Thompson and Katherine Christensen trs, Catholic University of America Press 1993) 76–84. Decretal collecting became a common practice in the second half of the twelfth century. Charles Duggan, *Twelfth-Century Decretal Collections and Their Importance in English History* (Athlone Press 1963). The first decretal collection to receive papal approval was the collection known as *Compilatio Tertia*, promulgated by Pope Innocent III in 1210. Harry Dondorp and Eltjo JH Schrage, "The Sources of Medieval Learned Law" in John W Cairns and Paul J du Plessis (eds) *The Creation of the Ius Commune: From Casus to Regula* (Edinburgh University Press 2010) 40.
[18] Peter Stein, *Roman Law in European History* (CUP 1999) 46.
[19] Clanchy, *Abelard* (n 14) 87.
[20] *Corpus Iuris Canonici*, vol 1, 1.
[21] James A Brundage, *Medieval Canon Law* (Longman 1995) 47.

was described by contemporaries as dialectical. Where rhetoric seeks to convince the speaker's audience to adopt the speaker's own opinions, dialectic seeks to find truth by putting two people with differing viewpoints in conversation, the ultimate goal being to reach a synthesis between two initially divergent viewpoints.

Medieval dialectic used authorities as a starting point. Contrary to popular belief, it was not Sir Isaac Newton who originated the image of a dwarf standing on the shoulder of a giant. It was rather a phrase John of Salisbury attributed to his teacher Bernard of Chartres, and described a twelfth- and thirteenth-century attitude to scholarship.[22] The authorities studied by the medieval schoolmen constituted the foundation of knowledge, but they were a foundation that could be built upon because medieval scholars could "see more and farther than our predecessors, not because we have keener vision or greater height, but because we are lifted up and borne aloft on their gigantic stature."[23] By working out the apparent contradictions of the fathers, the jurists, or the Bible, medieval scholars were able to see farther and lead people to a greater understanding of old texts. By resolving the cruxes of apparent conflict, scholars actually created new knowledge, creating an interesting dynamic between authority and what we would call creativity or innovation.

Dialectical reasoning became common in the schools partly because it represented a particular approach to truth. But dialectical reasoning was not just an epistemological approach to authority; it was, at the same time, a didactic strategy. Joseph Goering has suggested that we can make better sense of the masters of the twelfth and thirteenth centuries when we think of them primarily as teachers, rather than scholars. He suggests that their solutions to some of the apparent conflicts between authoritative texts were not necessarily meant to be *final* solutions to the problems, but *clever* solutions that would introduce students to the source texts as well as to the methods of reconciling apparently conflicting texts.[24] Goering analyzes the first distinction of Gratian's treatise on penance, a constituent part of the *Decretum*, which asks whether

---

[22] John of Salisbury, *The Metalogicon of John of Salisbury: A Twelfth-Century Defense of the Verbal and Logical Arts of the Trivium* (Daniel D McGarry tr, Martino Publishing 2015) 167 (Book III, c 4). Robert Merton traces the imagery of the giant and the dwarf back to Bernard, although he thinks that Bernard may have derived the idea that the younger generation builds upon the work of prior generations to create new knowledge from the 6th-century grammarian Priscian. Robert K Merton, *On the Shoulders of Giants: A Shandean Postscript*, (Vicennial edn, Harcourt Brace Jovanovich 1985) 194–95, 268. Newton, in his version, omits the dwarf. Ibid, 9.

[23] Ibid.

[24] Joseph Goering, "The Scholastic Turn (1100-1500): Penitential Theology and Law in the Schools" in Abigail Firey (ed), *A New History of Penance* (Brill 2008) 220, 224, 226 (hereafter Goering, "Scholastic Turn").

"contrition of the heart alone and secret satisfaction," without confession to a priest, is sufficient for the remission of sin.[25] He points out that one way to read Gratian is as a teacher pulling together the relevant texts and demonstrating his methodology, rather than as a scholar trying to authoritatively solve the problem. Although Gratian does come to a conclusion, that the authorities support the view that confession to a priest is required, he gives some indication that his purpose is not to shut the door on future discussion, but to open up possibilities for his students. Gratian ends his discussion of this problem by saying that "To which of these [opinions] one should preferably adhere, however, is reserved to the judgment of the reader. For both have wise and religious supporters."[26] He even cites some of the same texts for both sides of the argument, demonstrating that texts can be read in opposing ways.[27]

The *brocardica* literature was an example of this style of teaching, in which the master and students attempted to reconcile authorities. In texts such as the *Brocardica Dunelmensia*, students and teachers worked to demonstrate that the individual provisions of the *Digest, Codex, Institutes,* and even the *Decretum* and decretals, were all in perfect harmony with each other. Van de Wouw has suggested that the *Brocardica Dunelmensia* developed through a process of teaching, probably in the last decade of the twelfth century.[28] We can imagine a master sitting in a room, perhaps in Oxford, surrounded by students. Van de Wouw imagined the master presenting his students with a brocard, along with a few citations in support, and asking his students for additional citations *pro* and *contra*.[29] The master would probably also ask students to propose solutions. Second recensions of these texts often contained proposed solutions to the problems, and those solutions may have been the product of having taught from the first recension of the text.[30] Students in England's schools of higher learning would have devoted a portion of their time to reconciling texts that appeared to conflict with each other.

The drive to create harmony through dialectical reasoning was especially strong in the field of Roman law, particularly since the introduction to the

---

[25] "Utrum sola cordis contritione, et secreta satisfactione, absque oris confessione quisque possit Deo satisfacere ... " D.1 de cons. pr.; *Corpus Iuris Canonici*, vol 1, 1159; Atria A Larson (ed and tr), *Gratian's Tractatus De Penitentia: A New Latin Edition with English Translation* (Catholic University of America Press 2016) 3–4 (hereafter Gratian, *De Penitentia*).

[26] "Cum autem harum potius adherendum sit lectoris iudicio reservatur. Utraque enim fautores habet sapientes et religiosos." D.1 de cons. d.p.c.89; *Corpus Iuris Canonici*, vol 1, 1189; Gratian, *De Penitentia* (n 25) 86–87; Goering, "Scholastic Turn" (n 24) 224.

[27] Goering, "Scholastic Turn" (n 24) 224.

[28] Van de Wouw, "*Brocardica Dunelmensia*" (n 2) 240, 242.

[29] Ibid, 240–41.

[30] Kuttner, "Brocards" (n 5) 778.

*Digest*, the most studied of Justinian's texts in the medieval universities, stated outright that the texts of Roman law formed a harmonious system. An imperial constitution appended to the beginning of the *Digest* gave this advice to its reader:

> As for any contradiction occurring in this book, none such has found a place for itself, and none will be discovered by anyone who reflects upon the modes of diversity with a subtle mind. On the contrary, something will be found, even if obscurely expressed, which removes the objection of inconsistency, gives the matter a different aspect, and passes outside the limits of discord.[31]

Where the *Decretum* was an attempt to create harmony out of a large universe of discordant canons, the *Digest* claimed to be a closed system that had already been brought into harmony.[32] It challenged the reader to work through the apparent contradictions. The medieval jurist could thus find his marching orders in the *Digest*: to work through the apparent contradictions to show that Roman law really is the harmonious system it claims to be.

The *Brocardica* was merely a text that carried out Justinian's instructions to work out the apparent contradictions. Although the *brocardica* was a type of legal literature that one could find anywhere that Roman law was taught at the turn of the thirteenth century, these texts appear to have been especially popular among the English civilians. Peter Stein has argued that Vacarius and his students were fond of the work of the Bolognese jurist Johannes Bassianus, who emphasized the idea that law was a harmonious system and who taught in the *pro et contra* format.[33] The *Summa Codicis* and *Summa Institutionum* of Johannes' student Azo, so familiar to the authors of *Bracton*, are written in an expository format, but Azo also wrote in the *pro et contra* format. He wrote his own *brocardica*, which was sometimes attached to his other texts in

---

[31] "Contrarium autem aliquid in hoc codice positum nullum sibi locum vindicabit nec invenitur, si quis subtili animo diversitatis rationes excutiet: sed est aliquid novum inventum vel occulte positum, quod dissonantiae querellam dissoluit et aliam naturam inducit discordiae fines effugientem." D.Constitutio Tanta.15; *Digest of Justinian* (which is not paginated in this part of the text). I have made a few slight modifications to Watson's translation.

[32] Stephan Kuttner, *Harmony from Dissonance: An Interpretation of Medieval Canon Law* (Archabbey Press 1960) 20.

[33] Jason Taliadoros, *Law and Theology in Twelfth-Century England: The Works of Master Vacarius (c. 1115/20–c. 1200)* (Brepols 2006) 46 (hereafter Taliadoros, *Law and Theology*); Stein, "Vacarian School" (n 4) 26–28. The canonist Richard de Morins, known as Ricardus Anglicus, also wrote a *brocardica* based on the decretals, but did so when he was teaching at Bologna in the 1190s. He returned to England sometime before 1202, when he became prior of the important priory of Augustinian canons at Dunstable. He was involved in legal affairs until his death in 1242, serving regularly as a papal judge delegate. Robert C Figueira, "Morins, Richard de [called Ricardus Anglicus] (early 1160s–1242)" (ODNB, September 23, 2004) <www.oxforddnb.com/view/article/23518> accessed March 13, 2019.

manuscripts.[34] Moreover, the *Brocardica Dunelmensia* is not the only example of such a text created in England. Another *brocardica* of the twelfth century, known today as the *Brocardica Dolum per subsequentia purgari* after its first line, appears in six manuscripts, five of which reside in English libraries.[35]

The authors of *Bracton* may have spent part of their education in Roman law sitting in classrooms, working through the apparent contradictions in a *brocardica*. Indeed, the *Brocardica Dunelmensia*, likely a text of the 1190s, is probably a pretty good indication of the kinds of learning exercises someone like William of Raleigh could have engaged in as a student. When these justices turned to writing their own texts about their work in the king's courts, they employed the dialectic as a teaching method. Although *Bracton* is primarily written in the expository style of Azo's *summae*, the authors occasionally highlight important problems in the common law by pitting conflicting authorities against each other and attempting to reconcile those authorities. Sometimes those authorities are the kinds of authoritative texts a civilian would have reconciled in the schools: the texts of Justinian's *corpus*. Sometimes, however, the authors apply dialectical reasoning to a different type of text altogether: the cases decided in the royal courts and recorded on the plea rolls.

## Reconciling Roman Law in *Bracton*

The authors of *Bracton* had obviously learned the schools' methods of reconciliation, as dialectical reasoning is on display in the treatise. In the introduction to the section of the treatise on actions there is a passage, marked as an *addicio*, which I suspect was added to the margin of a manuscript by Henry of Bratton after he had completed his second recension of the treatise and then taken into the main text by a later copyist.[36] In this *addicio*, Bratton applies dialectical reasoning to the texts of Roman law.

---

[34] Kuttner, "Brocards" (n 5) 770.

[35] Erich Karl Matthias Schwaibold (ed), *Brocardica "Dolum Per Subsequentia Purgari": Eine Englische Sammlung von Argumenten des Römischen Rechts aus dem 12. Jahrhundert* (Vittorio Klostermann 1985) 4–19.

[36] This *addicio* actually appears in the margin of several manuscripts of the treatise. *Bracton*, vol 1, 385; Frederic William Maitland (ed), *Select Passages from the Works of Bracton and Azo* (SS vol 8, Bernard Quaritch 1895) 209 (hereafter Maitland (ed), *Bracton and Azo*). The passage appears in several of the manuscript traditions of the treatise, suggesting that it entered the manuscript tradition fairly early. *Bracton*, vol 1, 385. Although, as we have seen, some of the *addiciones* were composed of material from the first recension that was cut when the second recension was made, and then added back in by a later copyist, this *addicio* appears to be a later addition. It includes, among other things, a reference to a case that was heard *coram rege* in 1246 or 1247, well after William of Raleigh had retired from the courts, but while Bratton was sitting as a justice of that court. *Bracton*, vol 2, 323; CAF Meekings and

This *addicio* follows a discussion, probably written in one of the earlier phases of writing on the treatise, that treats the case in which a plaintiff brings several different actions against the same defendant at the same time.[37] The text says that "He may first put forward one, whichever he wishes, or proceed upon them all at the same time [except] in four cases."[38] The author relies on several civilian texts in crafting this passage. The base for this discussion is a procedural manual that began to circulate in 1216, the *Ordo Iudiciarius* of Tancred of Bologna.[39] Tancred was a student of Azo, and drew upon Azo's commentary on the eighth title of book three of the *Codex* for his discussion of the order for bringing actions.[40] Fritz Schulz demonstrated that the author of this passage in *Bracton* was relying primarily on Tancred, but that he also had access to Azo and occasionally altered the text to align more closely with Azo's discussion.[41] At times, he even went back to Azo's source, at one point altering the text to bring it into line with D.41.1.18 where Azo diverged from the source material.[42]

Tancred and Azo both state that, generally speaking, a plaintiff can bring as many actions as he wants to against the defendant all at once. If the plaintiff has two possible actions on the *same matter*, however, he must elect between them. Azo notes that there are certain instances where, although the plaintiff's actions all seem to be different, they actually decide the same thing, and therefore

---

David Crook, *King's Bench and Common Bench in the Reign of Henry III* (Selden Society 2010) 137 (hereafter Meekings and Crook, *King's Bench and Common Bench*).

---

[37] The textual history of this passage is tricky. Schulz pointed out words and sentences that appear to be misplaced. None are marked as *addiciones*, however. Perhaps they began as marginal notes in Raleigh's copy of the treatise that Bratton worked into the text imperfectly when he made his recension in the 1250s. For examples of material that Schulz believed to be marginal material imperfectly worked into the main text, see Fritz Schulz, "Critical Studies on Bracton's Treatise" (1943) 59 LQR 172, 177, 178 (hereafter Schulz, "Critical Studies").

[38] *Bracton*, vol 2, 322.

[39] Tancred's *Ordo* is available in a printed edition. Fridericus Bergmann (ed), *Pilii, Tancredi, Gratiae Libri de Iudiciorum Ordine* (Vandenhoeck and Ruprecht 1842) (hereafter Bergmann (ed), *Pilii, Tancredi, Gratiae*). It was a very influential text in the Middle Ages; it exists in over 100 manuscript copies. James A Brundage, *The Medieval Origins of the Legal Profession: Canonists, Civilians, and Courts* (University of Chicago Press 2008) 162. Tancred was the dominant figure at Bologna in the 1220s. Kenneth Pennington, "The Decretalists 1190 to 1234" in Wilfried Hartmann and Kenneth Pennington (eds), *The History of Medieval Canon Law in the Classical Period, 1140-1234* (Catholic University of America Press 2008) 237. He is also emblematic of the kinds of networks of texts and people that allowed Roman and canon law to circulate throughout Europe. Like Azo, he was Bolognese, so he did not travel far from home to undertake his studies. Two of his teachers at Bologna, however, were from farther afield: Lawrence of Spain and John of Wales. His *Ordo* travelled widely; it not only made it to England, but was also translated into German and French. Brundage, *Medieval Canon Law* (n 21) 227; Peter Landau, "The Development of Law" in David Luscombe and Jonathan Riley Smith (eds), *The New Cambridge Medieval History, vol. IV: c. 1024-c. 1198 Part I* (CUP 2005) 136.

[40] Schulz, "Critical Studies" (n 37) 176.

[41] Ibid.

[42] Ibid, 179.

should be treated as the same action.[43] The author of this passage in *Bracton* copies and adapts part of Tancred's discussion of this problem in a passage that blends Romanist and English terminology. He looks at four instances in which the plaintiff may not bring all of the actions he wishes to bring. He copies a section of Tancred's treatise discussing a hypothetical suit for the Titian estate and a right of way across the Sempronian estate, estates that are unlikely to have existed in thirteenth-century England.[44] But then he also includes clearly English examples; one of the cases he discusses is "where the actions proposed are such that one is destroyed by the election of the other, as where I sue in a proprietary action by writ of right and then wish to resort to a possessory one; I cannot, for to do so would be to impugn the first, since a proprietary action includes the possessory."[45] This refers back to a discussion a few pages earlier, in which the treatise explains the hierarchy of actions; once a plaintiff has brought an action on the ownership, or property, he cannot bring an action on the possession for the same thing, since the action on the ownership essentially included the action on possession.[46] Here the author inserts the writ of right, an English writ, as the proprietary action.

After that comes Bratton's long *addicio* to the text, which further discusses the problem of electing actions. This *addicio* appears to be an explanatory gloss on the material that comes before it. In this *addicio*, Bratton actually reconciles some texts from the *Digest* that appear to conflict with each other on the question of whether a plaintiff can bring two actions on the same facts:

And note *in fine* that when one has several concurrent actions for the same thing one must be brought, as *ff. quod metus causa, l. si mulier § si coactus* [D. 4.2.21.6] and *ff. de tributoria actione, l. quod in heredem § eligere* [D. 14.4.9.1]. But *ff. quorum legatorum, l. prima §quod autem* [D. 43.3.1.4] appears to be contrary, for there it is said that if two actions are available which the plaintiff knows to be available he may put them both forward with the protestation that he wishes to claim his thing by one of them; thus he may put forward the two actions without specification. The solution: when I am certain that both actions are available to me I am obliged to elect, as *ff. de tributoria, l. quod in heredem § eligere* [D. 14.4.9.1]. But if I do not know which may be available to me, I may then put my two actions forward in general words without specifying which, as in the contrary *lex*, as where my

[43] Maitland (ed), *Bracton and Azo* (n 36) 211; Azo, *Summae*, 167–69 (commentary on C.3.8).
[44] *Bracton*, vol 2, 322.
[45] *Bracton*, vol 2, 322–23.
[46] *Bracton*, vol 2, 320.

action depends upon an admission by my adversary; he is bound to declare, when asked, whether he holds as heir or as possessor, that I may know the action available to me as plaintiff, despite the general rule that no one is obliged to divulge the title upon which his possession rests, as *C. de heredibus l. cogi possessorem* [C. 3.31.11.6].[47]

Two provisions of the *Digest* appear to contradict another provision. Bratton demonstrates that they actually refer to different circumstances, providing the *solutio*, and even marking it as such, in true scholastic form. Bratton was not being wholly original here. Parts of this passage bear a striking similarity to parts of William of Drogheda's *Summa Aurea*. Most, but not all, of the citations in the *addicio* are drawn from one of two passages in Drogheda's *Summa*.[48] Other parts of the treatise borrow from Drogheda's text, which was probably only available from 1239 on.[49] Drogheda might have been a continuing connection, for Bratton and Raleigh, to the networks of people and texts that constituted the learned laws.[50] Drogheda was tied into these networks. He drew upon the latest civilian and canonist work in his treatise,

---

[47] "Et notandum in fine quod cum quis habeat plures actiones concurrentes de eadem re, una debet experiri, ut ff. quod metus causa, l. si mulier si coactus, et ff. de tributoria actione, l. quod in heredem eligere. Sed videtur contra ff. quorum legatorum, l. prima quod autem, ubi dicitur quod si duæ competant actiones quas actor sciat sibi competere, et protestatus fuerit ex una rem suam consequi velle, licebit ei, et ita potest indefinite proponere actiones. Solutio: Ubi certus sum duas mihi competere actiones eligere cogor, ut ff. de tributoria, l. quod in heredem eligere. Si autem ignorem quæ mihi competat, tunc sub generali verbo indefinite possum proponere actiones, ut in l. contraria. Vel ubi ex confessione adversarii dependet mea actio, cogitur adversarius exprimere cum fuerit interrogatus, utrum pro herede vel pro possessore possideat, ut sciatur per medium quæ actio mihi competat actori, licet titulum suæ possessionis dicere nemo cogatur, ut C. de heredibus l. cogi possessorem." *Bracton*, vol 2, 323.

[48] Thorne made the attribution when he edited the treatise. *Bracton*, vol 2, 323; William of Drogheda, *Die Summa Aurea des Wilhelmus de Drokeda* (Wagner 1914) 60, 290 (hereafter William of Drogheda, *Summa Aurea*). Bratton's citations are slightly off in some places. In the name of the *lex*, he substitutes *non utique* for Drogheda's *numquam* and *si servum* for Drogheda's *qui servum*. Bracton, vol 3, 323; William of Drogheda, *Summa Aurea* (n 48) 290. This may indicate that Bratton had Drogheda's text in front of him, as, in heavily abbreviated Latin, these would be easy mistakes to make. They may also provide us with evidence that Bratton had memorized portions of the *Digest*, even if imperfectly. Although the phrase "*non utique*" does not begin any of the fragments in book 47 of the *Digest*, it does appear within the first few words of 47.8.2.22 and 47.10.17.16. There are several fragments in book 44 of the *Digest* that begin not "*si servum,*" but "*si servus.*" D.44.3.4; D.44.4.5.4; D.44.5.2.2; D.44.6.2. Perhaps Bratton was combining a misreading of Drogheda's text, from a difficult-to-read manuscript, with his own imperfect memory of the *leges*.

[49] Jane E Sayers, "William of Drogheda and the English Canonists" in Peter Linehan (ed), *Proceedings of the Seventh International Congress of Medieval Canon Law* (Biblioteca Apostolica Vaticana 1988) 205, 206, 218 (hereafter Sayers, "William of Drogheda"); HG Richardson, "Studies in Bracton" (1948) 6 Traditio 61, 64.

[50] If they were not already acquainted with him, Raleigh and perhaps Bratton may have met Drogheda when he came before the court *coram rege* at Woodstock to have a deed recorded in 1237. Meekings and Crook, *King's Bench and Common Bench* (n 36) 31.

relying upon the *Decretals of Gregory IX*, compiled by the canonist Raymond de Peñafort at the direction of the pope, and available from 1234, as well as Roffredus of Benevento's *Libelli de iure civile*, probably available from 1235.[51] This *addicio* may, therefore, have been written into the margin to bring the treatise into line with the latest learned-laws texts, to add to the material borrowed from Azo and his student Tancred that had already been incorporated into the main text.

But even if Bratton borrowed this material from Drogheda, he did not borrow slavishly. Bratton's discussion of this problem in the *addicio* does not follow either of Drogheda's discussions of the same issue perfectly, and, although Bratton cites to many of the same texts, he uses them in different ways. Bratton reworked the material and demonstrated that he was just as committed to the project of reconciliation as Drogheda was. For one thing, Drogheda was not his only source; at the end of the addicio, Bratton works in citations to the *Decretum* and the *Codex* that he appears to have drawn from Tancred's *Ordo*.[52] Bratton may also have introduced some citations from his own memory. In the portion of the *addicio* quoted above, Bratton cites to three different provisions of the *Digest* and one of the *Codex*. Two of the provisions of the *Digest* are also cited by Drogheda in his passages on this issue. D.4.2.21.6 and C.3.31.11.6 are not, however. These may have been drawn from another civilian source, or may have been drawn from Bratton's own civilian learning. Bratton, or one of the other authors, had independent knowledge of the contents of C.3.31.11; it is quoted, without citation, in the tractate on defaults.[53] Bratton appears to have set out to solve some of the problems of Roman law on his own, and worked to reconcile those texts in his recension of the treatise.

[51] Sayers, "William of Drogheda" (n 49) 206.

[52] *Bracton* vol 2, 324.

[53] *Bracton*, vol 4, 169. C.3.31.11 is cited in Tancred, but in a section on an entirely different topic, nowhere near the passage in Tancred that Bratton draws from for this *addicio*. Bergmann (ed), *Pilii, Tancredi, Gratiae* (n 39) 194. Tancred is, therefore, unlikely to have been his source for C.3.31.11. I have been unable to find any citation to C.3.31.11 in Drogheda. I have not found any references to D.4.2.21.6 in Drogheda or Tancred, either. Later in the *addicio*, in a portion I have note quoted above, Bratton cites to D.39.4.16.13. I have not found any references to this *lex* in either Drogheda or Tancred. Maitland did not identify any of these three citations as being derived from Azo, either. Indeed, Maitland noted that although Azo wrote a "lengthy commentary" on C.3.31.11 in his *Summa Codicis*, "Bracton has not, to all appearances, borrowed from it." Maitland (ed), *Bracton and Azo* (n 36) 212. It is, of course, possible that Bratton was not supplying these citations himself, but was copying them from some other source. Sarah White has begun a project that will hopefully identify more of Bratton's civilian and canonist sources, so we may know more about this in the near future. Even if Bratton did draw this material from some other civilian text, he was, at the very least, doing some original work in combining these civilian sources.

## The Cases in *Bracton*

*Bracton* is, in many ways, meant to act as a bridge between the texts the authors encountered in the schools and the texts they would have produced as justices and clerks in the royal courts. Intertextual approaches to texts begin from the premise that no text can truly be understood as a closed system; every text is part of a broader universe of texts and derives its meaning from its relationship with other texts.[54] A text may be more or less explicit in its intertextuality. A book review, for instance, will explicitly quote, criticize, or interpret another text; the allusions to the writings of Ovid and St. Augustine in T.S. Eliot's poem *The Waste Land* are less clear on the surface of the poem. *Bracton* plays with its relationship with other texts in many different, and often very explicit, ways. At times it quotes or paraphrases texts of Roman and canon law in ways that the learned laws' initiates would recognize. It also draws texts of Roman and canon law and texts produced in the royal courts into the same universe. In *Bracton*, references to cases decided in the king's courts, often with specific citations to the roll on which they can be found, sit comfortably, side-by-side, with citations to the opinions of classical Roman jurists found in the *Digest*. *Bracton* brought these very different types of texts into proximity to each other.

Bratton actually hints, in the *addicio* discussed above, that he thought that the cases cited in the treatise were part of the same textual universe as the provisions of the *Digest* and *Codex*. The *addicio* goes on to treat several other instances in which the plaintiff cannot bring all of the actions he might wish against his opponent. Each fact-pattern is followed by a citation to some authoritative text. For example, Bratton, borrowing from Drogheda, tells us that "If they arise from different acts, then neither is destroyed by the other, as *ff. de privatis delictis, l. non utique* [D. 47.1.2] and *ff. de actionibus et obligationibus, l. si servum* [D. 44.7.34]."[55] In addition to including Drogheda's citations to the *Digest* and *Codex*, however, Bratton adds a few of his own, and not all of the authorities he cites are provisions of the *Digest* or *Codex*. One is a case:

> If one has impetrated two writs at the same time, provided he has not put them into operation, [he may elect one]; having chosen the one by which he wishes to proceed he cannot proceed on the second, if the other has been

---

[54] Judith Still and Michael Worton, "Introduction," in Michael Worton and Judith Still (eds), *Intertextuality: Theories and Practices* (Manchester University Press 1990) 1.

[55] *Bracton*, vol 2, 323. This material is out of order in Woodbine's Latin text. The translation has been amended by Thorne so that the citations go with the right material.

put into operation, before he has withdrawn from the first, as of the Abbot of Rievaulx and Peter of Savoy, *coram rege*.[56]

This refers to a case that was heard before the court *coram rege* in 1246 or 1247, while Bratton was a justice of that court.[57] He cites it in the same manner that he cites the provisions of the *Digest* and the *Codex* elsewhere in the *addicio*. This case, decided by the justices *coram rege*, is treated as equivalent to the provisions of the *Digest* and *Codex* that support the other statements of law made in this *addicio*.

Bratton's *addicio* is a bit of an outlier. Although the treatise contains quotations from more than 500 texts of Roman and canon law, it actually contains very few citations to them; there are only about thirty instances in which the authors of the treatise mark their Roman-law sources with a citation.[58] Bratton's *addicio* is the only instance in which any of the authors attempt to reconcile texts of Roman law to each other, as well as the only passage in which they attempt to reconcile texts of Roman law to decisions made in English cases. Since this *addicio* was likely added late in the process of writing the treatise, by Henry of Bratton, we might ask whether it can tell us anything about the earlier authors of the treatise and their understanding of the relationship between the authoritative texts of Roman law and cases decided in the king's courts. This may simply represent Henry of Bratton's understanding of cases.

Bratton's *addicio* is not the only example of the authors of the treatise treating the cases as if they are similar to the authoritative texts of Roman law, however. Throughout the treatise, in sections that were likely written in different stages of the writing process, the authors demonstrate, through their citation methods and the ways in which they manipulate the cases cited in the treatise, that they thought of them as texts that were similar or analogous to the authoritative texts of the learned laws.

The authors of *Bracton* made it fairly clear that they thought of these cases not simply as events that occurred in the royal courts, but as texts. In the *Note Book*, the justices abbreviated information specific to the case itself to transform it into an abstract fact-pattern, from which they could draw a generally applicable legal rule. In *Bracton*, they go one step further: they reduce the case

---

[56] *Bracton*, vol 2, 323.

[57] Meekings and Crook, *King's Bench and Common Bench* (n 36) 137. This case is also cited later in the treatise, in an *addicio* in the tractate on exceptions, where Bratton cites the case with more precision, as "among the pleas which follow the king in the thirty-first year, in a plea between Peter of Savoy and the Abbot of Rievaulx, concerning forges in the forest of Glaisdale." *Bracton*, vol 4, 289–90.

[58] See above, p 5, n.15.

to a citation. The way they construct those citations makes it clear that they are not simply citations to particular cases that occurred in the king's courts, but to the texts that record those cases. In the tractate on the assize *utrum*, one of the authors tells us that a conviction ought to lie if the twelve jurors hearing the case swear falsely, and that this "is proved in the roll of the eyre of the abbot of Reading and Martin of Pattishall in the fifth year of King Henry in the county of Gloucester, an assize, 'whether one hide of land,' around the beginning [of the roll]."[59] Note that the principle stated is proved not by the case, but "in the roll." *Bracton* provides other hints that the citations are meant to be citations to texts, rather than to cases. The citation gives several cues that would allow a reader of the treatise to find this specific case entry. It would have been fairly easy for someone with access to the roll of Pattishall's Gloucester eyre to find this case by scanning the cases, starting at the beginning of the roll, until he found those words. He tells us it is near the beginning of the roll. He also gives us some words that appeared in the first line of the roll. Two rolls survive from the 1221 Gloucester eyre, in which the Abbot of Reading and Martin of Pattishall sat as justices.[60] On the first membrane of one and the second membrane of the other, we find a case that begins "The same assize comes to recognize *whether one hide of land* . . ."[61] The first few words of the entry, "the same assize comes to recognize," would not have been very helpful in finding this case, as they are boilerplate that one would find in many entries. The author thus takes the first words that are fairly specific to the entry and makes them part of the citation.[62]

These elements, the reference to a portion of the roll and the use of a few words from the beginning of the entry, are common in the case citations found in the treatise. They would have helped the reader find the case on the roll, but they would have also drawn parallels for the reader between the texts produced by the king's courts and the authoritative texts of Roman law. The use of a few words from the beginning of a provision of law was a common way to cite in

[59] "Probatur in rotulo de itinere abbatis de Radinge et Martini de Pateshilla anno regis Henrici quinto in comitatu Gloucestriæ, assisa utrum una hida terræ, circa principium." *Bracton*, vol 3, 335.

[60] Doris M Stenton, *Rolls of the Justices in Eyre for Gloucestershire, Warwickshire, and Shropshire, 1221, 1222* (SS vol 59, Bernard Quaritch 1940) xiii–xiv, 23 (hereafter Stenton, *Gloucestershire, Warwickshire, and Shropshire*).

[61] "Eadem assisa venit recognitura si utrum i hida terre . . ." Ibid, 23 (no 77).

[62] This case is interesting because the author of this passage in *Bracton* uses it to prove that, if the jurors in a case brought by the assize *utrum* swear falsely, a jury of attaint can be called to convict them of swearing a false oath. *Bracton*, vol 3, 335. The case does not actually prove this point. The plaintiff admitted that the original assize had been taken in the third year of King John (1201–02). It had, by the time of the Gloucester eyre, been about two decades since that jury had given their verdict. Since the assize had been taken so long ago, the justices refused to hear the case without the special command of the king. They did not determine one way or the other whether an attaint would lie for an assize *utrum*. Stenton, *Gloucestershire, Warwickshire, and Shropshire* (n 60) 23–24.

the schools. A citation to the *Digest* would include the name of the title and the first few words of the fragment being cited. Thus, when one of the authors states that a possessory action must be heard before a proprietary action, and this "is proved by *ff. ad l. iul. de vi publica, l. si de vi,*" the reader would be able to find the passage from the series of clues the citation leaves.[63] This is a citation to the *Digest*. The mark "*ff.*" was the standard way of indicating a citation to the *Digest* in medieval texts. It would be followed by the name of the title, in this case book 48, title 6, titled "*Lex Iulia de vi publica*" in the text of the *Digest*. Then the citation gives "*l.*" for "*lex,*" the specific law that is being cited, and the first few words of the law, "*si de vi*" ("if it concerns force"), so the reader could either find that part of the text from memory—scholars often memorized the first words of many of the *leges* in the *Digest* so they could find them quickly—or by scanning the title. Indeed, the author of this passage may have been working from memory himself; his citation is actually a little off. [64]

The words that introduce case references are important for understanding the ways that the authors and thirteenth-century readers of the treatise would have understood those cases. The authors' choice of introductory words at times indicates that they were thinking about plea roll entries as the equivalent of the texts of the two laws. The authors of the treatise often speak of a point being "proved" by a case. When the treatise tells us that "a gift made of an advowson ought not be valid before the donor is in possession of the presentation," it also tells us that this "*is proved* in the roll of Michaelmas term in the eighth and the beginning of the ninth years of King Henry in the county of Bedford, concerning John de Trailly and the prior of Newnham, an assize of darrein presentment . . ."[65] The authors use the verb *probare* to connect the rule to the subsequent plea roll entry forty-six times in the received text of the treatise, i.e., in just under nine percent of the citations to the plea rolls.[66] They often connect the rule specifically to the text, as when they use the phrase "is

---

[63] "[P]robatur ff. ad l. iul. de vi publica, l. si de vi." *Bracton*, vol 2, 320.

[64] Usually a citation to the *Digest* would include the first words of the *fragment* being cited. The fragment was the level of organization below the title. It is so called because it represents a fragment of text taken from the work of an ancient Roman jurist. Here the *Bracton* authors are citing to a fragment from book 14 of Marcian's *Institutes*. The citation format for the fragment would be "*l. qui coetu.*" That could be followed by a citation to the section within the fragment, which in this case would be "*si de vi.*" The author of this passage went straight to the section citation, skipping the fragment. *Bracton*, vol 2, 320, n 8.

[65] The treatise continues on to summarize the case and then cite several others for the same or similar propositions. *Bracton*, vol 2, 163.

[66] In addition to the examples discussed, see *Bracton*, vol 2, 77, 97, 161, 249, 448; vol 3, 79, 107, 208, 209, 235, 281, 335, 360, 370, 372, 375, 376, 389, 403, 408; vol 4, 27, 29, 44, 95, 126, 139, 154, 161, 192, 193, 195, 196, 210, 225, 268, 270, 286, 297, 300, 313, 321, 336, 337, 366. *Probare* could mean *to test* in medieval Latin but the context in which it is placed makes it far more likely that the author is using it to mean *to prove* or *to approve*.

proved in the roll of," or, in one case, "is manifestly proved in the roll of . . ."[67] The authors might have said something along the lines of "this was proved when Martin of Pattishall made a judgment in such-and-such eyre," but for the *Bracton* authors it is not the event that proves the rule; it is the textual record of that event.

The "proved" language demonstrates that the authors of the treatise regarded plea roll entries as authoritative texts. It also demonstrates that they considered plea roll entries to be similar to the *leges* of the *Digest* and *Codex*. The treatise also uses this "proved" language to introduce citations to cases and citations to the authoritative texts of Roman law. As we saw above, one of the authors of the treatise, probably Raleigh, notes that a possessory action must be heard before a writ of right on the same facts, and that this "is proved by *ff. ad l. iul. de vi publica, l. si de vi* [D. 48.6.5.1]."[68] Raleigh and Bratton probably took this style from texts of the two laws. Azo regularly uses *probatur* to introduce *leges* from the *Digest* or *Codex*.[69] Drogheda likewise introduces citations to both Justinian's texts and papal decretals with the words *probatur* and *probantur*.[70] Even more prosaic phrases were probably borrowed from texts of the two laws. The vast majority of the case references in the treatise are introduced by the words *ut* (as) or *sicut* (just as). For example, one author tells us "dower may be constituted not only in lands and tenements acquired but in those to be acquired, if they are acquired or fall in during the life of the husband, as (*ut*) of Easter term in the seventh year of King Henry in the county of Somerset, concerning Emma, wife of William Dacy."[71] Although Azo used the "proved" language to introduce authoritative texts, he was actually much more likely to use "*ut*" to introduce one of his authorities, which suggests that even the *Bracton* authors' use of that ambiguous connector came out of their reading in the two laws.[72] The citation methods themselves were thus a way of equating

---

[67] "Probatur in rotulo . . ." *Bracton*, vol 2, 97, 163; vol 3, 235, 335, 408; vol 4, 29, 139, 154, 196. "Probatur manifeste in rotulo." *Bracton*, vol 3, 107.

[68] *Bracton*, vol 3, 320. Some of the other common introductory phrases appear in relation both to cases and to the two laws. In the tractate on acquiring dominion over things, the text at one point says "And this is established (*et ad hoc facit*) by a decretal in these words . . ." *Bracton*, vol 2, 185. The same introductory language is used at vol 2, 362 to introduce a provision of the *Codex* and at vol 2, 53 and vol 2, 429 to introduce provisions of the *Digest*. It is also used to introduce cases throughout the treatise. *Bracton*, vol 2, 191; vol 3, 110, 389, 397; vol 4, 29, 338, 354. Charlie Donahue has suggested to me that medieval *facit* citations may have served a different purpose from *ut* or *probatur* citations. *Facit* may have been used to indicate to the reader that the source being cited was not directly on point, and that some interpretation or comparison would be required to see the relevance to the issue at hand.

[69] See, e.g., Azo, *Summae*, 159–60.

[70] William of Drogheda, *Summa Aurea* (n 48) 2.

[71] "Item constitui potest dos non tantum in terris et tenementis perquisitis, sed etiam perquirendis, si perquisita fuerint vel acciderint in vita viri, ut de termino Paschæ anno regis Henrici septimo, comitatu Somersetiæ, de Emma quæ fuit uxor Willelmi Dacy." *Bracton*, vol 2, 268.

[72] See, e.g., Azo, *Summae*, 159–60.

the plea roll entry with the texts of Roman law, and of elevating the plea roll to a type of legal literature. The similarities in citation style and the fact that the authors placed these texts alongside each other imply that the authors of the treatise attributed a similar kind of authority to plea roll entries that they attributed to the texts of the learned laws. Either could be used to give authority to a statement made in the treatise.

## A Scholastic Approach to Cases

If the cases in the treatise were authoritative texts like the texts of Roman and canon law, then, ideally, they should not conflict with each other. They should form a harmonious system. Harmony was a principle that the authors of *Bracton* had in the backs of their minds as they worked on the treatise, and they occasionally brought the tools of dialectic to bear upon cases. In *Bracton's* tractate on the assize of darrein presentment,[73] there is a passage that references two cases of Martin of Pattishall:

> That in the eyre, in all assises . . . an essoin lies, and after the essoin a resummons, and after the resummons another essoin of absence on the king's service, provided the essoined person has his warrant by writ of the lord king, is proved in the last eyre of Martin of Pattishall in the county of Suffolk, an assise of mort d'ancestor beginning "If Ralph of Wadleysham." [But this could well be for this reason, because the tenant was resident outside the county and in the service of the lord king.] But the contrary may be found in the county of Kent [in the roll] of the eyre of Martin of Pattishall in the eleventh and the beginning of the twelfth years of King Henry, in Michaelmas term, that no resummons lies in the eyre.[74]

The passage starts by telling us how many delaying tactics a litigant being sued by an assize can use if he is being sued before the king's justices in eyre. The author tells us that one can use an essoin, a resummons, and then a second

---

[73] The tractate can be found at *Bracton*, vol 3, 205–44.

[74] "Item quod in itinere aliquando iacet essonium et post essonium resummonitio et iterum post resummonitionem essonium de servitio domini regis, dum tamen essoniatus warantum habeat per breve domini regis, praeter assisam ultimae praesentationis, quae excipitur ex certa causa et necessitate in omnibus assisis, probatur in ultimo itinere Martini de Pateshilla in comitatu Suffolciae, assisa mortis antecessoris, si Radulfus de Wadleghesham. Sed hoc bene potuit esse hoc ratione, quia tenens forte manens fuit extra comitatum et in servitio domini regis. Contrarium tamen inveniri poterit in comitatu Cantiae de itinere Martini de Pateshilla anno regis Henrici undecimo incipiente duodecimo de termino Sancti Michaelis quod in itinere nulla iacet resummonitio." *Bracton*, vol 3, 209.

essoin, and that we know this because it "is proved in the last eyre of Martin of Pattishall in the county of Suffolk, as assize of mort d'ancestor beginning 'If Ralph of Wadleysham.'"[75] But this was not the only way this type of case had been handled before, and it was not even the only way it had been handled by Martin of Pattishall. As the author of the passage tells us, "the contrary may be found in the county of Kent, of the eyre of Martin of Pattishall in the eleventh and the beginning of the twelfth years of King Henry, in Michaelmas term, that no resummons lies in the eyre."[76] The author thus presents us with two contradictory cases. If we are to follow previous practice, which case should we choose?

It would appear that at some later point, one of the authors of the treatise tried to solve this problem. A note on this case, set out in brackets above, was likely added to the margin of a copy of the treatise. This passage is not marked as an *addicio*, so the marginal material probably made its way into the main text before Bratton completed his recension of the treatise in the 1250s, and was inserted in what appears to be the wrong place, between these two cases. It is clumsily worked into the text, giving us the solution to the problem before it tells us what the problem is. The author of this note seeks to explain the reasoning behind the first case, telling us that "this could well be the reason [why there was a resummons in the case], because the tenant was resident outside the county and in the service of the lord king," implying that perhaps the first case cites not a general rule of procedure at the eyre, but an exception to that rule, that a resummons will lie if the tenant is resident outside the county or in the king's service, which were both generally sufficient reasons for an essoin.[77] In other words, the two cases can be reconciled if we accept that there were some peculiar circumstances in the first case. The author uses distinction to create harmony between two seemingly contradictory cases.

The treatise contains several other examples of the authors reconciling contradictory cases. In a passage of the tractate on defaults, one author cites a case holding that the view does not lie in a plea *de proparte sororum*, where a woman sues for her share of land that she has inherited together with her sisters in coparceny. The author then immediately states that "the contrary, however, that the view lies, appears of Michaelmas term in the second year of King Henry, after the war, in the county of Essex, of Matilda de Say and William de

[75] *Bracton*, vol 3, 209.
[76] *Bracton*, vol 3, 209.
[77] *Bracton*, vol 3, 209.

Mandeville."[78] The author presents a solution, however, by distinguishing the two cases based on the type of writ brought and the necessity of viewing the land in each case.[79] Likewise, in the tractate on exceptions, one of the authors provides a string of cases that have to do with when a writ of prohibition will lie against an ecclesiastical court. The author asserts that a writ of prohibition does not lie if the ecclesiastical court is hearing a case about tithes, but then says that "there is a case to the contrary with respect to tithes," citing to an eyre roll. The author then says "but it is resolved thus," and distinguishes the facts of "the first case, where the prohibition did not lie," from those of the second, where it did.[80]

It is worth noting that the authors' approach to cases is not quite the same as the modern notion of *stare decisis*. The authors of *Bracton* do not appear to be reconciling these cases out of a sense of fidelity to the court's prior decisions. Where the modern doctrine of *stare decisis* is primarily aimed at supplying the legal system with stability, stability was not the value the authors of *Bracton* were adhering to by citing to cases decided by the royal courts.[81] Rather, the cases cited in *Bracton* are authoritative in the same way the texts of Roman and canon law are authoritative. They form part of what should, ideally, be a harmonious system.[82] The authors of the treatise actually demonstrate a certain

---

[78] "Contrarium tamen videtur et quod visus iaceat, de termino Sancti Michaelis anno regis Henrici secundo post guerram comitatu Essexiae, de Matillide de Say et Willelmo de Maundeville." *Bracton*, vol 4, 181.

[79] *Bracton*, vol 4, 181.

[80] "Item locum non habebit prohibitio si de decimis agatur . . . Sed contra de decimis quod locum habeat prohibitio si decimæ petantur vel earum pretium ex venditione: ut de termino Sancti Michælis anno regis Henrici nono incipiente decimo comitatu Eboraci, de Ricardo persona Mapeltona. Sed hoc solvitur sic, quod in primo casu conventus fuit primus et principalis debitor, ubi locum non tenuit prohibitio, et in secundo casu conventi fuerunt fideiussores et implacitati cum ipse principalis debitor solvendo esset, et ubi post prohibitionem iudicatum fuit in foro seculari quod persona se caperet ad principalem debitorem qui solvendo fuit, et fideiussores inde quieti. Et unde videtur quod si principalis debitor solvendo non esset, quod persona agere posset in foro ecclesiastico contra fideiussores non obstante prohibitione." *Bracton* vol 4, 266–67.

[81] As the Ninth Circuit Court of Appeals put it, "*Stare decisis* is the policy of the court to stand by precedent; the term is but an abbreviation of *stare decisis et non quieta movere*—'to stand by and adhere to decisions and not disturb what is settled.'" *In re Osborne*, 76 F.3d 306, 309 (9th Cir. 1996).

[82] I therefore agree with David Ibbetson's assessment of the cases in the treatise insofar as the *Bracton* authors' focus was "not on the accretion of layers of law through series of legal decisions." I disagree, however, with his assessment that there is "nothing obviously normative about the use of these decisions; the mode of citation is wholly consistent with their being nothing more than illustrations of the way in which the rules had been applied in practice within the experience of the writer." David J Ibbetson, "Case Law and Doctrine: A Historical Perspective on the English Common Law" in Reiner Schulze and Ulrike Seif (eds), *Richterrecht und Rechtsfortbildung in der Europäischen Rechtsgemeinschaft* (Mohr Siebeck 2003) 30. Ibbetson's distinction between case law, which is about "fidelity to the past," and doctrinal thinking, which is about "fidelity to the system," is a useful one. The cases in *Bracton* are normative, but the way they are treated by the treatise's authors appears to me to show that they are about fidelity to the system rather than fidelity to the past. Ibid, 29. *Bracton* does twice quote Azo's formulation of a Roman principle, that a judge dealing with a novel case should make his decision by analogy to prior cases, working, as Azo puts it, "de similibus ad similia." *Bracton*, vol 2, 21; vol 4, 357;

discomfort when they are unable to achieve harmony. An author tells us at one point that when a tenant loses a case brought by writ of right by his default, he may still bring a new action to recover the land unless the case has reached a certain point in the proceedings, "until he has so put himself on the grand assise that the four knights have been summoned to choose twelve, according to some, and according to others until the twelve have been chosen."[83] An *addicio* to the text intervenes at this point to present two cases that "prove" that a defaulting litigant can still bring a new writ of right after the four knights have been chosen, but not after the twelve. But the author of the *addicio* is still troubled by this disagreement. He tells us that, in spite of the cases he has presented to support one side of the argument, "because of the disagreement of the ancients (*veteres*), nothing certain may be held as to what ought to be done if the default is made when the four knights have been summoned to choose, since some say one thing and some another."[84] Harmony appears to have been an aesthetic for this author. He is unable to work the decided cases into a coherent, harmonious system, and he finds that troubling.

## Conclusion

In *Bracton*, Raleigh and Bratton reduce the cases they find on the plea rolls to citations. They cite to them using formats very similar to those employed in texts of Roman and canon law, and intersperse citations to the plea rolls among citations to the authoritative texts of the *Digest* and *Codex*. They even employ the same types of reasoning to these texts that we find applied to the authoritative texts of Roman and canon law, attempting to create new rules by analogy to those already expressed in cases and to harmonize cases that appear to conflict. *Bracton* is, therefore, a text that brings together the texts studied in the schools and the texts produced by the royal courts. It makes the case that these texts are part of the same textual universe. The cases decided by judges and recorded on the plea rolls are texts of similar authority to the decrees of emperors and the opinions of jurists.

---

D.15.1.12; Horst Heinrich Jakobs, *De similibus ad similia bei Bracton und Azo* (Vittorio Klostermann 1996) 38. The concept of de similibus ad similia does not necessarily imply a concept of stare decisis.

[83] "Ita quod quatuor milites summoniti fuerint ad eligendum duodecim secundum quosdam, et secundum alios quousque duodecim electi fuerint." *Bracton*, vol 4, 154.

[84] "Propter dissensum vero antiquorum non poterit teneri aliquod certum quid fieri debeat si defalta facta fuerit cum quatuor milites sint summoniti ad eligendum, cum quidam dicant sic quidam contrarium." *Bracton*, vol 4, 154.

# 6

# The Genres of Authority

In both the *Note Book* and the *Bracton* treatise, Pattishall, Raleigh, and Bratton set out to constitute the plea roll entry in a new way. In the *Note Book*, they copied cases from the rolls, taking them out of their original context and deleting, replacing, or abbreviating certain types of case-specific information. In *Bracton*, they did not copy cases, but cited to cases, sometimes giving a summary of the case, but usually just providing the citation to the text of the plea roll as an authority for some abstract legal rule. In both texts, we can see the authors transforming the plea roll entry from an administrative text into a kind of legal literature, stylistically similar to the texts they would have encountered in the schools. In *Bracton*, in particular, the parallels between the cases and the authoritative texts of Roman law become very explicit both in the authors' citation practices and in their application of the techniques of dialectical reasoning to the texts.

Prior chapters have focused on how the justices used Roman models in their texts. This chapter will seek to explain why they did this. We will see in this chapter that the authors of *Bracton* identified the plea roll entry, a text they constructed as a text of authority, with the royal justice. *Bracton* implies that the justices themselves were authorities whose opinions mattered in the same way the opinions of the jurists of ancient Rome or the civilian and canonist jurists of the twelfth and thirteenth centuries mattered. To the authors of *Bracton*, the justice was the author of the plea roll entry, the authority behind its creation, just as Ulpian, Paul, and their contemporaries were the authorities behind the creation of the *leges* in the *Digest*. The authors of *Bracton* play with the different meanings of the word *iudicium* (judgment) in order to conflate the English justice with the Roman jurist. The English plea rolls used the word *iudicium* to denote the judgment of the court. As we shall see, the texts of Roman law also used it to denote a jurist's opinion. When a justice made a decision in an important case, he was giving his judgment in the sense of a ruling binding on the parties, but he was also giving his judgment in another sense: he was making a learned pronouncement of the law applicable in that case and similar ones. The authors of the treatise identify the plea rolls, the space where the justice's judgment is recorded, with *consilia* or *responsa*, the kinds of texts in which a

*Priests of the Law.* Thomas J. McSweeney, Oxford University Press (2019). © Thomas J. McSweeney.
DOI: 10.1093/oso/9780198845454.003.0007

jurist of the two laws offered his opinion. The cases were thus important to the justices who wrote *Bracton* not just because they provided authority, but also because they allowed these justices to think of themselves, the authors of those case records, as jurists.

## The Judgments of Jurists

*Bracton* has what appear to be two introductions, titled the *introductio* and the *prohemium auctoris* in the printed edition. We do not know for sure when either was written, or by whom. The first is reminiscent of the introductions to Justinian's *Institutes* and the *Glanvill* treatise. It borrows from both, as well as from Azo's *Summa on the Institutes*.[1] The second, the *prohemium*, is written in a standard scholastic format, the kind that one would find in a *summa* produced by a doctor of law or theology in the schools, and systematically explains the matter, intention, utility, branch of philosophy, and end of the work.[2] Paul Brand has argued that they were likely the work of different authors. He has made the case that the *prohemium* was likely written by Raleigh and that the *introductio* was added later by Bratton.[3] I am not as convinced that the two introductions were written by different people. It seems to me a possibility, but not a necessity, and there are reasons for thinking that the two were written by the same person.[4] Indeed, the *prohemium*, the part that Brand thought was more likely to be Raleigh's work, was probably added well into the process of writing and editing the treatise. It borrows heavily from William of Drogheda's *Summa Aurea*, and a version of the *Summa Aurea* that H.G. Richardson thought would only have been available sometime after 1239.[5] The parts that can be attributed to Drogheda are unlikely to be later additions, since they are integral to the text. If the *prohemium* was written sometime after 1239, it is still

---

[1] *Bracton*, vol 2, 19.

[2] *Bracton*, vol 2, 20.

[3] Paul Brand, "The Age of Bracton" in John Hudson (ed), *The History of English Law: Centenary Essays on "Pollock and Maitland"* (OUP 1996) 77 (hereafter Brand, "Age of Bracton").

[4] It is not entirely unusual for a text of the kind Raleigh and Bratton were writing to contain two introductions, written in different styles. Azo's *Summa Codicis*, a text upon which both introductions appear to rely, begins with a general introduction written in the same type of grandiose language used in the *introductio* to *Bracton* before moving into the matter, utility, and end of the work. Azo, *Summae*, 1–2. Moreover, there is some continuity between the two introductions to *Bracton*. Both the *introductio* and the *prohemium* rely on Azo's *Summae*. It could be that two different authors used the same texts to craft their introductions, but the fact that the same sources appear in both would seem to create a presumption of a single author.

[5] The *prohemium* quotes from a prefatory letter that only appears in three manuscripts of Drogheda's work, and that Richardson thought was a later addition to the text. HG Richardson, "Azo, Drogheda, and Bracton" (1944) 59 EHR 22, 39.

possible that it was added by Raleigh, but the likelihood that it was added by Bratton rises the later we can date a portion of the treatise. Raleigh, after all, retired from the court *coram rege* in 1239. The *introductio* is, unfortunately, more difficult to date. The texts that are quoted in the *introductio*—the *Institutes*, *Glanvill*, Azo's *summae*, and possibly Tancred's *Ordo Judiciarius*—all date to 1216 or earlier, so they give us no help in dating it.[6] All would have been available during the earliest stages of work on the treatise. It is unfortunate that we cannot be more precise, because the *introductio* makes some interesting statements about the treatise and how its author perceived it. Whoever he was and whenever he was writing, the author of the *introductio* attempts to characterize the English royal justices as jurists in the Roman-law mold. He does so by assimilating the types of texts produced by the justices to genres of texts that he knew from the schools.

The author of *introductio* claims to be the author of the treatise and indicates that his aim in writing the treatise is to curb the abuses of bad justices. He complains that the laws are often misapplied by "men of little wisdom and small learning who ascend the judgment seat before they have learned the laws."[7] When not being inadvertently misapplied, the laws are being willfully subverted by "the *maiores* who decide cases according to their own will rather than by the authority of the laws."[8] In order to fix these abuses and to "instruct the *minores*," who might counterbalance the unlearned and corrupt, the author of the treatise has "turned [his] mind to the ancient judgments (*veteres iudicia*) of the just, examining diligently, not without working long into the night watches, their deeds (*facta*), counsels (*consilia*), and responses (*responsa*)."[9] The words *iudicia, consilia*, and *responsa* are significant, in that they would have connected the work of English justices with the work of the jurists of Roman law. These words, and the *introductio* author's use of them, require careful examination.

The phrase "turned [his] mind to the ancient judgments of the just" is drawn from Azo's *Summa Institutionum*. The author did not copy word-for-word when he borrowed Azo's phrase, however. Azo explains to us in his *Summa* how Justinian's *Digest* came about. After Justinian had commissioned the *Codex*, "he turned his mind to the *immense volumes of ancient wisdom* (*immensa volumina veteris prudentiae*), a hopeless task, as if advancing through the middle of an

---

[6] *Bracton*, vol 2, 19.

[7] "Cum autem huiusmodi leges et consuetudines per insipientes et minus doctos, qui cathedram iudicandi ascendunt antequam leges didicerint." *Bracton*, vol 2, 19.

[8] "Multotiens pervertuntur a maioribus, qui potius proprio arbitrio quam legum auctoritate causas decidunt." *Bracton*, vol 2, 19.

[9] "[A]nimum erexi ad vetera iudicia iustorum, perscrutando diligenter non sine vigiliis et labore, facta ipsorum, consilia et responsa ... " *Bracton*, vol 2, 19.

abyss, he completed it by heavenly favor, and from nearly 2,000 books and 300,000 verses he composed one book which is called the *Digest* . . ."[10] The author of the *introductio* obviously relied on Azo, but he made some telling changes to the great jurist's formula. The "immense volumes of ancient wisdom" referenced in the *Digest* are treatises written by Roman jurists of the classical period, the first to third centuries A.D. The *Digest* excerpts fragments from them and reorganizes them by topic. The *Digest* is thus a collection of the opinions of jurists, given the force of a statute by an imperial decree that appears at the beginning of the work. Where Justinian had collected bits of the "immense volumes of ancient wisdom," the author of the *introductio* tells us that he has collected the "ancient judgments of the just."[11] What does he mean by this? Who are the just, and where can their judgments (*iudicia*) be found?

## The Genres of Juristic Literature

The word "*iudicium*" had several different meanings within the discourse of the learned laws. In the introduction to the lectures on the *Institutes* given in England sometime around 1200, the lecturer told his students that there are "five sources from which all law is derived."[12] Among these sources are the Twelve Tables, the actions established by "the authority of learned men," the praetorian edict, and imperial constitutions. The final source of law are the judgments (*iudicia*) of the jurists (*prudentes*) of the Roman Empire. The lecturer tells us that "As time went on, since the emperor was frequently occupied in wars, it was laid down that there should be some who gave answers on the law and that no judge should be allowed to go against their judgments (*iudiciis*), that is, their answers (*responsis*). This is the fifth source of law."[13]

[10] "Erexit postea animum suum ad immensa volumina veteris prudentiae, et opus desperatum, quasi per medium profundum vadens, coelesti favore adimplevit, et ex duobus paene milibus librorum et ex tricies centenis milibus versuum unicum librum composuit quem digestum appellavit." Azo, *Summae*, 1046; Frederic William Maitland (ed), *Select Passages from the Works of Bracton and Azo* (SS vol 8, Bernard Quaritch 1895) 16 (hereafter Maitland (ed), *Bracton and Azo*).

[11] It is worth noting that the author of this passage in *Bracton* puts himself in the place of Justinian. Where Azo is describing something Justinian did, the author of the *introductio* borrows the phrase to describe what *he* did in constructing the treatise. This might be considered a bit blasphemous.

[12] "Agit enim de iii. A quibus universum ius derivatur." The editors of the lectures, de Zulueta and Stein, thought that the "iii" contained in the manuscript was probably a scribal error, since the lecturer discusses five sources of law. Francis De Zulueta and Peter Stein (eds), *The Teaching of Roman Law in England around 1200* (Selden Society 1990) 2 (hereafter De Zulueta and Stein (eds), *Teaching of Roman Law*).

[13] "Tempore procedente, quia imperator multotiens finitimis bellis aduocabatur, constitutum est it essent qui de iure p. responderent, a quorum iudiciis, ide est responsis, nulli iudicum liceret recedere. Et hec est v. portio iuris." Ibid.

The word *iudicium* here thus refers to the opinion of a jurist. The lecturer explains that these *iudicia* or *responsa* of the jurists are the same ones that were put "into lucid harmony" by Justinian in the *Digest*.[14] The "ancient judgments of the just" in *Bracton's introductio* could thus be read, by someone trained in Roman law, as synonymous with the "immense volumes of ancient wisdom" mentioned in Azo. Those immense volumes were filled with the judgments of the just, and a thirteenth-century civilian likely would have understood the connection when he read *Bracton*.

There is further evidence that by using the word *iudicia*, the author of this passage was alluding to the opinions of jurists. The author's decision to modify Azo's phrase leads to a subtle shift in meaning. When Azo describes Justinian's process, it is a process of searching texts. The modified phrase in *Bracton* places the emphasis more squarely on the people who produced those texts, the "just" who produced the "judgments." The author of the *introductio* made it explicit that the authorities he was searching for were people, not just texts. At the same time, he refers to texts produced by those people. He refers not simply to the "judgments" of the just, but to a specific type of text that records those judgments, and the texts he refers to are types of texts that were produced by jurists. In full, the author says that "I have turned my mind to the ancient judgments of the just, examining diligently, not without working long into the night watches, their deeds (*facta*), counsels (*consilia*), and responses (*responsa*), and have collected whatever I found therein worthy of note into a *summa*."[15] It is important to note that the author of this passage in *Bracton* added the words *facta*, *consilia*, and *responsa*; they do not appear in the corresponding text in Azo. *Facta* is an unspecific term, simply meaning "things which have been done." *Consilia* and *responsa*, on the other hand, do refer to specific genres of writing in both classical Roman law and in medieval Roman and canon law. The two words, *consilia* and *responsa*, are essentially synonyms. A *consilium* is a piece of advice. When it is given in response to a request for advice, it is a *responsum*. In a legal setting, *consilia* and *responsa* referred to the legal opinions of jurists given in response to questions from magistrates or litigants.[16] William of Raleigh and Henry of Bratton would undoubtedly have known how these terms were used in both the texts of Justinian and in contemporary Roman-law practice. They

---

[14] "[I]n luculentam . . . consonantiam." Ibid.

[15] *Bracton*, vol 2, 20.

[16] Adolf Berger, *Encyclopedic Dictionary of Roman Law* (American Philosophical Society 1980) 681, "*Responsa Prudentium*" (Hereafter Berger, *Encyclopedic Dictionary*). In Classical Roman law, *consilium* generally referred to legal advice given to a magistrate by his council. Berger, *Encyclopedic Dictionary* (n 16) 408, "*Consilium magistratuum*." *Responsa* referred to answers to questions from litigants and others.

may have read the history of *responsa* found near the beginning of the *Digest*. The second title of the first book of the *Digest* describes the evolution of the law in Rome.[17] The title is called "The Origin of Law and of All the Magistracies and the Succession of the Jurists."[18] It contains a long segment on the history of law by the jurist Pomponius. After his account of the twelve tables, the development of statutes, and of the beginnings of the magistracies, Pomponius recounts the history of the jurists. A little less than half of the title is given over to an account of the "very many very great men" by whom "legal principles have been developed and passed down."[19] In the middle of this story of the heroes of the civil law, Pomponius gives an account of the development of *responsa*:

> [B]efore the time of Augustus the right of stating *responsa* (*respondendi ius*) at large was not granted by emperors, but the practice was that *responsa* were given by people who had confidence in their own studies. Nor did they always issue *responsa* under seal, but most commonly wrote themselves to the judges, or gave the testimony of a direct answer to those who consulted them. It was the deified Augustus who, in order to enhance the authority of the law, first established that *responsa* might be given under his authority. And from that time this [i.e., the right to issue *responsa* backed by the emperor's authority] began to be sought as a favor. As a consequence of this, our most excellent emperor Hadrian issued a rescript on an occasion when some men of praetorian rank were petitioning him for permission to grant *responsa*; he said that this [permission] was by custom not merely begged for but earned and that he [the emperor] would accordingly be delighted if whoever had faith in himself would prepare himself for giving *responsa* to the people at large.[20]

[17] This title is quoted in *Bracton* and was obviously known to at least one of the authors. *Bracton*, vol 2, 26 contains a reference to D.1.2.2.13, very close to the above quotation in the *Digest*. For citations to the first book of the *Digest*, see also *Bracton*, vol 2, 21, 30, 186, 304, 305; vol 3, 56, 128. The *introductio* itself contains a reference to the next title, specifically to D.1.3.1. *Bracton*, vol 2, 22.

[18] *Digest of Justinian*, vol 1, 3. "De origine iuris et omnium magistratuum et successione prudentium." D.1.2.

[19] *Digest of Justinian*, vol 1, 7. "Iuris civilis scientiam plurimi et maximi viri professi sunt: sed qui eorum maximae dignationis apud populum Romanum fuerunt, eorum in praesentia mentio habenda est, ut appareat, a quibus et qualibus haec iura orta et tradita sunt." D.1.2.35.

[20] *Digest of Justinian*, vol 1, 10. "Et, ut obiter sciamus, ante tempora Augusti publice respondendi ius non a principibus dabatur, sed qui fiduciam studiorum suorum habebant, consulentibus respondebant: neque responsa utique signata dabant, sed plerumque iudicibus ipsi scribebant, aut testabantur qui illos consulebant. Primus divus Augustus, ut maior iuris auctoritas haberetur, constituit, ut ex auctoritate eius responderent: et ex illo tempore peti hoc pro beneficio coepit. Et ideo optimus princeps Hadrianus, cum ab eo viri praetorii peterent, ut sibi liceret respondere, rescripsit eis hoc non peti, sed praestari solere et ideo, si quis fiduciam sui haberet, delectari se populo ad respondendum se praepararet." D.1.2.2.49. I have replaced Watson's "opinions" with "*responsa*" for clarity. In several places where the translation contains the noun "*responsa*," the *Digest* actually uses an equivalent verb. It is worth noting that Fritz Schulz argued that D.1.2.2, as it appears in the *Digest*, is probably the work

Immediately following this passage, Pomponius tells a story that focuses on a line of important jurists, ending his account with the succession of jurists who were granted the right to respond by the emperor.[21] The remainder of the *Digest* bears out Pomponius' reading of Roman law as the product of jurists with *auctoritas*, since the whole long work is composed of the writings of jurists.

Many of the elementary legal texts of the period placed the *responsa prudentium* among the fundamental sources of law. In Gratian's *Decretum*, they are one of five sources of Roman law.[22] Gratian drew his discussion of *responsa* from Isidore of Seville's *Etymologiae*, an encyclopedia of universal knowledge that was still widely read in the thirteenth century, and that probably would have been known by the authors of *Bracton*. In the *Institutes*, the *responsa prudentium* is one of six types of written law, or *ius scriptum*.[23] As noted above, the author of the English lectures on the *Institutes* specifically connected *responsa* with *iudicia*, just as *Bracton* did. For the lecturer, the *responsum* is the text that contains the *iudicium* of the jurist. He places the jurists' *iudicia*, contained in their *responsa*, among the "five sources from which all law is derived."[24]

The author of the *introductio* would, therefore, have been familiar with the notion that ancient jurists gave *responsa*, and even with the notion that the advice the jurist gave in a *responsum* would be called a *iudicium*.[25] He may also have been familiar with *responsa* as texts that were circulating in his own time. *Consilium* literature was current in the *Bracton* authors' time both in law and in medicine. The classic period for *consilia* would not come about until the fourteenth and fifteenth centuries, when collections of the *consilia* of (mostly Italian) jurists and physicians would circulate as texts with authority.[26] But despite the fact that the *consilium* collection would not flourish until the fourteenth

of several different people, and that parts are unlikely to have been written in Pomponius' time. That would not have been apparent to a thirteenth-century reader, however. Fritz Schulz, *History of Roman Legal Science* (Reprint edn, Clarendon Press 1967) 115–17.

[21] D.1.2.50–D.1.2.53.
[22] D. 2 c.5; Gratian, *The Treatise on Laws with the Ordinary Gloss* (Augustine Thompson and Katherine Christensen trs, Catholic University of America Press 1993) 8 (hereafter Gratian, *Treatise on Laws*).
[23] Inst.1.2.3; *Justinian's Institutes*, 37.
[24] De Zulueta and Stein (eds), *Teaching of Roman Law* (n 12) 2.
[25] The jurists were not alone in referring to the scholar's opinion as a *iudicium*. Some medical *consilia* of the late thirteenth and early fourteenth centuries use the term *iudicium* to refer to the physician's advice in the case. Jole Agrimi and Chiara Crisciani, *Les Consilia Médicaux* (Caroline Viola trs, Brepols 1994) 35.
[26] Sebasti Giralt, "The 'Consilia' Attributed to Arnau de Vilanova" (2002) 7 Early Science and Medicine 311, 345. Agrimi and Crisciani, *Consilia Médicaux* (n 25) 39.

century, the contemporary *consilium* genre must have been known in the cultural world of the *Bracton* authors. A *consilium* of Azo survives.[27] The *consilium* also appears in other types of literature. Andreas Capellanus' *De Amore*, a Latin treatise which Andreas probably wrote at the court of Champagne in the 1180s, shifts between several legal genres in teaching the ways of love to a young man named Walter.[28] Andreas teaches Walter how to win the love of different kinds of women through dialogues. His advice actually sounds quite a bit like advice for court procedure and pleading.[29] Andreas uses legal genres most explicitly, however, in chapter seven of Book II, which he titles "various judgments on love" (*variis iudiciis amoris*).[30] What follow are a number of texts, some written in the form of the judgment of a court and others in the form of a jurist's *responsum*. In each, a case is posed to a noble lady, who acts as a consulting jurist. Eleanor of Aquitaine, Isobel of Vermandois, Ermengarde of Narbonne, and Marie, Countess of Champagne, well-known and powerful women of the late twelfth century who were known for their connections with courtly literature, are all named in this text as consulting jurists on the laws of love. In Andreas' text, various nouns and verbs are used to describe the noble lady's response to the lovers, including terms that were familiar in the learned laws. In one case, we are given "the sentence (*sententia*) of Queen Eleanor pronounced (*respondit*) when she was consulted (*consulta*) on this matter," terminology that would have been familiar to a consulting jurist.[31] Some of the opinions are explicitly referred to as *responsa*.[32] The title, *variis iudiciis amoris* identifies the texts to come in the chapter as *iudicia*. The word *sententia* also appears in several of these cases.[33] *Sententia*, like *iudicium, consilium*, and *responsum*, was also used in the schools to refer to an authoritative opinion.[34] These *consilia*

[27] Azo, *Un Consulto D'azone Dell'anno 1205* (Luigi Chiappelli and Lodovico Zdekauer eds, Fratelli Bracali 1888).

[28] Andreas Capellanus, *Andreas Capellanus on Love* (PG Walsh trs, Duckworth 1982) (hereafter Andreas Capellanus, *On Love*).

[29] See ibid, 64–65, 86–87.

[30] Ibid, 250–71.

[31] The entire sentence reads "Huic autem mulieri reginae Alinoriae videtur obviare sententiae, quae super hoc negotio taliter consulta respondit." Ibid, 252–53 (no II).

[32] Ibid, 254 (no V), 262 (no XIII).

[33] Ibid, 252 (no II), 260 (no XII), 265 (no XV).

[34] Justinian's *Institutes* refers to the "*responsa prudentium*" as the "*sententiae et opiniones*" of those jurists who had been given the authority to respond by the emperor. Inst.1.2.8. The term *sententia* is also used to refer to the opinions of great thinkers in Peter Lombard's *Sentences*, the most important textbook in the field of theology throughout the middle ages. Giulio Silano, "Introduction" in Peter Lombard, *The Sentences, Book 1: The Mystery of the Trinity* (Giulio Silano trs, Pontifical Institute of Medieval Studies 2010) xxii. Richardson notes that the authors of *Bracton* often replaced the word *sententia* with the word *iudicium* when they borrowed passages from Tancred's *Ordo Iudiciarius*, suggesting that they recognized some equivalence between the terms. HG Richardson, "Studies in Bracton" (1948) 6 Traditio 61, 68–70.

are authoritative and binding in other cases, just like the *consilia* of the Roman jurists.[35] Indeed, although each problem is written in the form of a real-life dispute, the parties are turned into abstractions, just as they often were in papal decretals and *Bracton's Note Book*, hinting that their value lay in their applicability to similar cases. Thus, it is an unnamed "certain man (*quidam*)" who is "immoderately bound by love to a certain lady (*cuiusdam dominae*)."[36]

*On Love* is a very complex text. We do not know whether the authors of *Bracton* had read it or what they would have made of it if they had. But it does give us a sense of the semantic range terms such as *consilium, responsum,* and *iudicium* might have had in the twelfth and thirteenth centuries. Andreas used the form of the *consilium* in a humorous way, creating what were almost certainly fabricated cases on the laws of love in a text that shows signs that the author had his tongue firmly planted in his cheek when he was writing it. In order to do that and to make the text resonate with his audience, the *consilium* must have been a familiar form to those literate in Latin in the Northern French cultural context in which Andreas operated. The authors of *Bracton*, broadly speaking, shared this same cultural context. They were a group of educated Latin-literates who also spoke French and who could well have read literature produced in the courts of Northern France. If *consilia* were known to Andreas, they would likely have been known to the *Bracton* authors, who wrote about judicial cases in a manner so close to that used by Andreas to describe his cases on the laws of love.

## The Cases as *Judicia, Consilia,* and *Responsa*

The "ancient judgments of the just," which are manifested through their "*facta, consilia,* and *responsa*," smack of Roman law, and to genres of texts that were familiar to those who had studied it.[37] They would have evoked images of the jurist giving his authoritative opinion in a case. The author of the *introductio* implies that he began work on the treatise by turning his mind to these ancient judgments and that he "examin[ed] diligently, not without working long

---

[35] Some of them even cite to other *responsa* as precedents. Peter Goodrich, "Law in the Courts of Love: Andreas Capellanus and the Judgments of Love" (1996) 48 Stanford Law Review 633; Don A Monson, *Andreas Capellanus, Scholasticism, and the Courtly Tradition* (Catholic University of America Press 2005) 98.

[36] Andreas Capellanus, *On Love* (n 28) 250.

[37] Portions of this subsection have been adapted from Thomas McSweeney, "English Judges and Roman Jurists: The Civilian Learning Behind England's First Case Law" (2012) 84 Temple Law Review 827, 852–55 (hereafter McSweeney, "English Judges").

into the night watches, their *facta, consilia*, and *responsa*."[38] He then "collected whatever I found therein worthy of note into a *summa*."[39] He suggests that the process of collecting these texts was fundamental to the writing of the treatise, that the treatise is composed of these *iudicia, facta, consilia*, and *responsa*. Whether the *introductio* was the work of Martin of Pattishall or William of Raleigh, working to define the project at its beginning, or of Henry of Bratton, seeking to make sense of a completed treatise near the end of the process of revising it, we have to ask what part of the treatise the *introductio's* author was referring to when he spoke of the ancient judgments of the just, which he claims are so important to the project. Recall that the author of the *introductio* appears to have been rather deliberate in using these terms; they do not appear in the corresponding passage in Azo. What are these *iudicia, facta, consilia*, and *responsa* that the author thinks are so central to the treatise?

As we have seen, the phrases *iudicia, consilia*, and *responsa* could be and probably were understood by the author to mean the opinions of jurists excerpted from those "immense volumes of ancient wisdom" and placed in the *Digest*. The treatise does cite to the *Digest* a number of times, but it seems unlikely that the author of the *introductio* meant to imply that the opinions of the Roman jurists of old are the basis of the treatise. There are indications, however, that the various authors of the treatise associated the terms *judicium, consilium*, and *responsum* with the royal justices. In some parts of the treatise, the authors explicitly refer to some act as a *consilium* or a *responsum*, and it is usually in the context of a judge giving advice on a thorny legal matter. In the section on essoins, an author cites to the "response (*responso*) of William of Raleigh and Stephen of Seagrave made to Richard Duket, who sought their counsel (*consilium*) in this matter."[40] Duket was a royal justice. He had served as a clerk to the justiciars Geoffrey FitzPeter and Hubert de Burgh and was later appointed a justice on the same 1226 Yorkshire eyre, discussed in Chapter 3, where William of Raleigh and William of York served as clerks under Martin of Pattishall.[41] He saw service on the Common Bench, but apparently only for one term, Hilary, 1228, and acted as a justice in two eyres of

---

[38] "[E]go animum erexi ad vetera iudicia iustorum, perscrutando diligenter non sine vigiliis et labore, facta ipsorum, consilia et responsa . . ." *Bracton*, vol 2, 20.

[39] "[E]t quidquid inde nota dignum inveni in unam summam . . . compilavi." *Bracton*, vol 2, 20.

[40] "Ex responso Willelmi de Ralegha et S. de Segrave facto Ricardo Duket qui expetiit eorum consilium in hoc casu." *Bracton*, vol 4, 126.

[41] Doris M Stenton, *Pleas before the King or His Justices, 1198-1212, Volume 3* (SS vol 83, Bernard Quaritch 1966) cccxi–cccxiii. Duket merits three mentions in the *Bracton* treatise. All three relate to him receiving counsel from Martin of Pattishall or William of Raleigh on how to proceed in a case before him. *Bracton*, vol 2, 354, 360; vol 4, 126.

the early 1240s.[42] After 1235, Raleigh had ordered all of the other justices of the realm to reserve difficult questions to him, so it may have been in the late 1230s or early 1240s that Duket sought the advice of Raleigh and Seagrave, who were, in succession, the chief justices of the court *coram rege*. The authors of the treatise could, therefore, apply the terms *consilium* and *responsum* as easily to the advice the chief justice of the court *coram rege* gave to a fellow justice as they could to the opinions of Roman jurists.

The advice of justices appears throughout the treatise. Martin of Pattishall is featured prominently. This is not surprising, as Raleigh served him as a clerk for a number of years, referring to Martin as "my sometime lord" in a deed he wrote in 1235 or 1236.[43] The author tells us what Martin was accustomed to do in certain types of cases. For example, when "boundaries [were] destroyed or completely altered the lord Martin took an assise as of a free tenement, not as a trespass. For he used to say that one could not commit a more harmful disseisin than by destroying boundaries completely, or by moving or removing them."[44] In another part of the treatise, we are told what "is better, according to Martin."[45] In addition to his cases and sayings, other texts of Martin of Pattishall are quoted and referenced in the treatise, apparently as models for what future justices should do. His consultations to the ecclesiastical courts on issues of jurisdiction are preserved in three places.[46] Martin of Pattishall is not the only justice whose "sayings" are recorded. At one point the author of an *addicio* says that a particular doctrine having to do with curtsey "was wrongful according to Stephen of Seagrave," and that "He used to say that this law was misunderstood and misapplied . . ."[47] William of York is a popular arbiter of law for the author or authors. Indeed, his opinions often appear in *addiciones* that contradict the main text, suggesting that they were added by Henry of Bratton, perhaps in the margin of the treatise. In the middle of a discussion of descent to heirs, an *addicio* informs us that "there are some who say, and it is true, that mention must be made of a son who has died in the lifetime of his father, the

---

[42] CAF Meekings and David Crook, *King's Bench and Common Bench in the Reign of Henry III* (Selden Society 2010) 183 (hereafter Meekings and Crook, *King's Bench and Common Bench*); David Crook, *Records of the General Eyre* (Her Majesty's Stationery Office 1982) 102, 104.

[43] CAF Meekings, "Martin de Pateshull of Good Memory My Sometime Lord" (1974) 47 Bulletin of the Institute of Historical Research 224, 229, reprinted in *Studies in 13th Century Justice and Administration* (Hambledon Press, 1981) item XII (hereafter Meekings, "Sometime Lord").

[44] "Dominus tamen Martinus assisam cepit de divisis corruptis vel mutatis omnino sicut de libero et non sicut de transgressione. Dicebat enim quod non potuit quis magis iniuriosam facere disseisinam quam de terminis demoliendis omnino vel corrumpendis in parte vel amovendis." *Bracton*, vol 3, 128.

[45] *Bracton*, vol 3, 122.

[46] *Bracton*, vol 3, 373, 385; vol 4, 263.

[47] *Bracton*, vol 4, 360.

view of William of York."[48] In another *addicio* where the author complicates the primary text by admitting that "so [the rule stated above] seems to some, but to others the contrary seems true,"[49] he resolves the dispute by saying that this new, contrary opinion "was the reasoning of William of York, and it is good."[50]

The authors signal throughout the treatise that the words of individual justices are important. If justices can speak as individuals, they can also disagree with each other. The "some say . . . others say" (*quidam dicunt . . . alii dicunt*) formula that appears in so many scholastic texts makes its way into *Bracton*.[51] Sometimes the author resolves these disputes, either with his own solution or that of some judge.[52] There are some cases where one justice's opinion is preferred over another's. In one passage, an author tells us that, since serjeanties are not military fees in the same sense as a fee held by knight-service, the chief lord has no right to the marriage or wardship of the heir to a serjeanty,

> But the contrary may be seen concerning an abbess of Barking, among the pleas which follow the king in the [seventeenth] year of King Henry before William of Raleigh, who recovered the wardship and marriage of the heir of one of her tenants who held his tenement [in serjeanty] in the manor of Barking by the service of riding with her from manor to manor; *which Stephen of Seagrave did not approve*.[53]

Here William of Raleigh is put in opposition to both the author of this passage and to Stephen of Seagrave, whose opinion lines up with the author's own.[54]

The author of the *introductio* may, therefore, have been referring to the opinions of justices that appear throughout the treatise—and are occasionally marked as *consilia* and *responsa*—when he discussed the *iudicia, facta, consilia,* and *responsa* that he collected at the beginning of the project. He probably meant to cover more than just these opinions, however. He suggests that *iudicia* are central to the treatise and that the process of collecting them was a major

---

[48] "Sed sunt quidam qui dicunt, et verum est, quod de filio mortuo in vita patris oportet facere mentionem secundum Willelmum de Eboraco." *Bracton*, vol 4, 173.

[49] "Ut quibusdam videtur, sed aliis videtur contra." *Bracton*, vol 2, 367.

[50] "Et hæc fuit ratio W. de Eboraco et bona." *Bracton*, vol 2, 367. See also *Bracton*, vol 3, 66 for an example of a rule that is true "secundum W. de Eboraco."

[51] See *Bracton*, vol 2, 388, 403, 424, 432.

[52] See *Bracton*, vol 2, 251, for a case where the author resolves competing opinions by arguing that the latter opinion would create an absurd result.

[53] "Contrarium tamen habetur de quadam abbatissa de Berkinge inter placita quæ sequuntur regem anno regis Henrici—coram Willelmo de Raleigha, et quæ recuperavit custodiam et maritagium de herede cuiusdam tenentis sui, qui tenebat tenementum suum in manerio de Berkinge per servitium equitandi cum ea de manerio in manerium, quod quidem S. de Segrave non approbavit." *Bracton*, vol 2, 113 (emphasis mine).

[54] This seems to suggest that the author of this passage was not Raleigh.

part of the work. It is difficult to say that the scattered opinions of justices that appear throughout the treatise are a major part of it. Scholars have generally assumed that *iudicia* refers more specifically to the cases decided by English justices that are referenced in the treatise, and there is good reason to believe that they are correct.[55] The term *iudicium* itself hints at this interpretation, as it could actually refer to two different types of acts. As we have seen, it could refer to the act of giving a legal opinion, and was used in the lectures on the *Institutes* discussed above, as well as in *consilia* of the thirteenth century. But it could also refer to the act of making the final, authoritative decision in a case, one that could be backed up by the force of the secular authority. Today we use the term "judgment" primarily to refer to the latter; it is judges, not jurists, who hand down judgments. The word *iudicium* could be, and probably was, understood in this way by the author of the *introductio*. Texts of Roman and canon law often used the word *iudicium* to refer to a judicial proceeding more generally or the judge's final decision in that judicial proceeding more specifically.[56] It was also used in this way in the English royal courts. The *Bracton* authors use the word *iudicium* in this sense in several places.[57] The *prohemium*, for instance, indicates that the purpose of the treatise is to ennoble learners so they will be able to sit as judges and issue *iudicia*, which "are not of man, but of God, which is why the heart of a king who rules well is said to be in the hand of God."[58] It is through the judgment that both the royal and, by extension, the divine will are expressed. The judge sits "on the very seat of the king, on the throne of God," qualified by "so to speak," so as not to deify the justice.[59] The *prohemium*'s *iudicium* is God's speech mediated through the king and his delegate, the justice.

The opinions of justices and the cases from the plea rolls are presented in similar way throughout the treatise, suggesting that the authors of the treatise thought about them as similar texts. The *responsum* or *consilium* that Richard Duket requested from Raleigh and Seagrave, discussed above, is presented in the same format as many of the plea roll references in the treatise. The author makes no distinction between this response to Richard Duket and cases taken

---

[55] Brand, "Age of Bracton" (n 3) 77.

[56] See Kenneth Pennington, "Reform in 1215: *Magna Carta* and the Fourth Lateran Council" (2015) 97 Bulletin of the Institute of Medieval Canon Law, new series 97, 105.

[57] In addition to the *prohemium*, discussed below, see *Bracton*, vol 2, 304–05; vol 4, 136.

[58] "Utilitas autem est quia nobilitat addiscentes et honores conduplicat et profectus et facit eos principari in regno et sedere in aula regia et in sede ipsius regis quasi in throno dei, tribus et nationes, actores et reos, ordine dominabili iudicantes, vice regis quasi vice Ihesu Christi, cum rex sit vicarius dei. Iudicia enim non sunt hominis sed dei, et ideo cor regis bene regentis dicitur esse in manu dei." *Bracton*, vol 2, 20.

[59] *Bracton*, vol 2, 20.

directly from the rolls. He first states a rule of law—in this case that the knights sent to make a view of an essoin are considered a court of record—and then tells us that this is proved (*probatur*) by the *responsum*, in the same way he tells us, about one tenth of the time, that a rule is proved by such-and-such roll.[60]

When the author of the *introductio* said that the treatise was composed of the *iudicia, consilia,* and *responsa* of the just, he probably had a double meaning in mind, one that would be understood by a reader who was both versed in the workings of the courts and in the texts of Roman law. By playing with the multiple meanings of *iudicium*, the author of the *introductio* hinted that the justice acted as both judge and jurist when he gave judgment in the king's courts. A plea roll entry thus recorded the judgment of a judge in a particular case and also the judgment of a jurist on an issue of law. The author of the *introductio* places Pattishall and Seagrave on the same continuum as Paul and Ulpian and blends the roles of judge and jurist, both of which are present in the royal justice. He assimilates the plea roll entry to the jurist's *responsum*.

I want to be cautious in my claims about the cases cited in the treatise and how the authors understood them. It would be easy to interpret their thinking as more systematic than it actually was. It is important to keep in mind that the treatise had several authors and that those authors may have understood the role of the cases in different ways. When Pattishall, Raleigh, or whoever began the treatise first put his mind to those ancient judgments of the just, he may have had a different idea of why they were important to the treatise than Henry of Bratton did when he inserted the case of Peter of Savoy into a string of citations from the *Digest, Codex,* and *Decretals.* And it is even possible that the authors added cases without a fully formed theory of their role in the treatise.[61] There

---

[60] *Bracton*, vol 4, 126. Note that *consilium* was differentiated in professional usage from the practice of consultation by which the ecclesiastical courts could ask the royal courts whether they should proceed or desist in a case that might touch the royal jurisdiction. The authors denote that practice by the word *consultatio. Bracton*, vol 4, 263.

[61] It is also possible that cases were important to them for several different reasons. Frederic Cheyette pointed out that the case citations in *Bracton* could be fit into contemporary discourses about custom. In the schools of the thirteenth century, a number of scholars struggled with the question of how one proves custom. If a party to a case alleges that a custom exists, how does the court decide whether it exists or not? Cheyette quotes Azo for a position that he says had become "a commonplace of the Schools" by *Bracton*'s time, that a court could take the custom as proven if it could be shown "that someone claimed in court that the custom did not exist, and a judgment declared on the contrary that the custom did indeed exist." Frederic L Cheyette, "Custom, Case Law, and Medieval 'Constitutionalism': A Re-Examination" (1963) 78 Political Science Quarterly 362, 380. McSweeney, "English Judges" (n 37) 838–39, 842. Since the authors of *Bracton* treated English law as a form of custom or *ius non scriptum* in certain passages in the treatise, Cheyette surmised that they may have seen the cases as proof of the existence of certain customs. Ibid, 381. This view of the role of the cases in the treatise and the one I have presented are not mutually exclusive. Different authors could have held different opinions about the role of the cases or a single author could have thought that the cases served two purposes. The *iudicia* in the treatise could be both a jurist's opinion and proof of the existence of custom.

are certain themes that appear throughout the treatise, however. The plea roll entry is associated with the royal justice. It is treated in similar fashion to the *leges* found in Justinian's compilations. It would seem that the authors of the treatise had at least a vague sense that the plea roll entries were authoritative texts and that the justices of the royal courts were their authors.

## Texts and Communities

The authors of the treatise, by assimilating the plea rolls to the authoritative texts of Roman and canon law, were hinting that the authors of the plea rolls, the justices and clerks of the royal courts, were jurists. They were part of the culture of Roman and canon law that spanned Latin Christendom. Raleigh and Bratton were imagining that they were members of this cosmopolitan legal culture. They were trying to demonstrate that they had not left the world of the jurists when they left the schools, but had continued to work in one constituent part of that world, the courts of the English king. But the treatise is not simply an attempt to demonstrate that its *authors* were a part of the culture of Roman and canon law. It was also meant to draw its *readers* into that world.

The idea of an interpretive community originated in literary theory as a way to explain the deficiencies of previous theories that either posited that the meaning of a text is fixed in the text or that the meaning exists only in the subjective interpretation of the reader. One makes it difficult to explain why two people would ever disagree about the meaning of a text. The other makes it difficult to explain how one reading of a text could ever be superior to another. Stanley Fish has argued that the notion of an interpretive community solves this problem. The construction of meaning is not located in the text or in the individual, but in a community of people with shared understandings about how a text should be interpreted. This theory eliminates the problem of objective reading versus subjective intention because

the authorizing agency, the center of interpretive authority, is at once both and neither. An interpretive community is not objective because, as a bundle of interests, of particular purposes and goals, its perspective is interested rather than neutral; but by the very same reasoning, the meanings and texts produced by an interpretive community are not subjective because they do not proceed from an isolated individual but from a public and conventional point of view.[62]

---

[62] Stanley Fish, *Is there a Text in this Class? The Authority of Interpretive Communities* (Harvard University Press 1980) 14.

Fish is primarily concerned with the question of what authorizes us to interpret a text. His goal is to provide an underpinning to the project of literary criticism and to validate its practices. The concept of the interpretive community can be useful in thinking about *Bracton* if we turn it on its head and place the emphasis not on the meaning of the text, but on the community that supplies the meaning. Scholars such as Brian Stock and Richard Firth Green have done this in their work on what they call textual communities, a slight modification of Fish's concept of the interpretive community.[63] As Green describes them, textual communities are small, identifiable groups of people who identify with a set of particular texts and "evolve a distinctive way of using and interpreting these texts."[64]

*Bracton* seems designed to set the contours of a new textual community focused on texts such as *Bracton* and the plea rolls. As I argued in Chapter 1, *Bracton* was likely written with a small audience in mind. The ideal reader is a clerk of the courts with a high degree of knowledge of Roman and canon law. Such a reader would likely have understood what the *introductio* was trying to do. He likely would have known that the terms *iudicia, consilia,* and *responsa* were associated with the opinions of the Roman jurists in the early parts of the *Institutes*. He would have seen the parallel ways in which the treatise discusses and cites to the opinions of Martin of Pattishall and William of Raleigh, on the one hand, and to the opinions of Ulpian and Paul, on the other. The reader of the treatise would thus have been encouraged to bring together the two parts of his existence, as a scholar of Roman and canon law and as a justice or clerk in the king's courts, and to think about the texts he worked with in both of those spheres as equivalent. He would have been encouraged to bring the interpretive framework he had learned in the schools to bear on the plea rolls.

It would have required quite a stretch of the imagination to treat plea roll entries as if they were anything like the texts he had encountered in the schools—the *iudicia, consilia,* and *responsa* of jurists. The plea roll entry looked nothing like a *consilium* or *responsum*. It would not have been obvious to a reader of a plea roll entry that he could or should assimilate that entry to this civilian genre of legal literature. In order to turn the laconic plea rolls

---

[63] Brian Stock, *The Implications of Literacy: Written Language and Models of Interpretation in the Eleventh and Twelfth Centuries* (Princeton University Press 1983); Richard Firth Green, "Textual Production and Textual Communities" in Larry Scanlan (ed), *The Cambridge Companion to Medieval English Literature 1100-1500* (CUP 2009) 25–36 (hereafter Green, "Textual Communities").

[64] Green, "Textual Communities" (n 63) 29.

into *consilia* and *responsa*, their readers had to supply much of the meaning to those texts. *Bracton* invites the reader to make that leap, to imagine that the plea roll entry was a text similar in style and authority to a *lex* of the *Digest*. It invites the reader to approach those texts in a new way, to read them as if they contain not administrative facts, necessary to the smooth operation of the king's courts, but profound statements of law, the opinions of authoritative jurists. It is, in a sense, an invitation to become part of an interpretive community.

Through close examination of the plea roll citations in *Bracton* and the way they interact with the civilian and canonist sources cited in the text, we can start to get a sense for how the *Bracton* authors perceived plea roll entries, and how they wanted their colleagues in the royal courts to perceive them. The *Bracton* authors seem to have hoped that the texts would structure the community of the royal courts. New clerks should learn the law from the plea rolls. Great justices would be known by the texts they produced, be they the records of important cases, like those copied into the *Note Book* and cited in *Bracton*, or treatises based on those texts. The small community of justices and clerks in the royal courts would be held together by a common method of interpreting those texts, a method heavily inflected by the interpretive methods of the schools. The texts this community of people produced—the rolls, the plea roll collections, and *Bracton*—are not just evidence of the way this community constructed its identity; they are also the places where that identity was constructed.

The authors of *Bracton* were thus focused on their own small community in the royal courts. They wanted to shape it in their image. They had essentially borrowed a model of the legal professional from Roman and canon law. The justice or clerk should, ideally, emulate the jurist of Roman and canon law. He should be a learned teacher of law whose function was not merely to decide individual cases, but to expound the law of Latin Christendom through his writing. While Raleigh and Bratton do appear to have been focused on creating a professional culture specifically in the royal courts, their vision extended beyond the courts of their island realm. *Bracton* connects its readers to other groups of people across time and space. It connects them with the famous jurists of civil law at Bologna, who were giving their *iudicia* in the early thirteenth century. It connects them with the jurists of the ancient Roman past whose *iudicia* were recorded in the *Digest*. By assimilating the texts produced by justices and clerks in the courts of England with the texts produced by jurists in the centers of Latin legal culture, the authors of *Bracton* were staking a claim—on behalf of themselves and their imagined readers—to membership in the universal legal culture of Latin Christendom. They were not simply expounding the laws and customs of England. They were jurists of the universal law. *Bracton* is an attempt, by a group of justices in a particular time and space to imagine themselves as part of a universal culture.

# 7

# A New Plea Roll for a New Audience

By the 1250s, the circle of justices who wrote *Bracton* and created the *Note Book* had developed a legal literature based on the plea roll entry. William of Raleigh, Henry of Bratton, and others in their circle seem to have regarded the plea roll as an authoritative text, one that could be used as a foundation for dialectical reasoning. Raleigh and Bratton may have initially enjoyed some success in imparting their views on cases, authority, and the status of the royal justice on others within the judicial establishment. By the middle of the century, *Bracton* and the case collections may have been influencing people outside of the immediate circle of Raleigh and Bratton. As we saw in Chapter 1, Paul Brand has suggested that *Bracton* had its origin in some kind of oral program of instruction.[1] It is possible that Bratton was giving lectures, using *Bracton* as the foundation, in the 1250s. A lecture course on the law of king's courts appears to have existed by the 1270s at the latest, although it was not based upon *Bracton*.[2] An oral course of lectures on *Bracton* would explain the odd relationship that the treatise known as *Hengham Magna* bears to *Bracton*. *Hengham*—written sometime between 1260 and 1265, probably by John Blundel, a clerk of the Common Bench—follows *Bracton*'s organization but adopts none of its language.[3] If Blundel had *Bracton* laid out in front of him while he was working on his treatise, one would expect at least some of the language to come through. If Blundel was working from notes taken during a lecture based on *Bracton*, given for the clerks of the courts sometime in the 1250s or 1260s, the lack of any of *Bracton*'s language makes a bit more sense.

---

[1] Paul Brand, "Legal Education in England before the Inns of Court" in Jonathan A Bush and Alain Wijffels (eds), *Learning the Law: Teaching and the Transmission of English Law, 1150-1900* (Hambledon Press 1999) 57.

[2] Paul Brand, "Courtroom and Schoolroom: The Education of Lawyers in England Prior to 1400" in MCL, 62–64 (hereafter Brand, "Courtroom and Schoolroom").

[3] Thomas J McSweeney, "Creating a Literature for the King's Courts in the Later Thirteenth Century: Hengham Magna, Fet Asaver, and Bracton" (2016) 37 Journal of Legal History 41, 44, 50–52; Paul Brand, "*Hengham Magna*: A Thirteenth-Century English Common Law Treatise and Its Composition" in MCL, 388–89 (hereafter Brand, "*Hengham Magna*"). We do not know how this treatise eventually came to be attributed to the royal justice Ralph of Hengham, but it is unlikely that he was the author. Brand, "*Hengham Magna*" (n 3) 383–85.

*Priests of the Law.* Thomas J. McSweeney, Oxford University Press (2019). © Thomas J. McSweeney.
DOI: 10.1093/oso/9780198845454.003.00008

Other clerks of the court, apart from Blundel, may have had some exposure to *Bracton* in the middle decades of the thirteenth century. In the 1250s, someone connected with the central courts created a collection of cases decided by the Common Bench. The collection is titled *Casus et Judicia* (Cases and Judgments) and exists in only a single manuscript.[4] It bears a special relationship to another text that was copied into the manuscript, a register of judicial writs. Both were probably written by the same author, around the same time. Both *Casus et Judicia* and the register use the same method of citing to the records of the royal courts.[5] They also cover the same period of time; the dated writs in the register and the dated cases in *Casus et Judicia* all date to the period between 1250 and 1256. The writs and cases also come from the same court. All of the judicial writs in the register are returnable at the Common Bench, and all of the identified cases come from that court.[6] The register and the case collection were, therefore, likely part of a single project by someone working in the Common Bench who had ready access to judicial writs and plea rolls. He probably compiled his writs and cases sometime between 1256 and 1258.[7]

*Casus et Judicia* is a short text, filling only three folios in the manuscript and ten pages in the modern printed edition. It is written in Latin. It is a mix of statements of legal rules—"No one is obliged to warrant land except as it was on the day of the feoffment"—and entries written up in the form of illustrative cases.[8] Many reference specific cases on the rolls of the Common Bench. The cases described in *Casus et Judicia* are not copies of plea roll entries, but we know that they were taken directly from the roll because the citations tell us how and where to find the cases on the rolls, usually giving citations in the form "as of the quindene of St. John, in the thirty-sixth year, Essex. Emma."[9] The citation format is similar, although not identical, to that found in *Bracton*. *Bracton* generally gives the term and the year so that the reader can find the correct roll. Here the author gives the return day rather than the term during which the case was heard. A reader familiar with the workings of the royal courts would

---

[4] British Library MS Add 35179, fos 36–39. Elsa de Haas and GDG Hall (eds), *Early Registers of Writs* (SS vol 87, Bernard Quaritch 1970) lxi–lxiii (hereafter De Haas and Hall (eds), *Early Registers*); William Huse Dunham (ed), *Casus Placitorum and Reports of Cases in the King's Courts, 1272–1278* (SS vol 69, Bernard Quaritch 1952) xxvi–xxvii (discussion) and lxxv–lxxxiv (text) (hereafter Dunham (ed), *Casus Placitorum*).

[5] De Haas and Hall (eds), *Early Registers* (n 4) lxii.

[6] Ibid, lxiii. In addition to the cases identified by Hall, Paul Brand has found case number 3 in TNA KB 26/143, m 15d (Michaelmas 1250), number 19 in TNA KB 26/149, m 15d, and number 27 in TNA KB 26/154, m 19d.

[7] De Haas and Hall (eds), *Early Registers* (n 4) lxii.

[8] "Nemo debet warantizare terram nisi secundum quod fuit die feofamenti . . ." Dunham (ed), *Casus Placitorum* (n 4) lxxix (no 29).

[9] "[U]t de quindena Sancti J., anno xxxvi, Essex. Emma." Ibid, lxxvi (no 7).

know that the quindene of St. John is in Trinity term, allowing him to identify the proper roll of the Common Bench. The return day is actually a very useful piece of information, since plea rolls contained headings for the various return days within the term. This method is, therefore, somewhat more precise than the *Bracton* authors' method of telling the reader that the case is around the beginning, the middle, or the end of the roll.[10] The author also gives us the county, which would have been written in the margin next to the case on the roll, and the name of one of the parties, allowing the reader to pinpoint which case is being cited. In one case, he is even more specific, giving us the membrane of the roll on which the case can be found. He tells us "That in the assize of mort d'ancestor a resummons ought to be made through a default made after the essoin appears in the second folio of Saint Hilary, in year thirty-eight, Suffolk."[11] These citations tell us both that the author was working from the rolls himself and that he likely intended his readers to access the rolls. He was, therefore, like the authors of *Bracton*, probably a justice or clerk of the royal courts who was writing for justices and clerks of the royal courts.

The similarities to *Bracton* are probably not coincidence. The author of *Casus et Judicia* may have had access to a manuscript of *Bracton*. The formatting of several of the cases follows *Bracton*'s idiosyncratic style. The nineteenth case, for instance, reads:

> It is proper for the chief lord to distrain his tenement anywhere for his services, as for an aid for the marriage of his daughter, because although A holds of B and B [holds] the same land of C and B is held to C in something, it is proper that C distrain A through the tenement held of himself, although he holds other land, as of three weeks and of the octave and quindene of Saint John, in the thirty-sixth year, Bedfordshire, Wiltshire.[12]

---

[10] The rolls were becoming more voluminous by the 1250s, which may explain why the author of *Casus et Judicia* cited to particular return days rather than to the term of the court, as the authors of *Bracton* did. In the 1220s or 1230s, a citation to a particular term, perhaps with the added "around the beginning of the roll" or "around the end of the roll," was enough to locate the case without too much trouble. By the 1250s, it would have been considerably more difficult without a more precise citation.

[11] "Quod in assisa mortis antecessoris debeat fieri resummonitio per defaltam factam post essonium patet in secundo folio sancti Hyllarii, anno xxxviii. Suff." Dunham (ed), *Casus Placitorum* (n 4) lxxx (no 43). This citation is a bit odd. It is the only citation that includes the folio number. Clerks of the court usually did not refer to an individual membrane of the roll as a folio. That term was generally reserved for pages within books. The personnel of the courts generally referred to a single membrane of a roll as a *rotulus*, the same term they used for the roll as a whole. RF Hunnisett, "What is a Plea Roll?" (1988) 9 Journal of the Society of Archivists 109, 111–14.

[12] "Bene licet capitali domino distringere tenementum suum ubicumque pro servitio suo, ut pro auxilio ad filiam maritandum, quia licet A. teneat de B. et B. de C. eandem terram et B. teneatur C. in aliquo, bene licet C. distringere A. per tenementum de se tentum quamvis aliam terram habeat, ut de tertia septimana et de octabis et quindena Sancti Johannis, anno xxxvii, Bed. Will." Dunham (ed), *Casus Placitorum* (n 4) lxxvii.

The reference at the end is to an actual case decided in 1253 and contained on the roll of the Common Bench.[13] This summary of the case looks nothing like the entries one would find on the plea rolls concerning this case. The parties have been transformed from Hugh de Bretteville, William of Eastwick, and William Beauchamp into the abstract A, B, and C. Nor does it look much like the style of the *Note Book*. The plea roll entry is not copied, but digested and turned into a hypothetical case. The method of citing to a specific part of the roll used in *Casus et Judicia* is very similar to that in *Bracton*, however, and there are even close parallels in *Bracton* to the *Casus et Judicia* author's manner of transforming the case into a hypothetical. Take, for example, a passage on gifts in the treatise:

> Suppose that A. first demises for a term of years, and afterward, during the term, enfeoffs B. and puts him in possession, saving to the termor his term. Then, when he no longer retains anything except the bare lordship, A. enfeoffs the termor *de facto*. If B. ejects the termor at the conclusion of the term and puts himself in seisin by virtue of the first feoffment, restitution by the assise is not available to the termor, for A., since he had nothing except the bare lordship, could not cause him to have a free tenement. [But when this has been recognized by the assise, A. will be bound [to provide] his second feoffee with *escambium*, in that same proceeding and without any other writ, because of his fraud.] [If] the first feoffee, when he has once put himself in seisin, is ejected by the second feoffee, he will recover by the assise. That a gift is invalid when made by one who had nothing in demesne except bare *dominium*, that is, homage and service, you may have of Hilary term in the [eighteenth] year of king Henry in the county of Norfolk, of Cecilia de Stradesete and the Prior of the Hospital of Jerusalem.[14]

---

[13] TNA KB 26/149, m 15d (AALT IMG 0015d) <http://aalt.law.uh.edu/H3/KB26_149/0015d.htm> accessed March 13, 2019. This case is the second after the large blank space on the membrane, brought by Hugh de Bretteville against several defendants. I am grateful to Paul Brand for the identification. The entry in *Casus et Judicia* refers to a roll of the Common Bench made for a part of Trinity term, 1253. This particular roll begins partway through the term, around the octave of Holy Trinity, a return day at the end of June. TNA KB 26/149 m 1 (AALT IMG 0001) <http://aalt.law.uh.edu/H3/KB26_149/0001.htm>. The roll is divided into subsections for each return day. This entry says that the case was heard at three weeks and during the octave and quindene of St. John the Baptist. The case appears only in the section for the quindene of St. John the Baptist. The copyist was possibly approximating where the case appeared on the roll from memory, around the cases for three return days, three weeks after Trinity, the octave of St. John the Baptist, and the quindene of St. John the Baptist, which appear in that order on the roll. TNA KB 26/149, mm 12–15d.

[14] "Item esto quod A. primo dimiserit ad terminum annorum, et postea durante termino feoffaverit inde B. et in possessionem induxerit, salvo firmario termino suo: et cum nihil sibi retinuerit idem A. nisi tantum nudum dominium, de facto feoffat ipsum firmarium, si idem B. post terminum completum se ponat in seisinam ratione primi feoffamenti, et firmarium eiecerit, non competit firmario restitutio per assisam, quia ipse A. non potuit ei facere liberum tenementum cum non haberet nisi nudum

The parties are identified as A and B. The case is posed as a hypothetical fact pattern, until, at the end, we are told the rule that is illustrated in this fact pattern can be found in a case of the king's court.[15] We are even given a specific citation to the roll, just as in *Casus et Judicia*.

It is possible that *Casus et Judicia* was made by Henry of Bratton, and that this explains the similarities. This is unlikely, however, as the cases and writs found in *Casus et Judicia* and the associated register of writs are related to the Bench. Bratton never sat as a justice of that court. He was a justice of the court *coram rege* during the period when these cases were decided. The author may have been a clerk to one of the two justices who served continuously on the Bench from 1250 to 1256, Alan of Wassand and Roger of Thirkleby. Thirkleby was a Raleigh clerk, and may have passed along some of his former master's predilections.[16] The prothonotaries of the court, who kept the rolls and writs, would have had easy access to the materials necessary to create both *Casus et Judicia* and the register. We are now fairly sure that one prothonotary, John Blundel, appointed to that office in 1257, had literary aspirations, as he is the probable author of the treatise later known as *Hengham Magna*.[17]

Whoever he was, the author of *Casus et Judicia* provides us with some evidence that *Bracton* was circulating among the justices and clerks of the 1250s. This author was even emulating William of Raleigh and Henry of Bratton's method of reading the plea rolls as texts that contained legal principles, and that could be cited as authorities proving those principles. It would seem that Raleigh and Bratton's methods had moved outside of their immediate circle, and that searching the plea rolls for important cases had become part of the culture of the royal courts.

dominium. Sed hoc recognito per assisam tenebitur ipse A. secundo feoffato ad excambium in ipso iudicio sine alio brevi propter fraudem, cum ipse primo feoffatus cum semel se posuerit in seisinam per secundo feoffatum fuerit eiectus, et per assisam recuperaverit. Et quod non valet donatio ab eo facta qui nihil habuit in dominico nisi nudum dominium, scilicet homagium et servitium, habetis de termino Sancti Hillarii anno regis Henrici [octavo decimo?] comitatu Norfolciæ, de Cecilia de Stradesete et Priore Hospitalis Ierusalem." *Bracton*, vol 2, 92–93.

---

[15] The roll does not survive, but the case can be found in BNB, vol 2, 644–45. The fact patterns are not identical, but the case on the roll does involve a transfer of the land in demesne to one party and then an attempt to transfer it to a second party.

[16] Although recall that Thirkleby was the justice who said that "the civil court is polluted by the example of the ecclesiastical [court], and a brook is poisoned by a sulphurous fount." CM, vol 5, 211. He may not have had the same fondness for learned law that his master did.

[17] Cutting against Blundel's authorship is the fact that Blundel was not appointed to the position of prothonotary until the summer of 1257, after all of the cases contained in *Casus et Judicia* had been heard. Brand, "*Hengham Magna*" (n 3) 389.

## Internalizing *Bracton*: Writing Plea Rolls in the 1250s

There are two surviving rolls of special assizes taken by Henry of Bratton in the 1250s. Bratton's rolls are curious in several respects. Bratton included more legal content and more Roman-law terminology on his rolls than previous generations of justices had. He also actively edited his rolls. In some cases we can even see him changing the facts of a case in the editing process. We can make sense of Bratton's writing and editing process if we read it in the light of the culture of case collecting developed over the last three chapters. Between the 1220s and the 1250s William of Raleigh and Henry of Bratton had spent a good deal of their time—the time they were not spending writing plea rolls or issuing writs—excerpting cases from the plea rolls. In the process of excerpting and editing these cases, they re-constituted the plea roll entry as a type of legal literature. In *Bracton* they assimilated the plea roll entry to genres of texts they had encountered in their study of Roman and canon law, ascribing the same kind of authority to cases from the plea rolls that they ascribed to excerpts from the *Digest*. It would, therefore, be natural for Bratton to think of plea rolls as a type of legal literature that might be used to teach new clerks of the courts. In these assize rolls, we see what looks like Bratton crafting case records for an audience who would be interested in the legal principles those cases represented. Bratton may have had personal reasons for doing this. Bratton was part of a line of great justices; Martin of Pattishall and William of Raleigh were some of the most important justices of their generation. Their decisions had been excerpted into several collections and were celebrated in *Bracton*. In these rolls, we see Henry of Bratton trying to position himself as the obvious heir to the great justices Martin of Pattishall and William of Raleigh.

Much of Bratton's career as a justice was spent sitting on special assize commissions. The court *coram rege*, of which Bratton was a justice, kept roughly to the four judicial terms observed by the Common Bench by the 1250s.[18] When he was serving on the court *coram rege*, Bratton often used the vacations in-between to hear special assizes. A plaintiff who did not want to wait for the next eyre could pay for the king to commission justices to come to his county to hear his claim.[19] Between 1248 and 1267, the year before his death, Bratton

---

[18] Although the court *coram rege* did not keep to the terms quite as strictly as the Common Bench. The court *coram rege* often extended its work into the vacations. CRR, vol 16, xix. The court was hearing cases during the long vacation in 1237, 1239, 1240, and 1241. See CRR, vol 16, xxix–xxx, xxxvi, xxxvii, xli.

[19] CAF Meekings (ed), *The 1235 Surrey Eyre*, 3 vols (Surrey Record Society 1979) vol 1, 66–67 (hereafter Meekings (ed), *1235 Surrey Eyre*). For more on special assize commissions, see above, p 46.

regularly visited the Southwest of England—Somerset, Dorset, Cornwall, and his native Devon—on assize commissions.[20] We are fortunate to have two rolls of special assizes heard by Bratton in the 1250s.[21]

The power dynamics of these special assize commissions must have been complex. On the one hand, Henry of Bratton was being sent to the counties as an agent of royal authority. On the other hand, Bratton was firmly ensconced in the county communities of Devon, Cornwall, and Somerset. Bratton heard many of these assizes near his lay and ecclesiastical estates in Devon and Somerset. Justices were often sent to counties in which they had estates, and the reasons for this were partly practical.[22] A justice visiting his home county could presumably stay on his own estates while he was there, which would be cheaper than renting lodging. He could also check up on the management of his estates, especially important during the harvest, which took place during the courts' long vacation. There might have been other reasons for sending Bratton to these counties, however. He probably had personal or family connections with many of the litigants who came before his court. His commissions empowered him to select and appoint several locals to sit with him as justices. Bratton and his associates might have known something about the cases that were coming before them. They may also have had the connections necessary to arrange settlements. At the very least, having local notables on these commissions could have served to create a memory of the litigation and its outcome and to enhance the king's long reach with the authority of people who were rooted in the county community. These commissions, therefore, employed both royal power and the kind of local knowledge, authority, and expertise that we see in other thirteenth-century institutions, such as the eyre jury.

The most recent scholarly literature has tended to downplay Henry of Bratton's importance as a justice. When he was believed to have been the author of the treatise that bears his name, historians tended to treat him as if he were one of the great justices of his time, but now that he seems unlikely to have been the primary author of the treatise, as Nicholas Vincent puts it, Bratton's "place in the legal firmament has been reduced to that of a

---

[20] CAF Meekings and David Crook, *King's Bench and Common Bench in the Reign of Henry III* (Selden Society 2010) 130–33 (hereafter Meekings and Crook, *King's Bench and Common Bench*).

[21] TNA JUST 1/1178 and 1/1182.

[22] CAF Meekings, "Henry de Bracton, Canon of Wells" (1951-54) 26 N. & Q. for Somerset and Dorset 26 141, 142, reprinted in *Studies in 13th Century Justice and Administration* (Hambledon Press 1981), item VII (hereafter Meekings, "Canon of Wells").

second-rate camp follower."[23] It is true that he never quite made it to the top of the judicial establishment. Still, by the time Henry of Bratton heard these special assizes, he was an important person. In the 1240s, the generation of William of Raleigh and William of York was giving way to a new one. Raleigh retired from the court *coram rege* in 1239. His successor on the court *coram rege*, Stephen of Seagrave, who was cited approvingly in *Bracton*, retired to an Augustinian priory in 1241 and died shortly thereafter, to be replaced by Raleigh's former co-clerk, William of York.[24] William was elected bishop of Salisbury and retired from the court in December of 1246.[25] Shortly after William of York left the bench, Bratton became a justice of the court *coram rege* himself.[26] Although he was never named chief justice of that court, even during periods when there was no chief justice, Bratton often appears high in the order of precedence in royal documents.[27] Entries on the patent and close rolls for 1255 and 1256 even identify Bratton as a member of the king's council.[28] By the late 1240s he held a number of wealthy ecclesiastical benefices, including the rectory of Gosberton in Lincolnshire, a prebend of Wells Cathedral, and probably some kind of benefice in the diocese of Winchester. In 1245 Raleigh had given him one of two dispensations he had received from the pope. It allowed Bratton to hold three benefices with cure of souls, so he could safely hold three rectories and as many prebends, which did not carry the cure of souls, as he wished.[29] Bratton's rectory at Gosberton alone is said to have been worth close to sixty pounds, an income that would have been sufficient to endow a rather wealthy knight.[30] His prebend probably brought

[23] Nicholas Vincent, "Henry of Bratton (alias Bracton)" in Mark Hill and RH Helmholz (eds), *Great Christian Jurists in English History* (CUP 2017) 19 (hereafter Vincent, "Henry of Bratton").

[24] Ralph V Turner, *Men Raised from the Dust: Administrative Service and Upward Mobility in Angevin England* (University of Pennsylvania Press 1988) 134; *Bracton*, vol 2, 65, 113, 368; vol 3, 349; vol 4, 126, 161, 182, 360.

[25] Meekings and Crook, *King's Bench and Common Bench* (n 20) 73.

[26] Ibid, 80.

[27] He often appears ahead of other important royal officials. In the leap-year ordinance of 1256, Bratton is named after his colleagues on the court *coram rege*, but before Walter of Merton, who was the chancellor's deputy and in possession of the great seal at the time. CR 1254–56, 415; BNB, vol 1, 43. In a 1259 entry on the close roll specifying that only certain justices were to take special assize commissions, Bratton appears third, after Roger of Thirkleby and Henry of Bath, the chief justices of the Common Bench and the court *coram rege*, respectively. BNB, vol 1, 20.

[28] CPR 1247–58, 431; CR 1254–56, 230–1, 400.

[29] Meekings and Crook, *King's Bench and Common Bench* (n 20) 83–84, 89.

[30] Ibid, 84, 90. By the end of the century it was worth rather less. In the *Taxatio Ecclesiastica* of 1291 to 1292, it was said to be worth fifty marks. A mark was a unit equivalent to two-thirds of a pound. Fifty marks would, therefore, be equivalent to thirty-three pounds, six shillings, and eight pence. Jeff Denton and others, "Benefice of Gosberton" (*Taxatio* 2014) <www.hrionline.ac.uk/taxatio/benkey?benkey=LI. LK.HD.20> accessed March 3, 2019. From 1242, anyone with land yielding at least £20 of income per year could be forced to take up knighthood, giving us a sense of what was considered to be a knightly income. Peter Coss, *The Knight in Medieval England, 1000-1400* (Combined Books 1993) 61.

him about eight pounds per year in addition to that.[31] In 1254, Bratton was given the custody of and right to lodge himself in the earl of Derby's London houses, which were being held by the king during the minority of the deceased earl's heir.[32] At Binegar, where the parish church was attached to his Wells prebend, he had a mill, a mark of lordship in addition to a source of revenue, and a rabbit warren, a mark of special favor granted to him by William Longespée, an important magnate who held the lands, although not the title, of the earldom of Salisbury.[33] Bratton had gone from being a clerk who was probably paid out of his master's pocket and who likely shared lodgings with other clerks to a substantial landholder who enjoyed his own halls and chambers. He was not one of the great magnates of the realm, but he was a wealthy and important person who likely had some influence. His judgment likely carried quite a bit of weight when he came to the counties to hear cases.

These two rolls of Bratton's assizes are excellent sources for understanding Henry of Bratton for the simple reason that he was the only "professional" justice on the commissions. Bratton's commission gave him the authority to appoint two locals to sit with him as his associates. Bratton is thus the chief justice for purposes of these assizes, a role he never plays in any other records. He was probably in control of what transpired in court.[34] As in other plea rolls, the justices usually speak in the passive voice and only in indirect speech. We are told that litigants are questioned and that judgments are made, but we are rarely told by whom. When a question is asked or a judgment made on these two rolls, however, we can be reasonably certain that the actor is Henry of Bratton. These texts thus give us unique access to Bratton's thinking about the activities of the royal courts.

These texts also give us special insight into the judicial thinking of Henry of Bratton because they show us not what Bratton did in court, but his own representation of what he did in court, made after the fact when he had had some time to reflect on the implications of the cases he had heard. We can be certain that these rolls belonged to Bratton and not one of the other justices because he is the only justice who sat on every panel recorded in them, and they additionally record some business of the court *coram rege*. We can also be fairly sure that

---

[31] Jeff Denton and others, "Benefice of Whitchurch (Prebend)" (*Taxatio* 2014) <www.hrionline. ac.uk/taxatio/benkey?benkey=BW.BA.WC.29> accessed March 16, 2019; *Meekings* and Crook, *King's Bench and Common Bench* (n 20) 90; Meekings, "Canon of Wells" (n 22) 142.

[32] CPR 1247–58, 371.

[33] Meekings and Crook, *King's Bench and Common Bench* (n 20) 90.

[34] There has been no study of which I am aware of these locals chosen to sit on special assize commissions. It would be useful to know more about the role they played on the commissions, and whether the king expected them to merely act as local witnesses to the judgment, to lend some authority to it, or to actively participate in the proceedings.

Bratton played some role in crafting his plea rolls. Plea rolls were not verbatim records taken down while the case was going on and, as we saw in Chapter 4, there was likely some intermediate stage between the taking of notes in court and the drafting of the roll. There is evidence from the reign of Edward I that justices were involved in the process of crafting their rolls. During the corruption trials of several of Edward's justices in 1290, Chief Justice Hengham's clerk was accused of doctoring a plea roll entry after the fact.[35] This would be difficult to do without the changes being obvious on the face of the plea roll—with cancellations and writing in the margins—if there was not some editing process that preceded the final product. In 1306, the clerk Henry of Hales consulted Justices Howard and Stanton about the wording of an entry, suggesting that he was working on a final copy of the roll sometime after the case had taken place and wanted the justices' input.[36]

Assize rolls may have been kept differently than other kinds of rolls. Most plea rolls represented a series of cases that had been heard during a discrete period of time. Eyres sat for a limited period of time, and a clerk would keep his justice's roll for a specific eyre. At the Common Bench, rolls were kept by term of the court. They appear largely to have been kept by regnal year in the court *coram rege*, which did not have enough judicial business to fill a new roll for each term.[37] Bratton's assize rolls are different. Bratton kept them over a long period of time, adding new records as he was sent to take new assizes. These rolls were the accumulated record of many years. The entries are in many different hands. This could mean either that Bratton took different clerks with him at different times, or perhaps that he hired local clerks to work for him while he was away from the court *coram rege*.[38] These assize rolls are also far less orderly and neat than rolls from the central courts in the same period. They

---

[35] Paul Brand, "Medieval Legal Bureaucracy: The Clerks of the King's Courts in the Reign of Edward I" in MCL, 179.

[36] Ibid, 175; British Library MS Hargrave 375, fos 162r-v.

[37] *Bracton* usually cites to the rolls of the court *coram rege* by the regnal year alone, without any additional dating. See *Bracton*, vol 2, 103, 113. This suggests that the reader would be able to find the case, which was usually identified by the names of the parties in addition to the regnal year, simply by turning to the roll for that year. In reality, the surviving rolls do not run precisely according to the regnal year. Henry III's regnal year began on October 28, the anniversary of his coronation in 1216. The rolls of the court *coram rege* usually begin with the start of Michaelmas term, which could begin on either October 9 or 10. See CRR, vol 16, 219; CRR, vol 18, 127; CR Cheney and Michael Jones, *A Handbook of Dates for Students of British History* (Revised edn, CUP 2000) 137. Sometimes they began even earlier in the year. The roll of the court *coram rege* for 1242–1243 begins at the beginning of the long vacation in 1242 and runs into the long vacation of 1243. CRR, vol 17, 1, 79.

[38] For some examples of membranes where the handwriting changes from entry to entry, see TNA JUST 1/1178 m 1 (AALT IMG 326), m 2 (AALT IMG 330), m 3 (AALT IMG 331) <http://aalt.law. uh.edu/AALT3/JUST1/JUST1no1178/aJUST1no1178fronts/index.htm>; TNA JUST 1/1182 m 1 (AALT IMG 636), m 2 (AALT IMG 0638) <http://aalt.law.uh.edu/AALT3/JUST1/JUST1no1182/ aJUST1no1182fronts/index.htm>.

actually contain some cases that were not heard on assize commissions at all, but on the court *coram rege*, and hence should have been recorded on a *coram rege* roll.[39] There is also substantial evidence of editing on these rolls. It is probable that these two assize rolls were first drafts, meant to be copied eventually into a fair copy to be preserved.[40]

These rolls give us a unique glimpse into the way Bratton wanted to present himself. We can see evidence of Bratton shaping the case into the final form it will take on the roll, to be preserved for posterity. We can see in these rolls a justice striving to use the plea roll as a literary space. Although it was difficult to do in the context of the plea roll, Bratton found spaces on his roll that allowed the justice to speak to his audience. When he was unable to do this directly, he put Roman-law terms into the mouths of other parties, such as the litigants or the jurors. While staying within the confines of the plea roll genre, Bratton tried to turn his text into a legal text, and one that would have relevance to the new clerks who were learning their law from cases.

## Putting Words into a Litigant's Mouth: The Case of the Clyffords

In September of 1251, Bratton was sent to Devon on a special assize commission during the long vacation between Trinity and Michaelmas terms. The two Clyfford brothers, both claiming the same estate, came before Bratton.[41] John Clyfford had died and left his younger son, Geoffrey, holding his estate at Esterclyfford. John's first-born son, Roger, brought an assize of mort d'ancestor. Roger claimed that John had died seised of the land and that he was John's nearest heir, and should therefore have inherited the estate.[42] Geoffrey came and answered that his brother had no claim. Their father had given the land to Geoffrey during his lifetime and had therefore not been seised of it when he

---

[39] Meekings and Crook, *King's Bench and Common Bench* (n 20) 98, 107.

[40] Meekings and Crook note that Bratton's rolls "fall short of the standards of his contemporaries." Ibid, 141.

[41] In 1259, Bratton was instituted to the parish church of Combe in Teignhead by Giles Clyfford and his wife. Ibid, 132–33; OF Robinson (ed), *The Register of Walter Bronescombe, Bishop of Exeter, 1258-1280, Vol. 1* (Canterbury and York Society vol 82, Boydell and Brewer 1995) 31 (no 90). The ties of power and patronage between the royal courts, the Church, and the local community were complex.

[42] The assize of mort d'ancestor generally could not be used by two potential heirs, of the same bloodline, who were trying to claim the same inheritance. *Glanvill*, 155 (Book XIII, c. 11). It was therefore rarely used between brothers. In this case, however, the assize may have gone forward because Geoffrey was not claiming Esterclyfford as his inheritance. He was claiming it as a gift made during his father's life.

died. Geoffrey produced a charter from John purporting to record the transfer from John to Geoffrey.[43]

Roger admitted that John had made the charter but claimed that the charter was "completely empty" because John "never surrendered that land by body or by mind."[44] Rather, John "was always in seisin of that land together with the aforesaid Geoffrey."[45] Roger pointed out that it was John who sold the grain and stock from the land and "disposed of all other things through his will just as an owner (*dominus*)."[46] Since John had never actually allowed the land to leave his power, he had died seised of it.

This was a fairly common type of case. The assize of mort d'ancestor protected the eldest son's right to inherit his father's land, and most land could not be passed by will in the thirteenth century. A father who wanted to provide something for a younger son or even to disinherit a spendthrift, ne'er-do-well, or just plain unloved eldest son would need to transfer the land during his own lifetime. A transfer to a younger son would ensure that the father was not "seised as of fee" at his death, keeping the action outside of the wording of the assize. John had a charter drawn up to record all of the formalities of his gift to Geoffrey, but documentary evidence was not considered completely dispositive in thirteenth-century courts. It was merely written evidence of a corporeal transaction. One could therefore challenge a charter on the ground that it did not represent a real transaction. In John's charter to Geoffrey, John claimed that he had given up seisin of the land and had put Geoffrey into seisin. It was fairly common to include such a clause in a charter, stating explicitly that seisin had passed by the ceremony known as livery, which was required for a valid land transfer, but the charter did not prove that livery had actually been made.[47]

In Roger's response to the charter, we see Henry of Bratton's most significant intervention in the entry. Roger claimed that the charter was not an accurate account of events. Roger's precise words here, that John had never sent himself away from the land "by body or by mind" (*corpore nec animo*), are as important as they are improbable.[48] *Corpore et animo* is a significant

---

[43] TNA JUST 1/1178, m 11 (AALT IMG 348) <http://aalt.law.uh.edu/AALT3/JUST1/JUST1no1178/aJUST1no1178fronts/IMG_0348.htm>

[44] "Et Rogerus venit et dicit quod dicta carta non debet ei nocere. Quia ipsa penitus vacua est." Ibid. "Dictus Johannes numquam se dimisit de terra illa corpore nec animo." Ibid.

[45] "Ipse Johannes semper fuit in seisina in terra illa una cum predicto Galfrido." Ibid.

[46] "Vendit de blado de instauro et de omnibus aliis rebus disposuit per voluntate sua sicut dominus." Ibid.

[47] JM Kaye, *Medieval English Conveyances* (CUP 2009) 62–63 (hereafter Kaye, *Conveyances*).

[48] TNA JUST 1/1178, m 11 (AALT IMG 348) <http://aalt.law.uh.edu/AALT3/JUST1/JUST1no1178/aJUST1no1178fronts/IMG_0348.htm>.

phrase in the Roman law of property: the phrase appears in the *Institutes,* *Digest,* and *Codex,* Azo's *summae* and, most importantly, *Bracton,* where it occurs throughout the text.[49] At Roman law, one had to take *possessio* both *corpore* and *animo.*[50] *Animus,* or mind, is essentially intent. *Corpus,* or body, is the physical transfer of the thing. Once *possessio* had been obtained *corpore et animo,* it could only be lost *corpore et animo*: a possessor ejected from his land by force remained the legal possessor because he had only withdrawn in body, not in mind.[51]

It is always possible that Roger Clyfford knew that Henry of Bratton was the type of justice who would respond well to a Roman-law argument and made these arguments to impress him. It is also possible that Roger had a lawyer who knew that Bratton would respond well to these kinds of arguments. There certainly were serjeants for hire by the 1250s.[52] But to an extent, whether Roger Clyfford actually said these words or Henry of Bratton put them into his mouth when he wrote the roll is beside the point; even if Roger did use the phrase, it was Henry of Bratton and his clerks who decided what was to be included in the entry and what was to be excluded from it. They chose to include these words. But why? Perhaps using the Roman-law tag was simply second-nature to Bratton, who had possibly already begun work on his recension of *Bracton* and had probably, at the very least, learned from the treatise while serving as a clerk to William of Raleigh. *Animo nec corpore* could be a convenient shorthand for what Roger Clyfford or his serjeant had actually said. Bratton and his clerk were already translating from the French that was spoken in court to the Latin of the plea roll; they might easily translate Roger's words into civilian terminology, as well. Bratton may also have used this language to make the same point that he and Raleigh tried to make in *Bracton* and their plea roll collections: that the work they did in the royal courts was part of the larger legal tradition of Roman and canon law. Finally, he may have added it because he expected, or at least hoped, that his plea rolls would be excerpted to make future collections. The use of the familiar civilian tag, one that appears throughout *Bracton,* would make the case more useful as a tool for teaching the rules of possession.

---

[49] *Corpore et animo,* or some variation on it, appears in the *Bracton* treatise at *Bracton,* vol 2, 54, 96, 102, 107, 121, 122, 126, 130, 133, 134, 140, 225; vol 3, 14, 165, 247, 270; vol 4, 143.

[50] See D.41.2.3.1.

[51] Joshua Getzler, "Roman Ideas of Landownership" in Susan Bright and John Dewar (eds), *Land Law: Themes and Perspectives* (OUP 1998) 95–96.

[52] Paul Brand, *The Origins of the English Legal Profession* (Blackwell 1992) 54–67.

## Putting Words into the Jury's Mouth: The Manor of Liscombe

It is not difficult to believe that a litigant who came before Henry of Bratton—or, more likely, that litigant's lawyer—might have used some Roman-law terminology to impress him. It is somewhat more difficult to believe that the jurors would have had the learning or incentive to do the same. And yet Bratton records a Somerset jury speaking in the language of Roman law. A few months before the case of the Clyffords, in April, 1251, during the vacation between Hilary and Easter terms, Henry of Bratton was sitting at Milverton in Somerset. Milverton was a fairly sizeable town situated on Somerset's border with Devon, sitting just at the other end of the Exmoor from Bratton's home village of Bratton Fleming. When Bratton came to visit in 1251, it was home to a market and a parish church, which had become attached to a prebend in the chapter of Wells Cathedral and was held by Master William of St. Quentin, the archdeacon of Taunton and one of Bratton's fellow canons of Wells Cathedral.[53] Bratton chose two locals, Henry of Stawell and Roger FitzSimon, to sit with him as his fellow assize justices. The three justices heard the case of William of Polhamford, who brought an assize of novel disseisin claiming that William Rivers and his bailiffs had rented out some wasteland and meadow to Rivers' men to "till and denshire it," referring to a type of land reclamation native to Devon.[54] William of Polhamford claimed that this land belonged to his fee of Liscombe, not to William Rivers' fee of Winsford.[55]

The entry for this case exemplifies Bratton's approach to writing the plea rolls. Bratton adopted the textual aesthetics of the plea roll entries that were

---

[53] Diana E Greenway (ed), *Fasti Ecclesiae Anglicanae 1066-1300: Volume 7, Bath and Wells*, (Institute of Historical Research 2001) 63–64 (*British History Online*) <www.british-history.ac.uk/fasti-ecclesiae/1066-1300/vol7/pp63-64> accessed April 17, 2018.

[54] "Ad excolend[um] et ad faciend[um] baticium." TNA JUST 1/1178, m 2 (AALT IMG 328) <http://aalt.law.uh.edu/AALT3/JUST1/JUST1no1178/aJUST1no1178fronts/IMG_0328.htm> accessed March 13, 2019; Charles E H Chadwyck-Healey (ed and tr) *Somersetshire Pleas* (Harrison and Sons 1897) 392 (hereafter Chadwyck-Healey (ed and tr), *Somersetshire Pleas*). I am grateful to Chadwyck-Healey for his English translation of portions of these rolls, which aided me in reconstructing the Latin in places where the text is difficult to read. The case of the manor of Dulverton is particularly difficult to make out in places. His translation must be used in tandem with the rolls, however. Roll TNA JUST 1/1182 was misnumbered at the time Chadwyck-Healey made his translation.

Denshiring or devonshiring, also known as burn-beating, is a method of preparing fields for cultivation by paring off the turf and weeds, burning them, and using the ashes to fertilize the soil. "Denshire, v." (*OED Online*, March 2018) <www.oed.com/view/Entry/50031?redirectedFrom=denshiring> accessed April 17, 2018; "Bateicium, ~ia [OF bateiz]" (*Dictionary of Medieval Latin from British Sources*) <http://logeion.uchicago.edu/index.html#bateicium> accessed April 17, 2018.

[55] TNA JUST 1/1178, m 2 (AALT IMG 328) <http://aalt.law.uh.edu/AALT3/JUST1/JUST1no1178/aJUST1no1178fronts/IMG_0328.htm> accessed March 13, 2019; Chadwyck-Healey (ed and tr), *Somersetshire Pleas* (n 54) 393.

excerpted into plea roll collections as his model. We saw that when justices excerpted plea roll entries into collections, they tended to choose entries that were longer and included much more questioning of the jury than the standard entry. Like the excerpted plea roll entries, Bratton's case records are longer and more complete than most; this one runs to forty-five lines and takes up an entire side of a membrane.[56] Thirteenth-century juries could be asked to answer a very general question: Does A or B have the greater right? Did X disseise Y? Is Z the next heir? The entry in these types of cases will end with a yes or no answer: a general verdict. The jury's reasoning is not recorded in these cases. We only know that they decided one way or the other. Sometimes, however, the justices asked the jurors very specific questions. The justices could use the jurors' answers to these questions to make their own determination on the general question or to maneuver the jury toward a particular resolution of the case. Modern lawyers would call this a special verdict. It is between the lines of these specific questions that one can see the justices guiding the development of the law. When the jury was left alone to give a general verdict, much of the reasoning about right and wrong, about who should be in seisin and who should not, and about who should be found guilty and who should be acquitted, was left to that jury. Local norms found their way into the decisions of the courts through the jurors' own thoughts about what constituted disseisin. The jurors' reasoning in such cases was as inaccessible to the justice as it is to modern historians reading the rolls.

Bratton, however, chose to ask the jury a series of specific questions. But he also had to make the decision to present the case this way on the rolls. He might have recorded this case in the format of a general verdict. Legal historians have long suspected that many plea roll entries leave out key parts of the trial.[57] Many cases recorded as ending in general verdicts may have actually ended in special verdicts. In this case, Bratton chose both to control the contours of the transaction between justice and jury in court and to *represent* himself as controlling the contours of the transaction on the rolls. This allowed him to present the legal content of his case to his readers through the back-and-forth between justice and jury.

Bratton appears to have added his own flourishes to this entry. For instance, both of the parties to the suit had carried off furze, a plant that could be used for animal fodder and fuel, from the land. When Bratton asked the jurors which

[56] TNA JUST 1/1178, m 2 (AALT IMG 328) <http://aalt.law.uh.edu/AALT3/JUST1/JUST1no1178/aJUST1no1178fronts/IMG_0328.htm> March 13, 2019.
[57] SFC Milsom, *The Legal Framework of English Feudalism* (CUP 1976) 5.

of the litigants had carried it off justly and which had carried it off unjustly, the jurors responded:

> [I]t seems to them that the said William of Polhamford did this justly because the tenement is his, and that the said William Rivers did it unjustly because he has no right in the tenement nor any seisin otherwise than by his force and power . . . and that William Rivers could acquire nothing for himself *by such use in the tenement of another*.[58]

The phrase, "use in the tenement of another" (*usum in tenemento alieno*) smacks of civilian learning. It is possible that Bratton did not intend to use the words *usum* and *alieno* in a technical sense; *usum* can just mean "use" in a general sense and *alieno* is a way of saying that a thing belongs to someone else. He employs the word *usum*, however, in a way that aligns well with its technical usage in Roman law. Justinian's *Institutes* defines the *usus* as a "more restricted right than usufruct." The *usus* gives its holder the right to take "vegetables, fruit, flowers, hay, straw, and firewood for day to day needs," but not to harvest anything from the land to sell.[59] The Roman-law definition closely parallels what the jurors appear to have been trying to convey in their answer. The act they describe as *usus* was the act of carrying off the produce of the land, likely for the parties' own use. The "*in tenemento alieno*" language also has a civilian look to it. Book seven of the *Digest*, which discusses the usufruct and the related concept of *usus*, begins with a definition from the jurist Paul: "Usufruct is the right to use and enjoy the things of another (*alienis rebus*) without impairing their substance."[60] The "things" of the civilian text have become an English tenement or holding, but it seems probable that the author of this plea roll was thinking about civilian discussions of the use of things that belong to someone else and simply imported the language of the civilian texts to the context of the taking of produce from an English tenement. If the jurors actually said these things, they

---

[58] "Dicunt quod videtur eis quod predictus Willelmus de Polhamford hoc fecit juste quia tenementum illud suum est et quod predictus Willelmus de Ripariis hoc fecit injuste quia nichil juris habet in tenemento illo nec aliquam seisinam nisi per vim et potenciam suam et quia nichil juris haberet in tenemento illo nec justam seisinam . . . quod Willelmus de Ripariis nichil sibi adquirere possit per talem usum in tenemento alieno." TNA JUST 1/1178, m 2 (AALT IMG 328) <http://aalt.law.uh.edu/AALT3/JUST1/JUST1no1178/aJUST1no1178fronts/IMG_0328.htm> accessed March 13, 2019; Chadwyck-Healey (ed and tr), *Somersetshire Pleas* (n 54) 393.

[59] "Minus autem scilicet iuris in usu est quam in usu fructu. Namque is qui fundi nudum usum habet, nihil ulterius habere intellegitur, quam ut oleribus pomis floribus feno stramentis lignis ad usum cottidianum utatur." Inst.2.5.1; *Justinian's Institutes*, 63.

[60] "Usus fructus est ius alienis rebus utendi fruendi salva rerum substantia." D.7.1.1; *Digest of Justinian*, vol 1, 216. At least one of the authors of *Bracton* was probably familiar with title 1 of book 7 of the *Digest*, as the treatise appears to quote several chapters of this title. *Bracton*, vol 2, 28, 126; vol 3, 167.

were an improbably high-brow lot. Henry of Bratton, however, would certainly have known of the *usus* and that it was considered a right in the property of another person. He would have encountered it in the schools; the description of the *usus* found in the *Institutes* is expounded upon in the surviving English lectures on the *Institutes*.[61] He would also have encountered it in *Bracton*. The *nudus usus*, a phrase used to distinguish the *usus* from the usufruct in Roman law texts, appears three times in the *Bracton* treatise.[62] The phrase was therefore probably not used by the jurors, but added by Bratton himself.

Once again, Bratton may only have used this phrase as a convenient way of translating the jurors' French into Latin in a way that captured the meaning so that a clerk or justice trained in Roman law would understand the legal significance of what was said. Bratton may also have intended this entry to be used as a teaching text, however. Bratton found other spaces to explain the law in this entry, adding detail of a kind not usually found on the rolls. The entry explains elements of Bratton's decision that usually require no explanation on the rolls. At the end of most plea roll entries, the clerk tells us what damages, if any, were assessed against the losing party. Usually the entry ends with a brief "*dampnum xx s*" ("damages 20 shillings"), or something similar, as we see in other places on this roll. In this entry, however, the damages are not the end of it. This entry explains why the damages were assessed at that amount: "because for so much have they let that tenement, and they have received so much."[63] William Rivers had leased the land at issue, which the jury ultimately decided was not his to lease, to his men for twenty shillings. A passage of the *Bracton* treatise discusses the damages that accrue to the disseised party. To assess the damages, the jurors "ought to inquire what has been taken in issues, crops, and rents and other profits of the land and to estimate carefully what profit the disseisee would have had if he had not been ejected from the tenement," to make sure that the person who was disseised of the land received what he would have received from it had he not been disseised.[64] The justice should additionally make sure that the disseisors were not permitted to keep any of the profits they took from the land, "lest from another's loss they obtain gain or advantage."[65] *Bracton* was simply

[61] Francis de Zulueta and Peter Stein (eds), *The Teaching of Roman Law in England around 1200* (Selden Society 1990) 36.
[62] *Bracton*, vol 2, 102, 104, 127.
[63] "*Dampnum XX s. quia pro tanto locaverunt tenementum illud et tantum receperunt.*" TNA JUST 1/1178, m 2 (AALT IMG 328) <http://aalt.law.uh.edu/AALT3/JUST1/JUST1no1178/aJUST1no1178fronts/IMG_0328.htm> accessed March 13, 2019; Chadwyck-Healey (ed and tr), *Somersetshire Pleas* (n 54) 393.
[64] *Bracton*, vol 3, 76.
[65] "Et ita diligens esse debet in hac parte quod damna restituantur cum ipsa re, ne disseisitoribus in posterum ex negligentia eorum detur voluntas vel materia delinquendi per disseisinam, et ne ex alieno damno lucrum reportent vel commodum." *Bracton*, vol 3, 75.

stating the theory of damages for disseisin that was current in the royal courts of the middle of the thirteenth century.[66] The fact that Bratton awarded damages in the amount of the disseisor's profit was, therefore, unremarkable. What is unusual is that Bratton explained the reason for the damages on his roll. He did not need to do so; the rolls very rarely contained any explanation like this.

The entry also includes an explanation of the amercements assigned to the losing defendants. In the assize of novel disseisin, if the defendant lost, he was amerced as a punishment for making the disseisin.[67] William Rivers was not actually amerced in this case along with his bailiffs and his men, however. According to the entry, the jurors said "that the same William was not present, nor inciting" and William of Polhamford, the plaintiff, did not approach him to seek redress for the disseisin.[68] The entry then tells us that "Therefore William made no disseisin, and so he is quit of amercement."[69] These explanations could be useful if one of the parties later claimed that Bratton had made an error; he would be able to point to his roll to explain why the damages had been set at twenty shillings or why William Rivers had not been amerced while the other defendants had been. They are unusual on the plea rolls, however. On the other hand, these kinds of explanations could be very useful to someone learning the law. It would be useful to know that the tenant in William Rivers' situation, who had, through his bailiffs, let out the land, was not guilty of a disseisin if he had not been present for the making of the lease and had not incited the action. If Bratton wanted people to read these rolls as part of their legal education, it was important that he include these bits of information, which were not necessary to an administrator who was reading the rolls purely to see what damages he needed to collect.

### Rewriting the Facts to Make Better Law: The Manor of Dulverton

Henry of Bratton was not above completely rewriting the facts of a case when it suited him. The case of the manor of Dulverton is perhaps the most spectacular evidence of Bratton's intervention in the crafting of his assize rolls. In 1255,

---

[66] Donald Sutherland, *The Assize of Novel Disseisin* (Clarendon Press 1973) 52–53.
[67] Meekings (ed), *1235 Surrey Eyre* (n 19) vol 1, 70, 86.
[68] TNA JUST 1/1178, m 2 (AALT IMG 328) <http://aalt.law.uh.edu/AALT3/JUST1/JUST1no1178/aJUST1no1178fronts/IMG_0328.htm> accessed March 13, 2019; Chadwyck-Healey (ed and tr), *Somersetshire Pleas* (n 54) 394.
[69] Ibid.

Bratton was overturned by his colleagues on the court *coram rege*. The case of the manor of Dulverton shows us that one of Bratton's audiences was certainly his fellow justices. There was always the possibility that they would call on him to present the record of his case. In the case of the manor of Dulverton, however, Bratton re-crafted his roll after he had already been called to account by his colleagues on the judicial bench. He wanted to demonstrate that, if his colleagues had only read the case correctly, they would have come to the same conclusion he did. On the rolls and in the *Bracton* treatise, we see Bratton striking back by rewriting a case after his decision in it had already been overturned. The case of the manor of Dulverton thus provides us with the best evidence that Bratton was writing his rolls, at least in part, for an audience of future clerks and justices who would read them to learn the law.

Bratton's roll is confusing when it comes to the case of the manor of Dulverton, as it has been arranged and rearranged several times by the archivists. The membrane on which it appears does not bear a heading, so we do not know for certain where Bratton was sitting and when. He was probably sitting at South Petherton in Somerset, as the two cases that come immediately before this one bear the marginal notation "Sumers," "Periton."[70] This membrane should, therefore, probably follow the membrane that now appears at the end of the manuscript, which records assizes taken at South Petherton on September 5, 1255.[71] Once again Bratton was not far from home. South Petherton was a prosperous market town in southern Somerset just a few miles from the Fosse Way, an old Roman road. The Fosse Way ran close to the ecclesiastical estates at Binegar, about twenty-five miles north of South Petherton, which Bratton held as a prebendary canon of Wells Cathedral from about 1247.[72] Bratton had heard assizes at Shepton Mallet, very close to Binegar, a few days before, on August 30.[73]

The case of the manor of Dulverton began with an assize of mort d'ancestor brought by Roger of Reyni. Roger claimed one carucate of land, with its appurtenances, in Dulverton, on the border between Somerset and Devon, just on

---

[70] TNA JUST 1/1182, m 8.1 (AALT IMG 651, 652, 653) <http://aalt.law.uh.edu/AALT3/JUST1/JUST1no1182/aJUST1no1182fronts/index.htm> accessed March 13, 2019.

[71] TNA JUST 1/1182, m 9b (AALT IMG 680) <http://aalt.law.uh.edu/AALT3/JUST1/JUST1no1182/bJUST1no1182dorses/IMG_0680.htm> accessed March 13, 2019; Chadwyck-Healey (ed and tr), *Somersetshire Pleas* (n 54) 453.

[72] Meekings, "Canon of Wells" (n 22) 141–43.

[73] Meekings and Crook, *King's Bench and Common Bench* (n 20) 90. Chadwyck-Healey (ed and tr), *Somersetshire Pleas* (n 54) 444. The assizes at Shepton Mallet appear on membrane 7.1, where the first, cancelled, version of the case of the manor of Dulverton also appears. TNA JUST 1/1182, m 7 (AALT IMG 648) <http://aalt.law.uh.edu/AALT3/JUST1/JUST1no1182/aJUST1no1182fronts/IMG_0649.htm> accessed March 13, 2019.

the edge of the Exmoor. Roger claimed that his brother, Richard of Turberville, had died seised of the land. The Turbervilles were an important family in the region, a dynasty of tenants of the earl of Gloucester who held lands in the Welsh marches as well as in Devon and Somerset. Richard and Roger probably came from the junior branch of the family that appears to have dominated Dulverton. A Turberville had, at one point, controlled the advowson of the local parish church, a right which he granted to the priory of Augustinian canons at Taunton.[74]

The current holder of the land, Robert of Schete, produced a charter, given by the deceased Richard of Turberville, which said that Richard had made a gift of the manor of Dulverton to Robert during his lifetime. If this was true, it meant that Richard had not, in fact, been seised of the land when he died. The charter was given "a long time before the death of the same Richard."[75] In it, Richard transferred "all his land of Dulverton, with its appurtenances and liberties" to Robert "without any reservation, to be held and to be had by the same Robert and his heirs of the aforesaid Richard and his heirs by right of inheritance forever by the service of one pair of gloves, or one penny for all services except royal service."[76] Richard had thus given the land to Robert by subinfeudation, meaning that Richard would be Robert's lord. He had also given the land to Robert heritably, so Richard's heirs would be lords of Robert's heirs. If this was true, then our plaintiff, Roger of Reyni, would, at most, inherit the right to one pair of gloves every year, plus a few other lordly perquisites, from his brother.

Richard and Robert formalized this transfer through a final concord in the king's court. Richard and Robert brought a collusive suit. Robert obtained a writ of warranty of charter against Richard, which would force Richard to warrant the gift he had made in the charter to Robert. They made a fine, essentially meaning that they settled the case. This had two advantages. First, a final concord was the most secure form of land transfer one could make. Since it was memorialized in a judgment of the king's court, it was very difficult to attack,

---

[74] William Page (ed), *A History of the County of Somerset* (A Constable 1911) vol 2, 141.

[75] "Quia diu ante mortem ipsius Ricardi." TNA JUST 1/1182, m 8.1 (AALT IMG 653) <http://aalt. law.uh.edu/AALT3/JUST1/JUST1no1182/aJUST1no1182fronts/IMG_0653.htm> accessed March 13, 2019; Chadwyck-Healey (ed and tr), *Somersetshire Pleas* (n 54) 428.

[76] "Quod dedit ei totam terram suam de Dulverton cum omnibus pertinenciis suis et omnibus libertatibus sine aliquo retenemento tenendam et habendam eidem Roberto et heredibus suis de predicto Ricardo et heredibus suis iure heredetario ad perpetuum per servicium unius paris cyrotecharum vel unius denarii pro omni servicio salvo regali servicio." Ibid. The reservation of a pair of gloves as services was fairly common. Kaye, *Conveyances* (n 47) 140. The services were nominal in amount, but might serve a significant purpose: the annual ritual of handing over a pair of gloves could serve to remind Robert and Richard of the deal they had made.

even for third parties.[77] Second, a final concord produced a solid documentary record. The court produced a three-part chirograph, giving one copy to each of the parties and retaining its own copy, the foot.[78] The foot of the fine survives, so we know that this had all transpired fairly recently. That fine was made at Westminster in February of 1254, about nineteen months before Bratton heard this case.[79]

In that fine, Richard conceded that the whole manor of Dulverton, along with its appurtenances, belonged to Robert, essentially confirming Richard's charter to Robert. Then the fine records that Robert granted the manor back to Richard and his wife Matilda as part of the settlement of this collusive suit. The land that Richard had granted to Robert in the charter, Robert granted back to Richard in the fine. At the end of this drawn-out, expensive process, which included drawing up a charter, bringing a collusive lawsuit, purchasing a license from the king to make a fine, and obtaining a chirograph from the clerks of the king's court, all of which would have required fees and tips to the court and its clerks, the manor had returned to Richard of Turberville.

The gift from Robert back to Richard contained a few provisos, however. We do not know the parties' motivation for entering into this transaction, but this may have been an arrangement made upon Matilda's marriage to Richard of Turberville, as the gift from Robert of Schete to Richard of Turberville was made in *maritagium*. Robert of Schete was likely Matilda's father, or possibly brother. The *maritagium* most often took the form of a gift of land from the wife's family either to the husband alone or to the husband and wife together and their joint descendants. The goal was to endow this new marital unit with an estate that would revert back to the wife's family if issue failed.[80] In this case, however, it appears that the form of the *maritagium* was actually used to restrict the descent of land that the husband, Richard of Turberville, already held, because in this case Richard of Turberville conveyed the manor of Dulverton to Robert of Schete in fee and received it back, together with Matilda, in *maritagium*. This new grant was to "Richard and Matilda his wife . . . and to the heirs whom that same Richard shall have begotten of the aforesaid Matilda."[81] Where Richard

---

[77] Robert C Palmer, *The Whilton Dispute, 1264-1380: A Socio-Legal Study of Dispute Settlement in Medieval England* (Princeton University Press 1984) 52 (hereafter Palmer, *Whilton Dispute*).

[78] Chadwyck-Healey (ed and tr), *Somersetshire Pleas* (n 54) 429.

[79] Emanuel Green (ed), *Pedes Finium, Commonly Called Feet of Fines, for the County of Somerset, Richard I to Edward I* (Harrison and Sons 1892) 157.

[80] The husband and wife did not do homage for the land granted in *maritagium*. Homage was delayed until the entry of the third heir, meaning the couple's great-grandchild. According to *Glanvill* and *Bracton*, this allowed the land to revert to the wife's family if issue failed before the entry of the third heir. *Glanvill*, 93: *Bracton*, vol 2, 77; Kaye, *Conveyances* (n 47) 139.

[81] "Et pro hac etc. idem Robertus concessit predicto Ricardo et Matilda uxor eius predictam manerium cum pertinenciis habendum et tenendum eidem Ricardo et Matilda et heredibus quos idem

had apparently held Dulverton in his own name before this series of transactions, after Robert of Schete transferred the manor back to him, he held it together with his wife. This would protect Matilda if Richard predeceased her. If Richard had held Dulverton on his own, Matilda would only have been entitled to a life estate in one-third of Dulverton, her dower right, at Richard's death. But since Robert enfeoffed Richard and Matilda jointly in *maritagium*, Matilda would have the right to hold the whole of Dulverton for the rest of her life once Richard died.

Additionally, this grant was designed to ensure that, after Richard and Matilda had both died, the land would pass either to Matilda's and Richard's descendants or revert to Robert of Schete. If Robert's grant had simply been to Richard and his heirs, Richard's brother Roger could have inherited the manor of Dulverton at Richard's death. Instead, the grant was to his heirs *begotten by Matilda*, meaning that only descendants of Richard and Matilda could inherit Dulverton.[82] If Richard and Matilda died without descendants, then "the manor should revert to Robert and his heirs . . ."[83] It would seem that it was important to Robert of Schete that his descendants, through Matilda, would hold the manor of Dulverton. But Robert exacted a further price for this marriage: if Richard and Matilda had no issue, the manor of Dulverton would pass to Robert of Schete. Robert thus retained a reversion in the manor that would allow him to take it if Richard and Matilda's line died out. This is, of course, only one possible explanation of the motives for this complex series of transactions.[84] Bratton's roll does not tell us anything about the relationships between the parties, or why they entered into this transaction. Bratton does not seem to have been terribly interested in the family relationships and so does not tell us in this document why the parties would have wanted to enter into these complex transactions. He was much more interested in the legal points this case raised.

---

Ricardus de predicta Matilda procreaverit." TNA JUST 1/1182, m 8.1 (AALT IMG 652) <http://aalt.law.uh.edu/AALT3/JUST1/JUST1no1182/aJUST1no1182fronts/IMG_0652.htm> accessed March 13, 2019; Chadwyck-Healey (ed and tr), *Somersetshire Pleas* (n 54) 429. I have made minor amendments to Chadwyck-Healey's translation.

---

[82] Kaye, *Conveyances* (n 47) 137–40.

[83] "[M]anerium illud revertat ad predictum Robertum et heredes suos . . ." TNA JUST 1/1182, m 8.1 (AALT IMG 652) <http://aalt.law.uh.edu/AALT3/JUST1/JUST1no1182/aJUST1no1182fronts/IMG_0652.htm> accessed March 13, 2019; Chadwyck-Healey (ed and tr), *Somersetshire Pleas* (n 54) 429.

[84] Robert Palmer discusses a very similar grant and regrant made in 1290. In that case, the parties making the grant were involved in a longstanding dispute about the title to their land. They granted a reversion to Robert Burnel, the chancellor. The purpose of this grant was to give Burnel an interest in the land so he would help them to defend their title. Palmer, *Whilton Dispute* (n 77) 137–43.

Whatever the reason for making them, this series of transfers is a testament to the crafty conveyancing of English landholders in the thirteenth century. If Richard and Matilda died with living descendants, the land would pass to those descendants under the terms of the charter from Robert to Richard. If they died without descendants, the land would revert to Robert of Schete. Only in the event that Richard of Turberville died without heirs by Matilda and Robert of Schete died without any heirs at all, an unlikely occurrence, would the manor pass to Roger.

There was one further reservation in the grant from Robert to Richard. The roll says that "this concord was made saving to Robert and his heirs that they might have and hold the hundred of Dulverton as they held it before such concord was made."[85] A hundred was a division of land and people below the county level. Since the Anglo-Saxon period, each hundred had had a royally supervised communal court, where residents of the hundred could bring claims to be decided by their neighbors. Over the course of the twelfth and thirteenth centuries, many hundreds fell into private hands by royal grant. In these grants the hundred court was often attached to a manor, and the lord of that manor could collect the fines and fees generated by the court.[86] The court itself essentially became private property. This had happened to the hundred court of Dulverton, which had become attached to the manor. Richard had likely given the hundred court to Robert when he made the original charter, which had granted "all his land of Dulverton, with all its appurtenances and liberties, without any reservation."[87] Robert now retained it when he granted the land back to Richard. This would prove to be a crucial piece of information at a later stage of the case.

Robert probably thought that he had cinched his case. He was in seisin of the land and had good documents to prove that he should be in seisin. He was so confident in his seisin that he said he would be willing to forgo his claim based on the chirograph and fine and put the question of his seisin entirely to the jury.[88] The *Bracton* treatise does, after all, say that "since charters are

---

[85] "Et haec concordia facta fuit salvo predicto Roberto et heredibus suis quod possint habere et tenere hundredum de Dulverton' sic illud tenere antequam haec concordia facta esset." TNA JUST 1/1182, m 8.1 (AALT IMG 652) <http://aalt.law.uh.edu/AALT3/JUST1/JUST1no1182/aJUST1no1182fronts/IMG_0652.htm> accessed March 13, 2019; Chadwyck-Healey (ed and tr), *Somersetshire Pleas* (n 54) 429.

[86] Helen Cam, "*Manerium Cum Hundredo*: The Hundred and the Hundredal Manor" in Helen Cam (ed), *Liberties and Communities in Medieval England: Collected Studies in Local Administration and Topography* (Barnes and Noble 1963) 64–68.

[87] "[T]otam terram suam de Dulverton cum omnibus pertinenciis suis et omnibus libertatibus sine aliquo retenemento." TNA JUST 1/1182, m 8.1 (AALT IMG 652) <http://aalt.law.uh.edu/AALT3/JUST1/JUST1no1182/aJUST1no1182fronts/IMG_0652.htm> accessed March 13, 2019; Chadwyck-Healey (ed and tr), *Somersetshire Pleas* (n 54) 429.

[88] Ibid.

sometimes fraudulently drawn and gifts falsely taken to be made when they are not, recourse must therefore be had to the country and the neighborhood so that the truth may be declared."[89] This was not the end of the discussion, however. Roger claimed that the first transfer, his brother's transfer of the manor at Dulverton to Robert of Schete, was a fiction and that the records were fraudulent.[90] Roger maintained that, while his brother had given the charter and made the fine with Robert of Schete, as Robert claimed, he never handed the manor over to Robert. Richard of Turberville had therefore died seised of the land. If this sounds familiar, it is because it is precisely what Roger Clyfford had claimed in his case. Bratton may have had a special interest in these kinds of cases, as he appears to have paid special attention to the drafting of them on his roll.

At some later hearing of the case, at Bridgwater, about twenty miles northwest of South Petherton, Henry of Bratton called a jury of the neighborhood to say whether Richard had ever given up Dulverton before he died. At this stage of the proceedings, it turned out that Robert's confidence in his fine, chirograph, and seisin was misplaced. When the jury returned their verdict, they said that the deceased Richard did indeed give his charter to Robert of Schete, that he even took Robert's homage for the land and made the free tenants of the manor do homage to Robert, and that, as a final touch, he took Robert to the manor and placed him in seisin. Once Richard had brought Robert to the land, "they were together in the house of the aforesaid Richard for one night and on the next day they all went out, both Robert and Richard and the latter's wife, to the land of Robert at Combe."[91] Richard and Matilda's short vacation from Dulverton was presumably to give effect to the first grant, from Richard to Robert. They were taking themselves out of seisin of the land. Richard and his wife stayed with Robert for a while, and "when they had been out of seisin for some time," which a clerk wrote in the margin as "two months", Richard and his wife "returned and remained in seisin as before," giving effect to the terms of the second grant, from Robert back to Richard and his heirs by Matilda.[92]

---

[89] "Sed quoniam aliquando fraudulenter fiunt cartae et falso et finguntur donationes fieri, cum non fiant, ideo ad veritatem declarandam erit ad patriam et visnetum recurrendum." *Bracton*, vol 2, 59.

[90] Ibid.

[91] "Ita quod fuerunt simul in domo predicti Ricardi per unam noctem et in crastino recesserunt omnes tam predictus Robertus quam Ricardus et uxor sua ad terram ipsius Roberti apud Cumbe." TNA JUST 1/1182, m 8.1 (AALT IMG 652) <http://aalt.law.uh.edu/AALT3/JUST1/JUST1no1182/aJUST1no1182fronts/IMG_0652.htm> accessed March 13, 2019; Chadwyck-Healey (ed and tr), *Somersetshire Pleas* (n 54) 430.

[92] "Et cum predicti Ricardus et uxor sua sic essent extra seisinam per aliquod tempus (scilicet duos menses) redierunt et remanserunt in seisina ut prius." TNA JUST 1/1182, m 8.1 (AALT IMG 653) <http://aalt.law.uh.edu/AALT3/JUST1/JUST1no1182/aJUST1no1182fronts/IMG_0653.htm> accessed March 13, 2019; Chadwyck-Healey (ed and tr), *Somersetshire Pleas* (n 54) 430.

It is at this point that we begin to hear Bratton's voice on the roll, albeit in the passive voice and with no direct attribution to him. Bratton was not entirely satisfied with what the jury said and wanted further information. In particular, he wanted to know what happened during that two-month interval when Richard was off his land. As in the case of the Clyffords, Bratton asked a series of questions of the jury and recorded their answers. Bratton asked who remained on the land during that two-month interval between Richard of Turberville's departure for Combe and his return. The jurors said that Richard's *familia* and servants, not Robert's, remained in seisin. They had used Richard's ploughs to till the soil, a sign that they were acting as Richard's agents. He asked with whom the jurors associated the seisin of the manor. They said that they associated it with Richard, "and in all things they looked towards Richard."[93] The implication of the questions Bratton was asking was clear: if Richard had left the land, but had never actually given up control of it, the first transfer was a mere fiction and seisin remained with Richard until he died. If Richard was in seisin when he died then his brother, Roger, should have inherited it and could recover it by the assize of mort d'ancestor. All of those formalities that Richard and Robert had undertaken would avail them naught if Richard had never given up seisin of the land in the first place. After this series of leading questions, the jury finally said that Richard had died seised of the land. Bratton and his associates then awarded seisin of the land to Roger as Richard's nearest heir.[94]

In Chapter 4 we saw that the justices and clerks who were collecting cases from the plea rolls were particularly fond of certifications. Robert of Schete, apparently unhappy with his verdict, acquired a writ of *certiorari* to get the justices of the court *coram rege* to review the case. The justices then called the jurors to Westminster to certify their verdict sometime in the spring of 1256.[95]

---

[93] "Et quesiti nomine cuius utrum nomine Roberti vel predicti Ricardi dicunt quod seisina illa semper usi fuerunt nomine Ricardi et non nomine Roberti et per omnia fuerunt intendentes ipsi Ricardo . . ." Ibid

[94] Ibid.

[95] Chadwyck-Healey (ed and tr), *Somersetshire Pleas* (n 54) 431–32; Meekings and Crook, *King's Bench and Common Bench* (n 20)136. One of the three records of this certification says that it took place at Westminster. TNA JUST 1/1182, m 8.1 (AALT IMG 653) <http://aalt.law.uh.edu/AALT3/JUST1/JUST1no1182/aJUST1no1182fronts/IMG_0653.htm> accessed March 13, 2019. Another places it in the quindene of Easter, which would place the certification in the first week of May. TNA JUST 1/1182, m 8.2 (AALT IMG 654) <http://aalt.law.uh.edu/AALT3/JUST1/JUST1no1182/aJUST1no1182fronts/IMG_0654.htm> accessed March 13, 2019. It is unlikely that the court *coram rege* was hearing a case in Westminster in early May, as the court generally traveled with the king, and the king was at Windsor in early May. He did not arrive at Westminster until later in the month, either on May 22 or 23. CR 1254–56, 297–303, 309; CPR 1247–58, 471–73, 476. Since the certification was most likely heard before the court *coram rege*, not the Bench, either the place or the date is likely incorrect. Either mistake would have been fairly easy to make. It is possible that a clerk working from some notes on the certification accidentally expanded an abbreviated "W." to Westminster rather than Windsor. It is also possible that

In 1256, Bratton himself was sitting on the court *coram rege* along with Henry of Bath, Henry de la Mare, and Nicholas de Turri.[96] He had served with some of the justices of this court for a long time. Henry of Bath, the senior justice, may have been a close associate.[97] Nevertheless, the justices of the court *coram rege* partially overturned Henry of Bratton.

The certification proceedings for the manor of Dulverton may not have been the first thing on the justices' minds in the spring of 1256. William of York had just died at the end of January. He had served as chief justice of the court *coram rege* until 1247 and was actively involved in the legal affairs of the realm at least through 1251. Even as a bishop, he was occasionally asked for advice in resolving difficult cases.[98] He remained a presence for Bratton and his colleagues even after his retirement and the sitting justices of the court appear to have been close to him. Bratton's associates, Henry of Bath and Henry de la Mare, offered to stand as sureties for any debts William owed to the crown in order to allow his executors to move forward and administer the estate.[99] Bratton himself may have had some connection with William of York. His own master, William of Raleigh, had apparently formed a bond of some kind with the other William while the two were working so hard for Martin of Pattishall; William of York had been named one of the executors of William of Raleigh's will.[100] As we saw in Chapter 6, Bratton himself probably added several references to William of York's opinions to the *Bracton* treatise.[101] William was probably someone Bratton admired.

On May 9, Bratton and his associates together witnessed a royal mandate that fixed the method of calculating the length of a legal year during leap years, which cleared up an ambiguity in the administration of justice.[102] A defendant who successfully claimed the essoin of bed-sickness was given an adjournment of his case for a full year and a day. In leap years, it was

---

Bratton or his clerk misremembered the date. The correct return day, rather than the quindene of Easter, could have been five weeks after Easter, which would place the certification at a time when the court *coram rege* was in Westminster.

[96] Meekings and Crook, *King's Bench and Common Bench* (n 20) 120. Bratton was usually listed second among these justices in the witness lists for fines made before the court, just after Henry of Bath, the chief justice. Ibid, 43.

[97] Bratton disappeared from the court *coram rege* when Henry of Bath was removed as chief justice in February, 1251, and did not reappear on that court until Bath's reinstatement in the spring of 1253. Ibid, 102, 103, 107, 108.

[98] Ibid, 134.

[99] Ibid, 120.

[100] Ibid, 63.

[101] See above, p 197.

[102] Meekings and Crook, *King's Bench and Common Bench* (n 20) 121; CR 1254–56, 14–15.

important to know whether a year was reckoned for legal purposes as a period of 365 days, or whether the defendant got the benefit of that extra day in February.[103] Not all of the justices' business was this mundane, however. Some of the justices of the court *coram rege* were also involved in the *cause célèbre* of the time. In August of 1255, a boy named Hugh was found dead in Lincoln and the Jewish community of Lincoln was collectively accused of ritually murdering him.[104] The king and his officials initially treated this as a Jewish conspiracy; they thought that all of the Jews of Lincoln were involved, and that they had likely conspired with other Jews throughout England. Ninety-one Jews of Lincoln were rounded up and later sent to London according to Matthew Paris, who had no sympathy at all for the accused.[105] Several sources recount that, in November of 1255, eighteen of the Jews were summarily hanged after they refused to place themselves upon a jury composed exclusively of Christians.[106] The fate of the remaining members of the Jewish community of Lincoln remained in doubt through the spring of 1256. The justices of the court *coram rege*, as the king's legal advisers, were doubtless involved in this case. In March, Bratton's colleague on the court *coram rege*, Nicholas de Turri, was commissioned together with Roger of Thirkleby to make an inquiry into a Jewish school that had been run by one of the accused, in order to discover if any of the students had "fled on account of the death of the boy."[107] The remaining prisoners paid a large sum of money to Richard of Cornwall, the king's brother, to whom Henry had given custody of England's Jews, to intercede with the king, and they were freed on May 15, around the same time as the certification.[108]

---

[103] The king mandated that February 28 and 29 should be treated as a single day, so the essoined defendant would have the benefit of an extra day in a leap year. Ibid. This ran counter to the solution to the same problem laid out in *Bracton* and in one of the miscellaneous entries that have been added to what was originally the blank parchment at the end of the first half of the *Note Book*, that a year should always be reckoned as a period of 365 days and 6 hours. *Bracton*, vol 4, 91, 132–35; BNB, vol 1, 42; vol 3, 299–301 (no 1291).

[104] Haidee J Lorrey, "Hugh of Lincoln [St Hugh of Lincoln, Little St Hugh] (c. 1246–1255), supposed victim of crucifixion" (ODNB, September 23, 2004) <https://doi.org/10.1093/ref:odnb/14062> accessed March 13, 2019. I would like to thank my former student, Sarah Spencer, for bringing it to my attention that this trial was taking place around the same time as the certification in the case of the manor of Dulverton.

[105] Matthew Paris thought they were manifestly guilty, and that all the Jews of England shared in their guilt. CM, vol 5, 519.

[106] Joseph Jacobs, "Little St. Hugh of Lincoln" (1893-94) 1 Transactions of the Jewish Historical Society of England 89, 122 (hereafter Jacobs, "Little St. Hugh"); Gavin I Langmuir, "The Knight's Tale of Young Hugh of Lincoln" (1972) 47 Speculum 459, 478.

[107] Jacobs, "Little St. Hugh" (n 106) 124.

[108] Haidee J Lorrey, "Hugh of Lincoln [St Hugh of Lincoln, Little St Hugh] (c. 1246–1255), supposed victim of crucifixion" (ODNB, September 23, 2004) <https://doi.org/10.1093/ref:odnb/14062> accessed March 13, 2019.

Additionally, at the beginning of May, 1256, the king was headed towards a political disaster and at least one of the justices of the court *coram rege* was involved. The pope had been at war with the Hohenstaufen kings of Sicily for several years when he offered the crown of that kingdom to King Henry for his younger son, Edmund, in 1254. The offer was not a particularly good one; it required Henry to pay all the expenses incurred by the papacy in the prosecution of the war and to launch an invasion of Sicily to take the crown, since the pope was not actually in control of Sicily.[109] When the pope offered the same deal to Henry's brother, Richard of Cornwall, he is reputed to have paraphrased the Pope's offer as "I sell or give you the moon. Go up there and get it!"[110] Henry jumped at the offer, however, and did so without asking for the counsel of the realm first. By 1256 the king owed the papacy 135,000 marks, and failure to pay would result in his excommunication.[111] Henry presented this deal to the community of the realm as a *fait accompli* and then asked for the money to pay for it. In May of 1256, the king and council were preparing a mission to Rome to discuss the problems involved in raising the payment price. One of Bratton's associates, Henry de la Mare, was appointed to go to Rome as part of that delegation on May 15.[112] Bratton was therefore brought before his own associates at a time when the royal government was in turmoil and those associates were intimately involved in it. This is the context in which Bratton's case was heard in May of 1256.

The certification in the case of the manor of Dulverton is recorded on Bratton's roll. We can actually see Bratton's editing process and the conundrum he faced of how to present himself to future generations of clerks and justices. What exactly happened at Westminster in the case of the manor of Dulverton is not clear, because Bratton's plea roll, the only source for it, contains three separate accounts of what happened, all written in different hands. The first is written at the bottom of the membrane on which the main record of the case appears, in a very different hand from the body of the case. This *postea* to the case is actually written in the space on either side of two other, shorter records that appear at the bottom of the membrane.[113] It does not appear that the scribe lined the membrane before writing the *postea*, as the lines wander and are very close together, as if the author was trying to fit this record into a small space

[109]  JR Maddicott, *Simon De Montfort* (CUP 1994) 128.
[110]  "Vendo vel do tibi lunam, ascende et apprehende eam." CM, vol 5, 457.
[111]  Maddicott, *Simon De Montfort* (n 109) 128.
[112]  Meekings and Crook, *King's Bench and Common Bench* (n 20) 121.
[113]  A *postea* is an addition to a case that records some later stage of the proceeding. It was often added to the roll after the original record was made. The name *postea* comes from the fact that they usually begin with the Latin word *postea* (afterwards).

at the end of the parchment.[114] The second version appears in a much more legible hand on the back of a small slip of parchment that was attached to this membrane.[115] These two accounts of the certification vary from each other a bit, but in some respects are almost identical. In both, the justices start out by praising Henry of Bratton. They both make it clear that in the record Bratton showed them there is "no obscurity, nothing doubtful, nothing wanted, nor too little answered, but everything is plain and sufficiently examined, and according to the record, the judgment is just, and there was no place for certification, therefore the judgment stands."[116] Paradoxically, however, they turn from saying that Bratton left nothing out and that there is no need for certification to saying that, while Bratton had handled the issue of the manor correctly, he had completely forgotten to deal with the hundred court that was attached to the manor, and that this required certification.

A third account of the certification appears, in a different hand than both of the other two, on the other side of the attached slip of parchment.[117] This version confuses the matter even more. The first two versions agree that, when questioned during the certification proceeding, the jurors told the justices that Robert had collected the profits of the hundred court, but they were unsure whether Robert collected those profits for himself or on Richard's behalf. The first version then ends abruptly.[118] The second version, on the back of the slip of parchment, adds that "they believe for his own use rather than for Richard's" and, once again, ends abruptly.[119] According to the third version, however, the problem was not that Bratton forgot to deal with an important issue; it was, rather, that the jury lied. It says that when Henry of Bratton asked the jurors about the hundred court, the jurors were very sure about the profits from the

---

[114] TNA JUST 1/1182, m 8.1 (AALT IMG 653) <http://aalt.law.uh.edu/AALT3/JUST1/JUST1no1182/aJUST1no1182fronts/IMG_0653.htm> accessed March 13, 2019.
[115] TNA JUST 1/1182, m 8.2b (AALT IMG 654) <http://aalt.law.uh.edu/AALT3/JUST1/JUST1no1182/aJUST1no1182fronts/IMG_0654.htm> accessed March 13, 2019.
[116] "Et quia in recordo illo nihil obscurum nihil dubium nihil minus requisitum . . . sed omnia plana et sufficienter examinata et secundum recordum iustum iudicium et . . . non fuit locus certificationis ideo remaneat iudicium." TNA JUST 1/1182, m 8.1 (AALT IMG 653) <http://aalt.law.uh.edu/AALT3/JUST1/JUST1no1182/aJUST1no1182fronts/IMG_0653.htm> accessed March 13, 2019; TNA JUST 1/1182, m 8.2b (AALT IMG 654) <http://aalt.law.uh.edu/AALT3/JUST1/JUST1no1182/aJUST1no1182fronts/IMG_0654.htm> accessed March 13, 2019; Chadwyck-Healey (ed and tr), *Somersetshire Pleas* (n 54) 431.
[117] TNA JUST 1/1182, m 8.2 (AALT IMG 654) <http://aalt.law.uh.edu/AALT3/JUST1/JUST1no1182/aJUST1no1182fronts/IMG_0654.htm> accessed March 13, 2019.
[118] JUST 1/1182, m 8.1 (AALT IMG 653) <http://aalt.law.uh.edu/AALT3/JUST1/JUST1no1182/aJUST1no1182fronts/IMG_0653.htm> accessed March 13, 2019; Chadwyck-Healey (ed and tr), *Somersetshire Pleas* (n 54) 432.
[119] TNA JUST 1/1182, m 8.2b (AALT IMG 654) <http://aalt.law.uh.edu/AALT3/JUST1/JUST1no1182/aJUST1no1182fronts/IMG_0654.htm> accessed March 13, 2019; Chadwyck-Healey (ed and tr), *Somersetshire Pleas* (n 54) 432.

hundred court: they told Bratton that Robert had held it during Richard's life, but had given all of the profits to Richard, and did not take even a ha'penny from it.[120] In this version it was only when the case came to certification that the jurors changed their story and told the justices at Westminster that Robert took the profits from the hundred court. Only the third version contains a record of the judgment in the case: the justices resolved the case by splitting the difference, awarding the manor to Roger and the hundred court to Robert, partially undoing Bratton's resolution of the case.[121]

It is worth pausing to ask who exactly Bratton was writing for when he wrote these different versions of the certification. The rolls were supposed to be the administrative records of the court. They were supposed to record information that might be needed by the court or the parties at some later date. Did Bratton's record of the certification do that? Certainly if one of the parties later brought a writ on the same case—if Roger claimed the hundred court, for instance—Bratton's rolls would show that the court had heard the case already and decided to award the hundred court to Robert. But Bratton and his clerks, when they wrote several different versions of the certification, were not worried about getting the final resolution of the case right. Bratton and his clerks were worried about justifying Bratton's decision. They wanted to make the court's erroneous resolution of the case someone else's responsibility. In one version, Bratton did a good job with the manor, but forgot the hundred court; in the other, the resolution was not Bratton's fault at all, but the prevaricating jury's.[122]

In the versions of the certification that appear on his rolls, Bratton is concerned to demonstrate that the outcome was not his fault. It also seems, however, that Bratton thought that the court's solution, to give the manor to Roger and the hundred court to Robert, was incorrect. Bratton's colleagues on the court *coram rege* may have recognized that it was not an ideal legal solution to the problem; given how busy they were in the spring of 1256, they may have wanted to dispose of the case quickly. Their solution, giving each of the parties part of what they asked for, smacks of a compromise. Perhaps the justices

---

[120] "Juratores quesiti qualem seysinam idem Robertus habuit in vita ipsius Ricardi dixerunt quod idem Robertus tenuit aliquando hundredum illud et quesiti quis cepit explecia et proventus ejusdem hundredi dicunt quod predictus Ricardus quia dicunt quod [non] permittit quod idem Robertus aliquid inde perciperit quamdiu ipse viveret non ad valenciam unius oboli." TNA JUST 1/1182, m 8.2 (AALT IMG 655) <http://aalt.law.uh.edu/AALT3/JUST1/JUST1no1182/aJUST1no1182fronts/IMG_0655.htm> accessed March 13, 2019; Chadwyck-Healey (ed and tr), *Somersetshire Pleas* (n 54) 432.
[121] Ibid.
[122] This is not the only case in which Bratton justifies himself on his roll. In a 1252 case, Bratton similarly took pains to explain why he had not heard a case that was later heard by the court *coram rege* on certification. TNA JUST 1/1178, m 14d; Meekings and Crook, *King's Bench and Common Bench* (n 20) 140.

thought they could dispose of the case for good by giving each of the parties something, without giving too much thought to whether this was a legally defensible solution.

Henry of Bratton's rolls were not the final word on the case of the manor of Dulverton, however. The case makes an appearance in *Bracton*. It is marked as an *addicio*, suggesting that the later scribes probably found it in the margin of the *Bratton* recension of the treatise, a recension which may have already been complete at the time the case was heard on certification in 1256. Perhaps Bratton, returning to the treatise sometime in the late 1250s or early 1260s, added it to the margin. The treatise contains several discussions of the issue of gifts in which the donor does not fully withdraw from the land. Some of these passages were probably written in the earlier stages of drafting, when it was likely William of Raleigh working on the treatise. The issue appears to have been of particular concern for both Bratton and Raleigh. People who were trying to make an end run around the rules for inheritance of land, such as Richard of Turberville and John Clyfford, would make gifts by charter without doing effective livery of seisin. In *Bracton's* tractate on gifts, Raleigh had included a section titled, "How one ought to use his seisin," which he begins by telling the reader that even if someone has acquired land by gift he must then use the land in order to show that the gift is not "imaginary." An imaginary gift would be invalid.[123] As an example of an imaginary gift, Raleigh mentions the donor who withdraws from seisin of the land, but retains the profits. This gift is considered imaginary even if "homage has been taken, a charter made and seisin transferred with the proper ceremonies."[124] The fact that the donor failed to completely withdraw from the land demonstrates "that he did not withdraw from possession *animo* and *corpore*."[125] Again, we see the Roman doctrine of *animo et corpore* coming out in the writings of this circle of justices.

In the middle of this discussion of imaginary gifts we find the addition about the case of Roger of Reyni and Robert of Schete. Bratton begins the *addicio* with an additional example of a case where the donor has failed to completely withdraw from a gift: where the donor retains seisin or possession of some part, but not all, of the gift. Bratton even quotes a section of the *Digest*, an excerpt of an opinion of the jurist Paul, for the proposition that such a gift is invalid.[126] He

---

[123] "Cum autem possessio fuerit adquisita, quamvis donatarius statim habeat liberum tenementum, tamen ad declarationem possessionis ne imaginaria sit donatio, quamvis inducatur in vacuam possessionem, oportet uti seisina sua." *Bracton*, vol 2, 149–50.

[124] "Quamvis homagium et carta intervenerit et seisina cum solemnitate." *Bracton*, vol 2, 150.

[125] "Et videtur quod per talem usum a possessione non recessit animo neque corpore." *Bracton*, vol 2, 150.

[126] D.41.2.3.1. Bratton quotes the *Digest* to show that the donee can take possession of the entirety of the land without physically entering into all of it. One need not walk the boundaries to take possession

then tells the reader that "If the donee uses the appurtenances and the donor the principal thing, by his use the donor will retain the whole and the donee by his use acquire nothing, for it is either all or nothing, since the donor must have the intention of transferring the whole and the donee of accepting the whole."[127] The hundred court attached to the manor of Dulverton could be considered an appurtance. Bratton signals that he is thinking of this very case when he says that it was "badly decided to the contrary [in the case] between Roger of Reyny and Robert of Schute" because "it was held that by such use Robert retained the hundred, where Richard . . . had never withdrawn from the land to which the hundred was appurtenant."[128] Bratton, in true civilian fashion, gives us the "*solutio*" to the case: the fact that Robert held the hundred was irrelevant, because the manor and the hundred together constituted one, single gift, and Richard never gave up the manor. He had failed to withdraw from part of the gift. Therefore, the entire gift should have failed.[129]

Meekings and Crook have suggested that the heavy editing that we find on Bratton's assize rolls, some of which may actually be in Bratton's own hand, show that he was "anxious to ensure the correctness of the record, prepared to justify the correctness of his judgments."[130] This is probably true, but it is only part of the story. Bratton did insert material at various points on this roll to ensure that the record was complete.[131] It is hard to characterize Bratton's writing and re-writing of the case of the manor of Dulverton as an attempt to ensure the correctness of the record, however. There are discrepancies between the various accounts of the certification at Westminster and between those

*corpore.* Bratton adds to Paul's opinion that this is only the case if "the donor does not use it at all." In other words, if the donor retains possession of any part of the land, the donee's entry into possession of a part of it will be ineffective. *Bracton*, vol 2, 150.

[127] "Si autem donatarius in pertinentiis et donator in principali, donator totum retinebit per usum suum et donatarius per usum suum nihil adquirit, quia aut totum aut nihil, quia in animo donatoris esse deberet totum transferre et in animo donatarii totum recipere." *Bracton*, vol 2, 150.

[128] "Male actum in contrarium inter Rogerum de Reygny et Robertum de Schute, de terra de Dulvertona cum hundredo pertinente, ubi per talem usum adiudicatum fuit quod Robertus teneret et retineret hundredum propter usum de hundredo, ubi Ricardus frater Rogeri donator numquam recessit a terra ad quam hundredum pertinuit." *Bracton*, vol 2, 150–51. Bratton is critical of decisions of the court *coram rege* in other parts of the treatise, as well. In a discussion of gifts between husband and wife, an *addicio*, probably originally a marginal note made by Bratton, intervenes to say that "the contrary was done, and done badly from the error of the court" in a case decided *coram rege* in 1250. *Bracton*, vol 2, 98; Meekings and Crook, *King's Bench and Common Bench* (n 20) 135.

[129] *Bracton*, vol 2, 150–51.

[130] Meekings and Crook, *King's Bench and Common Bench* (n 20) 141.

[131] For interlinear insertions in what appears to be the same hand, likely Bratton's, that added some annotations to *Bracton's Note Book*, see TNA JUST 1/1178, m 19d (AALT IMG 408) <http://aalt.law.uh.edu/AALT3/JUST1/JUST1no1178/bJUST1no1178dorses/IMG_0408.htm> accessed March 13, 2019; TNA JUST 1/1178, m 20d (AALT IMG 409) <http://aalt.law.uh.edu/AALT3/JUST1/JUST1no1178/bJUST1no1178dorses/IMG_0409.htm> accessed March 13, 2019; Meekings and Crook, *King's Bench and Common Bench* (n 20) 141.

accounts and the record of the initial hearing of the case. One version of the certification must be false; either Bratton asked the jurors about the hundred court or he did not. And if Bratton did ask the jurors about the hundred court, why did he not record that question, and the jurors' answer, in his account of his original hearing of the case?

It is easier to characterize Bratton's editing as an attempt to justify the correctness of Bratton's judgments. This only raises a further question, however: justify it to whom? When Bratton wrote his self-justificatory accounts of the certification proceedings, the case had already been decided by the justices of the court *coram rege*. Bratton's editing makes more sense if we place it in the context of the practices of collecting and citing cases that had been fostered by Raleigh and by Bratton himself over the previous three decades. The case references in *Bracton* and in *Casus et Judicia* encouraged the reader to go to the rolls and read the case itself, often indicating where on the roll a particular case could be found. Bratton may have had this in mind when he took such pains to draft his version of the certification. Just as modern judges sometimes write their opinions with an audience of first-year law students in mind, hoping to be excerpted in casebooks, Bratton may have been writing this entry for justices and clerks who would read about the case in *Bracton* and then go to the rolls in search of the text. It was important that the case on the roll tell the right story and lead the reader to the right legal conclusion, even if it did not state the facts exactly as they happened in court.

Of course, Bratton's roll does not explain that retention of the seisin of a part of the gift is equivalent to the retention of the seisin of the whole. A clerk aspiring to be a justice would not have learned the rule on imaginary gifts—the reason why the case was badly decided, according to *Bracton*—from this roll. He would have to turn to *Bracton* for that. It is not clear why Bratton did not edit the roll to include some explanation of that rule. He could, perhaps, have edited the record of the original proceedings to include questions about the hundred court. Perhaps he could have found a space to make the point that the hundred court was irrelevant, and that questioning the jury about it would have been superfluous, because he had already found that Richard of Turberville had not withdrawn from the manor to which it was appurtenant. It may be that it was too difficult to find a space, within the confines of the plea roll entry, for Bratton to explain this high legal theory. It would not fit neatly into the justice's questions or the jury's answers. It may also be that Bratton intended the final version of his rolls to reflect the theory that the retention of a part renders the gift ineffective as to the whole. The roll does appear to be an incomplete draft. Perhaps he intended to edit both the account of the case and of the certification to be more consistent. Perhaps he did so. There may, at one time, have been a fair copy of this roll that included Bratton's final product and final decision about which version of the case to present on his rolls for posterity, but it is more probable that he never completed one. Bratton was ordered to deliver the rolls of Martin of Pattishall to the treasury in 1258, around the time the last case contained on these rolls was heard.[132] It may be that the treasury asked for his own rolls at the same time, and he may have been compelled to turn them in before he finished his fair copy.[133] Indeed, the disorderly state of the rolls seems to indicate that Bratton was in a bit of a rush when he turned them over.[134] Whatever happened, Bratton's rolls do not appear to have become the teaching texts that he hoped they would be.

## Conclusion

In his early experience as a clerk to William of Raleigh, Bratton learned that important justices had their cases excerpted and treated as authorities. Bratton might then have expected that his rolls would be read by future generations of clerks and justices and have wanted to paint a specific picture of himself. He wanted his rolls to be remembered as the opinions of a great jurist. We thus see Bratton constructing his rolls for an audience beyond the courtroom, an audience that would read his rolls for the legal principles contained in them, not just for information about the parties in the cases.

But what of Henry of Bratton? Was he successful in using the plea rolls to present himself as the jurist whom future generations of clerks and judges should look to as an authority? Bratton continued to serve as a justice of the court *coram rege* for about a year after the conclusion of the case of the manor of Dulverton, leaving that position for unknown reasons in 1257.[135] He continued to sit on assize commissions until his death in 1268, and seems to have been a trusted member of the judiciary. When he died in 1268, Bratton was chancellor of Exeter Cathedral, was a canon of Wells Cathedral, and held several additional ecclesiastical benefices, with a total income of over 100 pounds

---

[132] Meekings and Crook, *King's Bench and Common Bench* (n 20) 131.
[133] Ibid.
[134] Most of the membranes contain no heading, so we do not know when or where the cases on them were decided. They are filed in the wrong order, and even contain membranes that have nothing to do with Bratton's assizes. Two membranes from Bratton's *coram rege* rolls are included among them. Meekings, "Canon of Wells" (n 22) 143, n 5.
[135] Meekings and Crook, *King's Bench and Common Bench* (n 20) 129–30.

per year.[136] He was an important person at his death, but he was not remembered as a great jurist by subsequent generations. While some of his contemporaries, such as his co-clerk Roger of Thirkleby and his close associate Henry of Bath, are cited in the treatises of the later thirteenth century, Bratton never appears in them.[137] Bratton did become famous in a way, albeit not for the reason he would have thought. Ironically, it was for the *Bracton* treatise, most of which he did not write. It was attributed to him as early as 1278, perhaps because the treatise was found among his effects at his death.[138] If it was recognition as a learned jurist who knew his Roman law that he wanted, he got it in one manuscript of the treatise, copied about thirty years after his death, that named the treatise's author as "Henry of Bracton, doctor of civil and canon law and afterwards chief justice of King Henry for twenty years and more."[139] None of this is actually true, as far as we know, except perhaps in Henry of Bratton's dreams.

[136] For the benefices Bratton acquired in the 1250s and 1260s, see Vincent, "Henry of Bratton" (n 23) 23; Meekings and Crook, *King's Bench and Common Bench* (n 20) 132–33.

[137] The treatise known as *Hengham Magna*, which was probably written in the early 1260s, references the opinions of Bratton's associate Henry of Bath four times. William Huse Dunham (ed), *Radulphi de Hengham Summae* (CUP 1932) 23, 24, 30, 37. It also references a case heard before Roger of Thirkleby. Ibid, 46. For the dating of *Hengham Magna*, see Paul Brand, "*Hengham Magna*" (n 3) 389–90.

[138] Paul Brand, "The Age of Bracton" in John Hudson (ed), *The History of English Law: Centenary Essays on "Pollock and Maitland"* (OUP 1996) 74.

[139] "Explicit liber qui vocatur Bretun, et componebatur a quodam magistro Henrico de Bractone, doctore in iure civili et canonico, et postea iusticiario capitali Henrici regis per XX annos et amplius." Worcester Cathedral Library MS F 87; *Bracton*, vol 1, 18.

# Conclusion

## An End or a Beginning?

In the first half of the thirteenth century, a group of justices in England's royal courts spent a great deal of time reflecting on the work they were doing. In this time before the common law was yet the common law, when its nature was contestable, the justices and clerks in the circle of Martin of Pattishall, William of Raleigh, and Henry of Bratton wanted to show that it was a constituent part of the universal law of the Latin West. They worked to demonstrate, in *Bracton*, that the rules of the English courts could be understood within the framework of Roman law, even when particular rules conflicted. They also worked to demonstrate that the texts they were producing in the royal courts were analogous to the texts that jurists were producing in the schools. By taking plea roll entries out of their original context, generalizing them, placing them in a codex, glossing them, and citing them as if they were akin to the texts found in the *Digest*, the justices in the circle of Pattishall, Raleigh, and Bratton imbued their work with new meaning. The judgments of royal justices were the judgments of jurists. The work they did was not simply that of a judge or of a royal servant. It was the work of a *iuris prudens*, a jurist.

This book has argued that the common law's first professionals found their model of the legal professional in Roman and canon law. But was their vision of a legal professional a dead end? *Bracton* was an important text for the generations of justices, clerks, and lawyers who followed Henry of Bratton. In the 1250s and 1260s, while Bratton was still alive, there appears to have been a healthy engagement with the treatise. As we saw in Chapter 7, the collection of cases known as *Casus et Judicia* may have been made by someone who was familiar with *Bracton* and the plea roll collections.[1] The treatises *Hengham Magna* and *Fet Asaver*, both likely made by clerks of the royal courts, rely on *Bracton*.[2] Even in the last decades of the thirteenth century and the first decades of the fourteenth, *Bracton* seems to have had a strong following. Fifty-two manuscripts survive, and the vast majority of surviving manuscripts date to

---

[1] See above, pp 206–9.
[2] Thomas J McSweeney, "Creating a Literature for the King's Courts in the Later Thirteenth Century: Hengham Magna, Fet Asaver, and Bracton" (2016) 37 Journal of Legal History 41–71.

*Priests of the Law*. Thomas J. McSweeney, Oxford University Press (2019). © Thomas J. McSweeney.
DOI: 10.1093/oso/9780198845454.003.00009

this period.[3] In the last decade of the century, several treatise authors wrote texts that relied heavily on *Bracton*. The treatise known as *Cadit Assisa* is an excerpt from *Bracton's* tractate on the assize of mort d'ancestor.[4] An unknown author, possibly a lawyer named Matthew of the Exchequer, wrote an epitome of *Bracton* titled *Fleta* sometime around 1290. *Fleta* exists in full in only one manuscript.[5] A second epitome, called *Thornton*, was made by Gilbert de Thornton, the chief justice of the king's bench, around the same time.[6] *Britton*, also written sometime shortly after 1290, was written in French, rather than Latin, but incorporated many translated passages of *Bracton*.[7] Close to fifty manuscripts of this treatise survive.[8]

Bracton was being copied and adapted in the late thirteenth century, but by this time the justices who wrote *Bracton* and the plea roll collections had, for the most part, passed out of the memory of the people who worked in the central courts of the common law. Henry of Bratton or Henry of Bracton, by this time, was known only as the man whose name appeared in the treatise. We find no collections of his cases and his legal opinions are not recorded in the treatises of the last decades of the century. The grandiose introduction he gets in one of the manuscripts, "doctor of civil and canon law and chief justice in the courts of the king for twenty years and more," actually indicates that the creator of that manuscript knew little about him.[9] He was never chief justice of the Common Bench or court *coram rege*—or even of an eyre, for that matter—and is never referred to as a doctor or master in correspondence or the records of the royal courts. The real justice Henry of Bratton had, by this time, been transformed into the fictional Henry of Bracton. Martin of Pattishall and William of Raleigh fared little better. Their cases still appeared in copies of the treatise, but they were justices of an earlier age, and the justices of the later thirteenth century must have found these cases to be woefully out of date.[10] The authors

---

[3] Nicholas Vincent, "Henry of Bratton (*alias* Bracton)" in Mark Hill and RH Helmholz (eds), *Great Christian Jurists in English History* (CUP 2017) 24.

[4] See, e.g., Huntington Library MS 946, fos 54r–59r.

[5] Another manuscript contains a few passages from *Fleta*. David J Seipp, "Fleta (*fl.* 1290–1300)" (ODNB, September 23, 2004) <www.oxforddnb.com/view/article/9716> accessed March 13, 2019.

[6] SE Thorne, "Gilbert de Thornton's *Summa de Legibus*" (1947) 7 University of Toronto Law Journal 1, 4.

[7] For the dating of Britton, see Francis Morgan Nichols (ed), *Britton*, 2 vols (Clarendon Press 1865) vol 1, xviii.

[8] Its nineteenth-century editor knew of twenty-six manuscripts. Ibid, xlix–liii. Baker and Ringrose have identified an additional twenty-three that contain at least part of Britton. JH Baker and JS Ringrose, *A Catalogue of English Legal Manuscripts in Cambridge University Library* (Boydell Press 1996) 63.

[9] Worcester Cathedral Library MS F 87; *Bracton*, vol 1, 18.

[10] In 1291, the Earl of Gloucester asked that a search be made of the rolls from the eyres of justices "of former times (*de antiquis temporibus*) . . . for examples from the time of Martin of Pattishall and the other justices before and after him" to determine whether the wife of a felon who has abjured the realm but is still alive is allowed to claim land she held jointly with her husband. Paul Brand (ed), *The*

of *Thornton, Fleta*, and *Britton* cut the cases out of the treatise completely.[11] This act is more significant than it might at first seem. The practice of collecting cases from the plea rolls appears to have been important to the justices and clerks in the circle of Raleigh and Bratton. When they cited to cases in the treatise, they were making an argument about who they were. The authors of the epitomes of *Bracton* cut all of the cases and, more importantly, did not add any of their own. One would think that Gilbert de Thornton, a justice who was keeping his own rolls, might have substituted his own cases if collecting cases had been important to him. He did not.

After the early decades of the fourteenth century, *Bracton* became far less significant. People no longer had much interest in copying it. Engagement with Roman law declined markedly in the generations after Henry of Bratton's death. A small number of justices and serjeants studied Roman and canon law before going to work in the king's courts in the late thirteenth and early fourteenth centuries and the author of *Fleta* seems to have had access to the *Institutes*, as he added some of his own Roman learning to his treatise.[12] The justices and serjeants with Roman-law training appear to have been a small proportion of the total, however. Some of the terminology of Roman law made its way into the practice of the royal courts, but as David Seipp has demonstrated, it was generally re-purposed in very un-Roman ways, so that the use made of terms like *possessio* in the king's courts would have been unfamiliar and strange to a civilian or canonist.[13] Moreover, as educational courses in the common law developed in the second half of the thirteenth century, they appear to have focused on the particulars of pleading and procedure in the royal courts, not on

---

*Parliament Rolls of Medieval England, 1275-1504, vol. I: Edward I. 1275-1294* (Boydell & Brewer 2005) 246. It would seem that Martin of Pattishall was the quintessential justice "of former times" for the earl or his lawyers. Their knowledge of Pattishall may have come from the *Bracton* treatise. I would like to thank Paul Brand for bringing this to my attention.

---

[11] John Barton noted several writs and doctrines copied from *Bracton* into *Fleta* that were very old by the time *Fleta* was written. Barton used them as evidence that treatise authors did not necessarily agree with the latest law, and sometimes presented their own opinions as law, even if they did not reflect current practice. We might also read this as evidence of blind copying from *Bracton*, however. JL Barton, "The Authorship of *Bracton*: Again" (2009) 30 Journal of Legal History 117, 129, 151.

[12] Paul Brand, *The Origins of the English Legal Profession* (Blackwell 1992) 155; GO Sayles, "Introduction," in *Fleta, Volume IV: Book V and Book IV* (SS vol 99, Selden Society 1984) xx.

[13] David J Seipp, "Roman Legal Categories in the Early Common Law" in Thomas G Watkin (ed), *Legal Record and Historical Reality: Proceedings of the Eighth British Legal History Conference* (Hambledon Press 1989); David Seipp, "Bracton, the Year Books, and the 'Transformation of Elementary Legal Ideas' in the Early Common Law" (1989) 7 Law and History Review 175; David J Seipp, "The Concept of Property in the Early Common Law" (1994) 12 Law and History Review 29.

the higher-level questions of system and harmony that so concerned the civilians and the authors of *Bracton*.[14]

The ideal of a learned professional justice who had worked his way up from the clerkship did not survive the fourteenth century. The career path followed by Pattishall, Raleigh, and Bratton became less common as the thirteenth century progressed. Some justices, such as Ralph of Hengham, Hervey of Staunton, and John of Mettingham continued to rise to the bench through the clerkship.[15] From 1290, however, the king regularly appointed practicing lawyers to the Common Bench and the court *coram rege*.[16] By the middle of the fourteenth century, the crown was turning primarily to lawyers to fill vacancies on the judicial bench.[17] The community of justices and clerks focused on a particular set of textual practices envisioned by the *Bracton* authors could not have survived long, if it ever really came into being.

I do not think the attempts by the circle of Pattishall, Raleigh, and Bratton to re-think the nature of the common law and of the people who administered it were a complete dead end, however. John Dawson noted half a century ago that common-law systems are unique in treating their judges as the law's "living oracles."[18] In most civil-law systems, academic jurists are the oracles of the law, the people who drive legal development. *Bracton* may provide some clue as to how that divide came about. *Bracton* may even suggest that it was not, in its origin, much of a divide. In Northern Italy in the thirteenth century, judges were essentially subordinate to jurists. Judges sought counsel from jurists, requesting their *consilia* in difficult cases. In some places, local statutes provided that the judge was required to seek the counsel of a jurist if both parties requested consultation and even made the jurist's *consilium* binding on the

---

[14] Paul Brand, "Legal Education in England before the Inns of Court" in Jonathan A Bush and Alain Wijffels (eds), *Learning the Law: Teaching and the Transmission of English Law, 1150-1900* (Hambledon Press 1999) 51–84.

[15] Anthony Musson, *Medieval Law in Context: The Growth of Legal Consciousness from Magna Carta to the Peasants' Revolt* (Manchester University Press 2001) 46 (Musson, *Medieval Law in Context*); Paul Brand, "Mettingham, John of (d. 1301)" (ODNB, January 3, 2008) <www.oxforddnb.com/view/article/37608> accessed March 13, 2019.

[16] A few serjeants had served as justices before the 1290s. Laurence del Brok sat as a justice of the court *coram rege* for a short time in 1271. Richard of Boyland served regularly as an eyre justice between 1279 and 1289 and Alan of Walkingham served on the 1281-1282 Devon eyre. Paul Brand, "Edward I and the Transformation of the English Judiciary" in MCL, 158.

[17] Musson, *Medieval Law in Context* (n 15) at 46–47.

[18] John P Dawson, *The Oracles of the Law* (Reprint edn, Greenwood Press 1978) xi (hereafter Dawson, *Oracles*). The quotation actually comes from Blackstone's *Commentaries*. Blackstone says that the common law is comprised of general customs of the realm and then asks "how are these customs or maxims to be known, and by whom is their validity to be determined? The answer is by the judges in the several courts of justice. They are the depositary of the laws, the living oracles . . ." William Blackstone, *Commentaries on the Laws of England, Book 1: Of the Rights of Persons* (David Lemmings ed, OUP 2016) 52.

judge.[19] It was these *consilia*, not the decisions of the judges, that made law. *Consilia* were collected and studied, while judgments were not. Thus, the functions of interpreting the law and of applying the law were divided between two different groups. If, however, the English justices who wrote *Bracton* were simply combining the two functions of jurist and judge, and treating the judgments of justices as the *consilia* of jurists, the distance between the practices of continental law and English law may not have been as divergent at their origin as they appear to be today. If the judges came to be regarded as the common law's "living oracles" it may have been partly because they had attempted to class themselves among the jurists, the living oracles of the civil law.

I want to be appropriately cautious in making this claim. There have been almost 800 years of development in both the common law and the civil law since Martin of Pattishall or William of Raleigh sat down to begin writing *Bracton*. Much more recent developments, such as the concept of *stare decisis*, have encouraged common lawyers to look upon judges as the central figures of the common law.[20] The same is true of civil law. Dawson himself argued that the marginalization of the judge in favor of the jurist in the French legal system, which is often viewed as the quintessential civil-law system, was actually due to a reaction against the powerful judges of the last years of the *ancien régime*. The fact that jurists were more important than judges in the classical Roman law and in some of the civil-law systems of Europe may have helped it to take hold, but was not the primary driver.[21] Yet, this learned judicial culture that seems to have flourished in the royal courts at least through the 1260s may have encouraged people in England to think of judges as the central figures of the common law. At least within clerical and judicial circles themselves, *Bracton* appears to have fostered the idea of the learned justice. Senior clerks, like John Blundel, the probable author of *Hengham Magna*, may have been trying to create reputations for themselves by writing texts.[22] This may have continued through the end of the century. The justice Ralph of Hengham, who began his career in the royal courts as a judicial clerk, wrote a treatise called *Hengham Parva* in the 1280s or 1290s.[23] The justices who wrote *Bracton* and their attitudes to their work suggest that the divide between the judges of the common law and the jurists of the civil law was not so great in the thirteenth century. In this

---

[19] Dawson, *Oracles* (n 18) 139–40.

[20] To a medievalist, anything that has happened within the last two centuries seems recent.

[21] Dawson, *Oracles* (n 18) 371–400.

[22] For the attribution of the treatise to Blundel, see Paul Brand, "*Hengham Magna*: A Thirteenth-Century English Common Law Treatise and Its Composition" in MCL, 387–90.

[23] Paul Brand, "Hengham, Ralph (*b.* in or before 1235, *d.* 1311)" (ODNB, January 3, 2008) <www.oxforddnb.com/view/article/12924> accessed June 21, 2017.

formative period of the common law, when the justices were just beginning to establish themselves as the oracles of the law, those justices turned to Roman and canon law for models. In the image of the jurist, they found a model that could be adapted to the judge of the royal courts.

The search for origins is always a fraught endeavor, but Pattishall, Raleigh, and Bratton may have one final lesson for us. How we think about what it means to be a "lawyer" is important. At the moment, many within the American legal profession are pushing for a more practical approach to law, arguing that law schools teach too much legal theory and not enough practical skills. The authors of *Bracton* provide us with one vision of what it means to be a legal professional, and we can use them as a mirror for our own time. Pattishall, Raleigh, and Bratton thought their learning and their practice were intertwined. In this period, when the common law was contestable, these justices made the case for its independence by positing that it was an intellectual system, not simply an expression of royal or baronial will. They worked hard to systematize the things they were doing in the courts, to show that these procedures and practices constituted a body of knowledge. They also worked hard to demonstrate that they were not simply administrators, royal servants like the clerks and officials who worked in the exchequer. They rejected the notion that they were simply there to further the interests of their master. Pattishall, Raleigh, and Bratton worshipped justice and administered sacred rights. They were priests of the law.

# The Writing of the *Note Book*

I noted in Chapter 4 that the case collection known as *Bracton's Note Book*, British Library MS Add 12669, was probably only the last of a series of case collections made by the circle of Raleigh and Bratton. In this appendix, I will lay out the evidence for these earlier case collections. There are places in the text where three things coincide. First, there is a physical break in the manuscript: the scribe leaves a few pages blank. Second, the chronological ordering of the cases is interrupted. Third, the chronological ordering ends at a point that was significant in the career of William of Raleigh. Where these three things coincide, I argue, we are looking at a place where the creators of the *Note Book* finished copying from one earlier collection and began copying from another one.

As Samuel Thorne and H.G. Richardson suggested, *Bracton's Note Book* was probably not copied directly from the rolls. The best evidence for this are the entries that are assigned to the wrong term.[1] This would have been a very difficult mistake to make if the compiler of the *Note Book* had been working directly from the rolls. Richardson thought that the clerks who copied the *Note Book* were copying from "detached pieces of parchment, put into a rough order, containing entries already taken from the rolls and to some extent edited."[2] In other words, they were working not from the rolls themselves, but from a rough draft of the *Note Book*. Thorne suggested a different solution to the problem, however. Thorne thought that the *Note Book* may have been made from earlier collections. He noted, for instance, that at least some of the marginal glosses appear to have been copied from the source text, suggesting that the cases had already been glossed at the time they were copied into the *Note Book*. The glosses do not appear on the roll, however. That would seem to suggest a completed prior collection, not a series of drafts on scraps of parchment.[3] He suggested that the "nucleus" of the *Note Book* consists of a series of Common Bench cases that run from Easter term 1227 to Easter term 1234, and noted that the *coram rege* cases from 1234 to 1240 also seem to form a continuous series.[4] I think Thorne is largely correct, but I plan to flesh out his account of the prior collections and when and why they were made.

The *Note Book* is divided into two large sections. There is a break in the manuscript that mirrors a break in the text at folio 195. Material from the roll of the court *coram rege* for the twenty-fourth year of Henry III's reign (1239–1240) ends on 195.[5] At that point, the scribe apparently left three pages blank. They are now filled with miscellaneous materials, some in French and some in Latin, added by different hands, likely sometime after the *Note Book* was finished.[6] The text then turns back to the rolls with the roll from the Common Bench for

---

[1] *Bracton*, vol 3, xxxvii; HG Richardson, *Bracton: The Problem of His Text* (Bernard Quaritch 1965) 73–74 (hereafter Richardson, *Bracton*).

[2] Richardson, *Bracton* (n 1) 75.

[3] Many of the marginal notes are in the hand of the scribe who wrote the main text. Even those that are not may have been copied from an earlier text. Thorne shows that some of them contain elementary errors, which seem like the kinds of mistakes a copyist would make, not someone who was writing the text for the first time. *Bracton*, vol 3, xxxviii.

[4] *Bracton*, vol 3, xxxviii–xxxix.

[5] British Library MS Add 12269 fo 195; BNB, vol 3, 297. There is a marginal note next to entry 1289 that says "this assize is not from the roll." Ibid.

[6] Ibid, fos 195–96b; BNB, vol 3, 297–305.

Michaelmas, 1217 at folio 197.[7] There is no really compelling material reason for the scribe to have left a space of about three pages beginning at folio 195. There is no quire break. In fact, the scribe had just begun a new quire at folio 192. The next begins at folio 204.[8] There is, however, a change in the text at this point. The *Note Book* before folio 195 forms a continuous series of cases, first from the Common Bench from 1218 to 1234, in more or less chronological order, and then from the court *coram rege* between 1234 and 1240. After folio 195, the *Note Book* contains rolls from a few terms of the Common Bench not covered in the earlier section, and then rolls from eyres of Martin of Pattishall between 1221 and 1228. One way to explain this three-page gap is that the scribe had just finished copying from an already complete text and was signaling that he was moving on to something new. The materials up to 195 may, therefore, have been a complete case collection—made at some date after 1240, the date of the last of the cases, but before the *Note Book*—that was copied into the *Note Book* and then expanded upon with cases from rolls that had, for whatever reason, not been copied into the original collection. The part of the *Note Book* after folio 197 was probably also its own, separate collection, created to supplement the collection or collections that were copied into the first half of the *Note Book*, as the marginal notes in this part of the *Note Book* look like they were copied from another source just as the marginal notes in the first half.[9]

So far we have evidence for at least two collections that existed before the *Note Book*. There were probably several others. The first section of the *Note Book*, the part that runs up to folio 195, may actually have been copied not from one collection, but from several independent collections made at different times. Maitland noticed the first half of the *Note Book*'s not-quite-chronological organization. The text of the *Note Book* up to folio 46b consists of rolls of the Common Bench that have been placed in chronological order, from 1218 to 1228. Then there is one roll of 1220 placed at the very end of these rolls, out of order. The next quire begins on folio 47 with a roll of 1229, beginning the chronological march once again. The cases from that point on are once again chronological, up to 1232. Then, suddenly, cases from a roll of 1225 appear on 102b. When the cases from 1225 end on folio 105, the scribe then leaves the rest of the quire blank, before starting again on the tenth quire with a series of cases from rolls of the bench dating to between 1232 and 1234, which are in chronological order, once again until the end, when some anomalous rolls make their way into the text. The compilers must have been aware of this anomaly; they gave the cases from each roll a heading with the term of the court and the year. A roll that was out of order would have stood out to them.

Maitland thought that this strange ordering was the product of a writing process that took place over a very short period of time, where scribes were given rolls to work with and tried to put them in chronological order, but were occasionally required to add one they had missed.[10] Maitland also believed that the creators of the *Note Book* were working directly from the rolls. Since that is unlikely, another possibility presents itself: they were working from several earlier collections made in the circle of Martin of Pattishall and William of Raleigh. This theory is bolstered by the breaks in the text itself. There are breaks similar to the one at folio 195 at folios 46b and 105. In each case, one term ends and the scribe leaves some blank space before starting with a new roll. Neither of these breaks are quite as probative as the break at 195, as each one occurs near the end of a quire, a natural place to stop

[7]  BNB, vol 3, 305.
[8]  Ibid, vol 1, 62.
[9]  *Bracton*, vol 3, xxxviii.
[10]  BNB, vol 1, 63–64.

writing. In both of these cases, however, the same scribe seems to have continued on to the next quire; there is no obvious difference in the writing from one to the next.[11] That scribe still seems to have thought it advisable, for some reason, to begin a new quire rather than simply continuing with the one he was working on. That might suggest that the reason for the break has to do with a break in the text he is copying. In other places, the scribes happily continue a term from one quire to another.[12]

These breaks are significant, because they correspond exactly to the points in the text where the chronological ordering is disrupted. The first break, at folio 46b, comes at the end of the first chronological run of cases, from 1218 to 1228; the break comes immediately after the cases from the roll of 1220 that have been placed out of order.[13] The second, at 105, comes after the roll of 1225 anomalously inserted after a run of cases from 1229 to 1232.[14] The creators of the *Note Book* thus appear to have treated these chronological runs of cases, each with an anomalous roll at the end, as discrete units of text. If the scribes were working from multiple, independent collections, the breaks between these collections might have encouraged the scribes to think about them as separate, causing them to manifest the separation in their minds as physical breaks in the text.

There is further evidence that these may have been discrete collections. They also correspond to turning points in the career of William of Raleigh. It is perhaps significant that the first unit, which ends at Michaelmas term, 1228, corresponds to Martin of Pattishall's career as justice. Pattishall retired at the end of the following term of the court, Hilary 1229.[15] The first unit, therefore, may represent a case collection made shortly after Pattishall's retirement. Raleigh, as a new justice, may have wanted a collection of Pattishall's cases to have as a reference for himself now that he was sitting on the bench. He clearly revered Pattishall, as we can see from the many references to what he "used to say" in *Bracton*.[16] The second unit, which begins on a new quire at folio 47, lines up with the earliest phase of Raleigh's career as a justice. Raleigh ascended to the bench a little over two months after Pattishall's retirement, in early May of 1229, during Easter term.[17] The break between the first unit and the second admittedly does not line up perfectly with Pattishall's retirement and Raleigh's promotion: the first term represented in the second unit was actually Pattishall's last on the bench, Hilary term, 1229. This unit runs chronologically up to Easter term, 1232.[18] This, too, appears to line up with a significant moment in Raleigh's career. The bench was not in session for the two terms after Easter, Trinity, and most of Michaelmas, in 1232, as Raleigh and his associates were away on an eyre.[19] So this chronological unit ends when the Common Bench closed for the 1232 eyre. Although Raleigh had served on other eyres, the eyres of Trinity and Michaelmas 1232 were significant: they were the first in which Raleigh was appointed

---

[11] British Library MS Add 12269 fos 105b–106.

[12] At folio 192, i.e., a case from the roll of the court *coram rege* from Henry III's 23rd year straddles two quires. BNB, vol 3, 282 (no 1273).

[13] BNB, vol 2, 260.

[14] Ibid, 555.

[15] Alan Harding, "Pattishall, Martin of (*d.* 1229)" (ODNB, September 23, 2004) <www.oxforddnb. com/view/article/21542> accessed March 13, 2019.

[16] See *Bracton*, vol 2, 368; vol 3, 128.

[17] David Crook, "Raleigh, William of (*d.* 1250)" (ODNB) <www.oxforddnb.com/view/article/ 23042> accessed July 8, 2015; Ralph V Turner, *The English Judiciary in the Age of Glanvill and Bracton, c. 1176-1239* (CUP 1985) 195; CAF Meekings and David Crook, *King's Bench and Common Bench in the Reign of Henry III* (Selden Society 2010) 186 (hereafter Meekings and Crook, *King's Bench and Common Bench*).

[18] Cases from the roll of Trinity, 1225 appear at the end of this unit. British Library MS Add 12669 fos 102b–105b; BNB, vol 2, 540–55.

[19] David Crook, *Records of the General Eyre* (Her Majesty's Stationery Office 1982) 87–89.

chief justice of one of the circuits.[20] Perhaps Raleigh saw this as an appropriate time to create another collection.

The third unit, beginning with cases from Hilary term, 1233, is a short unit.[21] The chronological run of cases runs only to Easter term, 1234. After that, the roll of Michaelmas, 1232 is inserted—it apparently had been missed—and the eleventh quire ends.[22] When the twelfth quire begins on folio 132, it is with cases from the bench from 1224 and 1225.[23] Easter term, 1234, the last term of this third unit of the text, was also Raleigh's last term on the Common Bench. Raleigh was created chief justice of the newly reformed court *coram rege* at the end of May, 1234, towards the end of Easter term.[24] This third unit therefore contains cases heard by Raleigh after his promotion to chief justice of an eyre but before his promotion to chief justice of the court *coram rege*. Once again we see three things coinciding: a break in the chronological run of cases, a break in the manuscript (in this case, a quire break), and an important moment in Raleigh's career.

After this quire break, there is a fourth unit that contains cases from five terms of the Common Bench between 1224 and 1225. These terms are missing from the first unit, where they would otherwise belong, and were probably collected together to fill in gaps in earlier collections. Exactly when this was done, we cannot know. It could be that this unit was made after the 1234 collection was completed and it was noticed that there were gaps in the earlier collections. It may also have been tacked on to the front of the next collection when it was made. It runs to folio 161b, where there is no material break in the manuscript, which may suggest that it is continuous with the next collection.[25] After these cases end, another unit of cases, in chronological order, picks up. These are all rolls from the court *coram rege*, from 1234 to 1240, from Raleigh's elevation to chief justice of the court *coram rege* to his retirement to take up his bishopric. This unit finishes off the first section of the *Note Book*, ending at folio 195.[26]

The collections of cases up to 1234 were likely made by William of Raleigh, whose career coincides so well with the breaks in the manuscript, or by his clerks at his instruction. The collection of cases from 1234 to 1240, however, was likely not made by Raleigh, but by Henry of Bratton. The latest roll excerpted in the *Note Book*, the one that ends the first section of the *Note Book*, is the roll of the court *coram rege* for the twenty-fourth year of Henry III's reign, a regnal year that would have run from October 28, 1239 to October 27, 1240.[27] Raleigh retired in the spring of 1239, and therefore was no longer sitting on the court when this roll was made.[28] It does seem that Bratton stayed on for a time as a senior clerk in the court *coram rege* after his master's retirement from the court, and may have continued to keep the rolls under the new chief justice, Stephen of Seagrave.[29] The second-to-last roll represented in this unit of the *Note Book*, the roll of the court *coram rege* for 23 Henry III (1238–1239), started as Raleigh's roll, but appears to have been continued by Seagrave.[30]

---

[20] Ibid, 88.
[21] British Library MS Add 12669 fo 106; BNB, vol 2, 555.
[22] Ibid fo 131b; BNB, vol 1, 62; vol 2, 687.
[23] Ibid fo 132, BNB, vol 2, 687–719; vol 3, 1–123.
[24] Meekings and Crook, *King's Bench and Common Bench* (n 17) 49.
[25] BNB, vol 3, 123.
[26] Ibid, 298.
[27] Ibid, 285–97. C R Cheney and Michael Jones, *A Handbook of Dates for Students of British History* (Revised edn, CUP 2000) 33.
[28] Meekings and Crook, *King's Bench and Common Bench* (n 17) 50.
[29] See ibid, 51.
[30] Ibid, 61.

It is difficult to pinpoint when the *Note Book* itself was made, but there are a few clues. It was certainly not finished before 1240, the year of the last cases contained in the *Note Book*, and it appears to have been finished by 1256 at the latest.[31] There is some evidence to suggest a date before 1245. The miscellaneous material that appears on folios 195 through 196b, which appears to have been added after the *Note Book* was completed, includes a case from Martin of Pattishall's Lincolnshire eyre of 1226.[32] Cases from the 1226 Lincolnshire eyre are not otherwise included in the *Note Book*. This case probably made its way into the empty folios at the end of the first part of the *Note Book* because it had been relevant to the 1245 Lincolnshire eyre and had been searched out and copied onto the roll of that eyre, which survives.[33] Henry of Bratton was one of the justices on that eyre. It seems likely that Bratton became aware of the case through his work on that eyre and, perhaps shortly after the eyre, copied the entry into the *Note Book*. If Bratton was indeed copying this entry into the *Note Book* shortly after he became aware of it, that would suggest that the *Note Book* was complete by 1245.[34] The rolls of Seagrave included in the *Note Book* may also hint at when it was made. Seagrave appears to have taken his rolls with him when he retired. Seagrave's rolls appear to have been in the custody of the Abbot of Leicester and the Prior of Kenilworth in 1258, not in Henry of Bratton's custody.[35] Seagrave had probably left the rolls with the Abbot of Leicester when he died at the monastery in October of 1241, after taking the habit of an Augustinian canon.[36] If the last roll contained in the *Note Book* was Seagrave's, as seems probable, that would have given Bratton less than one year, from October of 1240 until Seagrave's departure from court for Leicester Abbey in September of 1241, to complete this collection of cases.[37] This may be the window in which the unit of the *Note Book* that covers Raleigh's time on the court *coram rege* was made. We cannot, however, be certain of this. The treasury's 1258 order to hand in the rolls of Seagrave, Pattishall, and Raleigh only referred to eyre rolls and bench rolls.[38] Seagrave may have left his *coram rege* rolls in the custody of the court *coram rege*, as Raleigh seems to have done when he retired. That would make a certain amount of sense, as the court would require some continuity in its records.

The markings that appear on many of Pattishall's and Raleigh's plea rolls are discussed in Chapter 4. The marked rolls often come from the same terms that are represented in the *Note Book*. These markings corroborate the theory that the *Note Book* was compiled from several collections. The rolls excerpted in the section of the *Note Book* before the break at folio 195

---

[31] One of the miscellaneous notes added after folio 195, which were likely added sometime after the manuscript was completed, is on how to count the extra day in a leap year. It explains the method that was in use before the leap-year ordinance of May 9, 1256. Bratton is listed among the witnesses to the ordinance. It seems unlikely that Bratton would have written the wrong version of the way to account for a leap year, so we can be fairly certain the *Note Book* was completed sometime before 1256. BNB, vol 1, 42–43.

[32] BNB, vol 3, 304–05 (no 1294).

[33] JUST 1/482, m 17, 'IMG 1770' (AALT) <http://aalt.law.uh.edu/AALT4/JUST1/JUST1no482/aJUST1no482fronts/IMG_1770.htm> accessed March 13, 2019. I would like to thank Paul Brand for this identification and suggestion.

[34] It is, of course, possible that Bratton copied the entry into the *Note Book* at some later date.

[35] The exchequer ordered the Abbot of Leicester and the Prior of Kenilworth to hand Seagrave's rolls over to the treasury for safekeeping in 1258. The exchequer, at least, thought Seagrave had taken his rolls with him when he retired. BNB, vol 1, 25; Ralph V Turner, *Men Raised from the Dust: Administrative Service and Upward Mobility in Angevin England* (University of Pennsylvania Press 1988) 134 (hereafter Turner, *Men Raised from the Dust*); TNA E368/14, m 12b (Exchequer Memoranda Roll, 1242).

[36] Turner, *Men Raised from the Dust* (n 35) 134.

[37] Ibid.

[38] For the text of the order, see GO Sayles (ed), *Select Cases in the Court of King's Bench under Edward I, Vol. 1* (SS vol 55, Bernard Quaritch 1936) cliv (text b).

bear different markings than the ones that are excerpted in the later part of the *Note Book*. Sixteen rolls from terms represented in the earlier part of the *Note Book* survive. Of those, all but one have the same kind of marking—a simple line down the side of each case to be copied.[39] The five surviving rolls for terms that appear in the portion of the *Note Book* after folio 195—again, with one exception—contain more elaborate markings, with subject headings written over the cases to be copied, the letter N (for *nota*), often worked into the side-lines, and the words *visus est* ("This has been seen") written at the tops of the membranes, presumably to note that the collector had already looked at this page and marked what, if anything, he wanted from it.[40] These differences in the markings appear to line up with the shift from the first to the second section of the *Note Book*.

This suggests that Raleigh used straight-line scoring when he made his early collections. Two rolls of the 1234–1240 collection of *coram rege* cases, a collection probably made by Bratton after Raleigh left the court, use this method of marking, as well. That suggests that either Raleigh was continuously marking interesting cases, as his rolls were being made, or that Henry of Bratton initially adopted his master's method of marking rolls when he made his first collection. If it was the latter, then Bratton appears to have developed a new style before he collected the cases that appear in the second half of the *Note Book*, which come from miscellaneous terms that had been missed in the first half. Bratton may have had even grander designs for the second half. The subject headings that appear over the cases to be excerpted hint that may have intended to arrange his collection by subject. In any event, Bratton's work does have the look of an attempt to supplement Raleigh's earlier collection or collections: the rolls that bear Bratton's markings and that ended up in the *Note Book* are all rolls that were left out of the earlier collections. Bratton seems to have had no desire to redo all the work that had been done with the rolls that were already represented in it.

The *Note Book* itself, which combined all of these earlier collections of Raleigh and Bratton, was probably Henry of Bratton's creation. It was, at the very least, in his hands at some point. Maitland noted that many of the marginal notes referenced cases, people, and places associated with Henry of Bratton. One even mentions Bratton.[41] Marginalia associated with Bratton appear in all parts of the *Note Book*. That would suggest that either Bratton annotated the earlier collections before they were copied into the *Note Book*, or that not all of the marginalia were copied from the earlier collections. Some may have been added later by Bratton. Maitland may have been wrong about the manner in which the *Note Book* was composed, but he was probably correct in his assessment that it was *Bracton's* note book.

At the end of his introduction to the *Note Book*, Maitland said

And now the question whether this Note Book was really Bracton's or no, must be left to the judgment of the learned world. An effort has here been made to state the evidence impartially; but of course I was happy in believing that his work was in my

---

[39] The exception is Michaelmas 1230. It is marked with the more elaborate markings discussed below. I must confess that I do not have an easy explanation for the appearance of the more elaborate markings in this roll. Doris M Stenton, *Rolls of the Justice in Eyre for Lincolnshire 1218-9 and Worcestershire 1221* (Selden Society 1934) lxxix. The other fourteen rolls, marked with straight lines, are, in the order they appear in the *Note Book*, those of Michaelmas 1219, Hilary and Easter 1220, Hilary and Easter 1228, Michaelmas 1228, Michaelmas 1220, Hilary 1229, Hilary 1230, Trinity 1230, Hilary 1231, Trinity 1225, Michaelmas 1233, Michaelmas 1232, Michaelmas 1224, *coram rege* 1236–1237, and *coram rege* 1237–1238. See ibid, lxxv–lxxxiii.

[40] Ibid. The exception is the roll of Pattishall's 1227 eyre in Kent, which appears in the second half of the *Note Book*, but contains straight-line markings only. Ibid, lxxxii. Perhaps it was marked for inclusion in an earlier collection, but missed for some reason. The other rolls that survive are those for Trinity 1220, Hilary and Easter 1221, Michaelmas 1223, and Michaelmas 1225. Ibid, lxxv–lxxvii.

[41] BNB, vol 1, 93–104.

hands, and my eyes may have been shut to facts which made against this pleasant belief. What is now to be wished is that some one will go through the book with the design of showing that it is not entitled to the name under which it is here published. Some one fact established by him, might make worthless every argument drawn from the manifold coincidences . . .[42]

Maitland presented us, as historians, with a model of humility. In the face of limited sources and complex problems, none of us alone can hope to solve the mysteries of the early common law. All we can hope is that we can shed a bit of light on the problems of these texts, which might allow some future scholar to shed even a bit more, using what is good in our work and correcting the egregious errors that become apparent as we discover new things. I have built this narrative of the *Note Book* on the work of scholars such as Maitland, Stenton, and Richardson, who, despite their marvelous work, I think got it wrong in certain respects. I hope my own work provides a starting point for someone else.

[42] Ibid, 116.

# Bibliography

## Cases Cited

*In re Osborne*, 76 F.3d 306 (9th Cir. 1996)
*Sveen v. Melin*, 138 S Ct 1815 (2018)

## Manuscript Sources

British Library MS Add 12669
British Library MS Add 35179
British Library MS Hargrave 375
Durham, Dean and Chapter Muniments, Fragment 30
Huntington Library MS 946
Lincoln's Inn MS Misc 738
TNA E368/14
TNA JUST 1/761
TNA JUST 1/1178
TNA JUST 1/1182
TNA KB 26/143
TNA KB 26/148
TNA KB 26/149
TNA KB 26/154
Worcester Cathedral Library MS. F. 87

## Primary Sources

"1217 Carta de Foresta (Charter of the Forest)" in DB Magraw, A Martinez, and Roy E Brownell (eds), *Magna Carta and the Rule of Law* (American Bar Association, 2014)
Andreas Capellanus, *Andreas Capellanus on Love* (PG Walsh trs, Duckworth 1982)
Amt, E and Church, SD (eds), *Dialogus De Scaccario, and Constitutio Domus Regis: The Dialogue of the Exchequer, and the Establishment of the Royal Household* (Clarendon Press 2007)
Azo, *Summa Codicis . . . (Institutionum et Digestorum) & Brocardica* (Vico Verlag 2008), reprint of *Summa Azonis Sive Locuples Iuris Civilis Thesaurus* (Venice 1581)
Azo, *Un Consulto D'azone Dell'anno 1205* (L Chiappelli and L Zdekauer eds, Fratelli Bracali 1888)
Bergmann, F (ed), *Pilii, Tancredi, Gratiae Libri de Iudiciorum Ordine* (Vandenhoeck and Ruprecht 1842)
Birks, P, and Mcleod, G (trs), *Justinian's Institutes* (Cornell University Press 1987)
Blackstone, W, *Commentaries on the Laws of England, Book 1: Of the Rights of Persons* (David Lemmings ed, OUP 2016)

Brand, P (ed), *The Earliest English Law Reports, Volume I: Common Bench Reports to 1284* (SS vol 111, Selden Society 1996)

Brand, P (ed), *The Parliament Rolls of Medieval England, 1275–1504, vol. I: Edward I. 1275–1294* (Boydell & Brewer 2005)

*Calendar of the Patent Rolls of the Reign of Henry III Preserved in the Public Record Office, 1232–1272*, 4 vols (His Majesty's Stationery Office 1906–13)

Clanchy, MT (ed), *The Roll and Writ File of the Berkshire Eyre of 1248* (SS vol 90, Selden Society 1973)

*Close Rolls of the Reign of Henry III Preserved in the Public Record Office*, 13 Vols (His Majesty's Stationery Office 1902–38)

Chadwyck Healey, CEH (ed and tr), *Somersetshire Pleas* (Harrison and Sons 1897)

*Curia Regis Rolls Preserved in the Public Record Office*, 20 vols (Her Majesty's Stationery Office 1922–2006)

De Haas, E, and Hall, GDG (eds), *Early Registers of Writs* (SS vol 87, Bernard Quaritch 1970)

De Zulueta, F (ed), *The Liber Pauperum of Vacarius* (SS vol 44, Bernard Quaritch 1927)

De Zulueta, F, and Stein, P (eds), *The Teaching of Roman Law in England around 1200* (Selden Society 1990)

Douglas, DC, and Greenaway, GW (eds), *English Historical Documents, Volume II: 1042–1189* (Eyre & Spottiswoode 1953)

Dunham, WH (ed), *Radulphi de Hengham Summae* (CUP 1932)

Dunham, WH (ed), *Casus Placitorum and Reports of Cases in the King's Courts, 1272–1278* (SS vol 69, Bernard Quaritch 1952)

Friedberg, E (ed), *Corpus Iuris Canonici*, 2 vols (Bernhard Tauchnitz 1879–81)

Friedburg, E (ed), *Quinque Compilationes Antiquae* (Bernard Tauchnitz 1882)

Gratian, *The Treatise on Laws with the Ordinary Gloss* (A Thompson and K Christensen trs, Catholic University of America Press 1993)

Green, E (ed), *Pedes Finium, Commonly Called Feet of Fines, for the County of Somerset, Richard I to Edward I* (Harrison and Sons 1892)

Henricus a Segusio, *Aurea Summa* (Cologne 1612)

Hall, GDG (ed and tr), *The Treatise on the Laws and Customs of the Realm of England Commonly Called Glanvill* (Reprint edn, Clarendon Press 2002)

Hardy, TD (ed), *Rotuli Litterarum Clausarum in Turri Londinensi Asservati*, 2 vols (Record Commission 1833–44)

Hardy, TD (ed), *Rotuli Litterarum Patentium in Turri Londinensi Asservati*, 2 vols (Record Commission 1835)

Jocelin of Brakelond, *Chronicle of the Abbey of Bury St. Edmunds* (D Greenway and J Sayers trs, OUP 1989)

John of Salisbury, *The Metalogicon of John of Salisbury: A Twelfth-Century Defense of the Verbal and Logical Arts of the Trivium* (DD McGarry tr, Martino Publishing 2015)

Kibler, W (ed), *Raoul De Cambrai* (S Kay tr, Livre de Poche 1996)

Larson, AA (ed and tr), *Gratian's Tractatus De Penitentia: A New Latin Edition with English Translation* (Catholic University of America Press 2016)

Luders, A, Tomlins, TE, France, J, Tauton, WE, and Raithby, J (eds), *The Statutes of the Realm: From Original Records, etc.* (1101–1713), 11 vols (London 1810–28)

Maitland, FW (ed), *Bracton's Note Book*, 3 vols (CJ Clay & sons 1887)

Matthew Paris, *Matthew Paris's English History*, 3 vols (JA Giles tr, Henry G Bohn 1852–54)

Matthew Paris, *Chronica Majora*, 7 vols (Henry Richard Luard ed, Rolls Series, Longmans & Co 1872–83)

Meekings, CAF (ed), *Crown Pleas of the Wiltshire Eyre, 1249* (Wiltshire Archaeological and Natural History Society 1961)

Meekings, CAF (ed), *The 1235 Surrey Eyre*, 3 vols (Surrey Record Society 1979)

Nichols, FM (ed), *Britton*, 2 vols (Clarendon Press 1865)

Robert Grosseteste, *Roberti Grosseteste Episcopis Quondam Lincolniensis Epistolae* (HR Luard ed, Longman, Green, Longman, and Roberts 1861)

Robert Grosseteste, *The Letters of Robert Grosseteste, Bishop of Lincoln* (FAC Mantello and J Goering trs, University of Toronto Press 2010)

Robinson, OF (ed), *The Register of Walter Bronescombe, Bishop of Exeter, 1258–1280, Vol. 1* (Canterbury and York Society vol 82, Boydell & Brewer 1995)

Roger of Howden, *Chronica Magistri Rogeri De Hovedene*, vol 3 (W Stubbs ed, Rolls series, Longman & Co 1870)

Sayles, GO (ed), *Select Cases in the Court of King's Bench under Edward I, Vol. 1* (SS vol 55, Bernard Quaritch 1936)

Sayles, GO, *Select Cases of Procedure without Writ under Henry III* (SS vol 60, Selden Society 1941)

Schwaibold, EKM (ed), *Brocardica "Dolum Per Subsequentia Purgari": Eine Englische Sammlung von Argumenten des Römischen Rechts aus dem 12. Jahrhundert* (Vittorio Klostermann 1985)

Shirley, WW (ed), *Royal and Other Historical Letters Illustrative of the Reign of Henry III, Vol. 1: 1216–1235* (London 1862)

Stenton, DM (ed), *Rolls of the Justices in Eyre for Lincolnshire 1218–9 and Worcestershire 1221* (SS vol 53, Bernard Quaritch 1934)

Stenton, DM (ed), *Rolls of the Justices in Eyre for Gloucestershire, Warwickshire, and Shropshire, 1221, 1222* (SS vol 59, Bernard Quaritch 1940)

Stenton, DM (ed), *Pleas before the King or His Justices, 1198–1212, Volume 3* (SS vol 83, Bernard Quaritch 1966)

Stenton, DM (ed), *Pleas before the King or His Justices, 1198–1212, Volume 4* (SS vol 84, Bernard Quaritch 1967)

Stubbs, W (ed), *Select Charters and Other Illustrations of English Constitutional History*, 2 vols (9th edn, Clarendon Press 1913)

Tardif, EJ (ed), *Coutumiers De Normandie* (Espérance Cagniard 1881)

Van de Wouw, H, *"Brocardica Dunelmensia"* (1991) 108 Zeitschrift der Savigny–Stiftung für Rechtsgeschichte: Romanistische Abteilung 235

Watson, A (tr), *The Digest of Justinian*, 4 vols (Revised edn, University of Pennsylvania Press 1998)

William of Drogheda, *Die Summa Aurea des Wilhelmus de Drokeda* (L Wahrmund ed, Wagner 1914)

Woodbine, GE (ed), and Thorne, SE (tr), *Bracton on the Laws and Customs of England*, 4 vols (Belknap Press 1968–77)

## Secondary Sources

Agrimi, J, and Crisciani, C, *Les Consilia Médicaux* (C Viola trs, Brepols 1994)

Baker, JH, *The Order of the Serjeants at Law* (Selden Society 1984)

Baker, JH, *An Introduction to English Legal History* (4th edn, Butterworths 2002)

Baker, JH, and Ringrose, JS, *A Catalogue of English Legal Manuscripts in Cambridge University Library* (Boydell Press 1996)

Barlow, F, *Thomas Becket* (Phoenix Press 1986)

Barnes, PM, "The Anstey Case" in PM Barnes and CF Slade (eds), *A Medieval Miscellany for Doris Mary Stenton* (Pipe Roll Society 1962)

Barrow, J, "The Education and Recruitment of Cathedral Canons in England and Germany 1100–1225" (1989) 20 Viator 117

Bartlett, R, *Gerald of Wales: A Voice of the Middle Ages* (New edn, Tempus 2006)

Barton, JL, "Bracton as a Civilian" (1967–68) 42 Tulane Law Review 555

Barton, JL, *Roman Law in England* (Ius Romanum Medii Aevi, Pars V, 13a, Typis Giuffrè 1971)

Barton, JL, "The Study of Civil Law before 1380" in JI Catto (ed), *The History of the University of Oxford, Volume I: The Early Oxford Schools* (Clarendon Press 1984)

Barton, JL, "The Mystery of Bracton" (1993) 14 Journal of Legal History 1

Barton, JL, "The Authorship of *Bracton*: Again" (2009) 30 Journal of Legal History 117

Beckerman, JS, "Law–Writing and Law Teaching: Treatise Evidence of the Formal Teaching of English Law in the Late Thirteenth Century" in JA Bush and A Wijffels (eds), *Learning the Law: Teaching and the Transmission of Law in England, 1150–1900* (Hambledon Press 1999)

Bellomo, M, *The Common Legal Past of Europe, 1000–1800*, (LG Cochrane tr, Catholic University of America Press 1995)

Berger, A, *Encyclopedic Dictionary of Roman Law* (American Philosophical Society 1953)

Berman, HJ, *Law and Revolution: The Formation of the Western Legal Tradition* (Harvard University Press 1983)

Bisson, TN, *The Crisis of the Twelfth Century: Power, Lordship, and the Origins of European Government* (Princeton University Press 2009)

Boyle, L, "The Curriculum of the Faculty of Canon Law at Oxford in the First Half of the Fourteenth Century" in *Oxford Studies Presented to Daniel Callus* (Clarendon Press 1964)

Boyle, L, "Canon Law Before 1380" in JI Catto (ed), *The History of the University of Oxford, Volume 1: The Early Oxford Schools* (OUP 1984)

Brand, P, *The Origins of the English Legal Profession* (Blackwell 1992)

Brand, P, *The Making of the Common Law* (Hambledon Press 1992)

Brand, P, "The Clerks of the King's Courts in the Reign of Edward I" in MCL

Brand, P, "Courtroom and Schoolroom: The Education of Lawyers in England Prior to 1400" in MCL

Brand, P, "Edward I and the Transformation of the English Judiciary" in MCL

Brand, P, "*Hengham Magna*: A Thirteenth–Century English Common Law Treatise and Its Composition" in MCL

Brand, P, "Ireland and the Literature of the Early Common Law" in MCL

Brand, P, "'*Multis Vigiliis Excogitatam et Inventam*': Henry II and the Creation of the English Common Law" in MCL

Brand, P, "The Birth and Early Development of a Colonial Judiciary: The Judges of the Lordship of Ireland, 1210–1377" in WN Osborough (ed), *Explorations in Law and History: Irish Legal History Society Discourses, 1988–1994* (Irish Academic Press 1995)

Brand, P, "The Age of Bracton" in John Hudson (ed), *The History of English Law: Centenary Essays on "Pollock and Maitland"* (British Academy 1996)

Brand, P, "Legal Education in England before the Inns of Court" in Jonathan A Bush and Alain Wijffels (eds), *Learning the Law: Teaching and the Transmission of English Law, 1150–1900* (Hambledon Press, 1999)

Brand, P, "The Languages of the Law in Later Medieval England" in DA Trotter (ed), *Multilingualism in Later Medieval Britain* (DS Brewer 2000)

Brand, P, *Kings, Barons, and Justices: The Making and Enforcement of Legislation in Thirteenth-Century England* (CUP 2003)

Brand, P, "Stewards, Bailiffs and the Emerging Legal Profession in Later Thirteenth-Century England" in R Evans (ed), *Lordship and Learning: Studies in Memory of Trevor Aston* (Boydell Press 2004)

Brand, P, "Hengham, Ralph (*b.* in or before 1235, *d.* 1311)" (ODNB, January 3, 2008) <www.oxforddnb.com/view/article/12924> accessed June 21, 2017

Brand, P, "Mettingham, John of (*d.* 1301)" (ODNB, January 3, 2008) <www.oxforddnb.com/view/article/37608> accessed March 13, 2019

Brand, P, "Law and Custom in the English Thirteenth Century Common Law" in P Anderson and M Münster-Swendsen (eds), *Custom: The Development and Use of a Legal Concept in the Middle Ages* (DJØF Publishing 2009)

Brand, P, "The Date and Authorship of Bracton: A Response" (2010) 31 Journal of Legal History 217

Brundage, JA, *Medieval Canon Law* (Longman 1995)

Brundage, JA, "Universities and the 'Ius Commune' in Medieval Europe" (2000) 11 Rivista internazionale di diritto comune 237

Brundage, JA, *The Medieval Origins of the Legal Profession: Canonists, Civilians, and Courts* (University of Chicago Press 2008)

Brunner, H, "The Sources of English Law" in *Select Essays in Anglo-American Legal History*, vol 2 (Little, Brown, and Company 1908)

Buckland, WW, and McNair, AD, *Roman Law and Common Law: A Comparison in Outline* (Revised edn, FH Lawson rev, CUP 1974)

Burger, M, *Bishops, Priests, and Diocesan Governance in Thirteenth-Century England: Reward and Punishment* (CUP 2014)

Cam, H, "*Manerium Cum Hundredo*: The Hundred and the Hundredal Manor" in H Cam (ed), *Liberties and Communities in Medieval England: Collected Studies in Local Administration and Topography* (Barnes and Noble 1963)

Calabresi, G, and Melamed, AD, "Property Rules, Liability Rules, and Inalienability: One View of the Cathedral" (1972) 85 Harvard Law Review 1089

Carpenter, DA, *The Minority of Henry III* (University of California Press 1990)

Carpenter, D, *Magna Carta* (Penguin 2015)

Carruthers, M, *The Book of Memory: A Study of Memory in Medieval Culture* (2nd edn, CUP 2008)

Catto, JI, "Citizens, Scholars, and Masters" in JI Catto (ed), *The History of the University of Oxford, Volume I: The Early Oxford Schools* (Clarendon Press 1984)

Cheney, CR, *From Becket to Langton* (Manchester University Press 1956)

Cheney, CR, and Jones, M, *A Handbook of Dates for Students of British History* (Revised edn, CUP 2000)

Cheyette, FL, "Custom, Case Law, and Medieval 'Constitutionalism': A Re-Examination" (1963) 78 Political Science Quarterly 362

Church, SD, "The 1210 Campaign in Ireland: Evidence for a Military Revolution?" in C Harper-Bill (ed), *Anglo-Norman Studies XX: Proceedings of the Battle Conference, 1997* (Boydell Press 1998)

Clanchy, MT, *From Memory to Written Record: England 1066-1307* (3rd edn, Wiley-Blackwell 2012)

Cobban, AB, *The Medieval English Universities: Oxford and Cambridge to c. 1500* (University of California Press 1988)

Cobban, AB, *English University Life in the Middle Ages* (Ohio State University Press 1999)

Coss, P, *The Knight in Medieval England, 1000–1400* (Combined Books 1993)

Crook, D, *Records of the General Eyre* (Her Majesty's Stationery Office 1982)

Crook, D, "Bath, Henry of (*d.* 1260)" (ODNB, January 3, 2008) <www.oxforddnb.com/view/article/1686> accessed March 13, 2019

Crook, D, "Raleigh, William of (*d.* 1250)" (ODNB, September 23, 2004) <www.oxforddnb.com/view/article/23042> accessed March 13, 2019

Crook, D, "Thirkleby [Thurkilbi], Roger of (*d.* 1260)" (ODNB, September 23, 2004) <www.oxforddnb.com/view/article/27401> accessed March 13, 2019

Crook, D, "York, William of (*d.* 1256)" (ODNB, January 3, 2008) <www.oxforddnb.com/view/article/29479> accessed March 13, 2019

Dawson, JP, *The Oracles of the Law* (Reprint edn, Greenwood Press 1978)

Denton, J, and others "Benefice of Gosberton" (*Taxatio* 2014) <www.hrionline.ac.uk/taxatio/benkey?benkey=LI.LK.HD.20> accessed March 3, 2019

Denton, J, and others, "Benefice of Whitchurch (Prebend)" (*Taxatio* 2014) <www.hrionline.ac.uk/taxatio/benkey?benkey=BW.BA.WC.29> accessed March 16, 2019

DeRolez, A, *The Paleography of Gothic Manuscript Books from the Twelfth to the Sixteenth Century* (CUP 2003)

Donahue, C, "*Ius Commune*, Canon Law, and Common Law in England" (1991–92) 66 Tulane Law Review 1745

Donahue, C, "Biology and the Origins of the Jury" (1999) 17 Law and History Review 591

Dondorp, H, and Schrage, EJH, "The Sources of Medieval Learned Law" in JW Cairns and PJ du Plessis (eds), *The Creation of the Ius Commune: From Casus to Regula* (Edinburgh University Press 2010)

Duggan, AJ, "Roman, Canon and Common Law in Twelfth–Century England: The Council of Northampton (1164) Re-Examined" (2010) 83 Historical Research 379

Duggan, C, *Twelfth–Century Decretal Collections and Their Importance in English History* (Athlone Press 1963)

Dukeminier, J, and others, *Property* (7th edn, Aspen, 2010)

Dunbabin, J, "Careers and Vocations" in JI Catto (ed), *The History of the University of Oxford, Volume I: The Early Oxford Schools* (Clarendon Press 1984)

Dunbabin, J, "From Clerk to Knight: Changing Orders" in C Harper–Bill and R Harvey (eds), *The Ideals and Practice of Medieval Knighthood II: Papers from the Third Strawberry Hill Conference* (Boydell Press 1988)

Edwards, K, *The English Secular Cathedrals in the Middle Ages: A Constitutional Study with Special Reference to the Fourteenth Century* (Manchester University Press 1967)

Evans–Jones, R, and MacCormack, G, "Obligations" in E Metzger (ed), *A Companion to Justinian's Institutes* (Cornell University Press 1998)

Feenstra, R, "'Legum doctor', 'legum professor', et 'magister' comme termes pour designer des juristes au moyen âge" in O Weijers (ed), *Actes du colloque terminologie de la vie intellectuelle au moyen âge* (Brepols 1988)

Fesefeldt, W, *Englische Staatstheorie des 13. Jahrhunderts: Henry de Bracton und Sein Werk* (Musterschmidt Verlag 1962)

Figueira, RC, "Morins, Richard de [called Ricardus Anglicus] (early 1160s–1242)" (ODNB, September 23, 2004) <www.oxforddnb.com/view/article/23518> accessed March 13, 2019

Fish, S, *Is there a Text in this Class? The Authority of Interpretive Communities* (Harvard University Press 1980)

Flower, CT, *Introduction to the Curia Regis Rolls, 1199–1230 A.D.* (SS vol 62, Bernard Quaritch 1944)

Fox, JC, "The Originals of the Great Charter of 1215" (1924) 39 EHR 321

Getzler, J, "Roman Ideas of Landownership" in S Bright and J Dewar (eds), *Land Law: Themes and Perspectives* (OUP 1998)

Getzler, J, *A History of Water Rights at Common Law* (OUP 2004)

Giralt, S, "The 'Consilia' Attributed to Arnau de Vilanova" (2002) 7 Early Science and Medicine 311

Goering, J, "The Scholastic Turn (1100–1500): Penitential Theology and Law in the Schools" in A Firey (ed), *A New History of Penance* (Brill 2008)

Goodrich, P, "Law in the Courts of Love: Andreas Capellanus and the Judgments of Love" (1996) 48 Stanford Law Review 633

Gouron, A "Introduction" in Azo, *Summae* (see Primary Sources above)

Grafton, A, *The Footnote: A Curious History* (Harvard University Press 1997)

Green, RF, "Textual Production and Textual Communities" in L Scanlan (ed), *The Cambridge Companion to Medieval English Literature 1100–1500* (CUP 2009)

Greenblatt, S, *Renaissance Self-Fashioning: From More to Shakespeare* (New edn, University of Chicago Press 2005)

Greenway, DE (ed), *Fasti Ecclesiae Anglicanae 1066–1300: Volume 7, Bath and Wells*, (Institute of Historical Research 2001) (*British History Online*) <www.british-history. ac.uk/fasti-ecclesiae/1066-1300/vol7/pp63-64> accessed April 17, 2018

Gurevich, A, *The Origins of European Individualism* (Katharine Judelson tr, Blackwell 1995)

Hall, GDG, review of *Curia Regis Rolls of the Reign of Henry III: 5–6 Henry III and 7–9 Henry III* (1958) 73 EHR 481

Hall, GDG, review of *Curia Regis Rolls of the Reign of Henry III: 9–10 Henry III* (1959) 74 EHR 107

Hall, GDG, review of *Curia Regis Rolls of the Reign of Henry III. Vol. xiii: 11–14 Henry III* (1962) 77 EHR 103

Hall, GDG, review of *Curia Regis Rolls of the Reign of Henry III, vol. xiv: 14–17 Henry III* (1964) 79 EHR 155

Harding, Alan, *England in the Thirteenth Century* (CUP 1993)

Harding, Alan, "Pattishall, Martin of (d. 1229)" (ODNB, September 23, 2004) <www. oxforddnb.com/view/article/21542> accessed March 13, 2019

Harvey, PDA, "The Manorial Reeve in Twelfth-Century England" in R Evans (ed), *Lordship and Learning: Studies in Memory of Trevor Aston* (Boydell Press 2004)

Helmholz, RH, "The Early History of the Grand Jury and Canon Law" (1983) 50 University of Chicago Law Review 613

Helmholz, RH, "Magna Carta and the *Ius Commune*" (1999) 66 University of Chicago Law Review 297

Helmholz, RH, *The Oxford History of the Laws of England, Volume I: The Canon Law and Ecclesiastical Jurisdiction from 597 to the 1640s* (OUP 2004)

Holt, JC, *Magna Carta* (3rd edn, CUP 2015)

Hudson, J, "Administration, Family, and Perceptions of the Past in Late Twelfth-Century England: Richard FitzNigel and the Dialogue of the Exchequer" in P Magdalino (ed), *The Perception of the Past in Twelfth-Century Europe* (Hambledon Press 1992)

Hudson, J, "Magna Carta, the *Ius Commune*, and English Common Law" in JS Loengard (ed), *Magna Carta and the England of King John* (Boydell Press 2010)

Hudson, J, *The Oxford History of the Laws of England, Volume II: 871–1216* (OUP 2012)

Hudson, J, "From the Articles of the Barons to Magna Carta" in Elisabeth van Houts (ed), *Anglo-Norman Studies XXXVIII: Proceedings of the Battle Conference, 2015* (Boydell Press 2016)

Hudson, J, *The Formation of the English Common Law* (2nd edn, Routledge 2018)

Hunnisett, RF, "What is a Plea Roll?" (1988) 9 Journal of the Society of Archivists 109

Hunt, RW, "The Preface to the *Speculum Ecclesiae* of Giraldus Cambrensis" (1977) 8 Viator 189

Hunt, W, "Seagrave, Sir Stephen of (*d.* 1241)" (Paul Brand rev, ODNB, September 23, 2004) <www.oxforddnb.com/view/article/25041> accessed March 13, 2019

Hurnard, ND, *The King's Pardon for Homicide before A.D. 1307* (Clarendon Press 1969)

Hyams, P, *King, Lords, and Peasants in Medieval England: The Common Law of Villeinage in the Twelfth and Thirteenth Centuries* (Clarendon Press 1980)

Ibbetson, DJ, "Case Law and Doctrine: A Historical Perspective on the English Common Law" in R Schulze and U Seif (eds), *Richterrecht und Rechtsfortbildung in der Europäischen Rechtsgemeinschaft* (Mohr Siebeck 2003)

Jacobs, J, "Little St. Hugh of Lincoln" (1893–94) 1 Transactions of the Jewish Historical Society of England 89

Jakobs, HH, *De similibus ad similia bei Bracton und Azo* (Vittorio Klostermann 1996)

Joüon des Longrais, F, "La portée politique des réformes d'Henry II en matière de saisine" (1936) 15 Revue historique de droit français et étranger, 4th Series 540

Kantorowicz, H, "The Quaestiones Disputatae of the Glossators" (1937–38) 16 Tijdschrift voor Rechtsgeschiedenis 4

Kaye, JM, *Medieval English Conveyances* (CUP 2009)

Kuskowski, AM, "The Birth of Common Law and the Invention of Legal Traditions" British Legal History Conference, University College London, July 7, 2017

Kuskowski, AM, *Law in the Vernacular: Composing Customary Law in Thirteenth Century France* (forthcoming)

Kuttner, S, and Rathbone, E, "Anglo–Norman Canonists of the Twelfth Century: An Introductory Study" (1949–51) 7 Traditio 279

Kuttner, S, *Harmony from Dissonance: An Interpretation of Medieval Canon Law* (Archabbey Press 1960)

Kuttner, S, "Réflections sur les Brocards des Glossateurs" in *Gratian and the Schools of Law, 1140–1234* (Variorum Reprints 1983)

Landau, P, "The Development of Law" in D Luscombe and J Riley Smith (eds), *The New Cambridge Medieval History, vol. IV: c. 1024–c. 1198 Part I* (CUP 2005)

Langmuir, GI, "The Knight's Tale of Young Hugh of Lincoln" (1972) 47 Speculum 459

Lawrence, CH, "The University in State and Church" in JI Catto (ed), *The History of the University of Oxford, Volume I: The Early Oxford Schools* (Clarendon Press 1984)

"Leges Anglorum Londoniis collectae (Leges Angl)" (Early English Laws 2019) <www.earlyenglishlaws.ac.uk/laws/texts/leges–angl/> accessed March 11, 2019

Le Goff, J, *Medieval Civilization, 400–1500* (J Barrow tr, Barnes & Noble Books 2000)

L'Engle, S, and Gibbs, R, *Illuminating the Law: Legal Manuscripts in Cambridge Collections* (Harvey Miller 2001)

Loengard, J, "The Assize of Nuisance: The Origins of an Action at Common Law" (1978) 37 Cambridge Law Journal 144

Lorrey, HJ, "Hugh of Lincoln [St Hugh of Lincoln, Little St Hugh] (c. 1246–1255), supposed victim of crucifixion" (ODNB, September 23, 2004) <https://doi.org/10.1093/ref:odnb/14062> accessed March 13, 2019

Maddicott, JR, "Magna Carta and the Local Community" (1984) 102 Past & Present 25

Maddicott, JR, *Simon de Montfort* (CUP 1994)

Macnair, M, "Vicinage and the Antecedents of the Jury" (1999) 17 Law and History Review 537

MacQueen, HL, *Common Law and Feudal Society in Medieval Scotland* (Edinburgh Classics Edition, Edinburgh University Press 2016)

Maine, HS, *Ancient Law* (16th edn, John Murray 1897)

Maitland, FW (ed), *Select Passages from the Works of Bracton and Azo* (SS vol 8, Bernard Quaritch 1895)

Maitland, FW, "The History of the Register of Original Writs" in HAL Fisher (ed), *The Collected Papers of Frederic William Maitland*, vol 2 (CUP 1911)

Marenbon, J, *Medieval Philosophy: An Historical and Philosophical Introduction* (Routledge 2007)

Mayali, L, "Ius Civile et Ius Commune dans la Tradition Juridique Médiévale" in J Krynen (ed), *Droit Romain, Jus Civile, et Droit Français* (Presses de l'Université des Sciences Sociales de Toulouse 1999)

Mayali, L, "Romanitas and Medieval Jurisprudence" in M Hoeflich (ed), *Lex et Romanitas: Essays for Alan Watson* (Robbins Collection 2000)

McDougall, S, *Royal Bastards: The Birth of Illegitimacy, 800–1230* (OUP 2017)

McSweeney, T, "*English Judges and Roman Jurists: The Civilian Learning Behind England's First Case Law*" (2012) 84 Temple Law Review 827

McSweeney, TJ, "Property before Property: Romanizing the English Law of Land" (2012) 60 Buffalo Law Review 1139

McSweeney, TJ, "The King's Courts and the King's Soul: Pardoning as Almsgiving in Medieval England" (2014) 50 Reading Medieval Studies 159

McSweeney, TJ, "Magna Carta, Civil Law, and Canon Law" in DB Magraw, A Martinez, and RE Brownell (eds), *Magna Carta and the Rule of Law* (American Bar Association 2014)

McSweeney, TJ, "Creating a Literature for the King's Courts in the Later Thirteenth Century: Hengham Magna, Fet Asaver, and Bracton" (2016) 37 Journal of Legal History 41

Meekings, CAF, "Six Letters Concerning the Eyres of 1226–8" (1950) 65 EHR 492

Meekings, CAF, "Henry de Bracton, Canon of Wells" (1951–54) 26 N. & Q. for Somerset and Dorset 141, reprinted in *Studies in 13th Century Justice and Administration* (Hambledon Press 1981), item VII

Meekings, CAF, "Martin Pateshull and William Raleigh" (1953) 26 *Bulletin of the Institute of Historical Research* 157, reprinted in *Studies in 13th Century Justice and Administration* (Hambledon Press, 1981), item XI

Meekings, CAF, "Adam Fitz William (d. 1238)" (1961) 34 Bulletin of the Institute of Historical Research 1

Meekings, CAF, "Martin de Pateshull of Good Memory My Sometime Lord" (1974) 47 *Bulletin of the Institute of Historical Research* 224, reprinted in *Studies in 13th Century Justice and Administration* (Hambledon Press, 1981), item XII

Meekings, CAF, "Introduction" in CRR, vol 15

Meekings, CAF, and Crook, D, *King's Bench and Common Bench in the Reign of Henry III* (Selden Society 2010)

Merton, RK, *On the Shoulders of Giants: A Shandean Postscript*, (Vicennial edn, Harcourt Brace Jovanovich 1985)

Carey Miller, DL, "Property" in Ernest Metzger (ed), *A Companion to Justinian's Institutes* (Cornell University Press 1998)

Milsom, SFC, *The Legal Framework of English Feudalism* (CUP 1976)

Moorman, JRH, *Church Life in England in the Thirteenth Century* (CUP 1946)

Musson, A, *Medieval Law in Context: The Growth of Legal Consciousness from Magna Carta to the Peasants' Revolt* (Manchester University Press 2001)

Novikoff, AJ, *The Medieval Culture of Disputation: Pedagogy, Practice, and Performance* (University of Pennsylvania Press 2013)

Orme, N, *English Schools in the Middle Ages* (Meuthen & Co 1973)

Orme, N, *Education in the West of England, 1066–1548* (Exeter University Press 1976)

Orme, N, *Medieval Schools: From Roman Britain to Renaissance England* (Yale University Press 2006)

Ourliac, P, and Gazzaniga, J, *Histoire Du Droit Privé Français De L'an Mil Au Code Civil* (Albin Michel 1985)

Packard, SR, "Miscellaneous Records of the Norman Exchequer" (1927) 12 Smith College Studies in History 1

Page, W (ed), *A History of the County of Somerset* (A Constable 1911)

Palmer, RC, *The Whilton Dispute, 1264–1380: A Social–Legal Study of Dispute Settlement in Medieval England* (Princeton University Press 1984)

Parkes, MB, *English Cursive Book Hands 1250–1500* (OUP 1969)

Pegues, F, "The Clericus in the Legal Administration of Thirteenth–Century England" (1956) 71 EHR 529

Pennington, K, "The 'Ius Commune', Suretyship and Magna Carta" (2000) 11 Rivista internazionale di diritto comune 255

Pennington, K, "The Decretalists 1190 to 1234" in W Hartmann and K Pennington (eds), *The History of Medieval Canon Law in the Classical Period, 1140–1234* (Catholic University of America Press 2008)

Pennington, K, "Reform in 1215: *Magna Carta* and the Fourth Lateran Council" (2015) 32 Bulletin of Medieval Canon Law, new series 97

Pennington, K, "*Legista sine canonibus parum valet, canonista sine legibus nihil*" (2017) 34 Bulletin of Medieval Canon Law 249

Platt, C, *The Abbeys & Priories of Medieval England* (Barnes & Noble 1996)

Plucknett, TFT, *Early English Legal Literature* (CUP 1958)

Pollock, F, and Maitland, FW, *The History of English Law before the Time of Edward I*, 2 vols (2nd edn, CUP 1898)

Powicke, FM, *King Henry III and the Lord Edward: The Community of the Realm in the Thirteenth Century* (OUP 1966)

Razi, Z, and Smith, RM, "The Origins of the English Manorial Court Rolls as a Written Record: A Puzzle" in Z Razi and RM Smith (eds), *Medieval Society and the Manor Court* (OUP 1996)

Radding, CM, and Clark, WW, *Medieval Architecture, Medieval Learning: Builders and Masters in the Age of Romanesque and Gothic* (Yale University Press 1992)

Reno, EA, "The Authoritative Text: Raymond of Penyafort's editing of the Decretals of Gregory IX (1234)" (PhD dissertation, Columbia University 2011)

Richardson, HG, "Business Training in Medieval Oxford" (1941) 46 The American Historical Review 259

Richardson, HG, "The Oxford Law School under John" (1941) 57 LQR 319

Richardson, HG, "The Schools of Northampton in the Twelfth Century" (1941) 56 EHR 595

Richardson, HG, "Azo, Drogheda, and Bracton" (1944) 59 EHR 22

Richardson, HG, "Tancred, Raymond, and Bracton" (1944) 59 EHR 376

Richardson, HG, "Studies in Bracton" (1948) 6 Traditio 61

Richardson, HG, *Bracton: The Problem of His Text* (Bernard Quaritch 1965)

Richardson, HG, and Sayles, GO, *Select Cases of Procedure Without Writ Under Henry III* (SS vol 60, Bernard Quaritch 1944)

Round, JH, "Bractoniana" (1916) 31 EHR 588

Rowberry, R, "The Origins and Development of Judicial Tenure 'During Good Behaviour' to 1485" in TR Baker (ed), *Law and Society in Later Medieval England and Ireland: Essays in Honour of Paul Brand* (Routledge 2018)

Sabapathy, J, *Officers and Accountability in Medieval England 1170–1300* (OUP 2014)

Sayers, J, *Papal Judges Delegate in the Province of Canterbury, 1198–1254: A Study in Ecclesiastical Jurisdiction and Administration* (OUP 1971)

Sayers, JE, "William of Drogheda and the English Canonists" in P Linehan (ed), *Proceedings of the Seventh International Congress of Medieval Canon Law* (Biblioteca Apostolica Vaticana 1988)

Sayers, JE, "Marlborough, Thomas of (d. 1236)" (ODNB, September 23, 2004) <www.oxforddnb.com/view/article/18077> accessed March 13, 2019

Sayles, GO, "Introduction" in *Fleta, Volume IV: Book V and Book IV* (SS vol 99, Selden Society 1984)

Seipp, D, "Bracton, the Year Books, and the 'Transformation of Elementary Legal Ideas' in the Early Common Law" (1989) 7 Law and History Review 175

Seipp, DJ, "Roman Legal Categories in the Early Common Law" in TG Watkin (ed), *Legal Record and Historical Reality: Proceedings of the Eighth British Legal History Conference* (Hambledon Press 1989)

Seipp, DJ, "The Concept of Property in the Early Common Law" (1994) 12 Law and History Review 29

Seipp, DJ, "Fleta (fl. 1290–1300)" (ODNB, September 23, 2004) <www.oxforddnb.com/view/article/9716> accessed March 13, 2019

Schulz, F, "Critical Studies on Bracton's Treatise" (1943) 59 LQR 172

Schulz, F, "Bracton as a Computist" (1945) 3 Traditio 265

Schulz, F, "Bracton on Kingship" (1945) 60 EHR 136

Schulz, F, *History of Roman Legal Science* (Reprint edn, Clarendon Press 1967)

Silano, G, "Introduction" in Peter Lombard, *The Sentences, Book 1: The Mystery of the Trinity* (G Silano trs, Pontifical Institute of Medieval Studies 2010)

Smalley, B, *The Study of the Bible in the Middle Ages* (Basil Blackwell 1952)

Smalley, B, *The Becket Conflict and the Schools: A Study of Intellectuals in Politics in the Twelfth Century* (Basil Blackwell 1973)

Southern, RW, "From Schools to University" in JI Catto (ed), *The History of the University of Oxford, Volume I: The Early Oxford Schools* (Clarendon Press 1984)

Stacey, RC, *Politics, Policy, and Finance under Henry III, 1216–1245* (Clarendon Press 1987)

Stacey, RC, "Kilkenny, William of (d. 1256)" (ODNB, September 23, 2004) <www.oxforddnb.com/view/article/15527> accessed March 13, 2019

Stacey, RC, *Law and the Imagination in Medieval Wales* (University of Pennsylvania Press 2018)

Stein, P, "Vacarius and the Civil Law" in CNL Brooke and others (eds), *Church and Government in the Middle Ages: Essays Presented to C.R. Cheney on His 70th Birthday* (CUP 1976)

Stein, P, "The Vacarian School" (1992) 13 Journal of Legal History 23

Stein, P, *Roman Law in European History* (CUP 1999)

Still, J, and Worton, M, "Introduction," in M Worton and J Still (eds), *Intertextuality: Theories and Practices* (Manchester University Press 1990)

Stock, B, *The Implications of Literacy: Written Language and Models of Interpretation in the Eleventh and Twelfth Centuries* (Princeton University Press 1983)

Sutherland, D, *The Assize of Novel Disseisin* (Clarendon Press 1973)

Taliadoros, J, *Law and Theology in Twelfth–Century England: The Works of Master Vacarius (c. 1115/20–c. 1200)* (Brepols 2006)

Tate, JC, "Ownership and Possession in the Early Common Law" (2006) 48 American Journal of Legal History 281

Thorne, SE, "Gilbert de Thornton's *Summa de Legibus*" (1947) 7 University of Toronto Law Journal 1

Tierney, B, "Bracton on Government" (1963) 38 Speculum 295

Turner, RV, *The English Judiciary in the Age of Glanvill and Bracton, c. 1176–1239* (CUP 1985)

Turner, RV, *Men Raised from the Dust: Administrative Service and Upward Mobility in Angevin England* (University of Pennsylvania Press 1988)

Turner, RV, "Clerical Judges in the English Secular Courts: The Ideal Versus the Reality" in *Judges, Administrators, and the Common Law in Angevin England* (Hambledon Press 1994)

Turner, RV, "The *Miles Literatus* in Twelfth- and Thirteenth-Century England: How Rare a Phenomenon?" in *Judges, Administrators, and the Common Law in Angevin England* (Hambledon Press 1994)

Turner, RV, "Roman Law in England Before the Time of Bracton" in *Judges, Administrators, and the Common Law in Angevin England* (Hambledon Press 1994)

Turner, RV, "Pattishall, Simon of (*d. c.*1217)" (ODNB, September 23, 2004) <www.oxforddnb.com/view/article/21544> accessed June 19, 2017

Van Caenegem, RC, *The Birth of the English Common Law* (2nd edn, CUP 1988)

Van Caenegem, RC, *An Historical Introduction to Private Law* (DEL Johnston tr, CUP 1992)

Van Liere, F, "The Study of Canon Law and the Eclipse of the Lincoln Schools, 1175–1225" (2003) 18 (1) History of Universities 1

Veach, C, *Lordship in Four Realms: The Lacy Family, 1166–1241* (Manchester University Press 2014)

Vincent, N, *Peter des Roches: An Alien in English Politics, 1205–1238* (CUP 1996)

Vincent, N, "Henry of Bratton (*alias* Bracton)" in M Hill and RH Helmholz (eds), *Great Christian Jurists in English History* (CUP 2017)

Williams, I, "A Medieval Book and Early–Modern Law: Bracton's Authority and Application in the Common Law c. 1550–1640" (2011) 79 Tijdschrift voor Rechtsgeschiedenis/Legal History Review 47

Winroth, A, *The Making of Gratian's Decretum* (CUP 2000)

Woodbine, GE, "The Roman Element in Bracton's De Adquirendo Rerum Dominio" (1922) 31 Yale Law Journal 827

Yale, DEC, "'Of No Mean Authority': Some Later Uses of Bracton" in MS Arnold and others (eds), *On the Laws and Customs of England: Essays in Honor of Samuel E. Thorne* (University of North Carolina Press 1981)

Young, CR, *The Royal Forests of Medieval England* (University of Pennsylvania Press 1979)

Zutshi, P, "When Did Cambridge Become a *Studium Generale*?" in K Pennington and MH Eichbauer (eds), *Law as Profession and Practice in Medieval Europe: Essays in Honor of James A. Brundage* (Routledge 2011)

# Index

Note: *For the benefit of digital users, indexed terms that span two pages (e.g., 52–53) may, on occasion, appear on only one of those pages.*

# Permissions

| Page | Quote reference | Credit |
|---|---|---|
| 1 | law is called.... sacred rights, Vol 2, 24 | BRACTON ON THE LAWS AND CUSTOMS OF ENGLAND, VOLUME II, translated, with revisions and notes, by Samuel E. Thorne, Cambridge, Mass.: The Belknap Press of Harvard University Press, Copyright © 1968 by the President and Fellows of Harvard College. |
| 14 | those born before espousals ... God and the Church, vol 4, 296 | BRACTON ON THE LAWS AND CUSTOMS OF ENGLAND, VOLUME IV, translated, with revisions and notes, by Samuel E. Thorne, Cambridge, Mass.: The Belknap Press of Harvard University Press, Copyright © 1977 by the President and Fellows of Harvard College. |
| 14 | prejudice to Holy Church, vol 4, 296 | BRACTON ON THE LAWS AND CUSTOMS OF ENGLAND, VOLUME IV, translated, with revisions and notes, by Samuel E. Thorne, Cambridge, Mass.: The Belknap Press of Harvard University Press, Copyright © 1977 by the President and Fellows of Harvard College. |
| 23 | Of the eyre of the bishop of Durham ... third year of King Henry, vol 3, 376 | BRACTON ON THE LAWS AND CUSTOMS OF ENGLAND, VOLUME III, translated, with revisions and notes, by Samuel E. Thorne, Cambridge, Mass.: The Belknap Press of Harvard University Press, Copyright © 1977 by the President and Fellows of Harvard College. |
| 23 | last eyre of Martin of Pattishall in Lincoln, vol 3, 389 | BRACTON ON THE LAWS AND CUSTOMS OF ENGLAND, VOLUME III, translated, with revisions and notes, by Samuel E. Thorne, Cambridge, Mass.: The Belknap Press of Harvard University Press, Copyright © 1977 by the President and Fellows of Harvard College. |
| 23 | these laws and customs ... authority of the laws, vol 2, 21 | BRACTON ON THE LAWS AND CUSTOMS OF ENGLAND, VOLUME II, translated, with revisions and notes, by Samuel E. Thorne, Cambridge, Mass.: The Belknap Press of Harvard University Press, Copyright © 1968 by the President and Fellows of Harvard College. |
| 61 | the utility ... since the king is God's vicar, vol 2, 20 | BRACTON ON THE LAWS AND CUSTOMS OF ENGLAND, VOLUME II, translated, with revisions and notes, by Samuel E. Thorne, Cambridge, Mass.: The Belknap Press of Harvard University Press, Copyright © 1968 by the President and Fellows of Harvard College. |
| 62 | the [art] of preparing records ... alleged and denied, vol 2, 20 | BRACTON ON THE LAWS AND CUSTOMS OF ENGLAND, VOLUME II, translated, with revisions and notes, by Samuel E. Thorne, Cambridge, Mass.: The Belknap Press of Harvard University Press, Copyright © 1968 by the President and Fellows of Harvard College. |

| Page | Quote reference | Credit |
| --- | --- | --- |
| 63 | The general intention ... and the good better, vol 2, 20 | BRACTON ON THE LAWS AND CUSTOMS OF ENGLAND, VOLUME II, translated, with revisions and notes, by Samuel E. Thorne, Cambridge, Mass.: The Belknap Press of Harvard University Press, Copyright © 1968 by the President and Fellows of Harvard College. |
| 63 | let the enrolment be made thus, vol 4, 209 | BRACTON ON THE LAWS AND CUSTOMS OF ENGLAND, VOLUME IV, translated, with revisions and notes, by Samuel E. Thorne, Cambridge, Mass.: The Belknap Press of Harvard University Press, Copyright © 1977 by the President and Fellows of Harvard College. |
| 63 | for the instruction ... said of enrolment, vol 4, 99 | BRACTON ON THE LAWS AND CUSTOMS OF ENGLAND, VOLUME IV, translated, with revisions and notes, by Samuel E. Thorne, Cambridge, Mass.: The Belknap Press of Harvard University Press, Copyright © 1977 by the President and Fellows of Harvard College. |
| 65 | can do nothing ... with respect to his sovereignty, vol 2, 305 | BRACTON ON THE LAWS AND CUSTOMS OF ENGLAND, VOLUME II, translated, with revisions and notes, by Samuel E. Thorne, Cambridge, Mass.: The Belknap Press of Harvard University Press, Copyright © 1968 by the President and Fellows of Harvard College. |
| 82 | Though in almost all lands ... unwritten law and custom, vol 2, 19 | BRACTON ON THE LAWS AND CUSTOMS OF ENGLAND, VOLUME II, translated, with revisions and notes, by Samuel E. Thorne, Cambridge, Mass.: The Belknap Press of Harvard University Press, Copyright © 1968 by the President and Fellows of Harvard College. |
| 89 | nothing relating ... relevant to this treatise, vol 2, 304 | BRACTON ON THE LAWS AND CUSTOMS OF ENGLAND, VOLUME II, translated, with revisions and notes, by Samuel E. Thorne, Cambridge, Mass.: The Belknap Press of Harvard University Press, Copyright © 1968 by the President and Fellows of Harvard College. |
| 102 | do right justice ... of the lord king, vol 2, 309 | BRACTON ON THE LAWS AND CUSTOMS OF ENGLAND, VOLUME II, translated, with revisions and notes, by Samuel E. Thorne, Cambridge, Mass.: The Belknap Press of Harvard University Press, Copyright © 1968 by the President and Fellows of Harvard College. |
| 107 | the king who wishes to rule rightly, vol 2, 19 | BRACTON ON THE LAWS AND CUSTOMS OF ENGLAND, VOLUME II, translated, with revisions and notes, by Samuel E. Thorne, Cambridge, Mass.: The Belknap Press of Harvard University Press, Copyright © 1968 by the President and Fellows of Harvard College. |
| 108 | lex agrees with English custom, vol 2, 101 | BRACTON ON THE LAWS AND CUSTOMS OF ENGLAND, VOLUME II, translated, with revisions and notes, by Samuel E. Thorne, Cambridge, Mass.: The Belknap Press of Harvard University Press, Copyright © 1968 by the President and Fellows of Harvard College. |

| Page | Quote reference | Credit |
|------|-----------------|--------|
| 108 | Though in almost all regions ... what usage has approved, vol 2, 19 | BRACTON ON THE LAWS AND CUSTOMS OF ENGLAND, VOLUME II, translated, with revisions and notes, by Samuel E. Thorne, Cambridge, Mass.: The Belknap Press of Harvard University Press, Copyright © 1968 by the President and Fellows of Harvard College. |
| 108 | where it is said that gifts ... unless condemnation follows, vol 2, 101 | BRACTON ON THE LAWS AND CUSTOMS OF ENGLAND, VOLUME II, translated, with revisions and notes, by Samuel E. Thorne, Cambridge, Mass.: The Belknap Press of Harvard University Press, Copyright © 1968 by the President and Fellows of Harvard College. |
| 110 | Nevertheless, it will not be absurd ... has the force of law, vol 2, 19 | BRACTON ON THE LAWS AND CUSTOMS OF ENGLAND, VOLUME II, translated, with revisions and notes, by Samuel E. Thorne, Cambridge, Mass.: The Belknap Press of Harvard University Press, Copyright © 1968 by the President and Fellows of Harvard College. |
| 112 | wild beasts ... or in the heavens, vol 2, 42 | BRACTON ON THE LAWS AND CUSTOMS OF ENGLAND, VOLUME II, translated, with revisions and notes, by Samuel E. Thorne, Cambridge, Mass.: The Belknap Press of Harvard University Press, Copyright © 1968 by the President and Fellows of Harvard College. |
| 112, *fn43* | unless custom or privilege rules to the contrary, vol 2, 42 | BRACTON ON THE LAWS AND CUSTOMS OF ENGLAND, VOLUME II, translated, with revisions and notes, by Samuel E. Thorne, Cambridge, Mass.: The Belknap Press of Harvard University Press, Copyright © 1968 by the President and Fellows of Harvard College. |
| 113 | things which by the natural law ... belong to no one, vol 2, 166-167 | BRACTON ON THE LAWS AND CUSTOMS OF ENGLAND, VOLUME II, translated, with revisions and notes, by Samuel E. Thorne, Cambridge, Mass.: The Belknap Press of Harvard University Press, Copyright © 1968 by the President and Fellows of Harvard College. |
| 115 | it is clear that actions ... from a mother, vol 2, 283 | BRACTON ON THE LAWS AND CUSTOMS OF ENGLAND, VOLUME II, translated, with revisions and notes, by Samuel E. Thorne, Cambridge, Mass.: The Belknap Press of Harvard University Press, Copyright © 1968 by the President and Fellows of Harvard College. |
| 116 | if seisin or possession ... revert to the ownership, vol 2, 184 | BRACTON ON THE LAWS AND CUSTOMS OF ENGLAND, VOLUME II, translated, with revisions and notes, by Samuel E. Thorne, Cambridge, Mass.: The Belknap Press of Harvard University Press, Copyright © 1968 by the President and Fellows of Harvard College. |
| 117 | We have spoken above ... ought to return to him, vol 4, 21 | BRACTON ON THE LAWS AND CUSTOMS OF ENGLAND, VOLUME IV, translated, with revisions and notes, by Samuel E. Thorne, Cambridge, Mass.: The Belknap Press of Harvard University Press, Copyright © 1977 by the President and Fellows of Harvard College. |

| Page | Quote reference | Credit |
| --- | --- | --- |
| 119 | has withdrawn from . . . by the assize, vol 2, 297 | BRACTON ON THE LAWS AND CUSTOMS OF ENGLAND, VOLUME II, translated, with revisions and notes, by Samuel E. Thorne, Cambridge, Mass.: The Belknap Press of Harvard University Press, Copyright © 1968 by the President and Fellows of Harvard College. |
| 120 | some are founded on the possession, others on ownership, 2, 294 | BRACTON ON THE LAWS AND CUSTOMS OF ENGLAND, VOLUME II, translated, with revisions and notes, by Samuel E. Thorne, Cambridge, Mass.: The Belknap. Press of Harvard University Press, Copyright © 1968 by the President and Fellows of Harvard College. |
| 121 | that is, of one's own . . . novel disseisin, vol 2, 294 | BRACTON ON THE LAWS AND CUSTOMS OF ENGLAND, VOLUME II, translated, with revisions and notes, by Samuel E. Thorne, Cambridge, Mass.: The Belknap Press of Harvard University Press, Copyright © 1968 by the President and Fellows of Harvard College. |
| 121 | is called the action unde vi . . . assize of novel disseisin, vol 2, 295 | BRACTON ON THE LAWS AND CUSTOMS OF ENGLAND, VOLUME II, translated, with revisions and notes, by Samuel E. Thorne, Cambridge, Mass.: The Belknap Press of Harvard University Press, Copyright © 1968 by the President and Fellows of Harvard College. |
| 121 | the hereditatis petitio possessoria . . . assize of mort d'ancestor, vol 2, 295 | BRACTON ON THE LAWS AND CUSTOMS OF ENGLAND, VOLUME II, translated, with revisions and notes, by Samuel E. Thorne, Cambridge, Mass.: The Belknap Press of Harvard University Press, Copyright © 1968 by the President and Fellows of Harvard College. |
| 121 | A thing may be . . . bare use, vol 2, 101 | BRACTON ON THE LAWS AND CUSTOMS OF ENGLAND, VOLUME II, translated, with revisions and notes, by Samuel E. Thorne, Cambridge, Mass.: The Belknap Press of Harvard University Press, Copyright © 1968 by the President and Fellows of Harvard College. |
| 123, *fn91* | the right . . . and seisin, vol 2, 123 | BRACTON ON THE LAWS AND CUSTOMS OF ENGLAND, VOLUME II, translated, with revisions and notes, by Samuel E. Thorne, Cambridge, Mass.: The Belknap Press of Harvard University Press, Copyright © 1968 by the President and Fellows of Harvard College. |
| 124 | pure right and the ownership, vol 2, 127 | BRACTON ON THE LAWS AND CUSTOMS OF ENGLAND, VOLUME II, translated, with revisions and notes, by Samuel E. Thorne, Cambridge, Mass.: The Belknap Press of Harvard University Press, Copyright © 1968 by the President and Fellows of Harvard College. |
| 124 | the pure right . . . usufruct, vol 2, 127 | BRACTON ON THE LAWS AND CUSTOMS OF ENGLAND, VOLUME II, translated, with revisions and notes, by Samuel E. Thorne, Cambridge, Mass.: The Belknap Press of Harvard University Press, Copyright © 1968 by the President and Fellows of Harvard College. |

| Page | Quote reference | Credit |
|------|-----------------|--------|
|  | For there is a right of possession . . . ought always to follow the ownership, vol 2, 24 | BRACTON ON THE LAWS AND CUSTOMS OF ENGLAND, VOLUME II, translated, with revisions and notes, by Samuel E. Thorne, Cambridge, Mass.: The Belknap Press of Harvard University Press, Copyright © 1968 by the President and Fellows of Harvard College. |
| 124 | There is possession which has nothing of right . . . free tenement with seisin. Vol 2, 122-123 | BRACTON ON THE LAWS AND CUSTOMS OF ENGLAND, VOLUME II, translated, with revisions and notes, by Samuel E. Thorne, Cambridge, Mass.: The Belknap Press of Harvard University Press, Copyright © 1968 by the President and Fellows of Harvard College. |
| 129 | is changed to a proprietary causa, vol 2, 123 | BRACTON ON THE LAWS AND CUSTOMS OF ENGLAND, VOLUME II, translated, with revisions and notes, by Samuel E. Thorne, Cambridge, Mass.: The Belknap Press of Harvard University Press, Copyright © 1968 by the President and Fellows of Harvard College. |
| 132-133 | how the ownership . . . acquisition of possession vol 3, 162 | BRACTON ON THE LAWS AND CUSTOMS OF ENGLAND, VOLUME III, translated, with revisions and notes, by Samuel E. Thorne, Cambridge, Mass.: The Belknap Press of Harvard University Press, Copyright © 1977 by the President and Fellows of Harvard College. |
| 133 | possession may be restored, vol 3, 162 | BRACTON ON THE LAWS AND CUSTOMS OF ENGLAND, VOLUME III, translated, with revisions and notes, by Samuel E. Thorne, Cambridge, Mass.: The Belknap Press of Harvard University Press, Copyright © 1977 by the President and Fellows of Harvard College. |
| 133 | how one is restored . . . appurtenant to a free tenement, vol 3, 162 | BRACTON ON THE LAWS AND CUSTOMS OF ENGLAND, VOLUME III, translated, with revisions and notes, by Samuel E. Thorne, Cambridge, Mass.: The Belknap Press of Harvard University Press, Copyright © 1977 by the President and Fellows of Harvard College. |
| 155, fn77 | wittingly swears otherwise than the matter in truth is, vol 3, 337 | BRACTON ON THE LAWS AND CUSTOMS OF ENGLAND, VOLUME III, translated, with revisions and notes, by Samuel E. Thorne, Cambridge, Mass.: The Belknap Press of Harvard University Press, Copyright © 1977 by the President and Fellows of Harvard College. |
| 156, fn77 | led astray by reasonable error, vol 3, 338 | BRACTON ON THE LAWS AND CUSTOMS OF ENGLAND, VOLUME III, translated, with revisions and notes, by Samuel E. Thorne, Cambridge, Mass.: The Belknap Press of Harvard University Press, Copyright © 1977 by the President and Fellows of Harvard College. |
| 174 | He may first put . . . in four cases, vol 2, 322 | BRACTON ON THE LAWS AND CUSTOMS OF ENGLAND, VOLUME II, translated, with revisions and notes, by Samuel E. Thorne, Cambridge, Mass.: The Belknap Press of Harvard University Press, Copyright © 1968 by the President and Fellows of Harvard College. |

| Page | Quote reference | Credit |
|------|-----------------|--------|
| 175 | where the actions proposed . . . includes the possessory, Vol 2, 322–323 | BRACTON ON THE LAWS AND CUSTOMS OF ENGLAND, VOLUME II, translated, with revisions and notes, by Samuel E. Thorne, Cambridge, Mass.: The Belknap Press of Harvard University Press, Copyright © 1968 by the President and Fellows of Harvard College. |
| 175–176 | And note in fine. . . possession rests, as C. 3.31.11.6, vol 2, 323 | BRACTON ON THE LAWS AND CUSTOMS OF ENGLAND, VOLUME II, translated, with revisions and notes, by Samuel E. Thorne, Cambridge, Mass.: The Belknap Press of Harvard University Press, Copyright © 1968 by the President and Fellows of Harvard College. |
| 178 | If they arise from different acts . . . and D. 44.7.34., vol 2, 323 | BRACTON ON THE LAWS AND CUSTOMS OF ENGLAND, VOLUME II, translated, with revisions and notes, by Samuel E. Thorne, Cambridge, Mass.: The Belknap Press of Harvard University Press, Copyright © 1968 by the President and Fellows of Harvard College. |
| 178-179 | If one has impetrated . . . coram rege, Vol 2, 323 | BRACTON ON THE LAWS AND CUSTOMS OF ENGLAND, VOLUME II, translated, with revisions and notes, by Samuel E. Thorne, Cambridge, Mass.: The Belknap Press of Harvard University Press, Copyright © 1968 by the President and Fellows of Harvard College. |
| 179, *fn57* | among the pleas . . . forest of Glaisdale, vol 4, 289-290 | BRACTON ON THE LAWS AND CUSTOMS OF ENGLAND, VOLUME IV, translated, with revisions and notes, by Samuel E. Thorne, Cambridge, Mass.: The Belknap Press of Harvard University Press, Copyright © 1977 by the President and Fellows of Harvard College. |
| 180 | whether one hide of land, around the beginning [of the roll].' Vol 3, 335 | BRACTON ON THE LAWS AND CUSTOMS OF ENGLAND, VOLUME III, translated, with revisions and notes, by Samuel E. Thorne, Cambridge, Mass.: The Belknap Press of Harvard University Press, Copyright © 1977 by the President and Fellows of Harvard College. |
| 181 | a gift made . . . an assize of darrein presentment, vol 2, 163 | BRACTON ON THE LAWS AND CUSTOMS OF ENGLAND, VOLUME II, translated, with revisions and notes, by Samuel E. Thorne, Cambridge, Mass.: The Belknap Press of Harvard University Press, Copyright © 1968 by the President and Fellows of Harvard College. |
| 182, *fn68* | And this is established . . . decretal in these words, vol 2, 185 | BRACTON ON THE LAWS AND CUSTOMS OF ENGLAND, VOLUME II, translated, with revisions and notes, by Samuel E. Thorne, Cambridge, Mass.: The Belknap Press of Harvard University Press, Copyright © 1968 by the President and Fellows of Harvard College. |
| 182 | dower may be constituted . . . wife of William Dacy, vol 2, 268 | BRACTON ON THE LAWS AND CUSTOMS OF ENGLAND, VOLUME II, translated, with revisions and notes, by Samuel E. Thorne, Cambridge, Mass.: The Belknap Press of Harvard University Press, Copyright © 1968 by the President and Fellows of Harvard College. |

| Page | Quote reference | Credit |
|---|---|---|
| 183 | That in the eyre ... that no resummons lies in the eyre, vol 3, 209 | BRACTON ON THE LAWS AND CUSTOMS OF ENGLAND, VOLUME III, translated, with revisions and notes, by Samuel E. Thorne, Cambridge, Mass.: The Belknap Press of Harvard University Press, Copyright © 1977 by the President and Fellows of Harvard College. |
| 185 | the contrary ... William de Mandeville, vol 4, 181 | BRACTON ON THE LAWS AND CUSTOMS OF ENGLAND, VOLUME IV, translated, with revisions and notes, by Samuel E. Thorne, Cambridge, Mass.: The Belknap Press of Harvard University Press, Copyright © 1977 by the President and Fellows of Harvard College. |
| 186 | until he has so put himself ... twelve have been chosen, vol 4, 154 | BRACTON ON THE LAWS AND CUSTOMS OF ENGLAND, VOLUME IV, translated, with revisions and notes, by Samuel E. Thorne, Cambridge, Mass.: The Belknap Press of Harvard University Press, Copyright © 1977 by the President and Fellows of Harvard College. |
| 186 | because of the disagreement ... and some another, vol 4, 154 | BRACTON ON THE LAWS AND CUSTOMS OF ENGLAND, VOLUME IV, translated, with revisions and notes, by Samuel E. Thorne, Cambridge, Mass.: The Belknap Press of Harvard University Press, Copyright © 1977 by the President and Fellows of Harvard College. |
| 189 | misapplied by the unwise and unlearned ... by the authority of the laws, vol 2, 19 | BRACTON ON THE LAWS AND CUSTOMS OF ENGLAND, VOLUME II, translated, with revisions and notes, by Samuel E. Thorne, Cambridge, Mass.: The Belknap Press of Harvard University Press, Copyright © 1968 by the President and Fellows of Harvard College. |
| 191 | I have turned my mind ... into a summa, vol 2, 20 | BRACTON ON THE LAWS AND CUSTOMS OF ENGLAND, VOLUME II, translated, with revisions and notes, by Samuel E. Thorne, Cambridge, Mass.: The Belknap Press of Harvard University Press, Copyright © 1968 by the President and Fellows of Harvard College. |
| 196 | response of William of Raleigh ... in this matter, vol 4, 126 | BRACTON ON THE LAWS AND CUSTOMS OF ENGLAND, VOLUME IV, translated, with revisions and notes, by Samuel E. Thorne, Cambridge, Mass.: The Belknap Press of Harvard University Press, Copyright © 1977 by the President and Fellows of Harvard College. |
| 197 | boundaries destroyed ... removing them, vol 3, 128 | BRACTON ON THE LAWS AND CUSTOMS OF ENGLAND, VOLUME III, translated, with revisions and notes, by Samuel E. Thorne, Cambridge, Mass.: The Belknap Press of Harvard University Press, Copyright © 1977 by the President and Fellows of Harvard College. |
| 197 | is better, according to Martin, vol 3, 122 | BRACTON ON THE LAWS AND CUSTOMS OF ENGLAND, VOLUME III, translated, with revisions and notes, by Samuel E. Thorne, Cambridge, Mass.: The Belknap Press of Harvard University Press, Copyright © 1977 by the President and Fellows of Harvard College. |

| Page | Quote reference | Credit |
| --- | --- | --- |
| 197 | was wrongful according to Stephen... misunderstood and misapplied, vol 4, 360 | BRACTON ON THE LAWS AND CUSTOMS OF ENGLAND, VOLUME IV, translated, with revisions and notes, by Samuel E. Thorne, Cambridge, Mass.: The Belknap Press of Harvard University Press, Copyright © 1977 by the President and Fellows of Harvard College. |
| 198 | so it seems... contrary seems true, vol 2, 367 | BRACTON ON THE LAWS AND CUSTOMS OF ENGLAND, VOLUME II, translated, with revisions and notes, by Samuel E. Thorne, Cambridge, Mass.: The Belknap Press of Harvard University Press, Copyright © 1968 by the President and Fellows of Harvard College. |
| 198 | was the reasoning... and it is good, vol 2, 367 | BRACTON ON THE LAWS AND CUSTOMS OF ENGLAND, VOLUME II, translated, with revisions and notes, by Samuel E. Thorne, Cambridge, Mass.: The Belknap Press of Harvard University Press, Copyright © 1968 by the President and Fellows of Harvard College. |
| 198 | But the contrary... *did not approve,* vol 2, 113 | BRACTON ON THE LAWS AND CUSTOMS OF ENGLAND, VOLUME II, translated, with revisions and notes, by Samuel E. Thorne, Cambridge, Mass.: The Belknap Press of Harvard University Press, Copyright © 1968 by the President and Fellows of Harvard College. |
| 199 | are not of man... hand of God, vol 2, 20 | BRACTON ON THE LAWS AND CUSTOMS OF ENGLAND, VOLUME II, translated, with revisions and notes, by Samuel E. Thorne, Cambridge, Mass.: The Belknap Press of Harvard University Press, Copyright © 1968 by the President and Fellows of Harvard College. |
| 208 | Suppose that A. ... Hospital of Jerusalem, vol 2, 92-93 | BRACTON ON THE LAWS AND CUSTOMS OF ENGLAND, VOLUME II, translated, with revisions and notes, by Samuel E. Thorne, Cambridge, Mass.: The Belknap Press of Harvard University Press, Copyright © 1968 by the President and Fellows of Harvard College. |
| 221 | ought to inquire... ejected from the tenement, vol 3, 76 | BRACTON ON THE LAWS AND CUSTOMS OF ENGLAND, VOLUME III, translated, with revisions and notes, by Samuel E. Thorne, Cambridge, Mass.: The Belknap Press of Harvard University Press, Copyright © 1977 by the President and Fellows of Harvard College. |
| 221 | lest from another's... gain or advantage, 3, 75 | BRACTON ON THE LAWS AND CUSTOMS OF ENGLAND, VOLUME III, translated, with revisions and notes, by Samuel E. Thorne, Cambridge, Mass.: The Belknap. Press of Harvard University Press, Copyright © 1977 by the President and Fellows of Harvard College. |
|  | since charters... truth may be declared, vol 2, 59 | BRACTON ON THE LAWS AND CUSTOMS OF ENGLAND, VOLUME II, translated, with revisions and notes, by Samuel E. Thorne, Cambridge, Mass.: The Belknap Press of Harvard University Press, Copyright © 1968 by the President and Fellows of Harvard College. |

| Page | Quote reference | Credit |
|------|----------------|--------|
| 228 | homage has been taken . . . proper ceremonies, vol 2, 150 | BRACTON ON THE LAWS AND CUSTOMS OF ENGLAND, VOLUME II, translated, with revisions and notes, by Samuel E. Thorne, Cambridge, Mass.: The Belknap Press of Harvard University Press, Copyright © 1968 by the President and Fellows of Harvard College. |
| 235 | that he did not withdraw . . . *animo* and *corpore*, vol 2, 150 | BRACTON ON THE LAWS AND CUSTOMS OF ENGLAND, VOLUME II, translated, with revisions and notes, by Samuel E. Thorne, Cambridge, Mass.: The Belknap Press of Harvard University Press, Copyright © 1968 by the President and Fellows of Harvard College. |
| 236 | If the donee . . . accepting the whole, vol 2, 150 | BRACTON ON THE LAWS AND CUSTOMS OF ENGLAND, VOLUME II, translated, with revisions and notes, by Samuel E. Thorne, Cambridge, Mass.: The Belknap Press of Harvard University Press, Copyright © 1968 by the President and Fellows of Harvard College. |
| 236 | badly decided . . . hundred was appurtenant, vol 2, 150 | BRACTON ON THE LAWS AND CUSTOMS OF ENGLAND, VOLUME II, translated, with revisions and notes, by Samuel E. Thorne, Cambridge, Mass.: The Belknap Press of Harvard University Press, Copyright © 1968 by the President and Fellows of Harvard College. |